DISCOVER
ITALY

W9-AZE-678

Copyright © **1996**, 1993 by Berlitz Publishing Co. Ltd, Berlitz House, Peterley Road, Oxford, OX4 2TX, England, and Berlitz Publishing Company, Inc., 257 Park Avenue South, New York, NY 10010, USA. All rights reserved. No part of this book may be reproduced or transmitted in any form or by any means, electronic or mechanical, including photocopying, recording or by any information storage and retrieval system without permission in writing from the publisher. Berlitz Trademark Reg. U.S. Patent Office and other countries.

Edited and designed by
D & N Publishing,
Ramsbury, Wiltshire.

Cartography by Carte Blanche,
Basingstoke, Hampshire.

Although we have made every effort to ensure the accuracy of all the information in this book, changes do occur. We cannot therefore take responsibility for facts, addresses and circumstances in general that are constantly subject to alteration.

If you have any new information, suggestions or corrections to contribute to this guide, we would like to hear from you. Please write to Berlitz Publishing at one of the above addresses.

Photographic Acknowledgements

Copyright © Kurt Amman 106; Berlitz Publishing Co. Ltd. 1, 11, 12, 21, 24, 32, 37, 40, 44, 46, 49, 66, 96, 103, 104, 105, 106, 107, 108, 109, 122, 126, 130, 136, 141, 144, 152, 153, 175, 179, 183, 185, 187, 189, 200, 201, 202, 207, 209, 210/211, 213, 217, 227, 231, 233, 237, 243, 244, 249, 250, 255, 258, 259, 262, 263, 265, 270, 272, 273, 274, 285, 286/7, 292/3, 294, 298, 300, 302, 303, 305, 310, 312, 314; Jason Best 55, 56, 62, 101, 139, 151, 155, 166, 308, 316, 320, 323; Cinematheque Suisse 195, 196, 197, 198; Columbia University Libraries, New York 245; Fiorepress, Turin 117, 118, 119, 120, 221; David Price-Goodfellow 48, 52, 168, 170, 173; National Italian Tourist Office 163, 205, 280; Jean Mohr 106, 108, 134, 142, 144; Natural Image, 132 (P Catherall), 319 (Bob Gibbons), 19, 53, 112, 158, 162 (Peter Wilson); Nature Photgraphers, 95, 99, 113, 125 (J M Sutherland); Prisma/Schuster GmbH 88/9, 268/9; Scala, Florence 110, 142, 143, 145, 146, 147, 148, 190/1, 215, 246; Neil Ray 6, 29, 39, 58, 85, 91, 161; Telegraph Colour Library 222, 228.

Front cover: Nervi, Riviera de Levante (Daniel Vittet/Berlitz Publishing).

Back cover: artist in Tuscan sunflower fields (Neil Ray).

Photograph previous page: Castelvecchio.

Phototypeset, originated and printed by C.S. Graphics, Singapore.

The Berlitz tick is used to indicate places or events of particular interest.

Berlitz

DISCOVER
ITALY

Jack Altman

and Jason Best

Contents

MAPS: Italy 4, 8; Rome's metro 18; Central Italy 84; Tuscany, Umbria and The Marches 128; The North-East 180; The North-West 224; The South 252; Sicily 296; Sardinia 307.
Town Plans: Florence 129; Genoa 242; Milan 225; Naples 253; Palermo 297; Pompeii 267; The Roman Forum 94; Rome 86–7; Turin 238; Venice 181; Verona 204.

Charting a Clear Course for a Holiday in Italy

Holidaying in Italy can be plain sailing once you know the ropes. However, the unprepared traveller confronted with the unfamiliar may feel like a mariner without a compass. Many aspects of Italian life take some getting used to, from the vagaries of Italian opening hours to the road code of Italian drivers. To save unnecessary anxiety and frustration, we offer this section of practical advice and information.

Climate

Stretching from the Alps to the latitude of Tunis, Italy has a climate as varied as its geography. In the Alpine region, winters are long and cold, but often sunny, while summers are short and pleasantly cool. The northern lakes and the Po valley see cold and foggy winters and warm and sunny summers. The rest of the country, even the Ligurian coast, enjoys mild weather in winter. Summers are dry and hot to scorching depending on how far south you go, but sea breezes often compensate for the torrid heat. The best time for a visit to the Ligurian and northern Adriatic coasts is May/June to September. Before or after this period it can be rather chilly. Many hotels will be closed and the resorts and beaches practically deserted. The best time to visit the cities of Italy is in spring or autumn—between April and June and again in September—when the weather is most pleasant and the streets less crowded.

If you are travelling in northern Italy in winter you will need boots and an overcoat, but in the south a lightweight coat will be adequate. During early spring and late autumn, you

A painter finds inspiration in a field of Tuscan sunflowers. Italy's rich artistic heritage, the greatest in the West, must also be a spur to creativity.

ITALY

FACTS AND FIGURES

GERMANY

FRANCE

AUSTRIA

HUNGARY

LIECHTENSTEIN

SWITZERLAND

SLOVENIA

▲ MONTE BIANCO

Aosta

Bolzano

Trento

Udine

Trieste

CROATIA

Como

Bergamo

Vicenza

Treviso

Milano

Brescia

Verona

Pavia

Cremona

Padova

Venezia

Torino

BOSNIA

Parma

Ferrara

Cuneo

Modena

Genova

Bologna

Ravenna

MONACO

San Remo

Lucca

Rimini

SAN MARINO

Pesaro

MARE LIGURE

Pisa

Firenze

Volterra

Arezzo

Ancona

San
Gimignano

Siena

Gubbio

Perugia

Assisi

Elba

Orvieto

Grosseto

Terni

Corse

Tarquinia

L'Aquila

Pescara

Civitavecchia

Tivoli

MARE ADRIATICO

Ostia

ROMA

Cassino

Foggia

Bari

Olbia

Napoli

Ruvo

Potenza

Taranto

Brindisi

Alghero

Sassari

Sorrento

Salerno

Paestum

Lecce

Gallipoli

Otranto

Oristano

Sardegna

MARE
TIRRENO

Cosenza

Cagliari

Catanzaro

Messina

Reggio di Calabria

Trapani

Palermo

Marsala

▲ MONTE ETNA

MARE IONIO

Sicilia

Caltanissetta

Catania

Agrigento

Siracusa

MARE

Ragusa

N

MEDITERRANEO

ALGERIA

MALTA

TUNISIA

| 0 | 160 km |
| 0 | 100 miles |

should bring light- to medium-weight clothing and rain wear for those brief, but torrential showers. Summer evenings can be cool, so don't forget to pack a jacket or wrap. All year round, comfortable walking shoes are indispensable. Casual wear is the general rule in most places, and few restaurants insist on a tie. Shorts and bare-backed dresses are frowned upon in churches, and women may have to cover their bare arms.

Passports and Visas

For a stay of up to three months, a valid passport is sufficient for citizens of Australia, Canada, New Zealand and USA. Visitors from Eire, the United Kingdom and other EC countries need only an identity card to enter Italy. Tourists from South Africa must have a visa.

Travel Documents for Motorists

To take a car into Italy, you must be at least 18 years old and should have a valid national driving licence accompanied by a translation (free from automobile associations) or an International Driving Permit. The pink EC driving licence, without translation, is accepted in Italy.

*M*ap of Italy
showing the main roads,
towns and features.

As a motorist, you should also have your vehicle registration papers and Green Card insurance (an extension to your regular insurance policy, making it valid for Italy). A Green Card is no longer compulsory for EC citizens but is strongly recommended. You can get a Green Card from your insurance agent or at most border points. If you plan to stay in Italy for more than 45 days, you must take out Italian insurance.

If the car you are driving is not your own, you must have the owner's written permission to drive the vehicle.

Drivers in Italy must carry a red warning triangle, which should be placed at least 30m (100ft) behind the car in the case of a breakdown. Red triangles can be hired from the frontier offices of the Italian Automobile Club (ACI). A set of spare bulbs is recommended.

Motorists should also have a national identity sticker for both cars and caravans (trailers).

Drivers of motorcycles need the same documents as car drivers, but no licence is required for motor scooters. (*See* also GETTING AROUND.)

Exporting Works of Art

If you are exporting archaeological relics or works of art, you should ensure that your dealer provides you with the proper receipts and a permit from the government. The illegal traffic in art works and relics is becoming an increasing problem for the Italian government and the visitor should take care not to add to it.

9

Pets

Dogs and cats must have a combined health and rabies inoculation certificate legalized by a veterinarian in the country of origin. It must be dated between 11 months and 20 days before entry into Italy.

Before taking your pet abroad, inquire whether there are any quarantine regulations that may apply on your return home.

Public Holidays

Banks, government offices, most shops and some museums and galleries are closed on the following days:

1 January	*Capodanno*
	New Year's Day
6 January	*Epifania*
	Epiphany
25 April	*Festa della Liberazione*
	Liberation Day
1 May	*Primo Maggio*
	May Day
15 August	*Ferragosto*
	Assumption Day
1 November	*Ognissanti*
	All Saint's Day
8 December	*L'Immacolata Concezione*
	Immaculate Conception
25 December	*Natale*
	Christmas Day
26 December	*Santo Stefano*
	St Stephen's Day
Moveable date:	*Lunedì di Pasqua*
	Easter Monday

Shops and offices also close on local feast days held in honour of a town's patron saint. In the main cities, these dates are: 25 April (S Marco), Venice; 24 June (S Giovanni Battista), Florence, Genoa and Turin; 29 June (SS Pietro e Paolo), Rome; 15 July (S Rosalia), Palermo; 19 September (S Gennaro), Naples; 4 October (S Petronio), Bologna; 30 October (S Saturnino), Cagliari; 3 November (S Giusto), Trieste; 6 December (S Nicola), Bari; and 7 December (S Ambrogio), Milan.

When a national holiday falls on a Thursday or a Tuesday, Italians may make a *ponte* (bridge) to the weekend and take the Friday or Monday off as well.

Time Differences

Italy follows Central European Time (GMT + 1). From the last Sunday in March to the last Sunday in September, clocks are put ahead one hour (GMT + 2).

Summer Time Chart:

Los Angeles	3 a.m.
New York	6 a.m.
London	11 a.m.
Rome	noon
Johannesburg	noon
Sydney	8 p.m.
Auckland	10 p.m.

Health and Medical Care

If your health-insurance policy does not cover you while abroad, take out a short-term policy with your insurance company, automobile association or travel agency before leaving home. Visitors from EC countries carrying the E111 form available from their local health centres are entitled to

A tranquil spot on the Po Delta. Visitors in Italy around the mid-August holiday of Ferragosto could be forgiven for thinking the whole country had closed down.

emergency medical and hospital treatment under the Italian social security system. The E111 form explains the steps you will need to take to obtain treatment in Italy.

If you are in need of medical care while staying in a hotel ask your hotel receptionist to help you find a doctor (or dentist) who speaks English. Local Health Units of the Italian National Health Service are listed in the telephone directory under *Unità Sanitaria Locale*. First-aid (*pronto soccorso*) services, with a doctor on duty, are found in all hospitals, as well as at airports, ports and all major railway stations.

Money Matters

Currency

Italy's monetary unit is the *lira* (plural *lire*, abbreviated L. or Lit.). Notes are issued for 1,000, 2,000, 5,000, 10,000, 50,000, 100,000. Coins are 10, 20, 50, 100, 200, 500. The first two coins are rare; you will find that shopkeepers usually round up amounts or, in some cases, give out sweets in place of very small change.

Credit Cards and Traveller's Cheques

Most hotels and many shops, service stations and restaurants honour the major international credit cards. Traveller's cheques are widely accepted, but you will get much better value if you exchange your cheques for *lire* at a bank or *cambio*. Take your passport or national identity card along when you go to cash a cheque. Eurocheques are fairly easily cashed in Italy.

Tax Refunds

Foreign visitors residing outside the EC will be refunded the IVA paid on larger purchases made in shops displaying the "Italy Tax Free" symbol: a red package attached to a balloon. Goods valued at L.605,000 or more qualify for the refund. Obtain a receipt from the shop, to show on departure, together with the goods, to a customs officer. Post the receipt in one of the special boxes to be found past the customs area at most international airports in Italy. Or send it by mail within 50 days of the date of purchase. A small service charge will be deducted from the refund.

A ruined castle and *a medieval bridge in the pretty village of Dolceacqua in Liguria, not far from the French border.*

Electric Current

In general, the electric current is 220-volt, 50-cycle AC, but 125-volt outlets still exist. The voltage might be indicated on the sockets in hotels, but it is best to ask, to avoid ruining your shaver or hair dryer. Voltage transformers can be purchased in electrical appliance shops in Italy, but it is easier to obtain one before leaving home. Italian plugs are round, so you may also need an adaptor plug. However, many shavers, hair dryers and travelling irons available internationally come with built-in adaptors and transformers.

Getting There

See your travel agent or the Italian Tourist Office in your country well before departure for help with timetables, budget and personal requirements.

By Air

Scheduled flights

Rome's Leonardo da Vinci (Fiumicino) and Milan's Linate and Malpensa airports (*see* below) are the main gateways to Italy, though certain direct, scheduled international flights operate into Bologna (Borgo Panigale), Genoa (Cristoforo Colombo), Naples (Capodichino), Pisa (Galileo Galilei), Turin (Caselle), Venice (Marco Polo), Sardinia (Elmas, near Cagliari) and Sicily (Punta Raisi, near Palermo). From Milan and Rome, there are regular scheduled flights to some 30 destinations within Italy.

Approximate flying times are: London–Rome 2½ hours, Los Angeles–Rome 15 hours, New York–Rome 8 hours, Sydney–Rome 26 hours.

Package tours

These are offered by a wide range of tour operators and travel agents, including the Compagnia Italiana Turismo (CIT), Italy's national travel agency and tour operator. You can choose an all-inclusive package (air fare, accommodation, sightseeing and airport transfers) or opt for an independent tour with the possibility to create your own itinerary. The majority of package tours from overseas start out in Rome and include a choice of guided tours throughout the country.

If you book a charter fare and plan to tour Italy independently, look into fly-drive possibilities with flight and car-hire included. The Italian National Tourist Office (*see* GUIDES AND TOURS) distributes lists of tour operators offering package tours and special-interest holidays, including language, art and architecture courses.

By Road

(*See also* TRAVEL DOCUMENTS FOR MOTORISTS.)

Cross-channel ferries link the UK with France, Belgium or Holland. From there you can put your car on a train to Milan (starting points include Boulogne, Paris and Cologne). If you are driving yourself, you will find that the excellent motorway network across the Continent is such that you can now drive from the Channel coast to the toe of Italy without ever leaving a motorway.

Motorways in Belgium and Germany are toll-free. In France, you pay according to the distance travelled. At the Swiss border, you have to buy a sticker (*vignette*), which is valid for the current year. This should be displayed on the windscreen. In Austria, tolls are only levied on a few motorways, including the Brenner Autobahn.

Car ferries also connect Italy with France, Malta, Tunisia, Greece, Turkey, Israel and Egypt.

By Coach

Eurolines operate regular coach services from major continental cities, as well as from London, to a number of destinations in Italy, including Turin, Milan, Venice, Bologna, Florence and Rome. The coaches are modern and there are stops for breaks and meals but it can still be a gruelling journey and the service is not especially cheap. In the UK, tickets may be booked through any National Express agent. Return tickets are valid for up to six months. Information on routes, timetables and fares may be obtained from: Eurolines, 13 Lower Regent Street, London SW1 4LR; tel. (071) 730 0202.

By Rail

(*See also* GETTING AROUND.)
The European national railways offer a wide range of bargain tickets. Many of the railpasses mentioned below must be obtained before leaving home.

The Eurailpass, an individual ticket available to people residing outside Europe, the CIS, Turkey and North Africa (Tunisia, Algeria, Morocco) is valid for first-class unlimited rail travel in 20 European countries, including travel on some private railways, buses and many ferry boats and steamers. The Eurail Youthpass for those under 26 years of age allows one or two months of unlimited second-class rail travel. Surcharges are imposed on fast trains like EuroCity (EC), InterCity (IC), Rapido (R) and TGV, and for certain ferry crossings during high season. The Eurail Flexipass, for North Americans, Mexicans, Australians and New Zealanders offers five days of unlimited first-class travel within a 15-day period; the 21-day pass permits nine days' travel. The Eurail Youth Flexipass allows 15 days of second-class travel inside two months.

For Europeans under 26 years of age the beloved *Interrail* ticket has been abandoned, and a new type of ticket called *Domino* has been introduced. Check with your travel agent for full details.

The shortest travel time between Paris and Rome is about 15 hours, between Munich and Venice approximately 9 hours and between Geneva and Milan just over 4 hours.

Getting Around

By Car

Driving in Italy can be a hair-raising experience for the uninitiated. Italian motorists are not reckless, they are simply attuned to a different concept of driving. If you observe the following ground rules and venture with prudence into the traffic whirlpool, you stand a good chance of coming out unscathed.

Glance round to right and left and in your rear-view mirror all the time; other drivers are doing the same, and they have developed quick reflexes.

Treat traffic lights which are theoretically in your favour and white lines across merging side streets with caution. Don't take priority for granted.

To make progress in a traffic jam, inch gently but confidently forward into the snarl-up. To wave on another driver, courteously letting him or her cut in ahead of you, is tantamount to abdicating your rights as a motorist.

Fuel and Oil

Foreign drivers can buy a concessionary package of Italian petrol

---

Auto-da-fé

Everyone knows that the Italians are car crazy. That they might actually be certifiable is suggested by reports of a new craze sweeping the young people of Rome: late-night car racing on the Via Cristoforo Colombo, the big dual carriageway leading into the city from the south. Romans may have the blood of chariot drivers coursing through their veins but this new phenomenon has less to do with Ben Hur than with James Dean. It seems the Roman hot-rodders take their inspiration from the "chicken-run" car duel in *Rebel Without a Cause*. Like Dean, several practitioners of this new cult have already died at the wheel.

coupons (which offer a discount of approximately 15 per cent on pump prices) and a motorway toll card. The fuel card (*Carta Carburante*) that is issued with the package makes you a temporary member of the Automobile Club d'Italia (ACI) and enables you to call upon its emergency services at any time (*see* ACCIDENTS AND BREAKDOWNS). The package may be obtained from the automobile associations in your own country, or at ACI frontier offices (in foreign currency only). The package is only available if you are driving a foreign-registered car, not if you are hiring a car in Italy itself.

Service stations abound in Italy, usually with at least one mechanic on duty. Most stations close on Sundays, and daily from 12 noon to 3 p.m., but many have self-service pumps for use if they are closed. Stations along the motorways are open 24 hours a day. Attendants expect a tip for special attention.

Fuel (*benzina*) is sold at prices set by the government and comes in super (98–100 octane), lead-free (95 octane), normal (86–88 octane) and diesel. Lead-free petrol is now common. Look for the pumps with green labels marked *Senza piombo* (without lead) or the abbreviation, *SP*.

Speed Limits

Speed limits in Italy are as follows: in built-up areas 50kph (31mph); outside built-up areas 90kph (56mph). On the *autostrada*, 130kph (80mph) on weekdays, 110kph (68mph) on weekends and holidays.

Fines for speeding are high. Always pay on the spot; if you don't you will be charged considerably more at a later date.

Rules of the Road

Drive on the right, pass on the left. When passing other vehicles, or remaining in the left-hand (passing) lane, keep your directional indicator flashing. Traffic on major roads has right of way over traffic entering from side roads, but this, like other traffic regulations, is frequently ignored, so beware. At intersections of roads of similar importance, the car on the right theoretically has the right of way.

Seat belts are compulsory, and you should drive with dipped (low-beam) headlights in tunnels.

In theory, the use of car horns is prohibited in towns and cities, but not outside built-up areas. In practice, Italian drivers make indiscriminate use of their horns. In fact, blowing one's horn is an Italian attitude, so don't get flustered when someone does it to you. Sound your own horn whenever it could help to warn other vehicles of your impending arrival.

Some city centres are totally or partially closed to private cars. You should remember that trams (streetcars) always have priority.

Road Conditions

The ACI (Automobile Club d'Italia) operates a 24-hour telephone assistance centre staffed with multi-lingual personnel who give information on road and weather conditions, petrol coupons, hotels and so on. Dial 44595, preceded by area code 06 if you call from outside Rome.

Autostrade

Italy's *autostrade* (motorways/expressways) are designed for fast and safe driving. Access signposts are green. A toll, varying according to vehicle size and distance travelled, is charged on most stretches except on sections near the largest cities and in certain areas in the south. In most cases, you take a ticket at the *autostrada* entrance station (usually from an automatic machine) and present it at the exit, but on some stretches the toll has to be paid at intermediate stages; on others, a flat fare is charged when entering the motorway. Keep a good supply of change for any automatic barriers you may encounter at motorway exits.

A pass called a *Viacard* can be used on the majority of Italian motorways and is obtainable from ACI offices, motorway toll booths and service areas. The card is currently available in two amounts: L50,000 and L90,000.

Service areas with restaurants or cafeterias, or both, are found at regular intervals along the motorways.

Accidents and Breakdowns

To report an accident, dial the all-purpose emergency number 113. There are emergency telephones on the motorways. Some have separate buttons for technical problems (indicated by a monkey wrench) and injuries (a red cross); press the button until a lamp lights up and wait for help. Others give information in four languages on how to request police, first-aid and breakdown assistance.

If you break down on any road in Italy, you can dial 116 for ACI assistance. You will, however, be charged so it is a good idea to take out international breakdown insurance before leaving home. Temporary membership of the ACI can be taken out at main frontier posts.

Spare parts are available for all popular makes of car; the ACI will give you the address of the nearest supplier.

Parking

In cities, the wisest course is to find a supervised parking place (*parcheggio custodito*) near your hotel, and leave your car there for the duration of your stay. There are authorized parking areas (*parcheggio a pagamento*), often near the main railway station, where you pay by the hour, as well as car parks (parking lots) outside the centre with bus connections into town. Many larger towns have multi-level parking garages (*autorimessa* or *garage*). In some city centres, street parking is metered. In a *Zona Disco*, you need a parking disc (*disco di sosta*), obtainable from service stations. Set it to show the time you arrived and it will indicate when you have to leave. Then display it in the car, visible through the windscreen (shield).

Don't leave your car in places marked by yellow-and-black stripes, or where it says *Zona Rimozione* (removal zone), *Zona Verde* (green zone) or *Zona Pedonale* (pedestrian zone), or in a *Sosta Vietata* (no parking) or *Divieto di Sosta* (no stopping) zone; if you park there, your car may be towed away, and you will have to pay a hefty fine to retrieve it.

Never leave valuables in a parked car. To discourage prospective thieves, remove any radios or cassette-players and leave the glove compartment open. Always lock car doors.

Road Signs

Most of the road signs you will see in Italy are international pictographs. The

LANGUAGE GUIDE at the back of the book contains some of the written signs you may come across.

By City Transport

Taxis (*tassì* or *taxi*) may be hailed in the street, picked up at a taxi rank or ordered by telephone. Ranks are listed in the yellow pages of the telephone directory under *Taxi*. Make sure that the meter is running. Extra charges for luggage and for trips at night, on holidays and to airports are posted inside every cab. Taxi drivers expect a 10 to 15 per cent tip. In Rome and other large cities, beware of the non-metered unlicensed taxis (*abusivi*), which charge much more than the normal taxi rates for trips in private cars.

As well as bus (*autobus*) services, some big cities operate trams or streetcars (called *tram* in Italian). Naples has four funicular (*funicolare*) routes. Rome, Milan and Naples are also served by underground/subway (*metropolitana*, abbreviated to *metro*) systems. In Venice there is no way to move on wheels; instead, there are diesel-powered water buses of various descriptions, as well as water taxis and gondolas.

At bus stops (*fermata*), signs indicate the numbers of the buses stopping there and the routes they serve. Buy tickets for buses and trams in advance at tobacconists, news-stands or bars. Board buses through the rear doors (marked *Salita*) and punch your ticket in the machine just inside; exit by the middle doors (marked *Uscita*). Metro tickets are available from machines at the stations.

Rome's orange buses are crowded on certain routes and during rush-hours, but they are an inexpensive means of transport. Tickets can be purchased singly or in books of ten; they are each valid for a period of ninety minutes. A *biglietto integrato* (BIG) lets you travel all day on buses and the metro; a cheaper ticket is valid for only half the day. Weekly tickets for tourists are on sale at the ATAC (Rome's transport authority) booth in Piazza dei Cinquecento, in front of the Stazione Termini, the central railway station. The ATAC booth also sells a useful city map indicating the bus network.

Rome's metro railway Line A (*see* map on following page) runs from Via Ottaviano, near the Vatican, south-east to Via Anagnina, stopping at more than 20 stations and passing in reach of many of the city's popular tourist sights. The intersecting Line B runs from Rebibbia in the north-east of the city through Stazione Termini to EUR in the south-west. Some trains branch off at Magliana and go to the coast, reaching Ostia Antica and Lido di Ostia. Metro stations are identified by a large red sign with a white letter *M*.

Rome's horse-drawn cabs (*carrozzelle*) have been a familiar sight in the capital for centuries. They can be found at many of the major tourist sites across the city, including St Peter's Square, the Spanish Steps and the Colosseum. Fares are not fixed, so it is usually best to agree a price with the driver before setting off.

Florence has about 40 main city and suburban bus routes. For information and a free bus map, go to the ATAF office at Piazza del Duomo 57r. Board buses at the rear and punch your ticket in the red machine by the door.

Milan is served by a comprehensive and efficient public transport system, comprising buses, trams and the city's metro system, the *Metropolitana Milanese*, which runs on three lines. Information and tourist tickets are available at the ATM office on the mezzanine floor of the Duomo metro station.

Naples has an integrated transport network of buses, trams, funiculars, suburban railways and a metro line, as well as ferries and numerous taxis. These will get you close to wherever you want to go in the city and its environs. To work out where you are going, get a good map and bus timetable from one of the local tourist information offices (sited in Piazza del Gesù, at the Mergellina dock, Castel dell'Ovo and in Piazza Garibaldi in front of the Central Station).

Venice's water buses (*vaporetti* and the smaller and faster *motoscafi*) ply the Grand Canal and shuttle between the islands. Operated by the ACTV

*M*ap of Rome's metro.

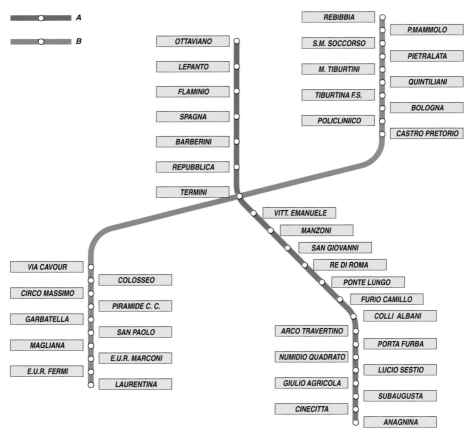

A pavement artist in San Gimignano shows that Tuscany continues to inspire portraits of the Madonna and Child.

(Venice's transport authority), the *vaporetti* are still a bargain considering the scenery. Tickets can be bought from bars and news-stands and at most stops. Apart from ordinary single tickets (buy one and get it punched in the machine on the landing stage before boarding or you will have to pay a surcharge), there are one-day and three-day tourist tickets. Venice has about ten water-taxi (*motoscafo di nolo*) stations. Although theoretically the rates are fixed, they tend to vary; agree on the fare in advance. This also applies to trips by gondola. Travelling by gondola is expensive but look out for the *traghetti*, public gondolas which ferry people across the Grand Canal;

they represent both a short cut and a bargain.

By Coach

Italy has a vast network of coach routes (long-distance buses) and each province has its own coach companies. Information on destinations and timetables is posted at coach terminals, usually situated near the town's railway station, and can be obtained from local or regional tourist offices. (*See* USEFUL NUMBERS AND ADDRESSES.) In remote rural areas and in the mountains, coaches prove a cheaper and faster means of transport than trains. However, between cities, trains provide the most efficient service.

By Train

The Italian State Railways (Ferrovie dello Stato, FS) operate an extensive network all over the country. Although the cost of train travel in Italy has been rising in recent years, it still represents a bargain when compared with prices in many other countries. Note that children under the age of 12 travel half-price; those under the age of 4 (not occupying a seat) travel free.

Italian trains can be extremely crowded, so it is advisable to make a reservation if you are planning a long journey. Buy your ticket in advance from a travel agency (bearing the FS emblem), as queues at railway stations can be interminable. If you have not booked, it is wise to arrive at the station at least 20 minutes before departure to be sure of catching your train.

Italian trains are classified according to speed, so choose your train carefully, as journey times (and ticket prices) vary a good deal. The following list describes the various types:

ETR 450 "Pendolino": fast and luxurious air-conditioned trains running between the main cities; first class only, reservation obligatory (ticket includes meal, newspapers and service).

EuroCity (EC) and Trans-Europe Express (TEE): international high-speed trains running between major European cities; first class only; reservation is obligatory and a fare surcharge payable.

InterCity: high-speed trains connecting the major Italian cities; first and second class; reservation and surcharge.

Espresso: long-distance express trains stopping at main stations, usually extremely crowded.

Diretto: slow trains stopping at most stations.

Locale: very slow local trains which stop at every station.

Tourists can take advantage of a number of reduced-rate passes on Italian railways. Anyone permanently residing outside Italy can buy a special Travel-at-Will ticket (Biglietto turistico libera circolazione, or BTLC) for unlimited first- or second-class rail travel during 8, 15, 21 or 30 days. With this ticket there are no supplements on the faster InterCity and Rapido trains, and no extra charge is made for seat reservations. The Flexi Card is similar to the Travel-at-Will tickets but, as its name suggests, more flexible and a good deal cheaper. It allows unlimited travel up to a certain number of days within a set period: 9 days (4 days travel); 21 days (8 days travel) and 30 days (12 days travel). The Biglietto Chilometrico is valid for two months of first- or second-class travel. It can be used by as many as five people, even if not related, for 20 trips totalling a maximum of 3,000km (1,864 miles), but supplements must be paid for Rapido and InterCity trains. The passes are available from major railway stations in Italy, but are cheaper to buy from travel agents in your home country.

By Boat

There are regular daily car ferries and hydrofoils connecting the mainland with Italy's many islands, both large and small. Sardinia and Sicily are particularly well served. Regular car ferries operate between Villa San Giovanni in Calabria to Messina in Sicily (journey time: 35 minutes) and from Reggio Calabria to Messina (50 minutes). Overnight car ferries run daily from Naples to Palermo, and several times a week in summer from Genoa to Palermo. Sardinia's major ports are connected to the mainland by frequent car-ferry services. The crossing time between Civitavecchia and Golfo Aranci in Sardinia is around seven hours.

If you are travelling by car or if you want a cabin, reserve long boat trips before leaving home, especially in high season (June to September).

Ferries and hydrofoils also operate between towns and sites on the northern lakes of Como, Garda and Maggiore. For information on schedules and fares, apply to a travel agency or the regional tourist office, or contact ACI's telephone assistance centre on (06) 44595.

By Plane

Alitalia, Italy's national airline, and its domestic affiliate ATI (Aero Trasporti Italiani) offer connections between a great number of Italian cities. Detailed information is available at travel agencies and Alitalia offices. Special fares are available for family groups, children, young people/students and senior citizens. Travellers can also take advantage of discounts on night flights and weekend tickets.

Hitch-hiking (*Autostop*)

Thumbing a ride is permitted everywhere except on motorways (expressways). If you do hitch-hike, it is always wiser to travel in pairs.

Car Hire

Hiring a car in Italy is expensive when compared with many other countries. It will probably be cheaper and more convenient to arrange car-hire in advance through your automobile association or through a company in your home country, or as part of a fly-drive package, such as the Alitalia-Avis Jet-drive scheme.

*G*enoa is a city with a long and proud maritime tradition. The birthplace of Christopher Columbus, it remains one of the great ports of the Mediterranean and the largest in Italy.

For those hiring a car in Italy itself, the major international firms have offices at airports, major railway stations, in town and city centres and at tourist resorts; they are listed in the *Yellow Pages* of the telephone directory under *Autonoleggio*. If you are staying in a hotel, your hotel representative may be able to recommend a less expensive local firm. Weekend rates and weekly unlimited mileage rates are usually available, and it is worth inquiring about any seasonal deals.

To hire a car, you must show your driving licence and passport or national identity card. The minimum age requirement varies from 18 to 25 depending on the company. You must have held a full licence for at least one year. A deposit is often required except by credit card holders; insurance is mandatory.

Large agencies will let you leave a rented car in another Italian or European city for an additional fee. You may be able to arrange to have your hire-car delivered to you. Note that

hiring a car with automatic transmission is more expensive and may have to be arranged in advance.

Chauffeur-driven cars can normally be hired at major rental companies. However, if you know your itinerary in advance, you should arrange for a package deal with your travel agent before departure.

Maps

Tourist offices give away basic street plans featuring a selection of local information. More detailed maps are on sale at news-stands. Look out for the publication date in a corner of the map to make sure it is the most up-to-date version available. There are many good maps of Italy, including those published by Hallwag, Kümmerly + Frey and Michelin. The Touring Club Italiano (TCI) produces excellent regional maps which can be purchased singly or in atlas form. They are available at bookshops, as are detailed hiking maps drawn to a scale of 1/25,000.

Guides and Tours

Local tourist offices and major hotels can help you find qualified guides and give you a list of guided tours. A selection of guides and interpreters is listed in the *Yellow Pages* of the telephone directory under the entry *Traduzione*, and local newspapers carry advertisements offering such services. There are also guides near most of the major tourist attractions, and portable cassette-players with commentaries in English can often be hired.

Ars longa, Vita brevis

Museum-going in Italy is not always simple. Even the local tourist office cannot always keep up with the changes in opening hours. Some museums are closed temporarily, for days, months or even years, for *restauro* (restoration). This is a blanket term covering budgetary problems for museum staff and modern security systems or genuine, long overdue programmes of renovation of the buildings and restoration of the paintings. Many ancient Roman monuments may also go into prolonged hiding under protective scaffolding.

When you do go to one of the really big museums like the Uffizi in Florence, the Vatican in Rome or Milan's Brera, treat it like Italy itself: unless you are a museum-fiend, don't try to do it all. Before you go in, look at the guide, study the museum plan in the lobby and head for the things you really want to see. Or, if you prefer the serendipity of coming across beautiful surprises, just wander around, but not for much more than an hour. Otherwise, you may get a sharp attack of visual overload and won't be able to tell the difference between a Fra Angelico and the sign for the fire extinguisher.

The Italian Tourist Agency (CIT) and many private firms offer morning, afternoon, half- and full-day city sightseeing tours, plus excursions to many points of interest.

Accommodation

Hotels (*Albergo*)

Italy's hotels span a broad range, from the opulent and palatial to the downright spartan. They are classified in five categories, graded by stars, from five (luxury) down to one. Rates vary according to region, location, season, class and services offered. They are fixed in agreement with the regional tourist board.

During high season and at Christmas and Easter, it is essential to book in advance in all the major tourist spots. In Venice it is wise to reserve all year round. Reservations may be made through travel agencies or by writing directly to the hotel. On the spot, regional tourist boards and local tourist offices can supply lists of hotels in their area but only in the smaller towns will they help you to reserve rooms. Most airports and major railway stations have hotel information desks which provide free advice and booking facilities.

Service charge, tourist tax and IVA (sales tax) are normally included in the room rate, but if prices are not listed as *tutto compreso* (all-inclusive), as much as 20 per cent can be added to your bill. The rate quoted for five- and four-star hotels is inclusive of air-conditioning charges, but you will hāve to pay extra for this facility (if available) in less expensive hotels. Breakfast is not usually included in the room rate.

In seaside or lakeside resorts, where many establishments are open only half the year, the low season is May–June and September in the north, a month earlier and later in the south. Note that during high season many resort hotels require guests to stay a minimum of three nights on half-board terms.

Pensioni

These are modest boarding houses, often with more character and a homelier atmosphere than hotels. They tend to offer fewer facilities and may not have a restaurant; when there is one, you could well be treated to some excellent Italian family cooking.

Motels

In Italy, motels are increasing in number and improving in service. Many have a swimming pool or private beach, tennis courts, and other facilities. The AGIP chain of motels offers reasonable facilities and covers much of the country, including Sicily and Sardinia.

Inns (*Locande*)

A *locanda* is generally an inexpensive country inn, providing basic accommodation. In some instances, the name may be given to a fine restaurant offering very comfortable lodging.

Villas and Apartments

Families staying for a week or longer in one locality may find it more convenient and economical, especially in the resorts, to rent a furnished villa or apartment. Many tour operators offer self-catering packages which include travel to and from Italy. Lists of operators are available from the Italian

National Tourist Office. In Italy, information is published in local newspapers. Regional and local tourist offices have their own lists of companies and agents arranging rental in the different areas.

Camping (*Campeggio*)

There are more than 2,000 official campsites in Italy, graded, like the hotels, by stars. Most of them are equipped with electricity, water and toilet facilities. Addresses and full details of amenities are given in the directory *Campeggi in Italia*, published annually by the Touring Club Italiano

A tent with a view.
The Florence skyline, with Brunelleschi's cathedral dome prominent, appears through the trees at this well-situated campsite.

(TCI). The directory is on sale in bookstores in Italy. A free list of sites, with location map, published by the Federcampeggio (Federazione Italiana del Campeggio e del Caravanning), is available from Federcampeggio, Via Vittorio Emanuele 11, Casella Postale 23, 50041 Calenzano (Florence); tel. (055) 882391; fax 8825918.

The list of campsites may also be available from the Italian State Tourist Board in your own country.

Campsites in Italy are mainly concentrated along the coast and around lakes, but all big cities have several sites accessible from the centre by car or public transport. They are listed in the *Yellow Pages* of the telephone directory under *Campeggi—Ostelli— Villaggi Turistici* (Campsites, Hostels, Tourist Villages). Seaside and lakeside camping grounds tend to be overcrowded in July and August. You are strongly advised to stick to the official sites.

To camp in the peak summer season, you should reserve in advance through the Centro Internazionale Prenotazioni Campeggio at the address for Federcampeggio listed above.

The International Camping Carnet, a pass that entitles holders to discounts and insurance coverage throughout Europe, is required at many campsites in Italy. It can be obtained either through your camping or automobile association or through the TCI or Federcampeggio.

If you enter Italy with a caravan, you should be able to show an inventory (with two copies) of the material and equipment in the caravan, listing items such as dishes and linen.

One-axle caravans on Italian roads may be no wider than 2.3m (7.5ft) and no longer than 6m (19.6ft), including tow hook. For two-axle caravans, the maximum width allowed is 2.5m (8.2ft) and maximum length 7.5m (24.6ft). The maximum height is 3m (9.8ft). The speed limit for cars towing caravans is 80kph (50mph) on main roads and 100kph (62mph) on motorways.

Youth Hostels

There are over 50 youth hostels (*ostello della gioventù*) in Italy, open to holders of membership cards issued by the International Youth Hostels Federation. Book well in advance if you plan to stay in one of the main tourist centres during high season. Membership cards and information are available from your national Youth Hostels Association and from the Associazione Italiana Alberghi per la Gioventù (AIG), the Italian Youth Hostels Association, at Via Cavour 44, 00184 Rome; tel. (06) 4871152; fax 4880492.

Farm Holidays

You can stay on a farm in Italy, in a spartan cottage, a modern farmhouse or a 17th-century castle, and enjoy threshing, grape-harvesting or mushroom-gathering, fishing, horse riding or golf. Contact Agriturist, the National Association for Rural Tourism: Corso Vittorio Emanuele 101, 00186 Rome; tel. (06) 6852342; fax 6852424.

Mountain Huts (*Rifugi Alpini*)

Those with a head for heights may care to explore lodgings in Italy's Alpine regions. There are around 500 huts in the mountain districts, most of them owned by the Italian Alpine Club (CAI). For lists of huts and further information, write to: Club Alpino Italiano, Via Fonseca Pimental 7, Milan; tel. (02) 26141378; fax 26141395.

Monasteries and Convents

Some Roman Catholic orders take in guests at very reasonable rates. They provide comfortable rooms as well as meals. For information, write to the tourist board in the region of your choice (*see* USEFUL NUMBERS AND ADDRESSES).

Day Hotels (*Alberghi Diurni*)

These handy establishments are not the kind of places to go if you want overnight accommodation. Instead, they offer practical facilities for low prices during the daytime. You can freshen up with a shower or bath, leave luggage or parcels, have a haircut, manicure or massage, have your laundry done or take a few hours' rest. Day hotels are generally situated in the city centres, in the vicinity of the main railway station.

Crime and Theft

Cases of violence against tourists are rare, but petty theft is an endless annoyance, and tourists are always easy targets for robbery. By taking a few simple precautions, you can reduce the risk or ease the pain and inconvenience caused by loss or theft of your belongings.

It is wise to leave unneeded documents and excess cash locked up in the hotel safe and keep what you take, including credit cards, in an inside pocket or a pouch inside your clothes. Handbags are particularly vulnerable; agile thieves, often operating in pairs on vespas or motorbikes, whisk past and snatch them from the shoulder, sometimes even cutting or breaking the straps to do so.

Be particularly attentive on crowded public transport and never leave bags or cameras unattended or out of sight at airports, railway stations, restaurants or beaches, even for a few seconds. Beware of begging children and don't let them distract your attention for a moment (by, for example, thrusting a cardboard sign at you to read); they are very adept pickpockets.

It is a good idea to make photocopies of your tickets, driving licence, passport and other vital documents in order to facilitate reporting a theft, should it happen, and obtaining replacements.

If you leave your car parked somewhere, lock it and empty it of everything, not only of valuables. Leave the glove compartment open, to discourage prospective thieves. Wherever possible, try to park in a garage or attended parking area.

When travelling overnight by train, keep the door and windows of sleeping car compartments locked.

Any loss or theft should be reported at once to the nearest police station, particularly for insurance purposes as your insurance company will need to see a copy of the police report.

Police

Italy's municipal police (*Vigili Urbani*), wear navy blue or white uniforms with shiny buttons and white helmets. They direct traffic and handle routine tasks. Some municipal police act as interpreters. Look for the special badge on their uniforms, which indicates the languages they speak.

The *Carabinieri*, dressed in dark blue uniforms with a red stripe, deal with serious crimes throughout the country; they are technically a part of the Italian army. The *Polizia di Stato* (national police), dressed in navy blue jackets and light blue trousers, deal with usual police matters; their headquarters are *La Questura*. Outside the towns, the *Polizia Stradale* patrol the roads.

The all-purpose emergency number, 113, will get you police assistance.

Emergencies

In an emergency you can phone the following numbers all over Italy 24 hours a day:
Emergency services:
ambulance, fire, police: 113
Carabinieri, for urgent
  police action: 112
Fire: 115
Road assistance (ACI): 116

Lost Property

Cynics say that anything lost in Italy is lost forever, but that is not necessarily true. Restaurants more often than not will have the briefcase, guide book or camera you left behind waiting for you at the cashier's desk. If you are not sure where the loss occurred, call the lost-property office (*ufficio oggetti rinvenuti* or *smarriti*). Report the loss of your passport or identity papers to your embassy or consulate.

Rome's general lost-property office is the Ufficio Oggetti Rinvenuti at Via Bettoni, 1; tel. 5816040. There are lost property offices at the Termini railway station, tel. 4730/6682 and at ATAC in Via Volturno, 65; tel. 4695. For losses on the metro, phone 57351.

In Florence, seek lost property at the Ufficio Oggetti Smarriti at Via Circondaria, 19; for property lost on trains, go to Piazza dell'Unità, 1.

Venice's general lost-property office is called the Ufficio all'Economato and is situated near the Rialto Bridge at Calle Loredam, Ca Farsetti 4136. The city's water-transport authority, ACTV, has a lost-property office at the St Angelo stop (No. 9) on the Grand Canal.

Complaints

Complaining is an Italian national pastime, but it can involve elaborate bureaucratic procedures once it passes beyond the verbal stage. The threat of a formal declaration to the police should be effective in such cases as overcharging for car repairs, but this will consume hours or even days of your visit.

To avoid problems in all situations, always establish the price in advance and make sure that any taxes or supplements are included. In hotels, restaurants and shops, complaints should be made to the manager (*direttore*) or proprietor (*proprietario*). Any complaint about a taxi fare should be settled by referring to the notice, in four languages, affixed by law in each taxi, specifying charges in excess of the meter rate.

Embassies and Consulates

Contact the embassy (*ambasciata*) or consulate (*consolato*) of your home country when in trouble (loss of passport, problems with the police, serious accidents). All the embassies are in Rome, while many countries also maintain consulates in other Italian cities. (For the addresses of embassies in Rome, *see* USEFUL NUMBERS AND ADDRESSES.)

Opening Hours

Opening hours vary from region to region, and sometimes even from district to district in the large cities. In true Mediterranean fashion, much of Italy shuts down, or at least slows down, in the hours after lunch. However, in Rome and in the northern cities, the modern business day is gradually creeping in, with a non-stop day operating at least in the city centre. The following opening hours should therefore just be looked upon as a guideline.

Banks are generally open from 8.30 a.m. to 1.30 p.m. and again for an hour or so in the afternoon, usually from 3 to 4 p.m., Monday to Friday.

Currency-exchange offices at airports and major railway stations are open till late in the evening and on Saturdays and Sundays.

Churches generally close for sightseeing at lunchtime, approximately noon to 3 p.m. or even later.

Museums and art galleries are usually open from 9 or 9.30 a.m. to 2, 3 or 4 p.m., and in some cases from 5 to 8 p.m., Tuesday to Saturday, and until 1 p.m. on Sundays. Closing day is generally Monday. If Monday is a holiday, it is possible that some museums and galleries may close the following day. It is best to check times locally before you set out.

Pharmacies are open 8.30 a.m. to 1 p.m. and 4–8 p.m. At least one in each district operates on a rota basis during the afternoon break, at night and at weekends. The addresses and opening schedule for duty pharmacies appear on every pharmacy door and in the local papers.

Post offices normally open from 8.30 a.m. to 2 p.m., Monday to Friday, until noon on Saturdays. Main post offices in the larger cities keep longer hours.

Shops open from 9 a.m. to 12.30 or 1 p.m. and from 3.30 or 4 to 7.30 or 8 p.m. In Milan and Turin, the lunch break is normally shorter and closing time earlier. Most shops close on Monday morning. Food stores generally open earlier, closing on Wednesday or Thursday afternoons. Shops in tourist resorts stay open all day, every day, in high season.

Communications

Post Offices (*Posta* or *Ufficio Postale*)

These are identified by a yellow sign with *PT* on black. Post offices handle telegrams, mail and money transfers. Postage stamps can also be purchased at tobacconists (*tabacchi*: look for the sign of a white *T* on a black rectangle) and at some hotels. Letter boxes are painted red; the slot marked *Per la Città* is for local mail only, while the one labelled *Altre Destinazioni* is for all other destinations. The slowness of the Italian postal service is a national scandal. Many businesses rely on fax or established international private courier services. The Vatican City maintains its own admirably efficient postal services, including post offices, stamps and letter boxes (painted blue). The rates are the same as those of the Italian Post Office.

Poste Restante/General Delivery

For a short stay it is not worth arranging to receive mail, as the post is so often slow. Nevertheless, you can have mail addressed to you in any town c/o Fermo Posta, Ufficio Postale Centrale, followed by the name of the town. Don't forget your passport for identification when you go to pick up mail. You will have to pay a small fee.

Telegrams (Telegramme)

These can be sent to destinations inside and outside Italy, as can telex messages. There is now a rapidly growing *telefax* (facsimile) service.

Parcels (Pacco)

Bureaucratic regulations about wrapping and sending packages from Italy

Wicker crafts in Tuscany. All across the country, Italians are adept at turning out functional and attractive products, from high-fashion to the most basic household article.

are so complicated that even the immensely knowledgeable hotel concierges might not know them all. Ask at a post office.

Telephone (*Telefono*)

Public telephones (*cabina telefonica*) are situated everywhere. Calls can also be made from bars and cafés, indicated by a yellow telephone sign outside. Older types of public payphones require tokens (*gettoni*), which are available at bars, tobacconists and from automatic dispensers sometimes installed next to the phone. More modern phones with three slots take both tokens and 100-,

200- and 500-lire coins. Some telephones are card-operated. Phone cards (*scheda telefonica*) of L.5,000 or 10,000 are available at some bars, tobacconists (*Tabacchi*), offices of Italy's telephone company, SIP (Società Italiana per l'Esercizio Telefonico) and post offices as well as from automatic distributors found in stations, airports and elsewhere. You can make long-distance and international calls from SIP offices, which are usually open from 7 a.m. to around 10 p.m.

Direct international calls can be made from telephones labelled *Teleselezione*. If you make a long-distance call in a hotel, expect to be heavily surcharged.

To make a call from a pay phone, insert the token or coin and lift the receiver. The normal dialling tone is a series of long dash sounds. A dot-dot-dot series means the central computer is overloaded; you will have to hang up and try again.

Area codes for main cities: Bari 080, Bologna 051, Catania 095, Florence 055, Genoa 010, Messina 090, Milan 02, Naples 081, Palermo 091, Rome 06, Turin 011, Trieste 040, Venice 041, Verona 045. Drop the 0 when dialling Italy from abroad.

To make a direct international call, dial 00, wait for a tone change, then dial the country's code, area code and subscriber's number. Some country codes:

Australia	(00) 61
Austria	(00) 43
Belgium	(00) 32
Canada	(00) 1
Denmark	(00) 45
Eire	(00) 35
India	(00) 91
Japan	(00) 81
Malta	(00) 356
Netherlands	(00) 31
New Zealand	(00) 64
Norway	(00) 47
Singapore	(00) 65
South Africa	(00) 27
Sweden	(00) 46
Switzerland	(00) 41
UK	(00) 44
USA	(00) 1
Germany	(00) 49

To telephone Italy from abroad, dial the international access code, then 39.

Charges for international phone calls within Europe are reduced between 10 p.m. and 8 a.m. on weekdays and all day on Sundays; for calls outside Europe, cheap-rate times are 11 p.m. to 8 a.m. and all day Sunday.

Some useful numbers:
Local and national enquiries: 12
Operator for Europe: 15
International enquiries: 176
Intercontinental operator: 170
Intercontinental enquiries: 1790

Eating

What to Eat

The classical cuisine of Tuscany and Bologna and the pizza and pasta dishes of Naples are available everywhere, but you can try other regional specialities as you travel around the country. Despite the plethora of sauces for the pasta, the essence of Italian cooking is its simplicity: fish cooked with perhaps just a touch of fennel; other seafood served straight, cold, as an hors d'œuvre; Florentine steak charcoal-grilled; vegetables sautéed without elaborate disguise, at most marinated in lemon, olive oil and pepper.

Any *trattoria* worth its olive oil will set out on a long table near the entrance a truly painterly display of its **antipasti** (hors d'œuvre). The best way to get to know the delicacies is to make up your own assortment (*antipasto misto*). Both attractive and tasty are the cold *peperoni*: red, yellow and green peppers grilled, skinned and marinated in olive oil and a little lemon juice. Mushrooms (*funghi*), baby marrows (*zucchini*), aubergines (*melanzane*), artichokes (*carciofi*) and sliced fennel (*finocchio*) are also served cold, with a dressing (*pinzimonio*). One of the most refreshing hors d'œuvre is the *mozzarella alla caprese*: slices of soft white buffalo cheese and tomato in a dressing of fresh basil and olive oil.

Try the tunny or tuna fish (*tonno*) with white beans and onions (*fagioli e cipolle*). Mixed seafood hors d'œuvre (*antipasto di mare*) may include scampi, prawns (*gamberi*), mussels (*cozze*) and fresh sardines (*sarde*), but also, chewily delicious squid (*calamari*) and octopus (*polipi*).

Ham from Parma or San Daniele (near Udine) is served paper-thin with melon (*prosciutto con melone*) or, even better, with fresh figs (*con fichi*). Most salami is mass-produced industrial sausage from Milan, but try the local product of Florence, Genoa, Naples and Bologna and look out for Ferrara's piquant *salame da sugo*.

Popular **soups** are mixed vegetable (*minestrone*) and clear soup (*brodo*), with an egg beaten into it (*stracciatella*).

Remember that Italian restaurants traditionally serve **pasta** as an introductory course, not as the main dish. While they won't go so far as to kill you, even the friendliest of restaurant owners will raise a sad eyebrow if you make a whole meal out of a plate of spaghetti.

It is said that there are as many different forms of Italian pasta noodles as there are French cheeses—some 360 at the last count, with new forms being created every year. Each sauce— tomato, cheese, cream, meat or fish— needs its own kind of noodle. In this land of painters and sculptors, the pasta's form and texture are an essential part of the taste.

Besides spaghetti and macaroni, the worldwide popularity of pasta has familiarized us with *tagliatelle* ribbon noodles (known in Rome as *fettuccine*); baked *lasagne* with layers of pasta, meat sauce and béchamel; rolled *cannelloni*; and stuffed *ravioli*. From there, you launch into the lusty poetry of *tortellini* and *cappelletti* (variations on *ravioli*), or curved *linguine*, flat *pappardelle*, quill-shaped *penne* and corrugated *rigatoni*. Discover the other 350 for yourselves.

> **Feasts Fit for Romans**
> Sometimes an Italian beanfeast is literally just that, a feast of beans. The Italian calendar is stuffed full of *sagre*, seasonal gastronomic feasts celebrating the typical food or wine of a particular district. The inhabitants of the province of Rome are especially partial to this form of celebration, which seems appropriate given their ancestors' reputation for gourmandizing. Almost every town and village in the province seems to have its own speciality. In Ariccia in September the locals tuck away suckingpig (*porchetta*), in Ladispoli it's artichokes in April (the *Sagra del carciofo*), while in Arsoli in September the order of the day is *fagioli*: beans. Camerata Nuova's Salsicciata celebrates sausages; Nemi honours its celebrated strawberries. Some of these festivals have genuine histories dating back centuries, others have only recently been cooked up by a canny local tourist board.

There are almost as many sauces. The most famous, of course, is *bolognese*, known more succinctly in Bologna itself as *ragù*. The best includes not only minced beef, tomato purée and onions but chopped chicken livers, ham, carrot, celery, white wine and, the vital ingredient in Bolognese cooking, nutmeg. Other popular sauces range from the simplest and spiciest *aglio e olio* (just garlic, olive oil and chilli peppers), *marinara* (tomato), *carbonara* (chopped bacon and eggs), *matriciana* (salt pork and tomato), Genoese *pesto* (basil and garlic ground up in olive oil with pine nuts and parmesan cheese) and *vongole* (clams and tomato), to the succulent *lepre* (hare in red wine) and startling *al nero*, yes, pasta blackened by the ink of the cuttlefish—wonderful. Don't be ashamed to ask whether Parmesan cheese should or should not be added.

For prince and peasant alike, the Po valley's ricefields have made **risotto** a worthy rival to pasta, particularly in and around Milan and Bergamo. The rice is cooked slowly in white wine, beef marrow, butter (not oil) and saffron, and served with Parmesan cheese. Delicious with mushrooms, chicken or seafood.

For the main dish, veal (*vitello*) has pride of place among the **meats**. Try the pan-fried cutlet (*costoletta*) Milanese-style in breadcrumbs, *scaloppine al limone* (veal fillets with lemon), *vitello tonnato* (veal in tunny fish

A tempting display of lobsters in a Venetian restaurant. With the Mediterranean coast never too far away, seafood dishes can be enjoyed all over Italy.

sauce), *alla fiorentina* (with a spinach sauce). The popular *saltimbocca* (literally "jump in the mouth") is an originally Roman veal-roll with ham, sage and Marsala, while *osso buco* is stewed veal shinbone. You will find calf's liver (*fegato di vitello*) served in a Marsala sauce, *alla milanese*; in breadcrumbs or *alla veneziana*; and thinly sliced, fried with onions in olive oil.

Beef (*manzo*), pork (*maiale*) and lamb (*agnello*) are most often served straightforward, charcoal-grilled or roast (*al forno*) but, particularly in the south where the beef may be less tender, the meat is cooked in a tomato and garlic sauce (*alla pizzaiola*).

The most common **chicken** dishes are grilled (*pollo alla diavola*); fillets with ham and cheese (*petti di pollo alla bolognese*); or, like veal, in a tunny fish sauce (*tonnato*).

All the **fish** that you see displayed as *antipasti* is prepared very simply— grilled, steamed or fried. You should

also look out for *spigola* (sea bass), *triglia* (red mullet), *pesce spada* (swordfish) and *coda di rospo* (angler fish). Be careful when ordering the *fritto misto*. Although this most often means a mixed fry of fish, it may be a mixture of breaded chicken breasts, calf's liver, veal and vegetables.

Aristocrats among the cooked **vegetables** are the big *Boletus* mushrooms (*funghi porcini*), which sometimes come stuffed (*ripieni*) with bacon, garlic, parsley and cheese. Try red peppers stewed with tomatoes (*peperonata*) or aubergine (*melanzane*) stuffed with anchovies, olives and capers. Baby onions (*cipolline*) and *zucchini* are both served sweet-and-sour (*agrodolce*). Vegetable accompaniments must be ordered separately, as they do not automatically come with the meat dish. What is available will depend on the season, but you are most likely to find spinach (*spinaci*), endives (*cicoria*), green beans (*fagioli*) done in butter and garlic, peas (*piselli*) and baby marrow (*zucchini*).

Of the **cheeses**, the famous Parmesan (*parmigiano*), far better than the exported product, is eaten separately, not just grated over soup or pasta. Try, too, the blue *gorgonzola*, *provolone* buffalo cheese, creamy Piedmontese *fontina*, the pungent cow's milk *taleggio* or ewe's milk *pecorino*. Roman *ricotta* can be sweetened with sugar and cinnamon.

Dessert means first and foremost *gelati*, the creamiest ice-cream in the world. This is generally better in an ice-cream parlour (*gelateria*) than the average *trattoria*. Serious connoisseurs send you to Parma and Bologna for the best, but they lower their voices when Neapolitans are around. The deliciously refreshing coffee- or fruit-flavoured *granita* has very little to do with that miserably insipid concoction that English dictionaries helplessly evoke as "water ice" (think *sorbet* and you're getting close).

Nothing varies more in quality than the Italian version of trifle; *zuppa inglese* (literally "English soup"). It may indeed be an extremely thick but sumptuous soup of fruit and cream and cake and Marsala or just a very disappointing sickly slice of cake. You may prefer the coffee trifle or *tirami sù* ("pick me up"). The *zabaglione* of whipped egg yolks, sugar and Marsala should be served warm or sent back.

Easier on the stomach is the fruit: grapes (*uva*), peaches (*pesche*), apricots (*albicocche*) and wonderful fresh figs (*fichi*), both black and green.

Regional Specialities

Though most regional delicacies have spread nationwide, a few specialities are still to be found principally in their place of origin.

Rome goes in for hearty meat dishes. If its *saltimbocca* veal-rolls have gone around the world, gourmets insist you must not wander too far from Piazza Navona to get a real *stufatino* beef stew or *coda alla vaccinara* (oxtail braised with vegetables). Romans also claim the best roast kid (*capretto*) or spring lamb (*abbacchio*). The capital's Jewish Ghetto originated the spectacular *carciofi alla giudea*; whole artichokes, crisply deep-fried, stem, heart, leaves and all.

Tuscany produces Italy's best chicken. Try *pollo alla cacciatora*, "hunter's style", with mushrooms, tomatoes, shallots, herbs and strips of ham. The flavoursome charcoal-grilled T-bone or rib steak (*bistecca alla fiorentina*) is often big enough to cover a whole plate and will serve two people, very, very happily. Hearty stomachs enjoy the *trippe alla fiorentina*; tripe with tomato, marjoram and parmesan cheese. On the coast, look out for the *cacciucco*; a spicy fish stew of red mullet, squid and crab in tomatoes, onions, garlic, Chianti and croûtons. *Baccalà* is a simpler but similarly spicy cod stew.

The cuisine of **Umbria** has great finesse. The roast pork (*porchetta*) is especially fragrant with fennel and other herbs, and look out for a succulent spit-roasted wild pigeon (*palombacce allo spiedo*). They are proud, too, of the *cacciotto* and *raviggiolo* ewe's cheese. In and around **Perugia**, the supreme pasta dish is *spaghetti ai tartufi neri* (with black truffles). Especially at Christmas time, the traditional *cappelletti in brodo* is served, a soup of ravioli stuffed with pork and veal.

Milan has contributed its risotto, breaded veal, *osso buco* and sweet *panettone* brioche to the nation. But it has kept for itself and its more robust visitors the *casoeula*; pork and sausages stewed in cabbage and other vegetables. Tough industrialists are weaned on *busecca alla milanese*; tripe with white beans. To fend off the autumn rains, the *polenta* maize-flour bread served with so many savoury **Lombardy** dishes becomes, as *polenta pasticciata*, a stout pie of mushrooms and white truffles in a béchamel sauce.

The herbs of **Liguria** make for some superb pasta sauces. The most famous of all, the basil of Genoa's *pesto*, is best with the local *trenette* (large size spaghetti). Rosemary is sprinkled on flat rounds of bread, *focaccia*, with olive oil; and wild aromatic greens are pounded together with ricotta cheese to make a delicious stuffing for the ravioli-like *pansoti*, which is always served with walnut sauce. The harvest of the land is just as important as that of the sea. On trattoria menus, *misto di mare* is followed by *misto di terra*.

Cooking in **Alto Adige** or South Tyrol is still predominantly Austrian-style and in German on the menu. The home-cured ham, *Speck*, is often served in the farmhouse manner; a chunk on a wooden board with a sharp knife for you to cut it yourself in paper-thin slices. Up in the mountains, you will appreciate the *Knödelsuppe*, a chicken or beef broth with dumplings of flour, breadcrumbs, onions, bacon, parsley and garlic. Austria meets Italy with *Spinatspätzle*, gnocchi-like spinach noodles sautéed with bacon and cream. **Friuli-Venezia Giulia** also continues the cuisine of the Austro-Hungarian empire: gulasch and barley soup. Here, the great ham is San Daniele. In **Trieste**, the seafood is excellent and the desserts, they claim, are as good as Vienna's, especially the apple *Strudel* and almond marzipan *mandorlato*.

In **Venice**, when you see someone smacking a cod against a gondola's mooring-post, likely as not it is being "tenderized" for the great *baccalà mantecato* (cream of dried cod), a smoother version of the French *brandade de morue*. The *grancevole*, beautiful red Adriatic spider-crabs, are treated more delicately as a centrepiece of Venetian seafood. Risotto is as popular here as in Lombardy, particularly with scampi or mussels, as well as the delightfully named *risi e bisi*; rice and green peas. An original creation of Harry's Bar, the rendezvous of the international smart set down by the Grand Canal, beef *carpaccio* is sliced raw and thin as Parma ham and served with an olive oil and mustard sauce. During Carnival time, have the mussel soup (*zuppa di peoci*) to resist the February mists. **Ravenna** can lay claim to the Adriatic's most bracing fish soup; *brodetto*, which is full of sea bass, squid, eel, red mullet and all kinds of shellfish.

Bologna has a position of leadership in Italian gastronomy similar to that of Lyon in France. Its old specialities are now the mainstays of the national cuisine, but some things are just not as good away from home: *tortellini* pasta coils stuffed with minced pork, veal, chicken and cheese; *costolette alla bolognese* (breaded veal cutlets with ham and cheese); and the monumental *lasagne verde*, baked green pasta with beef *ragù*, béchamel sauce and the all-important nutmeg. The key to the classic Bologna *mortadella* sausage is the flavouring of white wine and coriander. One of the great rice dishes of **Parma** is the *bomba di riso*; pigeons cooked in a risotto with their livers and giblets, tomato purée and, of course, parmesan. Parma's *prosciutto* (raw ham) is world famous. Real Parmesan cheese must be labelled *parmigiano-reggiano*.

Turin is famous for its *bollita*, a most aristocratic boiled beef dish, with sausage, chicken, white beans, cabbage, potatoes and a tomato sauce. Not to be confused with the *fondue* from across the Swiss border, the *fonduta* of Piedmont is a hot dip of buttery *fontina* cheese, cream, pepper and white truffles (more delicate than black).

In **Naples**, the tomato has been king since the Spaniards brought it here from America in the 16th century. It is there, deliciously, in the simplest pasta, the thinner *vermicelli* for which *alla napolitana* just means with a tomato sauce. It also dominates the greatest not-so-fast food ever invented, the *pizza*, for which the classic version also includes anchovies (*acciughe*), mozzarella cheese and oregano. A handy, purely local version is the *calzone*, pocket-size pizzas filled with ham and mozzarella and folded over in a half-moon. The seafood is excellent, especially the sea bass (*spigola*), swordfish (*pesce spada*), squid (*calamari*) and octopus (*polpi*). Have your morning coffee with a crisp Neapolitan *sfogliatella* croissant filled with sweet ricotta cheese.

The lamb of **Puglia** is a royal dish. Try the *agnello allo squero* spit-roasted on a fire of twigs perfumed with thyme and fine herbs; or *cutturidde*, baked with onion, parsley, tomatoes and sprinkled with pecorino cheese. *Gnemeridde* are chitterlings of baby lamb roasted or stewed with ham, cheese and herbs. On the Adriatic coast and the Gulf of Taranto, the seafood is excellent: squid and octopus in Bari; red mullet in Polignano; and oysters and mussels in Taranto. Two great fish soups: Gallipoli's sweet-and-sour with shellfish and white fish in a bouillon of tomatoes, onions and vinegar; or Brindisi's spicier version with sea bream, eel, squid and mussels.

The coastal resorts of **Sardinia** cook up a pungent fish soup (*cassola è pisci*) and roast eel (*anguidda arrustia*). Inland, kid (*capretto*) and suckling pig (*porceddù*) are roasted on the spit, as is the island's greatest delicacy, wild boar (*cinghiale*). There is a great variety of country bread, the best being the charcoal-baked *civriaxiu*. Try it with the local *pecorino* ewe's cheese.

Restaurants

You will find all types and classes of restaurant the length and breadth of Italy. In theory, an Italian *ristorante* is supposed to be a larger and more elaborate establishment than a family-style *trattoria* or a rustic *osteria*. However, this distinction is by no means always clear; a restaurant may call itself a simple *osteria*, for example, yet be among the grandest and most expensive establishments around.

Fast-food places abound in Italy, whether American-style burger joints or more traditional Italian institutions. Pizza may be a Neapolitan invention but you will find *pizzerie* all over the country, as well as small shops selling pizza by the slice (*a taglio*). A *rosticceria*, originally a shop specializing in grilled dishes, now provides tables for guests to eat on the premises. For a quick lunch-time snack, choose a *tavola calda*, a stand-up bar serving a variety of hot and cold dishes throughout the day, to take away or eat on the spot.

If you want to picnic in the park or out in the country and don't feel like preparing the food yourself, get your sandwiches made up for you at a local delicatessen (*pizzichieria*). Ask for *panino ripieno*, a bread roll filled with whatever sausage, cheese or salad you choose from the inviting display on the counter.

Italians still regard vegetarianism as a curious eccentricity, but a small number of vegetarian restaurants can be found in the major cities. Vegetarians touring Italy can obtain information about suitable establishments from the Associazione Vegetariana Italiana, Viale Gran Sasso 38, Milano.

In restaurants, lunch (*pranzo*) is normally served between 12.30 and 3 p.m., and dinner (*cena*) between 8 and 11 p.m. It is wise to book a table by telephone, particularly if you want to dine at peak hours (in cities around 1.30 and 9 p.m.; earlier in the country).

Restaurants display menus in the windows or just inside the door. Note that some meat and fish dishes are priced according to weight (*al etto*, per hectogram; sometimes indicated by the letters *SQ*), which can prove expensive. A cover charge (*pane e coperto*) and a service charge (*servizio*) is added to all restaurant bills, but it is customary to leave an additional 5 to 10 per cent tip for the waiter. Don't tip, however, in family-run establishments. All restaurants, no matter how modest, must now issue a formal receipt (*ricevuta fiscale*) indicating the tax (IVA). In theory, you can be stopped by the police as you leave the restaurant and fined if you are unable to present the receipt.

Drinking

Wines

Italian wine is much more than just Chianti, but it wouldn't be a catastrophe if that's all it was. The best Chianti Classico produced in an area of 70,000 hectares (175,000 acres) between **Florence** and **Siena** (*see* page 157) and

36

distinguished by the proud *gallo nero* (black cockerel) label will please the most discerning palate. In a Bordeaux-style bottle, it is a strong, full-bodied red with a fine bouquet. Whereas most Italian wines can and should be drunk young, the Chianti Classico ages very well. The best of the other Chianti reds, some in the more familiar fat basket-bottles, are *Rufina* and *Montalbano* and *Brolio*, distinguished by a cherub on the neck labels. (While straw is no guarantee of quality and authenticity, it is a fair rule-of-thumb that if the bottle's basket is *plastic*, the contents are similarly mass-produced and characterless.) Of **Tuscany's** other wines, the most appreciated reds are the earthy *Montepulciano* and rather dry *Brunello di Montalcino*. The best of the whites are the *Montecarlo* and *Vernaccia di San Gimignano*, both dry.

Orvieto in Umbria produces superb white wines, both dry and semi-dry. East of Rome in the **Alban Hills** is the refreshingly light *Frascati*. The famous *Est! Est! Est!* (*see* page 124) comes from **Montefiascone** on Lake Bolsena.

The very popular **Veneto** wines are centred around Verona and Lake Garda, notably the velvety *Valpolicella*, light and fruity, and the light *Bardolino*. *Soave* is a dry white with a faint almond flavour. The rosé *Chiaretto* comes from south of **Lake Garda** and another rosé, *Pinot Grigio*, from **Treviso**.

Piedmont boasts some of Italy's finest reds, notably the powerful, full-bodied *Barolo*, with its slight raspberry tang. *Barbera* can vary from the rich and full-bodied to the light and *frizzante* (slightly fizzy). *Barbaresco* is another notable red wine. From south of **Turin** comes the sparkling *Asti spumante*, a more than respectable alternative to champagne.

The *trulli* country of **Puglia** turns out some first-class white wines, most notably *Locorotondo* and *Martina Franca*. **Castel del Monte** produces fine red, white and rosé wines. If you like sweet wines, try **Trani's** *Moscato*.

Italy produces more different types of wine than any other country. Many fine wines are not known beyond their region of origin but Chianti is famous worldwide.

Among apéritifs, bitters such as *Campari* and *Punt e Mes* are refreshing with soda and lemon. For after-dinner **drinks**, try the anis-flavoured *sambuca* with a *mosca* coffee-bean (literally a fly) swimming in it or *grappa* eau-de-vie distilled from grapes, of which there are hundreds of different kinds, named after a grape or a village. Among the best are *grappa moscato* and *grappa di Barolo*.

Bars

With its shiny zinc counter, Gaggia coffee machine and air of brisk efficiency, the Italian bar is a functional place. Italians go there in the morning to kick-start the day with a bracing shot of caffeine and a rapidly consumed *cornetto* (croissant). Thereafter, the bar is a place to drop in and out of in the course of the daily round, somewhere to meet friends and down a quick drink rather than a place to stay and linger. Of course, there are bars where the locals do while away the hours, chatting and playing cards, but you are more likely to find them in rural areas and the more out-of-way parts of town than in the tourist centres.

Prices are cheapest if you follow the Italians' example and drink standing up at the bar. As soon as you sit down, the cost of your order goes up; prices are most expensive when you sit at an outside table. The different rates will be indicated on the price list (*listino prezzi*) behind the bar or cash-desk.

Unless you are sitting down, in most busy city centre bars you will have to pay for your drinks in advance at the *cassa* (cash-desk). Hand over the receipt (*scontrino*) at the bar and repeat your order. Italians usually proffer a small coin with the receipt.

There are a bewildering number of ways in which you can order a coffee in an Italian bar. The choice is by no means limited to *espresso* or *cappuccino*. Here is a brief guide:

caffè espresso: a small quantity of strong black coffee in a tiny cup.
doppio: double quantity.
lungo: slightly diluted with hot water.
corretto: espresso laced with a shot of spirits.
al vetro: in a little glass.
macchiato: "stained" with a drop of milk.
caffè latte: with a lot of milk.
latte macchiato: a glass of hot milk with coffee added.
cappuccino: served with frothed milk.
cappuccino freddo: iced coffee in a glass, a summer speciality.

If you want a decaffeinated version of any of the above, ask for *Caffè Hag* (a generic description in Italy, as well as a brand name).

Tea in an Italian bar is invariably disappointing (a cup of hot water with a tea-bag in the saucer), but there are a wide range of refreshing non-alcoholic drinks to sample. Try freshly squeezed citrus fruit drinks: *spremuta di arancia, di limone,* or *di pompelmo* (orange, lemon, and grapefruit); alternatively, you can have a *frullato*, a kind of milkshake made with chopped fresh fruit and milk, or a *granita*, a scoop of crushed ice flavoured with coffee or fruit.

Most bars serve a variety of snacks: the most common are *pannini* (filled rolls) and *tramezzini* (sandwiches). If you are in a *bar-pasticceria* you will have the pick of delicious cakes and pastries. Some bars have a *tavola calda* serving more substantial quick meals, which can be eaten on the spot or taken away.

On top of food and drink, many bars sell bus tickets, stamps and cigarettes; the ones displaying the yellow phone sign have a public telephone inside.

Festivals

Up and down the country, Italians express a deep-rooted sense of tradition through local festivals and games. Many of these customs boast centuries of uninterrupted observance, others have been revived in recent years. We offer here a far from exhaustive list of processions and festivities around the country.

January: *Piana degli Albanesi* (near Palermo): colourful Byzantine ritual for Epiphany.

February or early March: *Venice:* Carnival, masked balls and processions in magnificent costumes; *Viareggio:* Carnival; *Agrigento:* Almond Blossom Festival.

April: *Rome*: Pope's Easter Sunday blessing.

May: *Assisi*: Calendimaggio Christian and pagan festival; *Naples*: Miracle of San Gennaro (liquefaction of the saint's blood); *Camogli* (Riviera): *Sagra del Pesca*, communal fish-fry in giant pan; *Gubbio*: candle race, crossbow competition (*see* page 174); *Orvieto*: Pentecost feast of the Palombella (Holy Ghost).

June: *Pisa*: San Ranieri, jousting and torchlit regatta on Arno river; *Flo-*

Live snakes are draped over the statue of San Domenico in this procession held in May in the small town of Cocullo, south of L'Aquila.

rence: costumed medieval football game.

July: *Siena*: first Palio (2 July, *see* page 160); *Palermo*: Santa Rosalia; *Venice*: Redentore regatta; *Rimini:* Festival of the Sea; *Rome*: Noiantri street-festival in Trastevere (*see* page 111).

August: *Siena*: Second Palio (August 16).

September: *Arezzo*: Giostra del Saraceno (*see* page 164); *Venice*: Historical Regatta.

October: *Assisi*: Feast of St Francis; *Perugia*: Franciscan Mysteries.

December: *Rome*: Christmas food and toy market on Piazza Navona; *Assisi* and *Naples*: cribs in streets; *Alberobello*: celebrations in *trulli*.

Made in Italy: Designs for the Good Life

"At last—for the first time—I live," was the novelist Henry James's response to his first encounter with Italy. Who can say why the country and its people have that effect on visitors? Is it the sun-baked sensuality of the Mediterranean or the superabundance of supreme works of art? The glorious food and wine or the charm and good humour of the people? One thing is certain: the Italians have a natural aptitude for living well, a talent for pleasure, a knack for finding *la dolce vita* in the sourest of circumstances.

The Italians

Italians have a venerable tradition of having fun. Back in the time of the imperial Caesars, Roman citizens enjoyed some 200 feast-days a year. Modern Italy cannot lay claim to quite so much institutionalized merry-making, but wherever you go in the country today you are sure to come across a festival inspired by a local patron saint or a gastronomic feast (*sagra*) prompted by a local product. The saint's festival may stretch back into the mists of time

Roman and stranger, Italian and foreigner; everyone loves to hang out on Rome's celebrated Spanish Steps.

and have distinctly pagan overtones; the gastronomic feast may have been cooked up by the local tourist board a decade ago. What they have in common is that the locals take them seriously.

Take the example of Siena's Palio, the annual horse race contested between the city's 17 districts or *contrade*. No-one who has witnessed the passionate rivalry that goes into the race could possibly claim that the event was a stunt staged for the benefit of tourists. Real elation goes with victory for members of the winning *contrada*; true despondency accompanies defeat for the losers. Underpinning everything is a genuine sense of historical continuity. First held in 1260 to celebrate Siena's victory over the Florentines, the Palio has been performed in its modern form ever since 1659.

The same is true in Florence where the *calcio in costume*, an ancient version of football played in Renaissance costume between the city's four historic quarters, arouses fierce passions on and off the pitch. However, it is not a spirit that can be easily exported. When the *calcianti*, as the players are called, tried to stage a game in New York's Central Park it didn't look right.

"The *calcio in costume* could be a put up job," says Emilio Pucci, international fashion designer, local aristocrat and ceremonial head of the game. "But the game has a strong relevance to the city. After centuries the faces of the Florentines haven't changed. When the players get into their costumes you see modern faces becoming 16th-century faces. The surrounding streets, palaces, churches, the frescoes on the walls, all merge with the costumes. In Central Park it didn't come off. It needs every element of Florence to work."

If this suggests that there is some ineffable magic about Italy, well, it's probably true. When Vasari wanted to account for the emergence in Tuscany of the artists of genius who created the Renaissance, he suggested they were helped by "some subtle influence in the air of Italy".

It is not just in the art galleries, palaces and churches that you will notice the remarkable workings of this "subtle influence", it's apparent everywhere. It is visible in the sleek lines of a Ferrari, in the cut of an Armani suit and, above all, in the seemingly effortless sense of style displayed by the Italians you meet in the streets.

Eloquent Fingers

One spectator sport practised by 50 million Italians and watched by crowds of bemused foreigners, especially less expansive north Europeans and Americans, is the art of communication by gestures. Other peoples practise the art but none with quite the graceful flourish and eloquence of the Italians. The most Italian of all gestures is holding up pursed fingers, usually accompanied by a slightly anguished "*Cosa vuoi?*" ("What do you want?") or "*Cosa fai?*" ("What are you doing?"). Without a word, it often means: "You're crazy!" Beware of subtle nuances of interpretation. While a Spaniard pulling his earlobe is accusing you of sponging, an Italian is questioning a man's masculinity. A Frenchman stroking under his chin is calling you a bore, but an Italian may just be expressing an apologetic negative. The vertical horn-sign of the first and last fingers is universally recognized as "Cuckold!", but the same sign pointing horizontally is to protect you against the evil eye. Everybody knows the flourished forearm with clenched fist is a sexual insult, but don't be upset by the flattened hand raised sideways like a chopper to signify a departure.

You may wish to emulate them. Be warned, it is a difficult feat. Try to copy their dress sense and the way they carry off those vibrant colours, your chances of success are slight. The Mediterranean light, of course, has something to do with it, as countless holiday-makers discover when they unpack their new Italian wardrobe back home. Taken out of the context of sun-drenched piazzas and pavement cafés, the clothes just don't look the same: like the costumes of the *calcianti* in Central Park.

If life in Italy is beginning to sound all fun and games, a cross between a cakewalk and a cat-walk, a few words of warning are in order. *Il bel paese*, the beautiful country, has a down side.

The visitor may and probably will encounter traffic jams, noise and air pollution, petty street crime and museums with the shortest opening hours in Europe. The Italians themselves have to put up with (or participate in) widespread tax evasion, staggering levels of political corruption, a bitter North–South divide and the depredations of organized crime.

Just as the Italian driver, caught in a maelstrom of traffic, is adept at evading accidents, so do most Italians manage to steer clear of the hazards

that life sets in their way. The Italian flair for cheeky improvization is demonstrated by the enterprising Neapolitan who, when it became compulsory to wear car seat-belts in 1989, produced T-shirts imprinted with the image of a seat belt.

The anecdote also illustrates the typical Italian disregard for the edicts of the State. Centuries of oppression by foreign rulers before the unification of the country in the late 19th century, the scalding experience of Fascism under Mussolini and the sleazy chicanery of contemporary Italian politics have bred a powerful mistrust of authority.

Instead, Italians put their faith in an alternative institution: the family. From the Borgias of the Renaissance

Facts and Figures
Geography: The Italian landmass covers 301,245km² (116,228 square miles). The familiar boot-like silhouette stretches 1,200km (750 miles) from the north-west Alpine frontier with France to the south-east "heel" of Puglia. Below the three great lakes, Maggiore, Como and Garda, the fertile plain of the Po river separates the Alps from the rugged chain of the Apennines running like a wall down the middle of the peninsula to the arid and poorer south. Other major rivers are the Tiber at Rome, Arno in Tuscany and Adige in the Tyrolean Dolomites. Across the Adriatic to the east lies the rocky coastline of former Yugoslavia. Off the Tyrrhenian (west) coast are the mountainous islands of Sardinia (south of France's Corsica) and Sicily (off the boot's "toe"), the largest of the Mediterranean islands. Three major volcanoes in the south, Vesuvius, Stromboli and Sicily's Etna, are still active. Highest point: on Mont Blanc (Monte Bianco) 4,760m (15,617ft).
Population: 57.5 million.
Capital: Rome (pop. 2,800,000).
Major cities: Milan (1,425,000), Naples (1,200,000), Turin (1,000,000), Genoa (700,000), Palermo (735,000), Bologna (400,000), Florence (410,000), Catania (365,000), Bari (355,000), Venice (320,000).
Government: By its constitution of 1948, Italy is a republic of provinces grouped into 20 regions. A president with honorary rather than political powers is chosen by an Electoral Assembly of parliamentary and regional representatives. Government is in the hands of a Prime Minister and cabinet selected from among the parliament's Senate of 322 members and more powerful 630-strong Chamber of Deputies. A parliamentary mandate is 5 years.
Religion: 99% Catholic, 1% Protestant, Greek Orthodox, Jewish and Muslim.

to the siblings who run Benetton, the family has been the bedrock upon which success is founded in Italy. Today, over 90 per cent of Italian companies are still family-run, ranging from giant industrial concerns like Fiat (controlled by the Agnelli dynasty) down to small firms of artisans.

If the family rules Italy then the child, particularly when a boy, is king. Observe the way children are pampered and indulged in public. Parents travelling with children in Italy will notice their own offspring get this royal treatment, especially in restaurants. It comes as no surprise to learn that young Italians tend to remain living at home far longer than most of their European contemporaries.

That Italians do not seem to find the close-knit family claustrophobic is probably down to the ease they feel in one another's company and the

amount of time they spend out of doors.

You will see this in the easy conviviality of the *passeggiata*, the evening ritual whereby everyone in town strolls up and down the main street for the hour before dinner.

Italians tend to treat their public spaces as extensions of their private realms. When Napoleon spoke of Venice's Piazza San Marco as the finest drawing-room in Europe he was expressing an enduring truth about the Italian way of life. Italians have little regard for *la privacy*: both word and concept seem equally foreign to them. While the traditional Englishman's home is his castle, the average Italian is content with *un palazzo*: no, not a palace, usually, but a block of flats.

It helps, of course, that the Italians have such a facility for enjoying themselves. It's a bonhomie made all the more appealing by the fact that it doesn't need to be fuelled by alcohol. Italy may produce some of the best wines found in the world, Piedmont's Barolo or Tuscany's Brunello di Montalcino are two that come to mind, not to mention fierce liqueurs like *grappa*, but you will almost never see an Italian getting drunk, *ubriaco*.

So, whether you have come to Italy for the art and architecture or for the

*I*talians who marry in church must also celebrate their nuptials in commune—at the local town hall. When the ceremonies are over, a decorative backdrop for the wedding photographs is never hard to find.

beach resorts, you should make an effort to get to know the Italians: you will certainly find it rewarding.

As EM Forster wisely wrote in *A Room With a View* back in 1908: "The traveller who has gone to Italy to study the tactile values of Giotto, or the corruption of the Papacy, may return remembering nothing but the blue sky, and the men and women who live under it."

History

Italy as a nation has existed only since 1871. Before then, despite the peninsula's obvious geographical unity bounded by the Alps and the Mediterranean, its story is a fragmented tale of independent-minded cities, provinces and islands. Some carved out whole empires before sinking into relative oblivion, while others rose from obscurity to lead the people into modern nationhood.

We have abundant evidence of the ancient Etruscan, Greek and Roman communities in Italy, but know very little of the country's earlier, prehistoric settlers. Vestiges of dwellings survive: cabins on stilts in the frequently flooded Po valley; larger clay houses on the western marshlands of Tuscany and Sardinia's still visible domed dry-stone *nuraghi*. But the inhabitants? Perhaps North Africans and eastern Europeans peopled the Ligurian coast, while the Adriatic and south may have been settled from the Balkans and Asia Minor.

Nobody knows where the Etruscans came from. During the millennium before the Christian era, their civilization reached beyond Tuscany north to the Po valley and south towards Naples. At a time when Roman and other Latin tribes were still primitive, Etruscan society was aristocratic and highly sophisticated. Gold and other metal ornaments showed Greek influence, but the Etruscans' vaulted architecture was indigenous, as were their roads, canals and sewers.

Arriving in the 8th century BC, the Greeks set up city-states in eastern and southern Sicily, dominated by Syracuse, and others on the Italian mainland, at Naples, Paestum and Taranto. Pythagoras squared his hypotenuse in Calabria, and it was at Agrigento that Empedocles concluded the world was divided into four elements: fire, air, earth and water.

After defeats by Greeks in the south, Latins in the centre and Gallic invaders in the north, the Etruscan empire ended in the 4th century BC. As Greek colonial power weakened through Athens–Sparta rivalry back home and pressure from Carthaginians in Sicily, the vacuum was filled by an uppity confederation of Latin and Sabine tribes living on seven hills known collectively as Rome.

The Romans
Legend says Rome was founded by Romulus, sired with twin brother Remus by Mars of a Vestal Virgin and abandoned on the Palatine Hill to be suckled by a she-wolf. Historians agree that the site and traditional founding date of 753 BC are just about right.

Under Etruscan domination, Rome had been a monarchy until a revolt in 510 BC established a patrician republic which lasted five centuries. In contrast to other Italian cities weakened by internal rivalries and unstable government, Rome drew strength from a solid aristocracy of consuls and senate ruling over plebeians proud of their Roman citizenship and only rarely rebellious.

Romulus and Remus, the mythical founders of Rome, and the she-wolf that suckled them. Archaeological evidence of Iron Age settlements on hills above the Tiber suggests a historical basis for the legends of Rome's origins.

Recovering quickly from the Gallic invasion of 387 BC, the Romans took effective control of the peninsula by a military conquest reinforced by a network of roads with names that exist to this day: Via Appia, Flaminia, Aurelia. From chariots to Ferraris, Italians have always liked careering across the country on wheels.

Roman power extended around the Mediterranean with victory in the Punic Wars against Carthage and conquests in Macedonia, Asia Minor, Spain and southern France. The rest of Italy participated only by tax contributions to the war effort and minor

involvement in commerce and colonization. Resentment surfaced when former Etruscan or Greek cities such as Capua, Syracuse and Taranto supported Hannibal's invasion in 218 BC. Rome followed up defeat of the Carthaginians with large-scale massacres and enslavement of their Italian supporters. National solidarity was still a long way off.

Under Julius Caesar, provincial towns won the privileges of Roman citizenship. His reformist dictatorship, bypassing the senate to combat unemployment and ease the tax burden, made dangerous enemies. His assassi-nation on the Ides of March, 44 BC, led to civil war and the autocratic rule of his adopted son Augustus, who consolidated the empire.

Conquest of the Greeks accelerated rather than halted the influence of their culture in Italy. Romans infused Greek refinement with their own energy to create that unique mixture of elegance and realism, delicacy and strength that have remained the essence of Italian life and art.

In architecture, the Romans made a great leap forward from the Greek structures of columns and beams by developing the arch, vault and dome,

---

The Rise and Fall of a Noble Roman

Cunning politician, master of propaganda, great writer, all-conquering military genius and consummate seducer, Julius Caesar (100–44 BC) was supposed to become a priest. That was the career his patrician family mapped out for him, in the Temple of Jupiter, when he was just 13. But he soon got embroiled in Rome's brutal power-game. He married the daughter of Cinna, political enemy of the despotic general and consul Sulla. When the latter ordered him to divorce her, the young Caesar refused and fled to military service in Bithynia (part of modern Turkey).

He learned something of statecraft and court life during a homosexual relationship with the king, Nicomedes. After Sulla's death, he returned in 78 BC to enter Roman politics as a leader of the populist party, gaining public favour prosecuting cases of corruption among provincial governors. Dissatisfied with his oratory, he went to Rhodes to study rhetoric and was captured *en route* off the coast of Anatolia by pirates whom he promptly threatened to crucify. They laughed but let him go for a rich ransom he was able to prise out of local communities. He returned to capture the brigands, retrieved the ransom and crucified them.

He used lucrative postings in Spain to finance his political career back in Rome. As aedile in 65 BC, responsible for public order and buildings, he won huge popularity organizing a spectacular series of 320 gladiator duels, dressing the combatants in silver uniforms, unprecedented and crippling for the budget. His 60 BC triumvirate with Pompey and Crassus gave Pompey Caesar's daughter in marriage and Caesar the consulate in 59 and the proconsulate in Gaul and the eastern Adriatic from 58 to 49. His conquests there sealed his reputation as a great general. With Pompey asserting sole supremacy in Rome, Caesar returned to cross the Rubicon (the small river north of Rimini that separated Cisalpine Gaul from Italy), drive him out of Rome and crush his armies around the Mediterranean. Pausing to dally awhile with Cleopatra in Egypt, he returned to Rome in 44 BC to consolidate his power. But his popularity with the plebs provoked the anger of the Senate and the knives of Brutus and Cassius on the Ides of March.

A *Roman arch on the site of ancient Carsulae, near Todi in Umbria. Carsulae was an important station on the Via Flaminia, the Romans' great North Road, which led from the capital to Fano on the Adriatic coast.*

well suited to the needs of empire: basilicas for public administration, the new engineering of aqueducts and bridges, and triumphal arches for victorious armies. If they adopted the Greeks' gods by turning Zeus into Jupiter and Aphrodite into Venus, the cult placing the emperor at its apex served the interests of the Roman state.

In the centuries of imperial expansion, decline and fall, Italy took a back seat as power moved with the armies away from Rome east to Byzantium and north to Gaul or Germany.

Despite persecution under Nero in the 1st century AD, Christianity spread from Rome through southern Italy, later to the north. With Constantine (306–337) in Byzantium, Milan and then Ravenna became the capital of Italy. Christianity was made the state religion. At the end of the 4th century, Emperor Theodosius organized the Church into dioceses and declared paganism and heresy a crime. He himself was excommunicated by St Ambrose, Bishop of Milan, for massacring 7,000 rebels in Thessalonica. The position of Bishop of Rome as primate of the Western Church was asserted by Pope Leo I (440–461), tracing the succession back to St Peter.

The invasion of Attila's Huns and the sacking of Rome by Goths and Vandals brought an end to the Western Empire.

After the Empire

Wars between the Goths and Byzantines and new waves of invasions made Italian unity impossible.

The dual influence of Greek and Latin culture persisted. In the 6th century, Justinian reannexed Italy to his Byzantine Empire and codified Roman law as the state's legal system. Under Heraclius (610–641), Greek was extended to Italy as its official language.

Hellenistic and oriental influences were most evident in religion. Byzantine ritual coloured the Roman liturgy. The Roman basilica's long colonnaded nave leading to an apse gave way to the Greek cross with a central space surrounded by arches and topped by a dome. Sculptural reliefs flattened out to symbolic decorative, non-human forms, and painting and mosaics were bright in colour, but more rigid and formal. Spiritual pre-occupations turned away from the world's few joys and many woes in the present to mystic contemplation of the ineffable hereafter.

Much too ineffable for Italian tastes. The monastic movement founded by St Benedict in the 6th century re-asserted involvement in the realities of social life. The Benedictine order em-phasized moderation in the austerity of its food, clothing and sleep, not unlike

*R*avenna's well-preserved mosaics are testimony to the brilliance of Byzantine art. This 6th-century mosaic in Sant'Apollinare Nuovo shows the three magnificently costumed Magi bearing gifts for the infant Jesus.

the habits of any peasant of the times. Flagellation and similar rigours intro-duced into other Italian monasteries by the Irish monk Columbanus were soon modified by the gentler Benedictine rule.

Monasteries in Italy remained modest affairs, as bishops moved faster than abbots to take over lands laid waste by barbarian invasions. The Church ordered monasteries to forget secular matters and devote themselves to liturgy.

By the 8th century, the Byzantines held the balance of power with the Lombards (a Germanic tribe), who had invaded Italy in 568 and set up their capital at Pavia four years later. The Lombards controlled the interior in a loose confederation of fiercely in-dependent duchies. Lombard territory split Byzantine Italy up into segments ruled from the coasts: Veneto (Venice and its hinterland); Emilia (between

49

Ravenna and Modena); and Pentapolo (between Rimini and Perugia), plus Rome and Naples (with Sicily and Calabria).

In Rome, the highly political popes played the Lombard duchies off against those of the Byzantine Empire. They cited a forged document, the *Donation of Constantine*, supposedly bequeathing them political authority over all Italy. Seeking the powerful support of the Franks, Pope Leo III crowned their king, Charlemagne, ruler of the Holy Roman (in fact, mostly German) Empire, in 800. However, the pope had in turn to kneel in allegiance, and this exchange of spiritual blessing for military protection laid the seeds of future conflict between the papacy and the German emperors.

Venice, which was founded on its lagoons in the 6th century by refugees from Lombard raiders, prospered from a privileged relationship with Byzantium and an uninhibited readiness to trade with Muslims and other infidels further east. The enterprising merchants of Venice were only too happy to bring a little oriental spice and colour into the dour lives of Lombards in the Po valley and beyond the Alps to northern Europe.

Naples held on to its autonomy by prudently combining links with Rome and Constantinople. When Arabs conquered Sicily in the 9th century and turned to the mainland, Naples at first sought an alliance. However, as the invaders advanced towards Rome, Naples linked up with neighbouring Amalfi. Despite military expeditions by the Franks and Byzantines, the Arabs remained on the Italian scene for two centuries.

The Middle Ages

In the 11th century, the adventurous Normans put an end to Arab control of Sicily and southern Italy. Exploiting a natural genius for assimilating the useful elements of the local culture rather than indiscriminately imposing their own, they adopted Arab-style tax-collectors and customs officials and Byzantine fleet-admirals for their navy. At Palermo, churches and mosques stood side by side, feudal castles next to oriental palaces.

The Crusades against the Islamic threat to Christendom brought great prosperity to Italy's port cities. Pisa sided with the Normans in Sicily, and profits from its new commercial empire in the western Mediterranean paid for its cathedral, baptistery and famous Leaning Tower. Genoa's merchant empire spread from Algeria to Syria.

The supreme master of the art of playing all sides, Venice stayed out of the first Crusade to expand its trade with the East while ferrying pilgrims to Palestine. Later, when Byzantium threatened its eastern trading privileges, Venice persuaded the crusading armies to attack Constantinople in 1204, further strengthening its position.

The Po valley's economic expansion through land clearance and new irrigation works brought a decline of feudalism. Dukes, administrators and clergy lived in towns rather than isolated castles, absorbing the hinterland into communes, forerunners of the city-states.

The communes were strong enough to confine German Emperor Frederick Barbarossa's Italian ambitions to the south, where he secured Sicily for his Hohenstaufen heirs by marrying his son into the Norman royal family. Ruling from Palermo, Barbarossa's cultured but brutal grandson Frederick II (1194–1250) was a prototype for the future Renaissance prince.

His power struggle with the papacy divided the country into two highly volatile camps; Guelfs supporting the pope and Ghibellines supporting the emperor. The backbone of the Guelfs was in communes such as Florence and Genoa. In 1266, they financed the mercenary army of Charles d'Anjou to defeat the imperial forces and take the Sicilian throne. However, Palermo rose up against the French in the murderous Sicilian Vespers of 1282, when the locals massacred everyone who spoke Italian with a French accent and forced Charles to move his capital to Naples. The Sicilians offered their crown to the Spanish house of Aragon.

The Guelf-Ghibelline conflict became a pretext for settling family feuds (as in Shakespeare's *Romeo and Juliet*) or communal rivalries from which Genoa and Florence emerged stronger than ever. In Rome, dissolute popes repeatedly switched factions for temporary advantage and lost all political and moral authority in the process.

After two centuries of religious heresy, the Church needed a spiritual renewal, finding the perfect ally in Francis of Assisi (1182–1226), who was pious without being troublesomely militant. His sermons had immense popular appeal. He chose not to attack Church corruption but to preach instead the values of a Christ-like life. By involving religion in a love of nature, preaching even to sparrows, he appealed to an old pagan Italian tradition. The Franciscan order provided a much-needed, manageable revival. The architecture of the church built in his name at Assisi contradicted Francis's humble testament denouncing "temples of great dimension and rich ornament". Assisi's frescoes of the saint's life, painted by Giotto and Simone Martini, proved an immensely effective act of artistic propaganda against the prevalent libertinism and heresy.

Pope Joan

Over the years some fairly unlikely candidates have managed to clamber onto the papal throne but the strangest of them all must surely be Pope Joan.

According to medieval legend, Joan was an Englishwoman who disguised herself as a man in order to enter a monastery, the home of her lover, a Benedictine monk. Under the name John Anglus, she went with him to Athens and there learned Greek. When her lover died, Joan came to Rome and was made a professor. She won fame for her learning and eloquence, and on the death of Pope Leo IV in 855 was made pope, taking the name John VIII.

All this time Joan had managed to keep her true gender hidden, despite taking another lover. However, when her secret finally came out, it did so in a most dramatic way.

She was being carried in procession from St Peter's to San Giovanni in Laterano when she gave birth to a child. Mother and baby were promptly stoned to death by the enraged crowd and buried by the roadside. Notwithstanding this ignominious end to Joan's papal reign, her portrait, inscribed 'Joannes VIII, a woman of England', remained alongside the portraits of more legitimate popes in Siena Cathedral until 1592.

The pilgrimage church of San Francesco at Assisi was a major propaganda weapon in the Church's fight for the hearts and minds of the people.

The City-States

By the end of the 13th century, with the independent-minded communes growing into fully fledged city-states, Italy was clearly not to be subjugated to the will of one ruler.

The Middle Ages in Italy are far from being the murky era that many humanist scholars liked to contrast with the brilliance of the Renaissance. Bologna had founded Europe's first university, famous above all for its law studies, in the 11th century, followed by Padua, Naples, Modena, Siena, Salerno and Palermo. Unlike other Church-dominated European universities, sciences, medicine and law prevailed over theology.

In the absence of any political unification, it was the universities that awakened the national consciousness. Scholars travelling from town to town across the country needed a common tongue beyond the elitist Latin to break through the barriers of regional dialects. It had been a foreigner, German Emperor Frederick II, who launched the movement for a national language at his court in Palermo, but Dante Alighieri (1265–1321) provided the ardour, moral leadership, and unmatched literary example to bring it to fruition.

Genoa rose to challenge Venice's supremacy. It dislodged Pisa in the western Mediterranean, whittled away at Venice's hold on eastern ports, and set up colonies on the Black Sea for trade with Russia and the Far East. However, Genoa's 1381 participation in the ruinous Chioggia war on the Venetian lagoon exhausted its resources. Its newly formed Bank of St George had to sell off overseas colonies and ran the town like a private company for the benefit of a small local oligarchy seeking future prosperity as international financiers for the kings of Spain or France.

Venice rebounded to turn to the mainland, extending its Veneto territory from Padua across the Po valley as far as Bergamo. After relying exclusively on overseas trade, Venice created a new land-owning aristocracy through this expansion.

In its fertile Po valley, Milan prospered from trade with Germany, principally in textiles and armour. Escaping unscathed from the Great Plague of 1348 and subsequent epidemics, it built up a sound economic base and maintained a strong army with its plentiful manpower.

Florence was the first Italian town to mint its own gold coin (*fiorino* or florin), a prestigious instrument for trade in European markets. It also organized textile manufacture on a large-scale industrial basis. Although outside troops were called in to crush an uprising of the Ciompi (wool-workers), the people of Florence were well-fed and highly literate when compared with the rest of the country. The Medici emerged as the dominant

The Torre del Mangia, tall and slender 14th-century bell tower, rises above the Gothic Palazzo Pubblico, Siena's town hall down the centuries.

merchant family with Cosimo becoming the city's ruler in 1434. A building boom underlined the prosperity—Giotto's campanile was at last completed, as were Ghiberti's great baptistery doors, Brunelleschi's dome on the cathedral, and palaces by Alberti and Michelozzo.

Divided in the 14th century between the Spanish in Sicily and the French in Naples, southern Italy remained solidly feudal. Its almost exclusively agricultural economy suffered much more than the north from plague and famine. Landlords resorted to banditry in order to replenish their treasuries. If Palermo was in decline, Naples flourished as a brilliant cosmopolitan capital. In 1443, it was reunited in one kingdom with Sicily, under Alfonso of Aragon.

With the papacy in comfortable exile in Avignon since 1309, the brutal rule of the Orsini and Colonna families reduced Rome to a half-urban, half-rural backwater. Self-educated visionary Cola di Rienzo governed briefly in 1347 until the nobles drove him out. Thirty years later, the papacy returned.

The Renaissance

A new national fraternity of scholars with multiple expertise in the arts, sciences and in law emerged as itinerant consultants to rulers eager to make their city-states centres of cultural prestige and political propaganda.

Men like Leon Battista Alberti, architect-mathematician-poet, brought a new spirit of inquiry and scepticism. From their study and translation of the Greek philosophers, they developed principles of objective scientific research, independent of the political, religious or emotional bias characterizing medieval scholarship. The emphasis switched from heaven to earth. Leonardo da Vinci applied the new method to architecture, civil and military engineering, urban planning, geography and map-making. It was Giorgio Vasari, facile artist but first-rate chronicler of this cultural explosion, who dubbed it a *rinascita* or rebirth of the glories of Italy's Greco-Roman past. It proved, with the humanism of Leonardo and Michelangelo and the political realism of Machiavelli, to be the birth of our modern age. Including the blood and thunder.

For the creative ferment brought new horrors of war, assassination, persecution, plunder and rape. It was the heyday of the brilliant but lethal Spanish-Italian Borgias: lecherous Rodrigo, who became Pope Alexander VI, and his treacherous son Cesare, who stopped at nothing to control and expand the papal lands.

In Florence, where his family had to fight to hold on to their supremacy, Lorenzo de' Medici found time to encourage the art of Perugino, Ghirlandaio, Botticelli, the young Leonardo and tempestuous Michelangelo. However, decadence set in and Dominican preacher Girolamo Savonarola denounced the corruption of a Church and society more devoted to pagan classics than the Christian gospel. At the Carnival of 1497, he shamed the Florentines into throwing their "vanities" onto a giant fire in Piazza della Signoria. Clothes, jewellery and cosmetics were destroyed, but also books and paintings, with Botticelli contributing some of his own. Four years later, when Savonarola declined to test the validity of his apocalyptic prophesies with an ordeal by fire, he was arrested, hanged and burned anyway, in Piazza della Signoria.

On the international scene, the Turkish conquest of Constantinople in 1453 closed Genoa's Black Sea markets, but Venice worked out a new deal in Cyprus and even a *modus vivendi* in Constantinople itself. The Venetians' empire declined as they lost their taste for the adventure of commerce in favour of the safety of their land-holdings. From 1494 to 1530, the Spanish Habsburgs and the French turned Italy into a battleground for the Kingdom of Naples and the Duchy of Milan. Genoa threw in with the Spanish to give Emperor Charles V access, via Milan, to his German territories and later became a lucrative clearing-house for Spain's American silver. Rome was plundered by Imperial armies in 1527; the Medici were driven out of Florence and returned to power under tutelage of the Spanish, who won effective control of the whole country.

When the dust of war settled, it was the dazzling cultural achievements that left their mark on the age. The true father of Rome's High Renaissance, Pope Julius II (1503–13) began the new St Peter's and commissioned Michelangelo to paint the ceiling of the Vatican's Sistine Chapel and Raphael to decorate the Stanze. Architect Donato Bramante was nicknamed *maestro ruinante* because of all the ancient monuments he dismantled to make way for the pope's megalomaniac building plans. With the treasures uncovered in the process, Julius founded the Vatican's magnificent collection of ancient sculpture.

Michelangelo's Moses statue was designed for the monumental tomb (never completed) of the great Renaissance pope Julius II. Irascible and resolute, like the great Biblical lawgiver, Julius strove to assert the temporal and spiritual authority of the papacy.

Counter-Reformation

Badly shaken by the Protestant Reformation, the Church convoked the Council of Trent (north of Lake Garda) in 1545. Non-Italian bishops urged the Church to carry out its own reform, hoping to democratize relations with the pope. But the threat of Lutherans, Calvinists and other "heretics" shifted the emphasis to repression, culminating in the Counter-Reformation formally proclaimed in 1563. The Church reinforced the Holy Office's Inquisition and the Index to censor the arts. The Jesuits, founded in 1534, quickly became an army of militant theologians to combat heresy. Italian Protestants fled and Jews in Rome were shut up in a ghetto (50 years later than in Venice) and expelled from Genoa and Lucca.

Cardinal Carlo Borromeo, nephew of Pope Pius IV and Archbishop of Milan (1565–84), was the spiritual leader of Italy's Catholic revival. In alliance with the Jesuits, he weeded out corrupt clerics and what were, for him, the too soft Umiliati order of Catholic laymen. As a symbol of his crusading spirit, he consecrated the new Flamboyant Gothic cathedral, which took centuries to complete.

Art proved a major instrument of Counter-Reformation propaganda, but it had to undergo some important changes. The vigour and intellectual integrity of the High Renaissance had softened into Mannerism's stylized sophistication. Condemning the preoccupation with pagan gods and worldly decadence, the Church urged artists to deliver a strong, clear message to bring the troubled flock back to the fold. The Madonna and saints of Annibale Carracci attracted the faithful with a sensuous image of ideal beauty, while Caravaggio made a more brutal, but no less effective appeal with a proletarian Mary and grubby, barefoot Apostles. As the Church regained ground, it promoted a more triumphant image, epitomized by Bernini's baroque altar in St Peter's.

However, the self-confidence rang hollow when, in 1633, the Vatican ordered Galileo to deny the evidence of his own eyes, through the new telescope he had designed, and stop teaching that God's earth was only one of many planets in orbit around the sun.

After a 16th century in which Naples had become the largest town in Europe, and one of the liveliest, the

With its sweeping colonnades symbolizing outstretched arms, Bernini's majestic Piazza San Pietro was designed to embody the embrace of the Church.

south was increasingly oppressed and impoverished. The army had to crush revolts in Sicily and Naples against heavy taxes and conscription for Spain's wars in northern Europe.

Towards Nationhood

Lacking the solidarity to unite and too weak to resist by themselves, Italian kingdoms and duchies were reduced to convenient pawns in Europe's 18th-century dynastic power plays. At the end of the Wars of Spanish, Austrian and Polish Succession, the Austrians had taken over north Italy from the Spanish. The Age of Enlightenment engendered a new cultural ferment. The theatre of La Scala opened in Milan and the Fenice in Venice. Stimulated by the ideas of Voltaire, Rousseau and Diderot, intellectuals were more keenly aware of being Europeans, but also *Italians*, a national consciousness they promoted in the Milan magazine, *Il Caffè*.

The hopes of progressives were raised by Austrian reforms in Lombardy and Tuscany (where the Medici dynasty ended in 1737): fairer taxes, less Church influence in schools, more

public education, removal of the Inquisition, Jesuits, death penalty and instruments of torture. Outside the Austrian sphere of influence, Italy remained stolidly conservative. Venice stagnated under the rule of a small, entrenched élite, drawing nostalgic comfort from the city's petrified beauty as painted in the *vedute* of Guardi and Canaletto. The papacy in Rome had lost prestige with the dissolution of the Jesuits and the crippling loss of revenue from the Habsburg Church reforms. The south's aristocracy resisted all significant social reforms proposed by the Spanish. Don Carlos, a descendant of Louis XIV, saw himself as a southern Sun King, with Caserta Palace as his Versailles. He is best remembered for launching the excavations of Pompeii in 1748.

On the north-eastern Alpine frontier, a new state had appeared on the scene, destined to lead the movement to a united Italy. With Savoy split in the 16th century between France and Switzerland, its foothill region southeast of the Alps, Piedmont, had come into the Italian orbit. Side-stepping the stagnant economic burden of Spanish domination, the sparsely populated duchy expanded fast. Turin was little more than a fortified village of 40,000 inhabitants in 1600, but it rose to 93,000 a century later. The pragmatic dukes of Piedmont liked French-style absolutist monarchy but they tempered it with a parliament to bypass local fiefdoms. They copied Louis XIV's centralized administration and tax-collection and, by the 18th century, Turin was a sparkling royal capital built, quite unlike any other Italian city, in the classical French manner.

Napoleon Bonaparte was welcomed with his seductive ideas of Italian "independence" after driving out the Austrians and Spanish in 1797. However, the French soon proved just as great a burden on Italian treasuries to support their war effort and the Bonaparte family. If Napoleon did not exactly "liberate" Italy, he did shake up the old conservatism from Lombardy to Naples by creating new universities and high schools, streamlining the bureaucracy, creating a new legal system with his Napoleonic Code and generally awakening the forces of Italian nationalism. Clandestine political clubs like the *Carbonari* sprang up around the country.

Caution was the watchword among Italian rulers restored to their lands after Napoleon's defeat. Austria seized the occasion to add the Veneto to its Lombardy territories. The 1823 conclave of *zelanti* (zealot) cardinals elected arch-conservative Leo XII to help the papacy recover from its Napoleonic shock. On the lookout for any contagiously progressive movement, the Austrians helped Bourbon King Ferdinand of Naples crush an 1821 revolt for constitutional monarchy and foiled a similar uprising in Piedmont. The danger became clear in 1831 when insurrection spread through Bologna, Modena and Parma to the Papal States of central Italy. But the Austrians defeated a rebel government of "united Italian provinces", weakened by regional rivalries and conflicting personal ambitions.

The *Risorgimento*, or "resurrection" of national identity, took two conflicting paths. The Genoese-born Giuseppe Mazzini's *Giovine Italia* (Young Italy)

movement sought national unity by popular-based insurrection. He opposed Piedmontese patricians and intellectuals of the Moderates party seeking reform through a privilege-conscious confederation of Italian princes blessed by the papacy, with Piedmont providing the military muscle. They feared a new proletarian militancy among factory workers. Landowners bringing in cheap migrant labour faced mounting resentment. Food riots broke out in Lombardy, revolts in Tuscany, and southern peasants demanded a share-out of common land.

Giuseppe Verdi was the *Risorgimento's* towering artist. His operas'

*T*he Vittorio Emanuele
*II Monument in Rome was
erected between 1885 and 1911
as a proud symbol of Italian
unification. Its bombastic
appearance, however, has
aroused more derision than
patriotism.*

romantic humanism inspired fellow patriots, who saw in the *Nabucco* Freedom Chorus a positive call to action.

Outright rebellion erupted in Milan on 18 March 1848, a year during which there was revolution all over

Europe. Emissaries flew by balloon to nearby cities for reinforcements that freed Milan from the 14,000-strong Austrian garrison. The Venetians restored their republic, a Piedmontese army joined up with troops from Tuscany, the Papal States and Naples, and a new democratic Roman Republic was proclaimed. However, the hesitant Carlo Alberto of Piedmont gave the Austrians time to recover and Italian gains toppled like dominoes. National unity was again sabotaged by provincial rivalries.

Conceding the need for more reform, the new king of Piedmont, Vittorio Emanuele II, became a constitutional monarch with a moderate-dominated parliament. Prime Minister Count Camillo Benso di Cavour, a hard-nosed political realist, won over moderate left-wing support for a programme of free-trade capitalism and large-scale public works construction. Among the political exiles flocking to Piedmont was a veteran of the earlier revolts, Giuseppe Garibaldi.

With their French allies, Piedmont defeated Austria at Magenta and Solferino to secure Lombardy in 1859. A year later, Cavour negotiated the handover of Emilia and Tuscany, but it was the adventure of Garibaldi's Red Shirts that imposed the unification of the peninsula in 1860. With two steamers, antiquated artillery and L.94,000 in funds, Garibaldi set sail from Genoa with his "Expedition of the Thousand". The heroic Red Shirts seized Bourbon Sicily and crossed to the mainland. At Teano, outside Naples, they met up with Vittorio Emanuele, who was proclaimed King of Italy. National unity was completed with the annexation of Veneto in 1866 and Rome, the new capital, in 1871.

The Modern Era

Despite its extraordinary fragmented history, unified Italy took its place among modern nations as an unexceptional centralized state, careful to protect the interests of its industrial and financial establishment and granting reforms to the working classes only after pressure from their united action.

From their labours in France and Germany, where they were known as Europe's Chinamen, migrant Italian factory- and farm-workers brought back expert knowledge of union organization and strikes. In keeping with the Italians' traditional local attachments, their first unions were *camere del lavoro*, regionally based chambers of labour linking workers to their town or commune rather than their individual trade.

Both left and right wanted Italy to join the European race for colonies: their eyes fixed on Ethiopia and Libya. Conservatives supported expansion for reasons of national prestige. Socialists talked of Italy's "civilizing mission" in the Mediterranean, seeking to divert the flow of emigrants (heading increasingly to the Americas) to experimental collective land management in new African colonies in Tripoli and Cyrenaica.

At home, in addition to traditional textiles, industry was expanding fast in metallurgy, chemicals and machinery. The national love affair with cars had begun: from seven produced in 1900 and 70 in 1907, there were 9,200 rolling out of the factories by 1914, most of them from Fiat, founded in 1899.

59

With wily Prime Minister Giovanni Giolitti manoeuvring the forces of capital and labour, Italy began its 20th century in a blithe state of calm and prosperity known as *Italietta*: holidays by the sea or in the mountains, romantic operas like Puccini's *La Bohème* and *Madame Butterfly*, the first silent-movie extravaganzas of *The Last Days of Pompeii* and *Quo Vadis*, and relaxed conversations in city squares at the hour of the *passeggiata*, the evening walk. Avant-garde artists enraged by the smug bourgeoisie seemed harmless enough, futurists declared war on spaghetti and preferred the beauty of Maseratis and Alfa Romeos to that of Greek statues.

World War I

They were less amusing when hailing World War I as the "world's hygiene". Previously committed to a Triple Alliance with Austria and Germany, Italy remained neutral in 1914. The following year, acting with what Prime Minister Antonio Salandra acknowledged to be *sacro egoismo*, Italy signed a secret treaty to enter the war on the side of Britain and France in exchange for the post-war annexation of Austrian-held Trento, South Tyrol (now Alto Adige) and Trieste.

The people were at first cool to the war, despite the jingoism of flashy aristocratic aesthete Gabriele d'Annunzio and his friend, an ex-socialist newspaperman named Benito Mussolini. The Italian Army was the least well prepared of the combatants, lacking artillery, machine guns, trucks and properly trained officers, but the infantry showed remarkable courage in the trenches. After disaster at Caporetto, the Austro-German 1917 advance across the Veneto plain was held until the Italian counter-attack of October–November 1918 permitted a triumphant entry into Trento and Trieste.

For the peasant, worker and petit bourgeois, war in uniform was their first real experience of Italian nationality. Enthusiastic war-supporters like d'Annunzio, who had captured the popular imagination by flying over Vienna to drop propaganda leaflets, were acclaimed as patriots, while democrats and pacifist republicans were dismissed as defeatists. Parliament, which was denied knowledge of the secret war treaty till the Peace Conference of 1919, was exposed as impotent.

The Rise of Fascism

The left was in disarray. The Socialists won the elections but split over support for the Russian Revolution, leading to the formation in 1921 of the Italian Communist Party.

In an atmosphere of economic crisis—stagnant productivity, bank closures and rising unemployment—the conservatives wanted somebody tougher, more dynamic than eternally compromising old-style politicians. With black-shirted *Fasci Italiani di Combattimento* (Italian combat groups) beating up Slavs in Trieste and union-workers in Bologna, Mussolini fitted the bill. Threatened by the Fascists' March on Rome in 1922, King Vittorio Emanuele III invited Mussolini, *il Duce*, to form a government.

The now all-too-familiar process of totalitarianism set in: opposition leaders were assassinated and their parties, free unions and free press were all abolished. The Vatican did not complain, though it was upset when the fascist youth movement dissolved the Catholic Boy Scouts. After the Lateran Treaty of 1929 had created a separate Vatican state and perpetuated Catholicism as Italy's national religion with guaranteed religious education in the schools, Pope Pius XI even described Mussolini as a man sent by Providence.

Italian fascism remained a style rather than a coherent ideology, typified by the raised-arm salute replacing the "weakling" handshake, bombastic architecture and Mussolini's arrogant harangues from the Palazzo Venezia's "heroic balcony" in Rome. The Duce's motto of "Better to live one day as a lion than 100 years as a sheep" contrasted with the one he gave the country: "Believe, obey, fight." Neither lions nor sheep, most Italians survived with lip-service and good humour, while communists re-allied with socialists in the anti-fascist underground whose partisans linked up with the Allies during World War II.

In 1936, Mussolini diverted attention from the worsening economic climate at home with an invasion of Ethiopia and proclamation of the Italian Empire. Italian war planes joined Hitler's Luftwaffe on General Franco's side in the Spanish Civil War (5,000 Italian communists and socialists fought on the Republican side). In 1938, German-style racist legislation was introduced against the country's 57,000 Jews. The next year, Italy invaded Albania and, after France's collapse in June 1940, plunged with Germany into World War II. Its poorly equipped armies were defeated by the British in the African desert and by the mountain snows in the Balkans.

The Allies landed in Sicily in June, 1943, and liberated Rome one year later. Mussolini was toppled soon after the Allied landings but reinstated briefly as a German puppet in the north. He was eventually caught fleeing in German uniform to the Swiss border and was executed by an Italian mob in April, 1945.

Italy Today

The sordid hardships of post-war Italy—unemployment, the black market and prostitution—have been made graphically familiar through the brilliant neo-realist cinema of Rossellini and de Sica. However, the country soon recovered and, in undergoing rapid industrialization, changed its character from a predominantly agrarian society to an increasingly urban one. The 1950s and 60s were a period of economic boom; a time for the "sweet life" captured in Fellini's film *La Dolce Vita*.

While the Italians got on with enjoying their new-found prosperity, politics was left to perpetually changing coalitions dominated by the Christian Democrats. In 1963 the "opening to the left" allowed the Socialists into government but Italy's second largest party, the Communists (PCI), were frozen out by the Cold War.

The 1970s were Italy's *anni di piombo* (years of lead): a time of political terrorism by the extreme right and left. The country's darkest hour came in 1978 when the former Christian Democrat prime minister Aldo Moro was kidnapped and murdered by the Red Brigade.

By the early 1980s the terrorist threat was largely over, defeated in great measure by the *pentitismo* (repentance) of terrorists turned supergrasses. In 1982 the Italian football team won the World Cup, ushering in a period of renewed national self-confidence. But 1986 saw the moment of *il sorpasso*, when Italy claimed to have overtaken Britain as the world's fifth largest economic power.

The mood changed at the start of the new decade. As the economy faltered, deep-seated problems finally rose to the surface to trouble the nation. Italy's North–South divide grew increasingly bitter as voters in the prosperous North flocked to separatist parties like Umberto Bossi's Northern League, seduced by siren calls for an autonomous northern republic. Meanwhile, in the South, the Mafia flexed its muscles, brutally assassinating judges Giovanni Falcone and Paolo Borsellino in car bomb attacks in 1992. All over the country leading politicians were implicated in scandal after scandal, as more than 3,000 criminal investigations were launched for bribery, kickbacks and connivance with the Mafia.

In politics new figures began to emerge, and the 1994 general elections brought about the demise of the once-dominant Christian Democratic Party,

T he social, economic and political problems which beset modern Italy are no laughing matter, but Italians always seem to find ways of raising a smile.

while sweeping in the new 'Forza Italia' party, which is pledged to relaunch the Italian economy. A coalition government has been formed with the Federalist Northern League and the right-wing National Alliance Party.

Despite the uncertainties, Italians still manage to find reasons to be cheerful. The closer integration of the European Community appears to offer a safeguard for Italian unity and, while people may despair about state inefficiency and grumble about politicians, they themselves tackle the problems which life (and bureaucracy) sets in their paths, as they have always done, with boundless wit and ingenuity.

How To Use This Guide

The book includes descriptions of Italy's most important towns and regions. We have divided the country up into six areas, usually with a principal city as a focus or starting point: **Rome** for central Italy; **Florence** for Tuscany, Umbria and the Adriatic seaside resorts; **Venice** for Veneto, the Dolomites and Emilia's historic towns from Parma to Ravenna; **Milan** for Lombardy, Piedmont and the Italian Riviera; **Naples** for the south; and a separate section for the major islands of Sicily and Sardinia.

As always, we try to be representative rather than encyclopaedic in our coverage of the country. Given the sheer richness of Italy, our selection of places within these six areas is not in any way exhaustive (nor, by the same token, exhausting). Those who know something of Italy already will inevitably feel that a few of their favourite spots have been neglected (though they may also be grateful we have kept their secret), while they will find others they never dreamed of. Newcomers will have more than enough to choose from.

Depending on how much time you have for that all-important first taste, we suggest you try to visit at least two, perhaps even three of the regions. Those with a passion for the big cities can combine Rome or Milan with the artistic delights of Florence and Tuscany or the timeless romance of Venice. Yet for many, the key to Italy's Mediterranean soul is to be found in Naples and the south – and you can always cool off at the seaside resorts on the Riviera or the Adriatic.

The trick is in the mix: in exploring the variety and contrasts of north and south, and in combining the attractions of town and country and the different facets of Italy's daily life. While it would be a crime to ignore Italy's churches, palaces and museums, the best way to enjoy them is also to spend plenty of time lazing around in cafés, or on the beach or out in the country.

Many people cannot manage to go to Italy outside the major holiday periods: Easter, July and August. But if your options are more flexible, the most enjoyable months are May, June, September and October, especially for Rome, Venice and Tuscany. July and August can be almost unbearably hot and humid in the big cities, but some find a perverse ghostly pleasure in being in Rome on Ferragosto (on and around 15 August) when the city is abandoned to the cats and the crazy. And remember, during public holidays (*see* page 10), the Italians just close the country down.

Just the Essentials

Too much to see, too little time to see it all? For people on their first trip to Italy who don't want to miss the "musts", here's our list of the landmarks of Italian sightseeing.

Central Italy
Rome: Spanish Steps
—Trevi Fountain
—Piazza Navona
—Pantheon
—Colosseum
—Forum
—St Peter's basilica
—Sistine Chapel
Tivoli: Hadrian's Villa and Villa
 d'Este
Tarquinia: Etruscan town

Tuscany, Umbria and The Marches
Florence: Cathedral and baptistery
—Michelangelo's *David* in the
 Accademia
—Fra Angelico frescoes in San Marco
—Uffizi: museum
—Ponte Vecchio shops
—Masaccio frescoes in Santa Maria
 del Carmine
Pisa: Leaning Tower, cathedral
Chianti wine tour
San Gimignano fortified town
Siena: cathedral, summer Palio
Orvieto: cathedral, wines
Assisi: St Francis basilica
Perugia: Collegio del Cambio

The North-East
Venice: Grand Canal
—Piazza San Marco
—San Marco Basilica
—Doges' Palace
—Accademia gallery
—Rialto shops
—Murano glass factories
Padua: Giotto frescoes
Vicenza: Palladian villas
Verona: Roman arena
Rimini: beach resort
Ravenna: Byzantine mosaics
Bologna: cathedral and pinacoteca
Parma: Correggio frescoes

The North-West
Milan: Cathedral
—La Scala opera house
—Santa Maria delle Grazie: Leonardo
 da Vinci's *Last Supper*
—Brera museum
—Via Monte Napoleone shops
Pavia Charterhouse
Lakes: Garda, Como, Maggiore
Turin: Piazza San Carlo
—Cathedral
—Egyptian Museum
San Remo: casino resort
Cinque Terre: coastal villages
Portofino: sailing harbour
Genoa: Via Garibaldi palaces

The South
Naples: Santa Lucia port
—Spaccanapoli: popular district
—Archaeological museum, Pompeii
 treasures
—Capodimonte: art museum
Isle of Capri
Pompeii: ruins
Vesuvius: volcano
Amalfi coast
Gargano resorts
Alberobello *trulli*
Castellana grottoes
Castel del Monte fortress
Basilica in Bari
Basilica in Lecce
Matera: ravine cave-houses
Reggio di Calabria: Greek bronzes
Tropea: beach resort

The Islands
Sardinia: Costa Smeralda resorts
—Serra Orrios: prehistoric *nuraghi*
—Alghero resort, Neptune's Grotto
Sicily: Palermo: palace of the Normans
—Monreale: cathedral
—Agrigento: Greek temples
—Taormina resort

Going Places With Something Special in Mind

Italy is so rich in churches, castles, paintings, palaces, ruins and landscapes that you scarcely know where to begin. One way to avoid cultural indigestion is to choose a theme and organize your trip around it. No need to neglect everything else, but you can head straight for the things you most want to see and take in anything else along the way. Here are some suggestions.

The Greeks

By the 6th century BC the Greeks had established colonies in Sicily and southern Italy, of which magnificent ruins remain. Greek legends are also linked with places in Italy: Ulysses resisted the Sirens off the Sorrento Peninsula and avoided the perils of the rock of Scylla and the whirlpool of Charybdis in the Straits of Messina; and the gateway to the underground world of Hades lay in the volcanic Phlegrean Fields.

By foot, by car, by boat—the choice is yours. Italy offers a world of possibilities to the inquisitive traveller.

In Sicily
1 SYRACUSE
Cathedral, formerly Temple of Athena; Greek Theatre; Paradise Quarry; Archaeological Museum.

2 AGRIGENTO
Temple Valley.

3 SELINUNTE
Acropolis, temple.

4 SEGESTA
Hilltop theatre and temple.

5 PALERMO
Archaeological Museum.

On the Mainland
6 REGGIO DI CALABRIA

*M*ajestic ruins of the ancient Greek civilization.

Archaeological Museum: Riace Bronzes (warrior statues retrieved from the sea).

7 PAESTUM
Doric temples.

8 NAPLES
Archaeological Museum: Farnese Hercules and Greek mosaics, paintings and sculpture.

Byzantine Art

The transfer of imperial Roman power to Byzantium brought oriental influences into art in Italy and a naturalistic style that would later influence Italian painting.

RAVENNA
Mosaics in Mausoleum of Galla Placidia, Battistero Neoniano, and churches of Sant'Apollinare Nuovo and Sant'Apollinare in Classe; National Museum.

VENICE
Bejewelled Pala d'Oro and mosaics in St Mark's Basilica.

SICILY
Cefalù: cathedral mosaics. Palermo: mosaics in Martorana church. Monreale: cathedral mosaics.

Nuraghi in Sardinia

More than 7,000 prehistoric cone-shaped towers, built of huge stones, are scattered throughout Sardinia, dating back to between 1400 and 800 BC.

1 SASSARI
Museo Sanna: prehistoric material from *nuraghi*.

2 ALGHERO
Nuraghe Palmavera.

3 TORRALBA
Nuraghe Sant'Antine near Torralba, 35km (21 miles) south-east of Sassari, biggest of *nuraghi* consisting of tower encircled by triangular wall.

4 MACOMER
Nuraghe Santa Barbara.

5 BARUMINI
Nuraghe su Nuraxi, central tower, surrounded by wall and village huts.

6 CAGLIARI
Archaeological Museum: bronze statuettes and terracotta figurines from *nuraghi*.

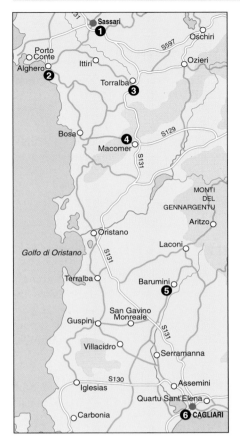

*P*rehistoric stone towers in Sardinia.

Romanesque Churches of Puglia

Architecture in the province of Puglia, which runs down the heel of Italy, was influenced by Norman rule and by the passage of the crusaders through its ports. You will find a magnificent series of Romanesque churches and cathedrals along the coast or slightly inland.

1 BARI
11th-century church and circular baptistery. Grandiose basilica of San Nicola, prototype of Romanesque churches in Puglia, with fine 12th-century episcopal throne.

2 BITONTO
Cathedral inspired by church of San Nicola in Bari; note imaginative carvings of animals on outside gallery and portal and richly sculpted pulpit in the interior.

3 MOLFETTA
12th-century Duomo Vecchio, surmounted by three pyramidal domes; interior combining Byzantine, Romanesque and Islamic features.

4 RUVO
Beautiful Romanesque cathedral, with triple portals, fine rose-window and bell tower.

5 TRANI
12th-century cathedral with magnificent bronze doors, right on the seafront.

6 BARLETTA
Romanesque cathedral with Gothic and Renaissance additions.

7 CANOSA
Cathedral: notable bishop's throne, supported by elephants; Norman tomb of Bohemond Guiscard in adjoining courtyard.

8 ALTAMURA
Cathedral with superb rose-window above portal carved with New Testament figures.

*R*omanesque churches
(1–9) and a chain of volcanoes
(10–13) in southern Italy.

9 TROIA
11th-century cathedral with lovely rose-window.

Volcanoes

A string of volcanoes lies along the south-west coast of Italy, part of a chain reaction linked to subsidence of the Tyrrhenian Sea. Some are still active.

10 VESUVIUS
Visit to crater edge; Eremo observatory; buried cities of Pompeii and Herculaneum.

11 PHLEGREAN FIELDS (CAMPI FLEGREI)
Volcanic area of hot springs west of Naples; gloomy Lago d'Averno, traditional mouth of hell; Solfatara crater near Pozzuoli.

12 ETNA
Crater visit from Catania or Taormina (conditions permitting); panorama.

13 STROMBOLI
Island volcano, still active.

Italian Gothic

The Gothic style, with pointed arches, vaulting and windows embellished by intricate tracery, developed in Italy in the 13th century and is often superimposed on Romanesque buildings.

1 ASSISI
Gothic additions to basilica of San Francesco; church of Santa Chiara.

2 BOLOGNA
Basilica of San Petronio.

3 FERRARA
Cathedral: Gothic upper part on Romanesque base.

4 FLORENCE
Palazzo Vecchio; Loggia della Signoria (dei Lanzi); cathedral and Giotto's campanile; churches of Santa Croce, Orsanmichele and Santa Maria Novella.

5 FOSSANOVA
Cistercian Abbey: church, cloisters and chapter house.

6 MILAN
Cathedral.

7 ORVIETO
Cathedral.

8 PAVIA
Carthusian charterhouse of La Certosa: Gothic with Renaissance sculpture.

9 PISA
Church of Santa Maria della Spina.

10 ROME
Church of Santa Maria sopra Minerva.

11 SIENA
Town hall; cathedral.

12 VENICE
Doges' Palace; Ca' d'Oro.

*I*ntricate Gothic
architecture.

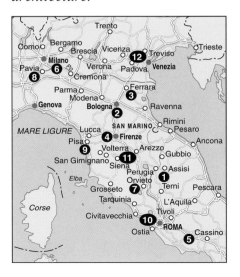

Major Baroque Monuments

The exuberant and sculptural Baroque style of architecture produced Italy's most theatrical churches, palaces, piazzas and fountains.

1 CASERTA
Royal Palace.

2 LECCE
Basilica of Santa Croce; Rosario church; Piazza del Duomo.

3 MILAN
Brera Museum.

4 NAPLES
St Martin's Carthusian monastery.

5 VENICE
Church of Santa Maria della Salute; Ca' Rezzonico; Ca' Pesaro.

6 ROME
Bernini colonnades in St Peter's Square; altar canopy in St Peter's; church of the Gesù; Borromini's Sant'Agnese in Agone and San Carlo alle Quattro Fontane; Palazzo Madama; Fountain of the Four Rivers in Piazza Navona; Trevi Fountain.

7 TURIN
Cathedral; Basilica di Superga; Palazzo Madama; church of San Lorenzo.

Caffès

Italy's *caffès* have traditionally been the meeting place for writers, artists, politicians and revolutionaries. Most of

*B*aroque (1–7) and Renaissance-style (13–23) architecture, with a break in a typical Italian caffè (8–12).

the big cities have their famous *caffè* rendezvous.

8 PADUA
Caffè Pedrocchi, where 19th-century Italian nationalists met to plot the downfall of Austrian rule.

9 ROME
Caffè Greco, for 200 years the favourite haunt of artists as varied as Mark Twain, Goethe, Byron and Fellini.

10 TRIESTE
Caffè degli Specchi (Piazza dell'Unità d'Italia).

11 TURIN
Caffès Baratti and Mulassano, elegant 19th-century coffee houses.

12 VENICE
Caffè Florian: red plush interior, open-air music on Piazza San Marco; rival Caffè Quadri, immediately opposite.

High Points of the Renaissance

The Renaissance, inspired by the classical traditions of Greece and Rome, was fostered by the Medici family in Florence in the 15th century and rapidly spread through northern Italy and down to Rome.

13 BERGAMO
Colleoni Chapel in multicoloured inlaid marble.

14 FERRARA
Spacious layout of Renaissance town planning; Renaissance palaces, including Palazzo di Ludovico il Moro.

15 FLORENCE
Baptistery; dome of cathedral; Spedale degli Innocenti; church of Santa Croce; churches of San Lorenzo and Santo Spirito; monastery of San Marco; Palazzo Medici-Riccardi; Palazzo Strozzi; Medici mausoleum at San Lorenzo.

16 MILAN
Portinari Chapel in basilica of Sant'-Eustorgio.

17 PAVIA
Carthusian monastery of La Certosa.

18 PERUGIA
Oratory of San Bernardino.

19 ROME
St Peter's basilica; Palazzo Farnese; Tempietto of San Pietro in Montorio; Campidoglio.

20 TIVOLI
Villa d'Este.

21 TODI
Church of Santa Maria della Consolazione.

22 URBINO
Ducal Palace.

23 VENICE
Palazzo Corner (Ca' Grande); Libreria Vecchia; churches of San Giorgio, Maggiore and Redentore.

Palladian Villas

The harmonious Renaissance buildings designed by Andrea Palladio in the 16th century set a whole new style and profoundly influenced the architecture of country houses in England and of plantation owners in the American Deep South. Country villas (by Palladio or his followers) can be visited by boat along the Brenta Canal from Venice and Padua or by road from Vicenza, Asolo, Padua and Rovigo.

1 VICENZA (PALLADIO'S HOME TOWN)
Basilica (enclosing Palazzo della Ragione); Teatro Olimpico; Palazzo Chiericati; Loggia del Capitaniato; houses in Corso Palladio.

2 FROM VICENZA
Villa Rotonda at Monte Berico; Villa Valmarana (frescoes by Tiepolo); Villa Godi near Lugo (early Palladio).

3 VENICE
Churches of San Giorgio Maggiore and Redentore.

4 FROM VENICE OR PADUA
Villa Foscari or La Malcontenta (Palladio); and Villa Gradenigo at Oriago,

Country villas and churches designed by Palladio and his followers.

73

Villa Widmann at Mira and Villa Nazionale or Pisani at Stra (Palladian-style).

5 FROM ASOLO
Palladio's Villa Barbaro-Volpi at Maser (Veronese frescoes) and Villa Emo at Fanzolo; sculptor Canova's domed mausoleum at Possagno.

6 FROM ROVIGO
Palladio's Villa Badoer and the Palladian-style Villa Bradagin at Fratta Polesine.

Medieval Walled Cities

In the delightful walled cities of northern Italy, the narrow streets, churches

Fortified cities (1–10) and colourful culture (11–18) in medieval Italy.

and palaces of the Middle Ages and the Renaissance are preserved within a formidable ring of fortifications.

1 LUCCA
Compact old Tuscan city, centre of medieval silk industry.

2 SAN GIMIGNANO
Fortified Tuscan hill town, bristling with tall towers.

3 VOLTERRA
City of Etruscan and Roman origin in the Tuscan hills.

4 SIENA
City on three hills, on which bitter battles were fought to ward off the Florentines.

5 MONTERIGGIONI (NEAR SIENA)
Its still-intact walls and towers were impressive enough to inspire verses of Dante's *Inferno*.

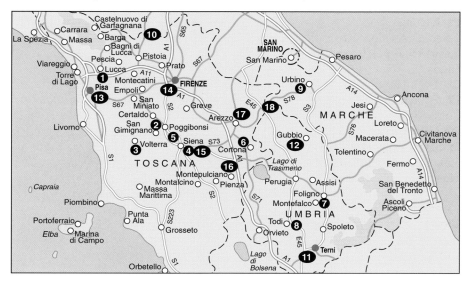

6 CORTONA
Medieval hill town, girdled by ramparts and guarded by fortress.

7 MONTEFALCO
Medieval town, perched on hill top.

8 TODI
Etruscan, Roman and medieval walls.

9 URBINO
Flourished as a haven of art under the dukes of Montefeltro.

10 MONTAGNANA
Ringed by brick walls and 24 towers.

Festivals in Tuscany and Umbria

All over Tuscany and Umbria, local pride and ancient traditions are expressed in colourful games and contests. Here are some of the most spectacular festivals.

11 NARNI
Corso all'Anello: "Ring Race" in honour of local patron saint held on 2nd Sunday in May.

12 GUBBIO
Corsa dei Ceri: locals race through the town carrying giant "candles" on 15 May. Palio della Balestra: crossbow contest held on last Sunday in May.

13 PISA
Gioco del Ponte: ancient "Push of War" held on a bridge over the Arno on the last Sunday in June.

14 FLORENCE
Calcio in Costume: ancient version of football played in Renaissance costume in June.

15 SIENA
Palio: world famous ancient horse races held on 2 July and 16 August.

16 MONTEPULCIANO
Bravio delle Botti: local teams push barrels up the town's steep main street on the last Sunday in August.

17 AREZZO
Giostra del Saraceno: jousting tournament held on the first Sunday in September.

18 SANSEPOLCRO
Palio della Balestra: crossbow contest with age-old rivals Gubbio held on 2nd Sunday in September.

The Medicis in Florence

The wealthy Medici banking family in Florence wielded power as dukes and popes and became munificent patrons of the arts under whom the Renaissance flowered.

1 PALAZZO MEDICI-RICCARDI
Palace built for Cosimo il Vecchio, who established Medici rule in Florence: Gozzoli frescoes of the *Journey of the Magi to Bethlehem* including portraits of Medici family members in kings' retinue; 17th-century ceiling showing *Apotheosis of the Medici* under Duke Cosimo III.

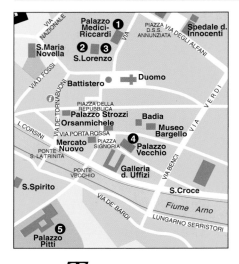

The wealthy and influential Medici family fostered the Renaissance in 15th-century Florence.

2 PIAZZA SAN LORENZO
Statue of Giovanni delle Bande Nere, father of Duke Cosimo I.

3 CHURCH OF SAN LORENZO
Built by successive Medicis, and adjoining Cappelle Medicee containing Medici tombs.

4 PALAZZO VECCHIO
Transformed from grim fortress into richly frescoed palace under Cosimo I; equestrian statue of Cosimo I in piazza outside.

5 PALAZZO PITTI
Palace to which Cosimo I later moved, hung with paintings collected by the Medici; portrait of Lorenzo the Magnificent and scenes of contemporary Florence in Ghirlandaio's frescoes in Santa Trinita's Cappella Sassetti.

National Parks

Italy's national parks are as diverse as the landscape of the country itself, from Alpine forests on the Swiss border to oak woods, southerly habitat of mouflon and deer.

GRAN PARADISO
Italy's oldest national park boasts a rich flora and fauna of Alpine flowers and plants, chamois, ibex and bird life in the Aosta Valley.

STELVIO
Mountainous national park in Lombardy and Trentino-Alto Adige on the Swiss border. Siberian, Scots and silver pines, golden eagles, deer.

ABRUZZO
National park east of Rome protecting the natural environment of the Central Apennines. Beech woods, brown bears, chamois and Apennine wolves.

CIRCEO
Italy's smallest national park, in Lazio, on the Tyrrhenian coast midway between Rome and Naples. Oak woods and Mediterranean shrub, water birds, deer and mouflon.

CALABRIA
Three mountain regions in the provinces of Reggio Calabria, Cosenza and Catanzaro. Pines, silver fir and beech, wolves, roe deer, wild boars.

Italian artists: Giotto (1–5), Leonardo da Vinci (6–9), Michelangelo (10 and 11) and Caravaggio (12–17).

Giotto, Father of Italian Painting

Giotto di Bondone (1266–1337), both architect and painter, was the first to give his backgrounds depth and his figures solidity and warmth.

1 PADUA
Cappella degli Scrovegni: magnificent frescoes of the *Life of Mary*, the *Annunciation*, the *Life and Passion of Christ* and the *Last Judgement*.

2 FLORENCE
Church of Santa Croce: frescoes of *St John* and *St Francis* in the Peruzzi and Bardi chapels.

3 ASSISI
Stunning frescoes of the *Life of St Francis* in both the Upper and the Lower Churches of the Basilica of St Francis.

4 BOLOGNA
Enthroned Madonna in Pinacoteca Nazionale.

5 ROME
Vatican Pinacoteca: the Stefaneschi triptych.

The Genius of Leonardo da Vinci

Leonardo da Vinci (1452–1519) was as brilliant a scientist and writer as he was an artist; his work inspired generations of European painters. You can see some of his greatest works in Florence and Milan.

6 FLORENCE
Adoration of the Magi and *Annunciation* in Uffizi Gallery.

7 VINCI
Casa Natale di Leonardo: house considered to be his birthplace, now preserved as a museum.

8 MILAN
Last Supper in refectory of church of Santa Maria delle Grazie; *Portrait of a Musician* in Pinacoteca Ambrosiana; and models of inventions in Museo Nazionale della Scienza e della Tecnica.

9 TURIN
Self-portrait (drawing) in Palazzo Reale.

The Versatility of Michelangelo

Michelangelo Buonarroti (1475–1564) excelled as painter, sculptor and architect. In Florence and Rome you can admire his consummate skill in all three spheres.

10 FLORENCE
Casa Buonarroti (Michelangelo Museum); statue of *David* in the Galleria dell'Accademia (a copy of it stands in the Piazza della Signoria); four unfinished statues of *Slaves* imprisoned in the marble also in the Galleria dell'Accademia; statue of *Bacchus* in Bargello Museum; *Pietà* in Museo dell'Opera del Duomo (originally intended for Michelangelo's own tomb but unfinished); New Sacristy of San Lorenzo; statues of Medici dukes and of allegorical figures of Day and Night, Dawn and Evening in Medici Chapels at San Lorenzo.

11 ROME
Dome of St Peter's; marble *Pietà* in recess to the right of basilica doors; ceiling and altar wall of Vatican's Sistine Chapel; Piazza del Campidoglio, laid out to Michelangelo's design; façade of Palazzo Farnese; statue of *Moses* in church of San Pietro in Vincoli.

The Art of Caravaggio

Michelangelo Merisi da Caravaggio (1571–1610) revolutionized religious painting by his use of realistic characters and settings and by dramatic effects such as the foreshortening and strong lighting of the main figures against dark backgrounds. He worked in Rome, Naples and Sicily.

12 ROME
Church of Santa Maria del Popolo: *Conversion of St Paul, Crucifixion of St Peter*; Quadreria della Galleria Borghese al San Michele: *Boy with a Basket of Fruit, The Sick Bacchus, David with the Head of Goliath* (the head of which is believed to be the artist's self-portrait); church of San Luigi dei Francesi: *St Matthew and the Angel, Calling of St*

Matthew, Martyrdom of St Matthew; church of Sant'Agostino: *Madonna of the Pilgrims*; Palazzo Barberini: *Judith with the Head of Holofernes*; Pinacoteca Capitolina: *St John the Baptist*; Vatican Pinacoteca: *Descent from the Cross*.

13 FLORENCE
Uffizi Gallery: *Head of Medusa*.

14 MILAN
Pinacoteca Ambrosiana: *Basket of Fruit*; Pinacoteca di Brera: *Supper at Emmaus*.

15 NAPLES
Capodimonte Gallery: *Seven Acts of Mercy* altarpiece, *Flagellation*.

16 MESSINA
National Museum: *Adoration of the Shepherds, Resurrection of Lazarus*.

17 SYRACUSE
Church of Santa Lucia: *Burial of St Lucy*.

Wine Tours

Italy has been producing wines since the time of the Etruscans. It is less well geared for wine-tasting than France, but you will find vineyard routes marked in Piedmont, the Chianti country south of Florence and the Alban Hills near Rome. Apart from visiting small cellars and big wine producers, look out for the sign *enoteca* (wine li-

Vineyards conveniently close to Rome.

brary), where you can taste and buy a variety of wines.

Alban Hills
The wine towers of the little towns of the Alban Hills known as the Castelli Romani offer you panoramic views and the chance to sample cool golden wines. You can take in the main towns in a day's outing from Rome.

1 FRASCATI
Hill town of 17th-century villas and gardens famous for its white wine.

2 GROTTAFERRATA
Abbey town with notable wines.

3 NEMI
Year-round wild mushrooms and strawberries to accompany local wine.

4 VELLETRI
Ancient wine-making town with ruins of Roman temple.

5 MARINO
Where the fountains spout wine at the grape harvest.

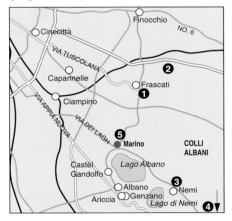

Home of the sparkling Asti Spumante.

Piedmont

South and east of Turin you can take a tour through the Langhe and Monferrato hills to taste some of Piedmont's most famous wines: the fruity red Barolo and Barbaresco and the lighter Barbera, or the white Asti and Gavi.

1 ALBA

Heart of wine and truffle country; wine tours include Barolo and the castle of Grinzane Cavour.

2 ASTI

Home of sparkling Asti Spumante: Italy's champagne.

3 PESSIONE (NEAR CHIERI)

Sampling of red and white vermouth on premises of Martini e Rossi; visit to wine-making museum.

Chianti Hills

Take the Chiantigiana vineyard road through the picturesque Chianti hills from Florence to Siena to taste Italy's most famous wine. Follow the *strada*

Italy's most famous wine.

del vino signs and try the red and white Chiantis at the wine-producing estates along the way. Cheaper wines are sold in the traditional straw-covered flask (now sadly often replaced by plastic) and the more expensive in straight-sided bottles.

1 SAN GIMIGNANO

Many-towered town famous for white Vernaccia wine.

2 SIENA

National Wine Library. Good place to buy.

3 MONTALCINO

Ancient walled town south of Siena, noted for full-bodied Brunello wine.

4 MONTEPULCIANO

Old hill-top town surrounded by vineyards producing ruby-red Vino Nobile.

5 GAIOLE

Centre of Chianti Classico, marked by black cockerel label; wine-tasting at abbey of Coltibuono.

6 RADDA

Chianti museum.

7 GREVE

Wide range of wines at the local *enoteca.*

Music and Theatre

Opera, concerts and music festivals featuring everything from classical to rock flourish throughout Italy, often against a backdrop of palaces, churches, cloisters or ancient ruins.

1 L'AQUILA
Concerts by Abruzzi Symphony Orchestra; chamber music in castle.

2 FLORENCE
Teatro Comunale for opera; Maggio Musicale classical music festival.

3 MILAN
Opera at La Scala; concerts by Italian Television's Milan Symphony Orchestra; Piccolo Teatro for stage productions.

4 NAPLES
San Carlo Theatre for opera; concerts

A variety of music and theatre to delight all tastes.

by Italian Television's Naples Symphony Orchestra.

5 PERUGIA
Chamber music in Palazzo dei Priori.

6 ROME
Teatro dell'Opera; open-air opera at Baths of Caracalla in summer (the use of this venue is under discussion); Accademia Nazionale di Santa Cecilia concerts in Accademia hall and Vatican Auditorium or open-air in Piazza del Campidoglio; symphony concerts by Italian Television's Rome Orchestra.

7 TURIN
Teatro Reggio for opera; symphony concerts by Italian Television's Turin Orchestra.

8 VENICE
La Fenice Theatre for opera and ballet; open-air concerts in courtyard of Doges' Palace.

9 VERONA
Open-air opera in old Roman arena.

Making the Most of a Short Stay in the Eternal City

A lifetime isn't enough to do justice to the Eternal City, reckon the Romans. With more than 2,500 years of history and culture behind them, they're probably right. Yet visitors with only a short stay in mind shouldn't feel daunted. The city certainly won't reveal all its secrets, but see just some of the sights and the shortest of sojourns is sure to prove rewarding.

The centre of Italy is the cradle of Latin civilization, the administrative headquarters of that ancient conglomerate known as the Roman Empire. Immediately surrounding Rome, Lazio is the old province of Latium. On the eastern flank of the Apennines, the Abruzzo region, of which the province of Molise is a recently created offshoot (1963), came under Roman domination in the 3rd century BC. While first-time visitors will want to

*T*elevision aerials *may bristle on the Rome skyline, but the great dome of St Peter's remains a timeless symbol of the Eternal City.*

spend most of their time in and around Rome, the wilderness of the Abruzzo National Park makes a pleasant excursion within fairly easy reach of Rome via the *autostrada*.

Rome (*Roma*)

Within and beyond its seven hills and along the winding banks of the River Tiber, Rome has four or five different personalities. There is the ancient Rome of the imperial ruins; the Catholic Rome of the Vatican and churches; the Renaissance city of Michelangelo and Raphael or the baroque of Bernini and Borromini; and a modern metropolis of interminable traffic jams, fashionable boutiques and cafés, but also

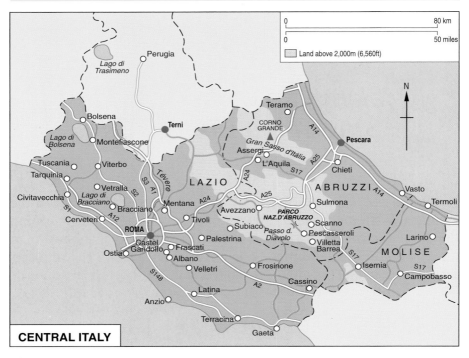

0 ——————————— 80 km
0 ——————————— 50 miles
☐ Land above 2,000m (6,560ft)

N

Perugia
Lago di Trasimeno
Bolsena
Lago di Bolsena
Montefiascone
Terni
CORNO GRANDE
Gran Sasso d'Itália
Assergi
Teramo
Pescara
A14
Tuscania
Tarquinia
Viterbo
Vetralla
L'Aquila
S17
Chieti
A25
Civitavecchia
Lago di Bracciano
Bracciano
Cerveteri
A12
LAZIO
Tévere
Mentana
A24
A25
ABRUZZI
A14
Vasto
Termoli
ROMA
Castel Gandolfo
Ostia
Frascati
Albano
Velletri
Tivoli
Avezzano
PARCO NAZ.D'ABRUZZO
Subiaco
Palestrina
Passo d. Diavolo
Sulmona
Scanno
Pescasseroli
Villetta Barrea
S17
Larino
MOLISE
Frosinone
Isernia
S17
Campobasso
Latina
Cassino
A2
Anzio
Terracina
Gaeta

CENTRAL ITALY

factories and high-rises in the industrial suburbs.

You may choose one, two or all of them, but none is easily separable from the others. Churches are built on the ruins of Roman baths or pagan temples. The T-shirted, designer-jeaned café crowd on Piazza Navona make a bizarre contrast with Bernini's grandiose 17th-century fountain. The secret of the Eternal City is that it has lived all its ages simultaneously. The road-building Caesars *knew* their descendants would be obsessed with cars.

Park yours, put on a pair of walking shoes and ease yourself into the city gently. Before you face the daunting challenge of the ancient city around the Colosseum or the formidable complex of the Vatican, we suggest you get to know the modern Romans' town.

Central Italy.

The Centre

Make an early start with breakfast on **Piazza del Popolo** at a veritable Roman institution, the meeting-place of the city's brighter spirits, the **Caffè Rosati** (and come back for an evening apéritif). Its terrace is a perfect vantage point for admiring the gracefully curving piazza as an exemplary piece of open-air urban theatre, designed in 1818 by Giuseppe Valadier, architect to Napoleon.

On the north side, the austere **Santa Maria del Popolo** is important for Raphael's Chigi Chapel, exquisite frescoes by Pinturicchio and, above all, two profoundly disturbing early 17th-century paintings by Caravaggio—the *Conversion of St Paul* and *Crucifixion* *of St Peter*—in the Cerasi Chapel left of the choir. Next to the church, an arched gateway marks what was the entrance to ancient Rome along the Via Flaminia, leading from Rimini on the Adriatic coast.

The **obelisk** in the centre, dating from the Egypt of Rameses II (13th century BC), was brought here from the Circus Maximus and re-erected by Pope Sixtus V in 1589. Rounding off the south side are the twin baroque churches, **Santa Maria dei Miracoli** and **Santa Maria in Montesanto**, completed by the 17th-century masters, Gianlorenzo Bernini and Carlo Fontana.

In spring the Spanish Steps are festooned with azaleas; all year round they are a favourite rendezvous for Romans and tourists alike.

Above the piazza to the east, the **Pincio** gardens offer a magical view of the city, especially at sunset. The Pincio promenade lined with pine trees and open-air restaurants takes you past **Villa Medici**, the home of French artists visiting on national scholarships, to the 16th-century French church, **Trinità dei Monti**.

Its twin belfries loom over the **Spanish Steps** (*Scalinata della Trinità dei Monti*), the eternal hang-out of guitar-playing youths, lovers and pedlars of trinkets and flowers. The pleasant daze induced on the three-tiered travertine staircase, festooned in spring with pink azaleas, was celebrated by John Keats as a "blissful cloud of summer indolence" before he died here in 1821. His house at the bottom of the Steps has been preserved as a museum.

Named after a palace used as the Spanish Embassy, the Steps and **Piazza di Spagna** are the heart of the

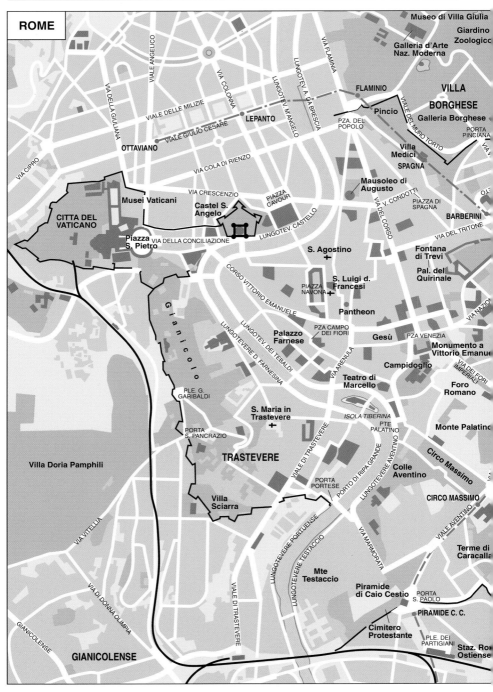

ROME

Museo di Villa Giulia

Giardino Zoologico

Galleria d'Arte
Naz. Moderna

VILLA
BORGHESE

FLAMINIO

Pincio

Galleria Borghese

PZA. DEL
POPOLO

Villa
Medici

PORTA
PINCIANA

SPAGNA

VIALE ANGELICO

VIA DELLA GIULIANA

VIALE DELLE MILIZIE

VIA COLONNA

LEPANTO

VIALE GIULIO CESARE

VIA FLAMINIA

LUNGOTEV. A DA BRESCIA

LUNGOTEV. M ANGELO

VIALE DEL MURO TORTO

OTTAVIANO

VIA CIPRO

VIA COLA DI RIENZO

Mausoleo di
Augusto

V. CONDOTTI

PIAZZA DI
SPAGNA

VIA CRESCENZIO

PIAZZA
CAVOUR

VIA DEL CORSO

BARBERINI

Musei Vaticani

Castel S.
Angelo

VIA DEL TRITONE

CITTA DEL
VATICANO

LUNGOTEV. CASTELLO

S. Agostino

Fontana
di Trevi

Piazza
S. Pietro

VIA DELLA CONCILIAZIONE

S. Luigi d.
Francesi

Pal. del
Quirinale

CORSO VITTORIO EMANUELE

PIAZZA
NAVONA

Pantheon

VIA NAZIO

Gianicolo

LUNGOTEV. DEI TEBALDI

LUNGOTEVERE D. FARNESINA

Palazzo
Farnese

PZA CAMPO
DEI FIORI

Gesù

PZA VENEZIA

Monumento a
Vittorio Emanue

VIA ARENULA

Campidoglio

VIA DEI FORI
IMPERIALI

Foro
Romano

PLE. G.
GARIBALDI

Teatro di
Marcello

S. Maria in
Trastevere

ISOLA TIBERINA

Monte Palatino

PORTA
S. PANCRAZIO

PTE
PALATINO

Villa Doria Pamphili

VIALE DI TRASTEVERE

TRASTEVERE

PORTA
PORTESE

Colle
Aventino

Circo Massimo

PORTO DI RIPA GRANDE

LUNGOTEVERE AVENTINO

CIRCO MASSIMO

Villa
Sciarra

VIALE AVENTINO

VIA VITELLIA

LUNGOTEVERE PORTUENSE

VIA MARMORATA

Terme di
Caracalla

VIA DI DONNA OLIMPIA

LUNGOTEVERE TESTACCIO

VIALE DI TRASTEVERE

Mte
Testaccio

Piramide
di Caio Cestio

PORTA
S. PAOLO

PIRAMIDE C. C.

GIANICOLENSE

Cimitero
Protestante

PLE. DEI
PARTIGIANI

Staz. Ro
Ostiense

GIANICOLENSE

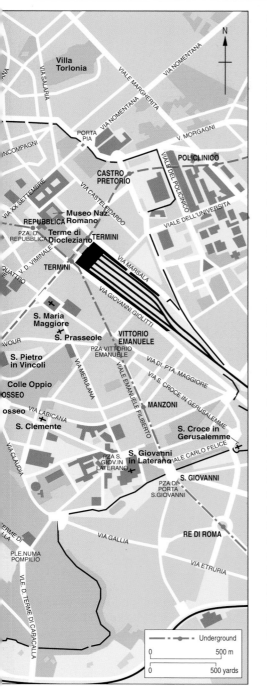

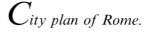

city's most fashionable shopping area, leading over to Via del Corso. The piazza's 17th-century boat-shaped marble fountain, **Fontana della Barcaccia**, is by Pietro Bernini, father of the great baroque master Gianlorenzo Bernini (some scholars credit the work to the more famous son). The venerable **Babington's Tea Rooms** is a relic of the days when Romans called the piazza the "English ghetto". More quintessentially Roman, on nearby Via Condotti, is the city's oldest coffee house, the 18th-century **Caffè Greco**. It's been popular, as you will see from pictures, busts and autographs, with Goethe, Byron, Baudelaire, Liszt, Gogol and Fellini.

The **Trevi Fountain** (*Fontana di Trevi*) benefited from Fellini's keen sense of baroque aesthetics when he dipped the sumptuous Anita Ekberg in its legendarily purifying waters in his film *La Dolce Vita*. Most people are content just to toss in a coin over their shoulder—a custom that is traditionally supposed to guarantee the thrower's return to Rome. Nicola Salvi's astounding 18th-century fountain is in fact a triumphal arch and palace façade (to the old Palazzo Poli) framing mythical creatures in a riot of rocks and pools, with a rearing horse symbolizing the ocean's turmoil and a calmer steed its tranquillity. Tucked away behind narrow alleys, this extravaganza is out of all proportion to its tiny piazza and no amount of signposts leading to it can prepare you for the marvellous shock of discovery. Romantics go at the dead of night, to be alone with its illumination.

City plan of Rome.

*T*he water that splashes over the sculpted rocks of Nicola Salvi's 18th-century rococo masterpiece, the Trevi Fountain, is reckoned to be the purest in Rome. Toss in a coin to ensure a return to the Eternal City.

That other symbol of the *dolce vita*, Via Veneto, has been deserted by its starlets and *paparazzi* and only the expensive cafés, shops and hotels remain.

On one of the seven hills of ancient Rome, the fortress-like **Palazzo del Quirinale**, once residence to popes fleeing the malarial swamps of the Vatican down by the Tiber, housed the king of Italy after 1870, and is now the

Rome's Monumental Blunder
Few edifices have known such universal
hostility as the Vittorio Emanuele Monument or "Vittoriano". Popularly known
as the "wedding cake" or "Rome's false
teeth", the bombastic colonnade with its
pedestrian equestrian bronzes and almost
unclimbable steps is a true monument of
urban catastrophe. Begun in 1885, the
40-year construction entailed the demo-
lition of a piece of the ancient Capitoline
Hill. Parts of the Palazzo Venezia were
dismantled for a clearer view. The gigantic proportions completely dwarf the
surrounding splendours of ancient
Rome and the dazzling white Brescia
marble clashes horribly with the city's
preference for gentle amber, ochre or
pink travertine.

presidential palace. The only embel-
lishment on its formidable façade is
Bernini's graceful porch, but its piazza
is worth the climb for the view over
the city towards the Vatican.

You could not miss **Piazza Venezia**
if you tried: and many do try, because
of its endless traffic jams and the
grotesque **Vittorio Emanuele Monument**, celebrating the first king of unified Italy with inimitable 19th-century
pomposity. North-west of the monument, the 15th-century **Palazzo Venezia**
is a fine example of severe but elegant
early Renaissance architecture, now
containing a museum of medieval and
Renaissance arms, furniture and
sculpture. Mussolini had his office
there and harangued his followers
from the balcony.

Behind Piazza Venezia, one staircase
leads steeply up to the austere 13th-
century **Santa Maria in Aracoeli**. Another, more graceful and gradual, takes
you up between statues of Castor and
Pollux to Michelangelo's beautifully
cambered square of the **Campidoglio**
(Capitoline Hill). This haven of quiet,
away from the traffic, forges a superb
link between the Renaissance and ancient Rome's most sacred site, where
sacrifices were made to Jupiter and
Juno. At the rear of the square is the
handsome 16th-century façade of the
Palazzo Senatorio (now the city hall),
flanked by the **Palazzo Nuovo** and

Palazzo dei Conservatori. These last two house the Capitoline Museums (*see* page 112). The grand bronze **equestrian statue of Marcus Aurelius**, which once stood in the centre of the square, has recently emerged from a lengthy restoration and is now sheltered behind glass in the Palazzo Nuovo.

The church of the **Gesù**, severe and relatively discreet on its own square west of Piazza Venezia, was a major element in the Jesuits' Counter-Reformation campaign. Begun as their Roman headquarters in 1568, its open ground-plan was the model for the congregational churches that were to regain popular support from the Protestants. While its façade is more sober than the exultant baroque churches put up as the movement gained momentum, the interior glorifies the new militancy in gleaming bronze, gold, marble and precious stones. Perhaps inevitably, the church's richest, almost overwhelming ornament is the **altar of St Ignatius of Loyola**, covering the tomb of the Jesuits' founder (in the left transept) with a profusion of lapis lazuli. The globe at the top is said to be the largest piece of this stone in the world.

In gentler contrast, the church of **Sant'Ignazio** stands in an enchanting

---

The Wind and the Devil

Piazza del Gesù is the windiest place in Rome, according to an amusing piece of folklore. The Devil and the Wind were out walking together one day when the Devil begged leave to go inside the church of the Gesù. He never reappeared, and the Wind has been waiting here for him ever since.

---

rococo stage-set of 18th-century houses. Inside, Andrea Pozzo (himself a Jesuit priest and designer of the saint's tomb at the Gesù) has painted a superb *trompe l'œil* ceiling fresco (1685) depicting St Ignatius's entry into paradise. Stand on a buff stone disk in the nave's centre aisle for the full effect of the celestial dome apparently rising above the transept.

The **Pantheon** (Piazza della Rotonda) is the best preserved monument of ancient Rome and rivals the Colosseum in its combination of quiet elegance and sheer massive power. Emperor Hadrian, its builder (around AD 120), achieved a marvel of engineering with its magnificent coffered dome, over 43m (142ft) in interior diameter (larger than St Peter's), borne by an intricate portico of pink and grey granite columns and arches. The bronze that once embellished it was taken away to make Bernini's canopy for the high altar in St Peter's. This "Temple of all the Gods" today contains the tombs of Renaissance deities such as Raphael and architect Baldassare Peruzzi and of kings Vittorio Emanuele II and Umberto I.

Caravaggio admirers will find some of his greatest masterpieces in the neighbourhood: the *St Matthew* trilogy in the fine baroque church of **San Luigi dei Francesi**, and the moving *Madonna of the Pilgrims* in the Renaissance church of **Sant'Agostino**.

Pause now at a café on that most serene of city squares, **Piazza Navona**. Nowhere in Rome is the spectacle of Italian street life more pleasantly indulged, thanks to an inspired collaboration of Roman genius across the ages. The elongated piazza was laid

*T*he Fountain of the Four Rivers, one of the most flamboyant creations of that baroque genius Gianlorenzo Bernini.

out around AD 90 by Emperor Domitian as an athletics stadium, *Circus Agonalis*—a sporting tradition continued in the Renaissance with jousting tournaments. The 17th century contributed its sublime baroque décor, and today, sages on the city council safeguard it as a pedestrian zone.

In the centre, Bernini's **Fountain of the Four Rivers** (*Fontana dei Fiumi*) celebrates the great rivers of the Americas (Río de la Plata), Europe (Danube), Asia (Ganges) and Africa (Nile). Romans who delight in Bernini's scorn for his rivals suggest that the Nile god covers his head rather than look at Borromini's church of **Sant'Agnese in Agone** and the river god of the Americas is poised to catch it in case it collapses. In fact, the fountain was completed several years before

Borromini's splendid, and structurally impeccable, façade and dome. Ecclesiastical tradition says the church was built on the ruins of a Roman brothel where St Agnes was stripped before being martyred.

The boisterous fruit and vegetable market on the **Campo dei Fiori** gives way in the afternoons to political meetings, admonished by the **statue** of philosopher Giordano Bruno. The Inquisition burned him alive here in 1600 for his preposterous idea that the universe was infinite, with many more galaxies than ours. An even more famous death occurred at nearby Piazza del Biscione, more precisely the restaurant Da Pancrazio, whose cellar shelters ruins of Pompey's Theatre where Julius Caesar was assassinated.

Only with a special appointment can you visit the glorious **Palazzo Farnese**, Rome's finest Renaissance palace. It was built by Antonio da Sangallo the Younger, Michelangelo and Giacomo della Porta, and now houses the French Embassy. A privileged few get in to see the ceremonial dining room's fabulous frescoes by Annibale Carracci. Since 1871 the French have leased the palace from the Italian government for the sum of one lira payable every year. In return the French provide a palace in Paris as Italy's embassy—very nice, too, but not exactly Michelangelo.

Narrow streets south-east of the Campo dei Fiori lead to the **Jewish Ghetto** near the ruins of the ancient Roman **Theatre of Marcellus** (*Teatro di Marcello*), the architectural model for the Colosseum. A permanent feature of Roman life for over 2,500 years but forced into a ghetto only in the 16th century, a small Jewish community still lives around Via del Portico d'Ottavia. The hefty neo-Babylonian synagogue, together with a small museum of Jewish history next door, is down by the river.

The Aventine

On the south-west rim of classical Rome, the Aventine is one of the original seven hills and remains above the city clamour a quiet residential sanctuary of villas and apartments in shady gardens of flowers and palms.

The Dominican basilica of **Santa Sabina**, on the hill's western edge, is noted for its admirable dignity and purity of line and the grace of its Roman columns. It was built on the site of a Roman matron's palace, honouring her martyrdom after she was converted to Christianity by her Greek slave. Make sure you see the beautiful carvings on the old cypress-wood west door.

A few steps away, enjoy the unusual **keyhole-view** through the garden door of the villa of the Knights of Malta (*Cavalieri di Malta*)—the distant dome of St Peter's, perfectly framed beyond an avenue of trees. Do it before the bus loads queue up.

At the foot of the Aventine near the Tiber, the little church of **Santa Maria in Cosmedin** was given to Rome's Greek colony in the Middle Ages. Its simple Romanesque façade and unadorned interior provide a stark contrast to the city's dominant baroque grandeur. Test your honesty in the portico's fierce-looking **Bocca della Verità** (Mouth of Truth). The ancient marble face, possibly once a well-cover, is said to bite the fingers off anyone

> **Saved by a Snake**
> In times of disaster the Senate of Ancient Rome turned for guidance to the collection of divine oracles known as the Sibylline Books. When Rome was afflicted by a great plague in 293 BC the books' advice, as interpreted by the professional soothsayers, was to send a ship to Epidaurus in Greece and bring back Aesculapius, the god of healing.
>
> The embassy returned to Rome with a statue of the god. As the ship sailed up the Tiber, to general rejoicing, a giant snake slipped overboard and swam to the Tiber Island. The people immediately hailed the serpent as the incarnation of Aesculapius himself. The pestilence abated and the grateful Romans built a temple to the god on the island, his new home. In memory of the manner of the god's arrival the whole island was faced with travertine and given the form of a ship. On the "stern" was carved in relief the figure of a snake.

telling a lie with his hand in the gaping mouth. Buy a copy at the church and test your friends back home.

Across the road, two of Rome's most charming and best-preserved temples stand on what was once part of the ancient cattle-market. The round one, with fluted marble columns, is wrongly called the **Temple of Vesta**, and was probably dedicated to Hercules, who never encouraged a cult of virgins. Its rectangular neighbour, known as the **Temple of Fortune**, is the victim of the classical scholars' equivalent of a typing error, as its presiding deity is now believed to have been Portunus, god of harbours, rather than Fortuna.

A sight for sore noses, over the Tiber embankment here, is the mouth of the **Cloaca Maxima**, ancient Rome's main drain still opening into the river near the Palatine Bridge.

South of the Aventine near Porta San Paolo, take time out to enjoy the serene beauty of the **Protestant Cemetery**, last resting place of John Keats (*see* page 85), and his friend Percy Bysshe Shelley, who was drowned in 1822 while sailing in the Bay of Spezia. Towering over the cemetery is Rome's only **pyramid**, incorporated into the city walls. A Roman colonial magistrate, Caius Cestius, commissioned it for his tomb in 12 BC on his return from a spell of duty in Egypt.

Classical Rome

The nucleus of classical Rome is around the Colosseum, with the Forum to the north-west and the Baths of Caracalla to the south. Don't be daunted: even the best-informed scholars find the monumental relics difficult to decipher. The mystery itself is more than half the charm of these vestiges of a vanished world. Take them in your stride, slower and more relaxed than ever when it comes to walking the ruins. Avoid the midday sun in the shadeless Forum and finish your visit with a picnic and siesta on the Palatine. Even if you are not an archaeology buff who wants to understand the meaning of every stone, it is worth at least an hour or two to stand among the debris of empire and wonder whether Fifth Avenue, Piccadilly, the Champs-Elysées or Red Square will look any better 2,000 years from now.

It says something about Rome's essential earthiness that, more than any inspirational church or opulent palace, it is the **Colosseum**—what Byron called "the gladiator's bloody circus"—that is the symbol of the city's eternity. Built in AD 80 by 20,000 slaves and prisoners, the four-tiered elliptical amphitheatre seated 50,000 spectators on stone benches. Flowing in and out of 80 arched passageways known as *vomitoria*, aristocrat and pleb alike came to see blood: bears, lions, tigers and leopards starved into fighting against each other, not to mention criminals, war captives and Christians. Gladiators butchered one another to the crowds' cries of *Jugula!* ("Slit his throat!")

For their churches and palaces, popes and princes have stripped the Colosseum of its precious marble, travertine and metal. They have left in the arena's basin a ruined maze of cells and corridors that funnelled men and beasts to the slaughter. The horror has disappeared beneath the moss and what remains is the thrill of the monument's endurance. As an old Anglo-Saxon prophecy goes: "While stands the Colosseum, Rome shall stand; when falls the Colosseum, Rome shall fall; and when Rome falls, with it shall fall the world."

The nearby **Arch of Constantine** celebrates the 4th-century emperor's victory over his imperial rival Maxentius at the Mulvian Bridge. The newly converted Constantine may have won the battle under the sign of the Cross but a cost-conscious Senate took fragments from monuments of earlier rulers— Trajan, Hadrian and Marcus Aurelius— complete with depictions of pagan rituals and sacrifices. Only a few reliefs, over the two outer arches, show the Christian Constantine.

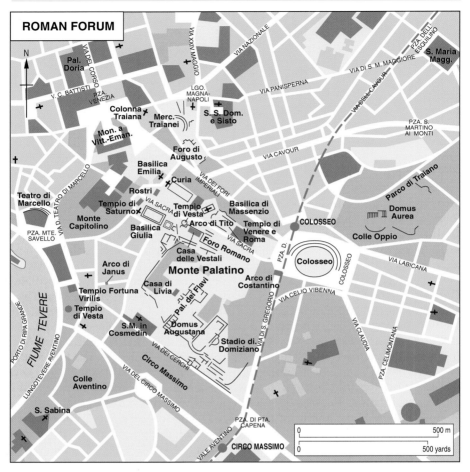

ROMAN FORUM

With an exhilarating leap of the imagination, you can stand among the columns, arches and porticoes of the **Roman Forum** and picture the hub of the great imperial city: the first in Europe to house a million inhabitants. Earthquake, fire, flood and the plunder of barbarians and Renaissance architects reduced the area to a muddy cow pasture until the excavations of the 19th century. Today, a detailed plan and the portable sound-guide rented at the entrance (on the Via dei

*T*he Roman Forum.

Fori Imperiali) will make sense of the apparent confusion and help you trace the layout of palaces, temples and market halls.

Start your tour at the western end, just below the Campidoglio's Palazzo Senatorio (*see* page 89). See above you how the arches of the Roman record office (*Tabularium*) have been incorporated into the rear of the Renaissance palace, with its modern municipal records on the other side of the wall. From here, look down the full length of the **Via Sacra** (Sacred Way), the route taken by victorious generals as they rode in triumphal procession to the foot of the Capitoline Hill, followed by the legions' standards, massed ranks of prisoners and carts piled with the spoils of conquest.

To remind us that this military might was backed by the right of law, part of the severe brick-built rectangular **Curia**, the home of the Roman Senate, still stands in the north-west

Originally a marshy valley between the Capitoline and Palatine hills until drained by the Etruscan king Tarquinius Priscus, the Forum developed from a marketplace into the political, religious and business centre of ancient Rome.

corner of the Forum. If London's House of Commons is the mother of parliaments, then the Curia's modest debating chamber was, in the words of writer HV Morton, the "venerable great-grandmother" of all parliaments.

In front of the Curia, a concrete shelter protects the underground site of the **Lapis Niger** (generally not on view), a black marble stone laid by Julius Caesar over the presumed grave of Romulus, the city's founder. Nearby are remains of the Basilica Julia law court and the **Rostra** orators' platform from which Mark Antony informed the people of Julius Caesar's assassination.

Two points at each end of the Rostra have special significance: the *Umbilicus Urbis Romae*, marking the traditional centre of Rome; and the *Miliarium Aureum* (Golden Milestone), which once recorded in gold letters the distances in miles from Rome to the provinces of the empire. Countless

Renaissance and baroque sculptors have drawn inspiration from the friezes on the **Arch of Septimius Severus** (honouring a 3rd-century emperor who died in York, England).

The **Temple of Saturn** doubled as state treasury and centre of the merry December debauchery known as the Saturnalia, the pagan precursor of Christmas. Three slender columns, the podium and a portion of the entablature denote the **Temple of Castor and Pollux**, built in 484 BC. It was dedicated to these twin sons of Jupiter (the Dioscuri) after they appeared on the battlefield at Lake Regillus to rally the Romans against the Latins and the Etruscans.

In the circular **Temple of Vesta**, the sacred flame perpetuating the Roman state was tended by six Vestal Virgins who, from childhood, observed a 30-year vow of chastity on pain of being buried alive if they broke it. At the end of the Via Sacra, the **Arch of Titus** commemorates the sack of Jerusalem in AD 70. Restored in 1821, it shows in magnificently carved relief the emperor's triumphal procession bearing the spoils of Jerusalem, among them the Jewish Temple's seven-branched golden candlestick and silver trumpets. Even today, many Jews will avoid walking through the arch that glorifies their tragedy.

Most impressive monument of the Imperial Forums, built as an adjunct to the Roman Forum in honour of Julius Caesar, Augustus, Trajan, Vespasian and Nerva, is the 30m- (98ft-) high **Trajan's Column** (AD 113). Celebrating Trajan's campaigns against the Dacians in what is today Romania, the minutely detailed friezes spiralling around the column constitute a veritable textbook of Roman warfare. St Peter's statue replaced the emperor's in 1587.

South of the Roman Forum, the **Palatine Hill** is Rome's legendary birthplace and today its most romantic garden, dotted with toppled columns among the wild flowers and spiny acanthus shrubs. Only rows of cypress trees and summer pavilions remain from the more formal botanical gardens laid out here in the 16th century by the Farnese family. They were following in the footsteps of the Roman aristocracy who in the time of the Republic had already made this a desirable residential district.

The so-called **House of Livia** is now believed to be that of her husband,

T rajan's Column was designed by one of the greatest architects of the ancient world, Apollodorus of Damascus.

Emperor Augustus, who lived here in characteristic modesty, but good taste. Small but graceful rooms retain remnants of the mosaic floors and a well-preserved wall painting of Zeus's love for a young priestess. Nearby, a circular Iron Age dwelling unearthed from the time of Rome's legendary beginnings is known as **Romulus's Hut** (*Casa di Romolo*).

The vast assemblage of ruins of the Domus Flavia include a basilica, throne room, banqueting hall, baths, porticoes and a fountain in the form of a maze. Together with the Domus Augustana alongside, the complex is known as the **Palace of Domitian**.

The last emperor to build on the Palatine was Septimius Severus. He carried the imperial palace to the very south-eastern end of the hill, so that his seven-storeyed **Domus Severiana** was the first glimpse of the capital for new arrivals. It was dismantled to build Renaissance Rome, and only the huge arcaded foundations remain.

Throughout the Palatine, the subterranean passageway of **Nero's Cryptoporticus** links the palaces. In the dim light you can make out stucco decorations on the ceilings and walls.

Back up above ground, from grassy knolls enjoy the fine views back over the Colosseum or southward over the great **Circus Maximus**, where chariot races were held for crowds of up to 200,000.

A kilometre south of the Colosseum, the huge 3rd-century **Baths of Caracalla** (*Terme di Caracalla*) were built for 1,600 people to bathe in considerable style and luxury. Imagine the still-impressive brick walls covered in coloured marble, some of which you can see today adorning the fountain basins of Piazza Farnese in front of the French Embassy (*see* page 91). The baths and gymnasia were of alabaster and granite, profusely decorated with statues and frescoes. Public bathing was a prolonged social event as merchants and senators passed from the *caldarium* (hot room) to cool down in the *tepidarium* and *frigidarium*. Until 1994 the *caldarium* was used as the stage for spectacular open-air operas. It is vast enough for processions of elephants, camels and four-horse chariots. Unless measures are taken to protect the monument however, the concerts will have to end.

South of the baths begins the **Appian Way** (Via Appia Antica), over which the Roman legions marched on their way to Brindisi to set sail for the Levant and North Africa. On either side lie the ruins of sepulchres of 20 generations of patrician families. The chapel of **Domine Quo Vadis** marks the site where St Peter is said to have encountered Christ as he fled Nero's persecution in Rome and asked "Whither goest thou, Lord?" (*Domine, Quo Vadis?*).

Further along the Appia Antica, within a short distance of each other, are three of Rome's most celebrated **catacombs**: St Callixtus, St Sebastian, and Domitilla. About 6 million early Christians, including many martyrs, saints, and several 3rd- and 4th-century popes, were buried in some 50 of these vast underground cemeteries. Knowledgeable guides take you into a labyrinth of damp and musty-smelling tunnels and chambers burrowed into the soft volcanic tufa rock, sometimes six levels deep (claustrophobes abstain). Paintings and carvings adorn the catacombs with precious examples of early Christian art.

The Vatican

The power of Rome endures both in the spirituality evoked by every stone of St Peter's Basilica and in the almost physical awe inspired by the splendours of the Vatican Palace. At their best, the popes and cardinals replaced military conquest by moral leadership and persuasion; at their worst, they could show the same hunger for political power and worldly wealth as any Caesar. A visit to the Vatican is an object lesson for the faithful and sceptic alike.

Named after the hill on which it stands and which in the Middle Ages was surrounded by a malarial swamp, the Vatican has been a papal residence for over 600 years, but a sovereign state independent of Italy only since the Lateran Pact of 1929.

If you have the time, try to visit St Peter's and the museums of the

Latin Lives

So, Latin is a dead language, is it? Not quite. A team of sixteen Vatican linguists have spent four years giving it artificial respiration. They have come up with the first-ever Latin dictionary really to get to grips with the 20th century: two volumes containing 10,000 modern and technical words, embracing everything from washing machines to cover girls. An *escariorum lavator* is a washing machine, while a *machinatio aeri purgando* (machine to clean the air) is an air-conditioning system. Hijacking is *aeronavis abstractio a prestituto cursu* (the theft of an aeroplane from its established destination). UFOs are *coruscantes disci per convexacaeli volantes* (shining convex discs flying across the sky). And a cover girl? Not even this modern phenomenon could stump the Vatican team. She is an *exterioris pagine puella*.

Seeing the Pope

When he's not in Bogotá or Bangkok, it is possible to see the pope in person at the Vatican. He normally holds a public audience every Wednesday at 11 a.m. (10 a.m. in summer), either in a large modern audience hall or down in St Peter's Square (and sometimes at his summer residence at Castel Gandolfo). An invitation to a papal audience may be obtained from the Pontifical Prefect's Office (open Monday to Saturday in the morning) through the bronze gates in St Peter's Square. A visitor's bishop at home can arrange a private audience.

On Sundays at noon, the pope appears at the window of his apartments in the Apostolic Palace (right of the basilica, overlooking the square), delivers a brief homily, says the Angelus and blesses the crowd below. On a few major holy days, the pontiff celebrates high mass in St Peter's.

Vatican Palace on separate days. The riches here pose the city's biggest threat of fatigue and visual overload. In any case, it's a good idea to divide your visit in two with a relaxed lunch. Check opening times: the Vatican museums are usually open all day around Easter and in the summer months, but close at 1.45 p.m. the rest of the year.

Best of all, have a picnic and siesta in the nearby gardens of the **Janiculum Hill** (*Gianicolo*) where, in the more stormy times of the *Risorgimento*, as an equestrian statue proclaims, Garibaldi fought one of his fiercest battles.

To appreciate the unique panorama of St Peter's and its square, take your courage in both feet and walk. Start out by crossing the Tiber to the **Castel Sant'Angelo**, originally Hadrian's mausoleum built in AD 139. Its name derives from Pope Gregory's vision of

The Castel Sant' Angelo, imperial tomb and papal fortress, has witnessed some of the bloodiest episodes in Rome's history. It is also the setting for the climax of Puccini's opera Tosca, *when the heroine hurls herself to her death from the battlements.*

the Archangel Michael—now represented by a statue on top—heralding the end of a plague in 590. (If you are walking all the way, take the pretty **Ponte Sant'Angelo**, adorned by ten Bernini angels.) It was 6th-century barbarians who commandeered the massive round pile as a fortress, using ancient statues as missiles to hurl on the heads of their enemies below. Linked to the Vatican by a thick-walled passage, it served as a hide-out for popes in times of danger, notably Pope Clement VII, who holed up here for a month during the sack of Rome by Habsburg troops in 1527.

After the grimness of the exterior, it comes as a surprise to step into the luxurious surroundings of the old **Papal Apartments**. Lavish frescoes cover the walls and ceilings of rooms hung with masterpieces by Dosso Dossi, Nicolas Poussin and Lorenzo Lotto. Set away by itself off the Courtyard of Alexander VI is an exquisite **papal bathroom** painted with delicate designs over every inch of its walls. A harsh jolt brings you back to reality as you enter the **dungeons**, scene of torture and executions, where famous prisoners languished—among them philosopher Giordano Bruno and sculptor-goldsmith Benvenuto Cellini.

In **St Peter's Square** (Piazza San Pietro), his greatest creation, Bernini has performed one of the world's most exciting pieces of architectural orchestration. The sweeping curves of the colonnades reach out to Rome and to the whole world, *urbi et orbi*, to draw the flood of pilgrims into the bosom of the church beyond. In a rare opportunity for concentrated effort by one man on such a gigantic project, Bernini's 284 travertine columns, 88 pilasters and 140 statues of the saints were completed in just 11 years, from 1656 to 1667. Stand on one of the two circular paving stones set between the **obelisk** and the square's twin 17th-century **fountains** to appreciate the harmony of the quadruple rows of Doric columns, so perfectly aligned that they seem like a single row. The purity of Bernini's work here refutes the popular conception of baroque as being nothing but overblown extravagance.

The great risk of the Renaissance lay in what would happen if too many of those geniuses got involved in the same project. For instance, **St Peter's Basilica**. The largest of all Catholic churches and by any standards a grandiose achievement, it inevitably suffers from the competing visions of all the architects called in to collaborate. Bramante, Giuliano da Sangallo, Raphael, Baldassare Peruzzi, Michelangelo, Domenico Fontana, Giacomo della Porta, and Carlo Maderno were all involved—each adding, subtracting and modifying, often with a pope looking over his shoulder.

From 1506 to 1626, it changed from the simple ground plan of a Greek cross, with four arms of equal length, as favoured by Bramante and his arch-enemy Michelangelo, to the final form of Maderno's Latin cross extended by a long nave, as demanded by the popes of the Counter-Reformation. One result is that Maderno's porticoed façade and nave obstruct a clear view of Michelangelo's dome from the square.

The church's dimensions are impressive: 212m (695ft) exterior length, 187m (613ft) inside length; 132.5m (435ft) to the tip of the dome, whose interior diameter is a mighty 42.45m (139ft).

As you go in, notice the keys of St Peter inlaid in the doorway paving. Set in the floor by the centre door is the large round slab of red porphyry where Charlemagne knelt for his coronation as Holy Roman Emperor in 800 (*see* page 50).

The basilica's most treasured work of art is Michelangelo's sublime **Pietà**: Mary with the dead Jesus on her lap. This can be found in its own chapel to the right of the entrance. The artist was only 24, young and justly proud enough to append his signature (the only surviving example), visible on the Madonna's sash. Since a religious fanatic attacked it with a hammer some years ago, the statue is protected by bullet-proof glass.

Reverence can cause damage, too: on a 13th-century blackened bronze **statue of St Peter**, attributed to Florentine architect-sculptor Arnolfo di Cambio, the lips and fingers of countless pilgrims have worn away its toes.

Beneath the dome, Bernini's great **baldacchino** (canopy), cast out of bronze beams taken from the Pantheon's portico (*see* page 90), protects the high altar, built right over St Peter's tomb and reserved for the pope's mass. In the apse beyond, the baroque master gives full vent to his exuberance with his bronze and marble **Cathedra of St Peter**, throne of the

Apostle's successors. It is crowned by a *gloria* in which the dove of the Holy Spirit is lit up on sunny days from a window at the back.

It should come as no surprise that, as the greatest patron that painters, sculptors and architects have ever known, the Catholic Church should house in its headquarters one of the world's richest collections of art. The **Vatican Palace** contains eight museums, five galleries, the Apostolic Library, the Borgia Apartments, the Sistine Chapel and Raphael Rooms. Shuttle buses run regularly from St Peter's Square to the museum entrance.

If you want at all costs to avoid the Sistine's day-long crowds, go straight there first thing in the morning (don't forget your binoculars for details on the ceiling). In any case, you can't miss it—arrows point the way. There are also many marvels to see *en route.*

With the booty from the ruthless dismantling of ancient monuments to make way for the Renaissance city in the 16th century, the **Museo Pio-Clementino** has assembled a wonderful collection of Roman and Greek art. Most celebrated is the tortured *Laocoön* group (from Rhodes, 1st century BC–1st century AD), only recently returned more closely to its pristine state by the removal of one son's pathetically outstretched arm added by overzealous 16th-century restorers.

The **Gregorian-Etruscan Museum** displays some of archaeology's most exciting finds from a 7th-century BC Etruscan burial mound at Cerveteri (*see* page 123). Among the finely worked jewellery is an ornate gold brooch decorated with lions and ducklings. Look, too, for the bronze statue

*T*his magnificent spiral ramp, built in 1932, leads the visitor into one of the greatest collections of art and antiquities in the world: the Vatican Museums.

of a sprightly Etruscan warrior, the *Mars of Todi* (4th century BC).

Pope Julius II took a calculated risk in 1509 when he called in a relatively untried 26-year-old to do the interior decoration of his new apartments. The result was the four **Raphael Rooms** (*Stanze di Raffaello*). In the central Stanza della Segnatura are the two masterly frescoes, *Disputation over the Holy Sacrament* and the *School of Athens*, contrasting theological and philosophical wisdom. The *Disputation* unites biblical figures with historical pillars of the faith such as Pope

Gregory and Thomas Aquinas, but also the painter Fra Angelico and the divine Dante. At the centre of the *School*, Raphael is believed to have given the red-coated Plato the features of Leonardo da Vinci, while portraying Michelangelo as the thoughtful Heraclitus, seated in the foreground.

In stark contrast to Raphael's grand manner, look out for the gentle beauty of Fra Angelico's frescoes in the **Chapel of Nicholas V** (signposted as *Cappella del Beato Angelico*). The lives of Saints Lawrence and Stephen are depicted in delicately subdued pinks and blues.

The richly decorated **Borgia Apartments** contain, in addition to Pinturicchio's frescoes (with portraits of lusty Pope Alexander VI and his notorious son Cesare and daughter Lucrezia), the modern religious art collection of Paul VI. The latter includes Rodin bronzes, Picasso ceramics, Matisse's Madonna sketches and designs for ecclesiastical robes and, perhaps unexpectedly, a grotesque Francis Bacon pope.

Nothing can prepare you for the visual shock of the **Sistine Chapel** (*Cappella Sistina*), built for Sixtus IV in the 15th century. Even the discomfort of the throngs of visitors (silence requested) seems to yield to the power of Michelangelo's ceiling, his *Last Judgement*, and the other wall frescoes of Botticelli, Pinturicchio, Ghirlandaio and Signorelli. In this private chapel, where the cardinals hold their conclave to elect a new pope, the glory of the Catholic Church achieves its finest artistic expression.

The chapel portrays nothing less than the story of man, in three parts: from Adam to Noah; the giving of the Law to Moses; and from the birth of Jesus to the Last Judgement. On Michelangelo's **ceiling**, you can make out the celebrated outstretched finger of man's creation, the drunkenness of Noah, the turmoil of the Flood, but most overwhelming of all, particularly now that the colours are so fresh and vivid after the recent restoration, is the impression of the whole. This is best appreciated looking back from the bench by the chapel's exit.

On the chapel's altar wall is Michelangelo's tempestuous *Last Judgement*, painted 23 years after the ceiling, when he was 52 and imbued with deep religious soul-searching. An almost naked Jesus dispenses justice more like a stern, even fierce, classical god-hero than the conventionally gentle biblical figure. The artist's agonizing self-portrait can be made out in the flayed skin of St Bartholomew, to the right below Jesus.

Working Solo on the Ceiling

As might be imagined, painting the Sistine ceiling wasn't easy. Michelangelo, a sculptor in marble with only a little oil-painting behind him, had never before done a fresco (wall-painting on damp plaster). Preferring his inexperience to their incompetence, he fired his seven assistants in the first couple of weeks and continued alone for four years, from 1508 to 1512. Contrary to legend, he did not lie on his back, but painted erect on tiptoe, bent backwards "like a Syrian bow", with Pope Julius II climbing the scaffolding to check on progress and threatening to throw him off his platform if he didn't hurry up. "I'm not in a good place," he wrote to a friend, "and I'm no painter."

Italian Architecture

Leaving to one side the temples of the Greek colonies in southern Italy, indigenous Italian architecture begins with the **Etruscans.** But their bitter rivals, the Romans, left little standing beyond a few town ramparts, at Tarquinia and Cortona, with an occasional sturdy arched gateway, as at Volterra or Perugia. Domestic building seems to have been of wood and baked clay, rather than stone. Their monumental tombs were hewn from underground rock.

To the Greek architecture of horizontals and verticals, with roof-entablatures sitting squarely on a structure of columns, the **Romans** added the rounded forms of arches, vaults and domes. Columns, preferably of the ornate Corinthian order, were reduced to a decorative element often sunk into the walls. The use of brick and concrete made large domes and vaults possible as early as Pompeii's Stabian Baths in the 2nd century B.C. Some 300 years later, the capital's great domed Pantheon achieved a summit in Roman architecture, both as a feat of large-scale engineering and a masterpiece of simple, harmonious proportions.

The most typical public building, the *basilica*, was the precursor of the Christian church, a nave separated by columns from side aisles, with an apse at the end. The characteristic rounded forms appeared in triumphal arches and elliptical amphitheatres

The Pantheon, Rome

Sant'Apollinare in Classe,
Ravenna

Santa Maria Maggiore, Rome

San Marco, Venice

such as Verona's Arena and
Rome's Colosseum. Residences
were of three kinds: one-storey
domus town-houses like those
at Pompeii, with street façade
left plain or let out as shops
and interior built around an
atrium and one or more
peristyle courtyards; multi-
storey _insula_ apartment houses;
and a more sprawling suburban
or country _villa_ of porticoes
and colonnades, of which the
most sophisticated example is
Hadrian's residence at Tivoli.

Even after centuries of
remodelling, Rome's **Early
Christian** churches, such as
Santa Sabina or Santa Maria
Maggiore, remain pure models
of the imperial basilica, using
columns and entablatures from
pagan temples. The 5th- and
6th-century brick edifices of
Ravenna show both the
Byzantine influence in Galla
Placidia's cruciform Mausoleum
and the octagonal church of
San Vitale and the Roman
inspiration of the
Sant'Apollinare Nuovo basilica.

Cathedral and Leaning Tower, Pisa

Blind arcades and a soaring campanile make their appearance here as basic elements of Italian architecture.

Venice's San Marco basilica (rebuilt 1063) offers the country's most spectacular version of the Byzantine Greek-cross pattern in which four domes surround a central dome over the high altar. Here the ornament is emphatically oriental, but the campanile reminds us we're in the west.

The dominant **Romanesque** style of the 11th century was set by Pisa's cathedral (begun 1063), with its façade of tiered arcades above three porches. The cathedral's combination with baptistery and free-standing campanile launched the Italian taste for architectural "stage-set". While the ornate façade arcading spread through Tuscany, notably in Lucca and Massa Marittima, a more austere version of Pisa cathedral's sloping silhouette is to be found down in Puglia, where Bari's San Nicola (1087)

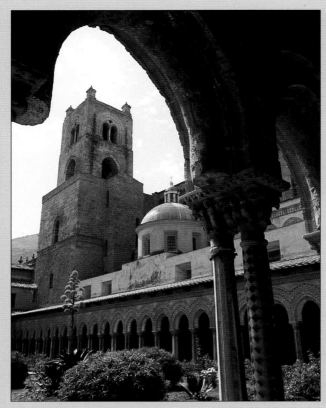

(Above) Detail of Palazzo Vecchio, Florence

(Left) Monreale, Sicily

(Below) Palazzo Vecchio, Florence

set the tone for the cathedrals along the Adriatic coast. Elsewhere in southern Italy, notably in Palermo, Monreale and Amalfi, the Normans added elements of Islamic architecture, with honeycomb ornament in the interiors and interlocking arches around the cloisters.

In the church of San Miniato (largely 12th century) and its façade of pink alabaster slabs framed in green and white, Florentine Romanesque (sometimes called proto-Renaissance) is characteristically more concerned with harmony of colour and clarity of line than with the intricate sculptural delicacies of Pisan design.

A feature of civic Romanesque is the tower as status symbol, prominent in San Gimignano but also in Bologna. Venice maintains a Byzantine flavour in such palaces as the Fondaco dei Turchi.

Emperor Frederick II of Hohenstaufen marked the

Doges' Palace, Venice

south Italian landscape with the **Gothic** style of his fortresses, most brilliantly with the octagonal Castel del Monte in Puglia (1240). Just as formidable was Florence's government building, Palazzo Vecchio (1298), a solid fortress with minimal space for windows. As usual, Siena plumps for something less severe in its Palazzo Pubblico (1297), and its Campo established the pattern for city squares in southern Tuscany— Arezzo, Volterra and Montepulciano. Monumental fountains, such as Perugia's or Siena's Fonte Gaia, became a fundamental element of the urban landscape.

Italy's greatest Gothic churches are at Siena (1284) and Orvieto (1310), where the façades' polychrome marble or mosaics create a "pictorial" impact rather than the sculptural and more purely architectural effects of French or German Gothic. In Assisi's San Francesco (1228), we see even more emphatically how

the Italians were just not interested in Gothic's ability to reduce walls to a minimum with spacious arcades; what they wanted was good wall space for vast frescoes of the life of St. Francis. Bologna's lofty San Petronio cathedral is closest in spirit to northern European Gothic. If Florence's cathedral is a hodgepodge victim of procrastination, Giotto's campanile remains the country's finest single Gothic monument. In the hands of the Venetians, Gothic arcades as in the Doges' Palace were light and airy, decorative work closer to the goldsmith's art than the builder's.

The Flamboyant Gothic of Milan cathedral (begun 1386, but finished only in 1856) goes the whole flamboyant hog, while the Charterhouse of Pavia (begun 1396) happily carries its ornate façade into the Renaissance era.

The stability and poise of imperial Rome were the keynotes of **Renaissance** architecture, and it was in

Charterhouse, Pavia
Pazzi Chapel, Florence

St. Peter's, Rome

Piazza Navona fountain, Rome

15th-century Florence, not in the ancient capital, that these qualities were first to be found. The spirit is epitomized in Filippo Brunelleschi's Foundlings' Hospital (*Spedale degli Innocenti*, designed in 1419), with its graceful arcades of slender columns and Andrea della Robbia's elegant roundels decorating the abutments. The cathedral's grandiose dome is considered the architect's masterpiece, but the full serenity of his work is perhaps better appreciated in Santa Croce's Pazzi Chapel (1429). Florence's Renaissance palace façades are still forbiddingly fortress-like—the Palazzo Strozzi and Michelozzo's Palazzo Medici—if more decorative in their inner courtyards. The contrast is most striking in Laurana's Palazzo Ducale in Urbino (1460s).

Rome itself at first stuck more ponderously to imperial Roman design—compare the arcades of the Colosseum with those of the Palazzo Venezia's courtyard (1470). Northern Renaissance is more ornate: Como's cathedral, town halls at Brescia and Verona, and Sansovino's magnificent library in Venice (1532).

With the power-shift to Rome, the High Renaissance asserted a more monumental dimension with Bramante's grandiose design for St. Peter's, Raphael's Villa Madama and Peruzzi's Villa Farnesina. In Florence, the restless Michelangelo carried the trend into highly stylized **Mannerism** with his Medici Chapel and Laurentian Library (*Biblioteca Laurenziana*, 1520s). Andrea Palladio imposed a personal elegance on Renaissance and Mannerist

style with his villas in and around Vicenza and his churches for Venice.

Baroque architects were the unabashed servants of the Counter-Reformation, affirming Rome's authority with such churches as Vignola's deliberately imposing Gesù in Rome (1568). In the next generation, Bernini (1598–1680) made the point most eloquently with his all-embracing square for St. Peter's, *baldacchino* and throne inside, in addition to his exquisite oval-plan Sant' Andrea al Quirinale and the superb fountain for the Piazza Navona. His rival, the more tortured Borromini (1599–1667), combined the masterly technique of all Baroque's complexities with an inspired sense of spatial harmony—beautifully realized in the San

Casa Castiglioni, Milan

Carlo alle Quattro Fontane (1637–41) with its concave-convex façade and honeycomb dome and the even more intricate Sant'Ivo della Sapienza (1660).

In Turin, Guarini carried complex design to its outer limits with his church of San Lorenzo and an eight-pointed star cupola for the cathedral's Chapel of the Holy Shroud (*Capella della Santa Sindone*, 1668). In the next century, Turin toned down its Baroque with Juvarra's Palazzo Madama and elegantly subdued Superga church. Exuberant design appealed to the southern mentality, most spectacularly in Vanvitelli's Caserta palace (1752) for the kings of Naples, and in Puglia the splendidly carved façades of Lecce's churches and town-houses.

Highlights of the **neo-classical** style after the French Revolution were Padua's Caffè Pedrocchi (1816) and Naples' Teatro San Carlo (1817). In 1861, Milan's Galleria Vittorio Emanuele celebrated the commercial use of the industrial age's iron and glass.

For Italy, the ornate Art Nouveau style which ushered in the **20th century** was known as *Liberty*, after the styles set by the London department store, typified by Giuseppe Sommaruga's Casa Castiglioni in Milan. In architecture, the rhetorical Futurists were more theoreticians than builders, emphasizing the lines and materials of the machine age (achieved with gusto a couple of generations later with Paris's Pompidou Centre built by Renzo Piano, of Genoa, and Florence-born Briton, Richard Rogers). Stylish Rationalists managed to modify the Fascist taste for bombast in their social buildings—Terragni's Novocomum apartments in Como, 1927, and Michelucci's Santa Maria Novella railway station in Florence, 1933. Pier Luigi Nervi is perhaps the most celebrated of modern Italian architects, exposing structural elements in his Florence sports stadium or Orbetello aeroplane hangar, or drawing shapes and rhythmic patterns from nature, as in his Pirelli skyscraper in Milan. Gae Aulenti brings old and new together with her bold restructuring for Venice's Palazzo Grassi.

Amid all the Vatican's treasures, the 15 rooms of the **Picture Gallery** (*Pinacoteca Vaticana*), in a separate wing of the palace, sometimes get short shrift. This collection of ten centuries of paintings should not be overlooked, and art-lovers may even want to devote a separate visit. Among the most important are works by Giotto, Fra Angelico, Perugino, Raphael's *Transfiguration* (his last great work), Leonardo da Vinci's unfinished *St Jerome*, Bellini's *Pietà* and Caravaggio's *Descent from the Cross*.

The neighbourhood south of the Vatican, **Trastevere**, literally "across the Tiber" has long been renowned as the most popular quarter of Rome. Here, ordinary people, who like the Cockneys in London consider themselves the original citizens, uphold ancient traditions and customs. It is good to wander among the narrow streets and markets to sample the authentic life of the city, highlighted by the July *Noiantri* (We Others) street festival of music and fireworks down by the river.

Inevitably, "popular" and "authentic" became chic and the ambience is now somewhat diluted by a certain smart set moving in and, inevitably, raising the rents. But the true Trasteverini hang on, mainly in the area immediately around **Santa Maria in Trastevere**, reputedly the oldest church in the city. Its foundation may date back to the 3rd century, but the present structure is the work of Pope Innocent II, himself a Trasteverino, around 1130. A wonderful Byzantine-influenced **mosaic** of Mary enthroned with Jesus decorates the domed ceiling of the apse. The city's liveliest fruit and vegetable market is to be found on **Piazza di San Cosimato**.

Other Museums

The **Galleria Borghese** is housed in a handsome baroque villa inspired originally by Hadrian's Villa at Tivoli (*see* pages 115–16), but with its Italian formal gardens now transformed into an English-style landscaped park. This great collection includes outstanding sculptures by Bernini and paintings by Raphael, Correggio, Titian, Caravaggio, Botticelli, Rubens, Dürer and Cranach. (The Galleria Borghese has been undergoing restoration for some years now, and only part of it is open to the public. The gallery's paintings have been transferred to the Quadereria della Galleria Borghese al San Michele in Via di San Michele 22, across the river in Trastevere. It is open all day from Tuesday to Saturday.)

Villa Giulia, 16th-century pleasure palace of a pope (Viale delle Belle Arti north-west of the Villa Borghese), provides a handsome setting for Italy's finest museum of **Etruscan art**. Keys to the mystery of this pre-Roman civilization are to be found in the wealth of detail of their everyday life revealed by the personal possessions buried with the dead in their tombs.

Next to replicas of the round stone burial mounds, built like huts, are rooms exhibiting the tombs' contents: bronze statuettes of warriors in full battle dress; shields, weapons and chariots (even the skeletons of two horses); gold, silver and ivory jewellery; decorative vases mass-imported by the Etruscans from Greece; and a host of everyday cooking utensils, mirrors and combs. One of the most beautiful sculptures is a life-size terracotta for a sarcophagus lid of a blissful young couple reclining on a banquet couch.

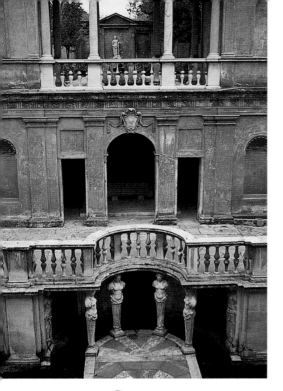

a fine Rubens *Romulus and Remus* and Caravaggio's louche *St John the Baptist* and sprightly *Fortune Teller*.

The **Palazzo Barberini** (Via delle Quattro Fontane), another architectural battleground for arch-rivals Borromini and Bernini, is worth a visit as much for its splendid baroque décor as for its collection of paintings. They come together in the palace's Great Hall with Pietro da Cortona's dazzling ceiling fresco, *Triumph of Divine Providence*. Notable in the collections are a Fra Angelico triptych, Raphael's *La Fornarina* (believed to be a portrait of the painter's mistress), Caravaggio's harrowing *Judith and Holofernes*, and works by Titian, Tintoretto and El Greco.

Other Churches

It is impossible even to count all the churches worth visiting in Rome, many of which it is most enjoyable to stumble on by accident. We suggest a few of the best:

Originally built in the 5th century on the Esquiline Hill site of a Roman temple to the goddess Juno, **Santa Maria Maggiore** is the largest of the churches dedicated to the Virgin Mary and a great favourite with pilgrims. They come, especially at Christmas time, to admire relics of the **holy crib** from Bethlehem. In the Oratory of the Crib (*Oratorio del Presepio*), are the moving 13th-century sculptures of Joseph, the Three Kings, the ox and the ass by Arnolfo di Cambio (Mary and the child Jesus are 16th-century additions). The most spectacular art treasures of the church are its gorgeous 5th-century **mosaics**, 36 Old Testament scenes high on the walls (don't forget

Originally built as a summer villa for Pope Julius III between 1551 and 1553, the Villa Giulia now houses Rome's magnificent museum of Etruscan art.

The **Capitoline Museums**, in the palaces of the Campidoglio, have extensive collections of sculpture excavated from ancient Rome. In the Palazzo dei Conservatori is the most celebrated piece, the superb Etruscan bronze **She-Wolf** (*Lupa Capitolina*), symbol of the city. The wolf dates from around the 5th century BC, but the little Romulus and Remus that she is suckling are Renaissance additions by Pollaiuolo. The **Picture Gallery** (*Pinacoteca Capitolina*) has important Venetian works by Bellini, Titian, Tintoretto, Lotto and Veronese, as well as the binoculars) and a triumphant Mary and Jesus enthroned over the high altar. The coffered Renaissance ceiling glitters with the gold of the first shipments from the Americas.

In a nearby side street, **Santa Prassede** is unprepossessing from the outside but enchanting in the intimacy of its interior. The delicate 9th-century mosaics of Jesus and four angels make the **Chapel of St Zeno** the city's most important Byzantine monument. To the right of the chapel is a fragment of rare jasper said to come from the column to which Jesus was tied for his flagellation. Notice, too, the fine mosaic of Jesus and the New Jerusalem over the chancel.

San Pietro in Vincoli (St Peter in Chains) might not attract a second look (and might even prefer it that way, given the hordes of visitors) if it did not contain one of the greatest of Michelangelo's sculptures, his formidable **Moses**. Intended for St Peter's Basilica as part of Michelangelo's botched project for Pope Julius II's tomb, the statue of the great biblical figure sits in awesome majesty at the centre of the monument. You can imagine how grandiose the original plan must have been when you realize from his sideward stare that Moses was supposed to be just a corner figure facing the centre. The horns on his head continue a traditional medieval mistranslation of the Hebrew for halo-like rays of light. On each side, the comparatively passive figures of Jacob's wives—a prayerful Rachel and melancholy Leah—were Michelangelo's last completed sculptures.

San Giovanni in Laterano (St John Lateran) is regarded as the mother church of the Catholic world (it is the seat of the pope as Bishop of Rome). The original 4th-century church predated even the first St Peter's by a few years. On a wooden table incorporated in the high altar, Peter himself is believed to have celebrated mass. The present basilica, little more than 300 years old, is at least the fifth on this site, but the bronze central doors date back to ancient Rome when they graced the entrance to the Curia. (Those you see in the Forum now are copies.)

*G*iovanni di Stefano's ornate Gothic canopy rises over the high altar of San Giovanni in Laterano. The canopy contains silver reliquaries purported to hold the heads of Saints Peter and Paul.

Transformed by Borromini in the 17th century, the interior, in predominantly sober whites and greys, remains a decidedly restrained form of baroque, enlivened only by the coloured marble inlays of the paving. Statues of the Apostles in recesses along the nave are the work of pupils of Bernini. The octagonal **baptistery**, with its fine 5th- and 7th-century mosaics, was built over the baths of Constantine's second wife Fausta, the site of Rome's first baptisms.

San Paolo fuori le Mura (St Paul's Outside the Walls), Rome's largest basilica after St Peter's, was built by Constantine in 314 and enlarged by Valentinian II and Theodosius. Astonishingly, it survived until destroyed by fire in 1823. Reconstruction has restored some of its original splendour. Salvaged from the fire, the **tabernacle** of 13th-century sculptor Arnolfo di Cambio decorates the high altar over the burial place of St Paul. Rest awhile in the Benedictine **cloister** designed by Pietro Vassalletto, master of the cosmatesque style of inlaid marble. Slender spiral columns glitter with green, red and gold mosaic, enclosing a garden of roses and a gently rippling fountain.

A descent of the three levels of **San Clemente** takes you back to the very beginnings of the Christian era. The present 12th-century church preserves its basilica form with three naves divided by ancient columns. Note the Romanesque pulpit, paschal candle, episcopal throne and a fine **mosaic** in the apse. To the right of the nave, steps lead down to the **4th-century basilica**, its Romanesque frescoes sadly fading fast. An ancient stairway goes further

underground to a maze of corridors and chambers believed to be the home of St Clement himself. An uncomfortably close neighbour for this third successor to St Peter as pope is a pagan **temple of Mithras** (*Mithraeum*). A well-preserved sculpture shows the Persian god of light slaying a bull. The sound of trickling water from a nearby stream echoes eerily through these subterranean chambers as it drains off into the Cloaca Maxima.

Lazio

The excursions made today into the Lazio hinterland around Rome are those that the ancient Romans themselves made to vacation homes by the sea or nearby lakes.

Tivoli

Follow the old Roman chariot road (repaved) of Via Tiburtina 30km (19 miles) east of the capital to the haunting ruins of **Hadrian's Villa** (*Villa Adriana*), near the picturesque town of Tivoli, at the foot of the Sabine Hills. Sprawling across 70 hectares (173 acres), this retirement hideaway of the

At Tivoli, east of Rome, Emperor Hadrian laid out the largest and most luxurious villa built in the Roman Empire.

great emperor-builder was designed to recapture some of the architectural marvels of his empire, especially the Greece he loved above all else—a travel notebook for his old age.

Barbarians and museum curators have removed most of the villa's treasures, but a stroll through the remaining pillars, arches and mosaic fragments in gardens running wild among the olive trees, cypresses and pines can be marvellously evocative of a lost world.

Start with the villa's excellent scale model. The monumental baths, separate Latin and Greek libraries, Greek theatre, temples and pavilions together make up the home of a man who drew no distinction between the pleasures of mind and body. In the centre, the enchanting **Villa dell'Isola**, a pavilion surrounded by a little reflecting pool and circular portico, epitomizes all the magic of the place.

In Tivoli, overlooking the Roman plain, the **Villa d'Este** is a 16th-century counterpart to Hadrian's Villa, celebrating all the extravagance of the late Renaissance. The house, home of Cardinal Ippolito II d'Este, plays second fiddle to its **gardens**: alleys of cypresses and soaring fountains (500 in all, including Bernini's *Bicchierone*), grottoes, waterfalls and reflecting pools.

Subiaco

Two monasteries on the wooded mountain above the town mark the site where St Benedict came with his twin sister Scholastica at the end of the 5th century to meditate, devising the rule for what was to become the Benedictine monastic order. A pretty 2½km (2-mile) drive west of town along a winding road shaded by holm oaks

brings you to the **Monastero di Santa Scolastica** with three graceful cloisters. Two kilometres (1½ miles) further on is the **Monastero di San Benedetto**. Here, 15th-century frescoes of the Umbrian school decorate a corridor leading to the **upper church**, with a fine Gothic pulpit. Stairs by the altar lead down to a series of chapels built into the rock of the mountain and making up the **lower church**. Superb 13th-century frescoes depict the Madonna, St Benedict and Pope Innocent III and the only known portrait of St Francis of Assisi painted in his lifetime. At the lowest level is the cave of Benedict's meditation, **Sacro Speco**.

Palestrina

The World War II bombs that destroyed much of the town also did archaeologists the signal favour of uncovering important ruins of the 2nd-century BC Temple of **Fortuna Primigenia** (Fortune the First-Born). The sanctuary was actually a complex of temples spread out on the terraced slopes of the Prenestini Hills above the town. Views over the mountains and across the Albano Hills are superb. The 17th-century **Palazzo Barberini** stands on the site of the main temple of Fortuna, making amends now by housing a fine **museum** of the sanctuary's statues, bronzes, terracottas and jewellery found in the adjacent necropolis. Among the ruins of the lower sanctuary is a grotto where the temple's oracle was consulted. As birthplace of the great 16th-century composer of polyphonic church music, Giovanni Pierluigi da Palestrina, the town has erected a modern statue to him on **Piazza Regina Margherita**.

THE ETRUSCANS

Above: Sculpted architrave

Below: Sarcophagus from Tarquinia

When the all-conquering Romans decided to wipe out any trace of their Etruscan rivals from the face of the earth, they did a very thorough job, leaving only a few city walls and gates around Tuscany and Umbria. But luckily, they didn't think of going *below* the earth to wipe out the Etruscans' "cities of the dead". It's in the richly decorated and furnished tombs of Tarquinia and Cerveteri that we gather our only tangible knowledge of this mysterious people who dominated central Italy from the 9th to the 4th century B.C.

Where did they come from? Over the Alps from beyond the steppes or via the sea from Asia Minor? Or were they in Italy all the time, an indigenous people blurring their ethnic origins by intermarrying with invaders? All we know, from the few linguistic hints deciphered from inscriptions on tombs and pottery, is that their language, unlike those of Italy's other peoples, was not a member of our own Indo-European group.

By the testimony of the Greeks who traded with them and the Romans who fought them for control of the peninsula, they were a

Left: Etruscan warrior in bronze

Above: Bronze head of a woman

pleasure-loving people, intelligent and talented enough to create a considerable civilization, but not ambitious to found a real empire. At the height of their power in the 6th century B.C., Etruscan lands reached across Tuscany to the Po valley and down a narrowing strip to Campania. Like all traders in those times, they apparently indulged in a little piracy, but didn't extend their aggressivity to actual overseas conquest (apart from a brief occupation of eastern Corsica). Organized as 12 highly independent-minded cities in a confederation that met near Lake Bolsena for religious festivals rather than political concertation, Etruria never formed a single nation.

The major source of their wealth was the iron and copper mined in the Etruscan hills and the island of Elba. Typical of their priorities in life, they traded metal tools and weapons for the Phoenicians' and Greeks' jewels, gold, silver, ivory and rich ornamental pottery. Their goldsmiths achieved superb delicacy in their work, intricately granulated for fine detail in brooches, earrings and necklaces—using the surplus for dentistry.

They enjoyed rich crops of grain and didn't wait for the Greeks to teach them the nourishing value of olives or the joys of the grape. And it was the Etruscans, before the Romans, who deserve our everlasting gratitude for showing those talented fellows from Gaul how to make wine.

In those earnest days of their rise to empire, the Romans were scornful of the Etruscans' propensity for the delights of the good life—banquets, games, dancing, music to accompany their every pursuit, whether boxing, baking bread or even whipping a slave. They were held to be inordinately sensual, making hetero- or homosexual love in public.

What bothered the macho Greeks and Romans most was the prominent status accorded

Etruscan ornaments and household implements: small vase, wine ladle, perfume holder

to Etruscan women. Unlike their early Roman counterparts, Etruscan women might be property owners. At dinner, they actually reclined beside their men. Greek historian Theopompus snorted: "They dine not with their husbands, but with any man present; and they toast to anyone they want to." A tomb-engraving shows a man and woman in a wrestling match. Another depicts a woman telling her male opponent in a table game: "I'm going to beat you." He replies: "I believe you are." The tenderness of husband and wife is a frequent theme of their sculpture, as is the seated mother and child, a precursor of the Christian Madonna rarely to be found in Roman art.

The Etruscans' religion was one of fatalism, accepting their destinies as foretold by haruspices, soothsayers who read the future in the livers of sheep, or in the chance interventions of lightning. The liver, like the heavens, was divided into 16 regions, each ruled by a separate deity. To beseech the intervention of a particular god for a specific

Medusa in mosaic, from the museum in Volterra

health disorder, the Etruscans brought to their shrines *ex voto* miniature terracotta arms, legs and livers (like the French to this day, they attributed many of their problems to a crisis of the liver). Model genitals, breasts and uteruses were also deposited to enhance fertility or perhaps fend off venereal disease.

Prolonged prosperity and easy living were not without anguish. By the 5th century B.C., their religion began to adopt sombre Greek concepts of a diabolical underworld, which became more prevalent later as they went into political decline. Etruscan kings had ruled in Rome itself until 509 B.C. They built the Cloaca Maxima sewers to drain the marshes on the site of the Forum. On the Capitoline Hill, they erected the first great temple to Jupiter. But fatalistically, they saw the Roman conquest as inevitable. Priests interpreted unusual insect swarms as signs of the "last Etruscan century". By 90 B.C. the Etruscans had become Roman citizens.

Bridging the transition: an Etruscan/Roman street in Vulcia

Alban Hills and Castel Gandolfo

The region immediately south-east of Rome is known locally as the **Castelli Romani** (Roman Castles), for the fortified hill-top refuges built during the medieval civil wars. Today, it is just the summer heat that drives the Romans out on day-trips to the vineyards of the Alban hills and lakes. The country villages of **Frascati**, **Grottaferrata**, **Marino** and **Rocca di Papa** make delightful stops, not least of all for a cool glass of their estimable white wine, especially during the autumn grape-harvest festivals.

The pope has his summer palace at **Castel Gandolfo**, on the shores of Lake Albano. He holds audience on Wednesdays from mid-July to early September and blesses the thousands of pilgrims on Sundays at noon. In the mellow microclimate of the nearby **Lake Nemi**, strawberries are grown all year round and served—with cream or lemon juice—in Nemi's village park.

Abbey of Montecassino

The monastery founded by St Benedict in 529, from which the great Benedictine order was launched across Europe, stands once again on its mountain, 516m (1,692ft) above the town of Cassino.

Its total destruction by Allied bombs in 1944 was the latest of a series of devastations over the centuries. The Lombards levelled the first building in 581, the Arabs smashed the second in 833, an earthquake razed a third reconstruction in 1349. By modern times, the edifice was largely Renaissance and neoclassical in style and that is the appearance it has resumed in the metic-

---

The Tragedy of Montecassino

To halt the Allied advance north through Italy, 15 German divisions held the Gustav Line across the peninsula, passing through the town of Cassino. In early 1944, twelve Allied divisions—two American, four French, four British Commonwealth and two Polish—were practically paralysed. Their leaders were convinced that the Germans had, in that mountain-top monastery rising from the plain, an impregnable position. Francis Tuker, commanding a division of Indian and Gurkha troops that was to launch the first assault on Montecassino, asked for a concentrated air bombardment to "neutralize" the monastery. On the night of 15 February, the ancient monument was annihilated. But there had been no German forces inside. Only after the bombardment did their paratroops move in, making of the rubble a much more formidable obstacle. Repelling attack after attack, they held out for another three months before being driven out by renewed air bombardments. The Poles took over on 18 May, having lost nearly 4,000 men in the effort.

In his memoirs, Winston Churchill wrote of the tour he made of the abandoned Cassino front in August: "The monastery towered up, a dominating ruin. Anyone could see the tactical significance of this stately crag and building which for so many weeks played its part in stopping our advance."

---

ulous post-war restoration seen today. Of the three cloisters, two, like the abbey's church itself, are in the 18th-century style, flanking the splendid **central cloister** rebuilt to Bramante's 16th-century design. The view over the plain to the Tyrrhenian Sea is magnificent.

The **British Military Cemetery** lies 1km (less than a mile) south of

Cassino, on the road to Sant'Angelo. The **German Cemetery** is on the Cairo road, 3km (2 miles) to the north. The **Polish Cemetery** is on Monte Cassino just below the monastery.

Ostia Antica

Set among cypress and pine trees, the ruins of the seaport and naval base of ancient Rome reveal more about the people's daily life and building methods than do those of the capital. Ostia lies on the Tyrrhenian coast at the mouth (*ostium*) of the Tiber, 23km (14 miles) south-west of Rome.

With sea-going vessels unable to reach the capital along the shallow Tiber, Ostia's barges brought Rome its vital supplies. As excavations have

*T*hese evocative ruins
*are all that remains of Ostia
Antica, Rome's ancient seaport,
which flourished between the 4th
century BC and the 4th century
AD. Silting of the Tiber has left
Ostia 3km (1½ miles) inland.*

revealed, this commerce created a prosperous town of warehouses, offices, apartment blocks known as *insulae* (islands), and grander houses, decorated with mosaics and murals.

The porticoed **Piazzale delle Corporazioni** (Corporation Square) housed 70 commercial offices around a central temple to Ceres, goddess of agriculture. Set in the pavement, mottoes and emblems in mosaic tell of grain-wholesalers, caulkers, rope makers and shipowners trading here from many foreign parts. Climb the tiered seats of the nearby **theatre** for a view over the ruined city.

The **House of Cupid and Psyche** presents a typical private dwelling, with marble-paved rooms built round a central garden courtyard. Nearby, a small **museum** traces the history of Ostia with locally excavated statues, busts and frescoes.

Avoid the polluted grey sand beaches of neighbouring Lido di Ostia, the nearest beach resort to Rome. The cheerful open-air restaurants are a safer bet.

If you do want to swim in the Mediterranean or nurture a suntan, try **Fregene**, immediately west of Rome. It is no luxury riviera, but the sandy beaches against a backdrop of pleasant pine groves are cleaner than those at Ostia.

North of Rome off Via Claudia, a cooler, more secluded swim is to be had in the crystal-clear waters of **Lake Bracciano**, surrounded by olive groves and beaches of reeds and black volcanic sand.

Tarquinia and Northern Lazio

The A12 *autostrada* and the old Via Aurelia (which ends up in Arles in French Provence) lead to **Tarquinia**. The most important of the original 12 towns of the Etruscan confederation, the town dominated Rome in its heyday of the 7th and 6th centuries BC. Today, the paintings and sculptures found in its **necropolis** of over 5,700 tombs provide fascinating evidence of the brilliant Etruscan civilization. Visits to the tombs, outside town, are organized from the **National Museum**, housed in the fine 15th-century Gothic-Renaissance Palazzo Vitelleschi as you enter Tarquinia. The museum exhibits sarcophagi, Etruscan and imported Greek vases and some of the best wall-paintings, in reconstructed tombs. Displayed in a room by itself, the prize of the collection is the *Winged Horses* sculpture from Tarquinia's Ara della Regina Temple.

On your way to Tarquinia you pass the Etruscan necropolis of **Cerveteri**, where the scores of tombs discovered represent every kind of burial from the early shaft and pit graves to tumuli, dating from the 7th to 1st centuries BC.

These later mounds often contain several chambers, carved into the volcanic tufa in the shape of wooden Etruscan homes. Stucco decorations and rock carvings represent the weapons, hunting equipment, domestic animals and even household pots and pans that the Etruscans felt they would need in the after-life. Before going, check at the Villa Giulia museum in Rome that the Cerveteri necropolis is open, as the tombs are often closed to the public and cannot be visited without special permission.

The **Museo Nazionale di Cerveteri**, housed in a 16th-century castle, displays in chronological order a rich array of objects from the tombs, including sarcophagi, sculptures, wall-paintings and vases.

Tuscania is a quiet little fortified town, recovering now from an earthquake in 1971 which luckily did not harm its two Romanesque churches on the eastern outskirts (the Tourist Office on Piazza Basile will get you the keys). Built from the 8th to the 12th centuries, **San Pietro** stands at the back of a grassy courtyard with Etruscan sarcophagi, beside two crumbling medieval towers. The sober interior has Byzantine-style frescoes, an 11th-century altar canopy and a **crypt** built on Etruscan and ancient Roman pillars. The Romanesque tower and rose window of **Santa Maria Maggiore**'s façade have a similar simple beauty.

Drive up to **Montefiascone** for the lovely view from its Rocca dei Papi gardens over Lake Bolsena. The church of San Flaviano at the bottom of the town's hill has some richly sculpted capitals on its massive columns.

This Is It
In the days before guide books began giving stars to hotels and restaurants, Bishop Johannes Fugger of Augsburg sent out an advance man for his trip to Rome to mark the inns where the wine was good. The code word was "*est*": roughly "this is it". The fellow raved over the wine of Montefiascone, exclaiming: "*Est, est, est!*" The bishop drank and he drank and he drank, right into his grave. You'll find the tomb in San Flaviano's third chapel on the left, with its merry Latin inscription explaining the delicious cause of death. *Est, Est, Est* is what they have called the wine ever since.

In the restful charm of its medieval quarters, **Viterbo** makes a good overnight stop. The oldest neighbourhood, with narrow streets and little market squares, is around Via San Pellegrino. On equally attractive Piazza San Lorenzo, the Palazzo Papale has an impressive 13th-century Gothic loggia. It stands opposite the cathedral, which has an intriguing mixture of Gothic campanile (bell tower) and Renaissance façade with a Romanesque interior.

Abruzzo

As a tonic for polluted lungs and street-weary limbs, plunge into the cool fresh air and mountain greenery of the exhilarating nature reserve of the **Abruzzo National Park** (via the Pescina exit on the A25 *autostrada*). The Abruzzo plateau is the highest in the Apennines, excellent for climbers and hikers, and the national park protects magnificent forests of beech, maple and silver birch trees. Wildlife is abundant: brown bear, wolves, rare Abruzzo chamois, foxes, badgers and red squirrels. Bird-watchers can see golden eagles, yellow-billed Alpine choughs and little firecrests, while even the most cloth-eared city-slicker might catch the drumming of a woodpecker.

Enter the park near the wild 1,400m- (4,600ft-) high **Passo del Diavolo** (Devil's Pass) overlooking the Fucino valley and, to the north, affording a spectacular panorama of the Gran Sasso d'Italia plateau, the Apennines' rooftop. Nine kilometres (6 miles) south at **Pescasseroli** is the park administration Visitor's Centre, at which you can get camping permits and maps for hiking. A ski resort in winter, the town also has a nature museum, botanical garden and small zoo. Drive east to **Villetta Barrea** with its attractive villas bordering Lago di Barrea.

Outside the park lies the pretty lake and popular summer resort of Scanno, where the village women still wear the handsome but rather austere regional costume.

L'Aquila
The capital of Abruzzo is a sober, serious town of long, wide avenues that makes a good base for hikers or climbers heading for the Gran Sasso mountains. Founded by Emperor Frederick II in 1240 as a bastion against the papal forces, the town commemorates the 99 legendary castles of its origins with a 99-spout fountain of grotesque masks, the **Fontana delle Novantanove Cannelle**, placed at the Porta Rivera on the western outskirts of town.

The lively centre of town is a crossroads rather than a piazza, the

*T*he Abruzzo National Park preserves the natural flora and fauna of the Central Apennines. Brown bears and wolves are among the wildlife (the latter more easily heard than seen). The park's fragile ecology is threatened by a different kind of predator—man.

Quattro Cantoni. However, **Via Sassa** offers the most attractive collection of medieval, Renaissance and baroque buildings in a town hard hit by earthquake. One of the town's most impressive churches is the 15th-century **San Bernardino** basilica, with a Renaissance façade and rich baroque interior containing a notable Andrea della Robbia ceramic of the Madonna's coronation in the second chapel to the right.

On the north-east corner of town, visit the **Museo Nazionale d'Abruzzo** housed in a massive 16th-century castle. It has a fine collection of Abruzzo medieval painting and sculpture and representative works of the 17th and 18th centuries by Roman and Neapolitan artists: Mattia Preti, Andrea Vaccaro, Bernardo Cavallino and Francesco Solimena.

From here take Via Strinella outside the city walls south to the fine Romanesque-Gothic church of **Santa Maria di Collemaggio**, distinguished by a handsome red and white stone façade with three rose windows above three Romanesque portals.

Hikers and climbers wanting to tackle the **Gran Sasso d'Italia**, the highest range in the Apennines, should head for **Assergi** (good for buying or renting equipment), 17km (10 miles) north-east along the *autostrada*. Another 4km (3 miles) beyond the town, the cable car (*funivia*) from the Fonte Cerreto station will take you up to "base camp" at **Campo Imperatore**, 2,130m (6,990ft). You can also drive up. In 1943, Mussolini was held prisoner in the hotel here until daringly kidnapped by German paratroops. The most ambitious climb in these parts is the **Corno Grande**, a three-peaked mountain topping off at 2,912m (9,557ft).

Art to Stimulate the Mind, Landscapes to Soothe the Spirit

Art lovers flock to Tuscany to learn the elusive secret of that "subtle influence in the air" which inspired the great artists of the Renaissance. Pisa, Siena and the region's other city-states all played their part but it was in Florence that European civilization was born anew. Visitors find a tranquil spirituality in the serene landscapes of neighbouring Umbria—the influence, no doubt, of the region's great saints, Francis, Clare and Benedict.

Light is the secret of the region's magic. In that apparently miraculous collision of imagination and intellect that sparked the Renaissance in 15th-century Florence, its painters and architects had the constant inspiration of the dramatic changes in Tuscan light from dawn to dusk. More than anywhere else in the country, Tuscany and Umbria present that ideal green Italian landscape, dotted with pink stone hilltop towns, where cypress-tree sentinels watch over the olive groves and vineyards below.

*B*runelleschi's graceful *redbrick cupola for the cathedral of Santa Maria del Fiore dominates the Florence skyline.*

With careful timing, modern visitors can capture a glimpse of that miracle of light in Tuscany and Umbria. Arrive early in the morning for a first look across the hills to the grey-stone towers of San Gimignano, but come to Siena's Piazza del Campo at sunset. Pisa's dazzling white marble is at its best in the noonday sun, but late afternoon is the blessed moment for the brilliant façade of Orvieto's cathedral.

Florence (*Firenze*)

First-time visitors may want to stay in the thick of the fray, but veterans may prefer to enjoy the treasures of Florence by driving in from a vantage-point like Fiesole (*see* pages 152–53) or

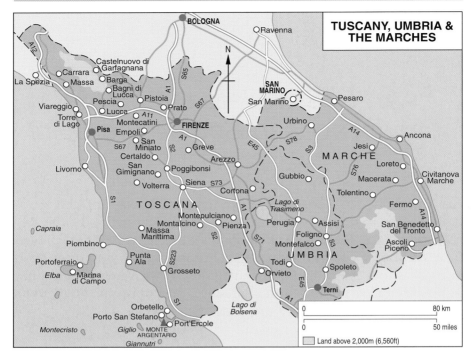

TUSCANY, UMBRIA & THE MARCHES

Land above 2,000m (6,560ft)

*T*uscany, Umbria and the Marches.

one of the other nearby hill towns. Despite the magnificence of its monuments and museums, the city, particularly in the heat of summer, is less amenable to "hanging around" in than Venice; and the people, in their courteous but cool reserve, are less seductive than Romans or Neapolitans.

Our itineraries divide the city's heart into four quarters: from the Duomo north to San Marco; from Piazza della Signoria, the Palazzo Vecchio and the Uffizi east to Santa Croce; from Mercato Nuovo west to Santa Maria Novella; and south of the Arno around the Pitti Palace and Piazzale Michelangelo.

From the Duomo to San Marco

The **Duomo** (cathedral), officially Santa Maria del Fiore, proclaims the inordinate but certainly justified civic pride of the Florentines. It was started around 1296 to designs by the great Gothic architect Arnolfo di Cambio, but was not consecrated until 1436. The imposing green, white and rose marble façade only received its finishing touches in the second half of the 19th century, some six centuries after work on the cathedral had begun.

The first of its glories is the freestanding **campanile**, based on a design by Giotto. The 85m (267ft) bell tower is decorated on its lowest storey with two rows of hexagonal bas-reliefs sculpted by Andrea Pisano and Luca della Robbia from Giotto's drawings. Characteristic of the city's civic

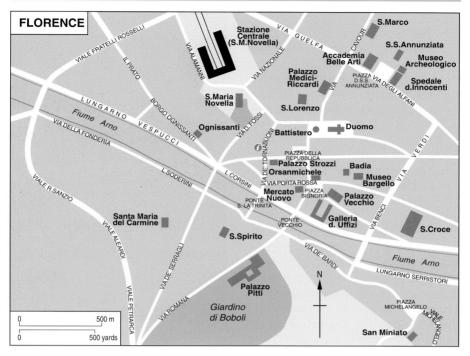

FLORENCE

City plan of Florence.

consciousness, they portray the *Life of Man* from Adam's creation to the rise of civilization through the arts and sciences—music, architecture, metallurgy and the like—which were, pursued so earnestly by the Florentine guilds that commissioned the work.

The originals of these artworks have been removed to the safety of the nearby cathedral museum (*see* below), leaving copies behind to weather the car fumes and acid rain. The statues of *Prophets* and *Sibyls*, some by Donatello, which decorate the niches of the bell tower's second storey have also been replaced by copies.

The cathedral's crowning masterpiece is, of course, Brunelleschi's grandiose redbrick **cupola**. With its eight white stone ribs curving to the marble lantern at the top, it is the city's sym-

bol, visible not only all over Florence but also from far beyond in the Tuscan hills. Completed in 1436, it measures 45.5m (149ft) in diameter and the 463 steps to its top (entrance inside the church, in the north aisle) climb in comfortable stages to reveal glimpses of the surrounding city, different views of the cathedral's interior and fascinating close-ups of the dome's structure. Brunelleschi's original wooden model is displayed in the cathedral museum, along with some of the specially designed building machinery which enabled him to pull off this tremendous feat of Renaissance engineering.

The interior of the Duomo appears stark and austere in contrast with its dazzling exterior. But look out, in the third bay on the north aisle, for Paolo Uccello's statue-like **equestrian painting** of the 14th-century English mercenary Sir John Hawkwood (unpronounceable for Italians, so known as Giovanni Acuto). After brilliant performances in the 100 Years' War in France, Sir John obtained what modern-day footballers would call an "independent transfer" to Florence as a *condottiere*. His "fee" included tax-exemption, state funeral and cathedral monument.

Opposite the cathedral's west façade is the octagonal 12th-century Romanesque **baptistery** of San Giovanni (St John), long celebrated for the magnificent bas-reliefs of its **bronze doors**. The oldest, facing south and telling the story of John the Baptist, were designed by Andrea Pisano in 1318. A century later, Lorenzo Ghiberti won the competition to design the great north and east doors, devoted respectively to the life of Jesus and scenes from the Old Testament. Michelangelo said the latter, facing the Duomo, were good enough to adorn the entrance to heaven and they have been known ever since as the *Doors of Paradise*. Among the losing candidates was Filippo Brunelleschi, who thereafter devoted himself to architecture. (In the Bargello, *see* page 138, you can compare his bronze model with Ghiberti's.) Byzantine-style mosaics inside the cupola include scenes from the *Creation*, *Life of St John* and a *Last Judgement*.

The original panels for the baptistery's great bronze doors, along with many of the Duomo's finest works of art, are to be found in the cathedral museum, **Museo dell'Opera del Duomo**

*T*he Gothic art of Andrea Pisano adorns the gilded bronze south door of the Baptistery in Florence.

(Piazza del Duomo, 9). Two rooms on the ground floor are devoted to Brunelleschi and contain wooden models of the cathedral's dome and lantern, as well as some of the original ropes and pulleys, wheels and capstans, and other such equipment used in their construction.

On the stair landing you will come across Michelangelo's unfinished *Pietà* of the dead Jesus in his mother's arms. The sculpture gives an impression of tragic agony rather than the pathos portrayed by the earlier *Pietà* in St Peter's in Rome (*see* page 100). Michelangelo originally conceived the group for his tomb and represented himself in the figure of Nicodemus. Flaws in the marble so enraged the artist that he hurled a hammer at it, destroying a part, which had to be restored. The rather insipid Mary Magdalen was added by a pupil.

A very different Mary Magdalen is to be found on the first floor of the museum. Donatello's **wooden statue** of the penitent Magdalen in old age is a sombre and haunting work. Much more light-hearted in tone are the jolly boys and girls singing, dancing and playing musical instruments on the two magnificent **choir galleries** in the same room. Dating from the 1430s, these *cantorie* were originally created for the Duomo; one is by Luca della Robbia, the other by Donatello.

Something of the might of the Medici family can be sensed in their massive palace, north-west of the cathedral, the 15th-century **Palazzo Medici-Riccardi**. Now Florence's prefecture, the formidable edifice, with its rough ashlar stone façade smoothing out in the upper storeys, set the style for the city's Renaissance palaces. The ground floor originally had an open loggia at the corner for the family banking business.

After a rest in the quiet little garden of orange trees beyond the main courtyard, visit the upstairs chapel for Benozzo Gozzoli's 15th-century **fresco** of the *Journey of the Magi to Bethlehem*. It portrays the Medici clan led by a youthful Lorenzo the Magnificent processing on horseback through an enchanting Tuscan landscape. Gozzoli has included his self-portrait in the crowd of figures to the left of Lorenzo; you can spot his signature in gold on his red hat.

Just across the square is the family church of **San Lorenzo** designed by Brunelleschi. Funds ran out before Michelangelo's planned façade could embellish the austere barn-like exterior. Inside, you will see the Medici family arms set in the floor in front of the altar. Brunelleschi is at his most elegant in the **Old Sacristy** at the end of the left transept, decorated with four Donatello wall-medallions.

Adjoining the church but with a separate entrance in Piazza Madonna degli Aldobrandini are the **Medici Chapels** (*Cappelle Medicee*), monuments to the splendour and decadence of the dynasty. The **Princes' Chapel** (*Cappella dei Principi*) is a piece of 17th-century baroque bombast in oppressive dark marble, for which the altar was not completed, appropriately enough, until 1939. At the end of a corridor, the summit of Medici power is celebrated in Michelangelo's superb **New Sacristy**, conceived as a pendant to Brunelleschi's in the church. Lorenzo the Magnificent and his brother Giuliano lie in simple tombs beneath the sculptor's *Madonna and Child*, flanked by lesser artists' statues of the family saints Cosmas and Damian. Michelangelo's greatest work here is reserved for two minor members of the family: Lorenzo's grandson, the Duke of Urbino, who is portrayed as a pensive Roman soldier above two allegorical figures of *Twilight* and *Dawn*; and his son, the Duke of Nemours, who appears warrior-like above figures of *Night* and *Day*.

For a moment of peace, wander through the handsome **Laurentian Library** (*Biblioteca Laurenziana*) to the left of the church entrance. The library was built to designs by Michelangelo to house the priceless collection of books and manuscripts begun by Cosimo the Elder, including the famous 5th-century *Virgil codex*. Michelangelo also designed the inlaid wooden desks used to display the manuscripts.

The Dominican Monastery of **San Marco** provides the exquisite setting for a museum largely devoted to the paintings of Fra Angelico (1387–1455), who lived here as a monk. Off the cloister, with its ancient cedar tree, are some of his finest works, notably a *Descent from the Cross* altarpiece from the church of Santa Trinità and miniatures of the life of Jesus. In the small refectory is a stately Ghirlandaio mural of the *Last Supper*, a popular subject for monastic dining rooms. In the monks' cells upstairs, the frescoes of the man Italians call Beato (Blessed) Angelico were intended to be inspirational rather than decorative. His celebrated *Annunciation* faces the top of the stairs (compare the simpler version in cell 3) while other outstanding works include the mystic *Transfiguration* in cell 6 and *Jesus Mocked* in cell 7. The Prior's Quarters in the second dormitory (cells 12, 13 and 14) were the home of fire-and-brimstone preacher Girolamo Savonarola from 1481 until his death in 1498 (*see* page 54). You can see some of his belongings, a portrait by fellow-monk Fra Bartolomeo and the picture of his burning at the stake.

As a museum conceived primarily for students of Florentine painting from the 13th to the 16th century, the **Accademia Gallery** (Via Ricasoli, 60) is an important adjunct to the Uffizi (*see*

pages 136–138). But it is a single work of art that draws visitors here like a magnet: Michelangelo's great **David**. Completed in 1504 when Michelangelo was 29, the statue depicts the hero in repose; but infused with all the contained energy needed to hurl that stone at Goliath. The gallery's collection of works by Michelangelo also includes four unfinished *Slaves* or *Prisoners*, originally intended by the sculptor to

Colourful pageantry surrounds Florence's historic football game, the calcio *in costume. Citizens in 16th-century dress parade through the city streets before the game (a cross between rugby, wrestling and American football without the padding) is played.*

form part of the monumental tomb for Pope Julius II. In their incomplete state, the writhing figures appear to be struggling to free themselves from the confines of the stone.

In **Piazza Santissima Annunziata**, Brunelleschi produced a consummate piece of Renaissance urban planning and a pioneering example of the piazza as stage-set. He designed the graceful colonnade of nine arches for the **Spedale degli Innocenti**, hospital for foundlings, symbolized by the charming little babes in Andrea della Robbia's roundels above the arches. Michelozzo's later Santissima Annunziata church, together with the 17th-century fountains and equestrian statue of Grand Duke Ferdinando, preserve the harmonies of the master's overall design.

Adjoining the hospital, the **Museo Archeologico** (Via della Colonna, 36) houses one of Italy's most important collections of Egyptian, Greek and Etruscan antiquities. Among its highlights: the celebrated Greek *François Vase*; two remarkable Etruscan bronzes, the *Chimera* and *Arringatore* (orator); and an Egyptian granite sculpture (14th century BC) of a divine cow giving milk to a pharaoh.

Piazza della Signoria to Santa Croce

Flanked by the city's most elegant shoe shops, the quarter's main street retains the tradition of its medieval name, Via de' Calzaiuoli (stocking- and shoe-makers).

If the tall, rectangular block of **Orsanmichele** looks more like a grain silo than the church it's supposed to be, that's because it was once both.

Florentines always liked combining faith and business and rebuilt the oratory to St Michael in the 14th century to house a wheat exchange, with arches in place of the present ground-floor windows and a granary upstairs. For 14 niches overlooking the streets, the guilds commissioned **statues** of their patron saints from Florence's greatest talents, a landmark in Renaissance sculpture. Look out for Ghiberti's vigorous bronze of the city's patron *St John* (east wall, on Via de' Calzaiuoli) and *St Matthew*, the bankers' tax-collector-turned-Apostle (west); Donatello's *St George*, the armourers' dragon-killer (north, a bronze cast of a marble original now in the Bargello) and *St Mark*, whose vividly sculpted robes do credit to the linen-drapers he protects (south); and Nanni di Banco's outstanding conspiratorial group of *Four Crowned Martyrs* for the sculptors' own guild of stonemasons and woodworkers (north). In the interior is Andrea Orcagna's elaborate 14th-century Gothic **tabernacle** with a *Madonna* painted by Bernardo Daddi.

Piazza della Signoria is Florence's civic centre. Site of the town hall (*Palazzo Vecchio* or *della Signoria*) since 1299, the square bustles in all seasons, not least because it leads to the richest of Italy's art museums, the Uffizi. At the south end of the square is the 14th-century arcaded **Loggia della Signoria** or dei Lanzi, transformed from the city fathers' ceremonial grandstand into a guardroom for Swiss mercenary *Landsknechte*. It shelters several masterpieces, including Benvenuto Cellini's bronze **Perseus** brandishing the severed head of

Put on a Pedestal

Almost as beautiful as the statue of Perseus are the little figures of Jupiter, Minerva, Mercury and Danae around the base. To keep Duke Cosimo's wife, Eleonora of Toledo, from taking them for her private apartments—"they'll risk being spoilt down in the piazza," she said—Cellini soldered them firmly to the pedestal. But the art custodians of Florence have now decided the Duchess was right, replaced them with copies and put Cellini's originals in the Bargello.

Medusa. In one inspired moment, the Renaissance braggart has combined the legendary technical wizardry he loved to show off as a goldsmith with undeniable sculptural beauty.

Also in the Loggia, the spiralling *Rape of the Sabines* of Giambologna (actually a Flemish artist named Jean Boulogne) is another piece of dazzling virtuosity. But the Loggia's statues are gradually being replaced by copies, while the originals are removed to the non-polluted safety of museums.

In a piazza that is a veritable sculpture garden, more statuary graces the orator's platform along the town hall's sober façade. A weathered copy of Michelangelo's *David* occupies the spot directly beneath the palace tower where the original was set in 1504 by the Florentine Republic as a symbol of the city's fierce independence. Standing against a hostile world of cruel Philistines, Florentines loved to identify with the beauty and courage of the poetic young giant-killer.

The Florentine sculptor Baccio Bandinelli strove throughout his career to emulate Michelangelo, but his *Hercules and Cacus*, commissioned by Cosimo I, cannot help looking clumsy

T hanks to his scandalous autobiography, Benvenuto Cellini is remembered as much for his outrageous love affairs and murderous quarrels as for the exquisite artistry revealed in works like this.

alongside the *David*. To the left is a copy of Donatello's *Marzocco*, Florence's heraldic lion, next to a copy of his bronze of *Judith and Holofernes*, which always made the Medici uneasy with its theme of a tyrant decapitated. (The originals are in the Bargello and Palazzo Vecchio respectively.) Beyond these statues lies Ammanati's huge and lumpen Neptune Fountain, nicknamed by the Florentines "*il Biancone*" (the big white one), and Giambologna's stately bronze equestrian statue of Cosimo I.

Piazza della Signoria was the venue for Savonarola's notorious "bonfire of the vanities" in 1497. At the urging of the apocalyptic Dominican preacher, the Florentines cast "immoral luxuries", including books, jewellery, clothes and paintings, into a giant fire in the middle of the square. Botticelli was one of those who took part, flinging some of his own paintings onto the purifying flames. But Savonarola's hold over the city did not last for long. Denounced as a heretic by the Inquisition, he was hanged and burned at the stake here in the piazza the following year. A commemorative stone in front of the fountain marks the spot where the execution took place.

The **Palazzo Vecchio**, or Palazzo della Signoria, appears as much a fortress as a palace. After Arnolfo di Cambio's austere Italian Gothic exterior, the first inner courtyard comes as a gentle contrast. It was remodelled by Michelozzo in 1453, while the ornate stucco and frescoes were added by Vasari for a Medici wedding in the 1560s. Vasari also designed the porphyry fountain in the centre, which bears a copy of Verrocchio's delightful

---

A Strategist of Statecraft

If the Medici had listened to Niccolò Machiavelli (1469–1527) instead of jailing and torturing him, they might have stayed in power a great deal longer. As the roving ambassador for the Florentine republic, he had spent a lot of time not only with Cesare Borgia and Pope Julius II, but also with France's Louis XII. There he learned to appreciate the advantages of a large-scale rough, tough absolutist monarchy over the more refined subtleties of all those little Italian states. What he analysed in *The Prince* and *Discourses* (written in his enforced retirement after 1512 and diplomatically dedicated to the Medici) was not a theory for an ideal state and perfect prince, but the real state as he had observed it, with its actual strengths and weaknesses, and the successful prince able to exploit them. He wanted above all a state freed of foreign domination.

All he got for his trouble, in 1526, was a humiliating job inspecting the city walls. Given the chance to fight with the pope's League of Cognac against the Holy Roman Emperor Charles V, Machiavelli left Florence until the fall of the Medicis encouraged him to return in the hope of reclaiming his old post in the chancery. The Florentines, remembering his collaboration with the Medicis, would have none of it. Overcome by disappointment, he died within a month.

---

bronze cherub (the original can be seen inside the palace).

Upstairs, the **Salone dei Cinquecento** was built in 1495 for Savonarola's short-lived Republican Council before serving as Duke Cosimo's throne room and, three centuries later, the chamber of Italy's first national parliament. The décor celebrates Florentine power— Vasari's frescoes of victories over Siena and Pisa and Michelangelo's *Victory* statue, designed originally for Pope Julius II's tomb and set here to honour the Grand Duke of Tuscany. On the second floor, the **Sala dei Gigli** (Hall of the Lilies) is brilliantly decorated in blues and golds with vivid Ghirlandaio frescoes of Roman and early Christian history. It adjoins the **Chancery** (*cancelleria*) where Niccolò Machiavelli served as secretary to the Florentine Republic. Santi di Tito's portrait of the young philosopher is hard to reconcile with the popular image of the cynical and pragmatic author of *The Prince*. Far more

*G*iotto broke decisively from the stiff forms of Byzantine art to bring a new humanity to images of the Madonna and Child.

straightforward is the original of Verrocchio's cherub cuddling a dolphin like a baby doll.

The **Uffizi** museum of Italian and European painting stretches in a long U-shape from the Palazzo Vecchio down to the Arno river and back. Duke Cosimo had Vasari design it in 1560 as a series of government offices (*uffici*, hence the name), a mint for the city's florin and workshops for the Medici's craftsmen.

That makes a lot of museum, but a great one that it would be sad to renounce through visual fatigue. We won't burden you with guilt by telling you "not to miss" this or to "be sure" to see that, but just signal some of what really is worth seeing. See all or only half a dozen, stop for an occasional peek out the window over the Arno and Ponte Vecchio bridge, and rendezvous later at the museum's roof-garden café above the Loggia della Signoria.

Constant reorganization makes it hazardous to specify room numbers, but the paintings are exhibited chronologically by schools from the 13th to the 18th century. Here are some of the highlights:

Giotto breathes a warm humanity into his *Madonna Enthroned* (1300) that distinguishes it from the more formal pictures of the subject by Cimabue and Duccio in the same room. See also Giotto's Madonna polyptych. Some 30 years later, the *Annunciation* triptych of **Simone Martini**, with Mary shying away from archangel Gabriel, has the characteristic elegance and poetry of the Sienese school.

Paolo Uccello shows a dream-like, almost surrealist obsession with his (unsolved) problems of perspective and merry-go-round horses in his *Battle of San Romano* (1456). It contrasts with the cool dignity of **Piero della Francesca** in his *Federico da Montefeltro and wife Battista* (1465), portrayed against their Urbino landscape.

In his graceful *Primavera* (1478) and the almost too famous but undyingly delightful *Birth of Venus*, **Botticelli** achieves an enchanting mixture of sensuality and purity. His Flemish contemporary, **Hugo van der Goes** is more down to earth in the realism of his *Adoration of the Shepherds*, which influenced Florentine painters like **Ghirlandaio**; compare here his *Adoration of the Magi*.

In the *Baptism of Christ* (1470) of **Verrocchio**, you can see the earliest identified work of his pupil, **Leonardo da Vinci**: the background landscape and the angel on the left, beautiful enough to reduce his companion angel to wide-eyed jealousy and Verrocchio to giving up painting for sculpture. Leonardo's *Annunciation* of a few years later already shows his characteristic gentle tone and feeling for precise detail, and the *Adoration of the Magi*, left unfinished by his departure for Milan (1481), reveals his revolutionary power of psychological observation.

The octagonal **Tribuna** was designed by Buontalenti in 1584 to show off the most highly prized objects in the Medici collection. With its mother-of-pearl inlaid ceiling and pavement of *pietre dure*, the room is itself a work of art. The beautiful **octagonal table**, especially made for the Tribuna over a period of 16 years, displays a marble copy of the 4th-century BC *Aphrodite*

of Cnidos. Around the walls are portraits of the Medici family by their court painter **Bronzino**. Look out for his elegantly Mannerist portrayal of Cosimo's Spanish wife Eleonora of Toledo and their chubby baby son.

The northern European rooms include a splendid *Portrait of His Father* (1490) by **Albrecht Dürer**; *Adam and Eve* (1528) by **Lucas Cranach**; *Richard Southwell* by **Hans Holbein**; and a moving *Mater Dolorosa* by **Joos van Cleve**.

In the mystic *Holy Allegory* (1490) of **Giovanni Bellini**, we can appreciate the typical Venetian serenity even without understanding its symbols.

The only **Michelangelo** in the Uffizi is the *Holy Family* roundel (1504), his earliest painting, decidedly sculptural in the group's solid plastic qualities. Without Michelangelo's strength and torment or Leonardo's complexity, the third of Italy's three Renaissance giants, **Raphael**, brings his own powers of both clarity and restraint to the *Madonna of the Goldfinch* and a revealing *Self-Portrait*.

Titian has a superbly sensual *Venus of Urbino*, less Greek goddess than the prince's mistress she probably was, and an equally disturbing *Flora* (1515). Some are also upset by the eroticism of **Parmigianino** in his strange but undeniably graceful *Madonna with the Long Neck* (1534). Look also at her fingers, which are a masterpiece of the sophisticated and subsequently decadent Mannerism that followed the High Renaissance.

There is an intriguing ambiguity to the half-naked peasant youth posing as a *Bacchus* for **Caravaggio**, but nothing complicated about the robust sexiness of the **Rubens** *Bacchanale*. Compare Caravaggio's mastery of *chiaroscuro* (the play of light and dark) in the service of realism in his violent *Abraham and Isaac* (1590) with the more contemplative style of **Rembrandt** in his *Old Rabbi* (1658) and other portraits.

Time for that refreshment on the roof-garden.

For a change from all this fine art, try the **Science History Museum** (*Museo di Storia della Scienza*, Piazza dei Giudici, 1), where you'll find Galileo's telescopes, his (pickled) middle finger and an Edison phonograph.

Designed in the late 13th century by Arnolfo di Cambio but with a neo-Gothic façade added in 1863, the church of **Santa Croce** (east of the Uffizi) has an important series of Giotto **frescoes**. The pathos shines through the heavily restored paintings of *St Francis* in the Bardi Chapel, to the right of the apse, and *St John* in the Peruzzi Chapel next door. In a chapel in the left transept, the wooden **Crucifixion** by Donatello (1425) is in affecting naturalistic contrast to the Renaissance idealism of the time.

The church is also revered by Florentines as the last resting place of many great Italians. Galileo, Machiavelli, Ghiberti and composer Rossini are all buried here. **Michelangelo's tomb** (right aisle, second bay) was designed by Vasari, with symbolic statues of *Painting*, *Sculpture* and *Architecture* mourning beneath a bust of the artist (89 when he died). Michelangelo wanted the tomb surmounted by the *Pietà*, now in the cathedral museum (*see* page 130–31), but the Florentines nearly didn't even get his body: they had to smuggle it out of Rome in a bale of sacking. For Dante, they have to be content with a cenotaph, as Ravenna, his burial place, refuses to part with his remains.

At the back of the cloister of Santa Croce's Franciscan monastery adjoining the church, Brunelleschi's **Pazzi Chapel** is a little gem of Renaissance elegance. Its spaciousness is enhanced by geometric patterns of dark stone against whitewashed walls. Brunelleschi preferred Luca della Robbia's subdued glazed ceramic roundels to Donatello's too-competitive wall medallions in the Old Sacristy of San Lorenzo. The most cherished treasure in the Santa Croce **museum** is Cimabue's 13th-century *Crucifixion* rescued and painstakingly restored after the town's 1966 flood.

The ominous 13th-century fortress of the **Bargello** (Via del Proconsole, 4) was Florence's first town hall and a very unpleasant prison under the jurisdiction of the Police Chief or Bargello, before becoming the National Museum of sculpture. The old armoury is now the **Michelangelo Hall**, greeting you with a most unhappy bust of the master by Daniele da Volterra. Michelangelo's works here include a marble bust of *Brutus*, a *Virgin and Child* marble roundel and an early *Drunken Bacchus* (1497). Compare Sansovino's more decorous *Bacchus* of 20 years later. Among the Cellini **bronzes** is an imposing bust of his master, Duke Cosimo. The **General Council Hall** is dominated by the works of Donatello: his vigorous *St George* intended for the Orsanmichele (*see* page 133); two statues of *David*, doubting in marble, naked and restless in bronze; and the stone *Marzocco* lion, the town's symbol from the Palazzo

Vecchio. You can also see the two bronze panels submitted for the baptistery doors competition by Brunelleschi, the loser, and Ghiberti, the winner (*see* page 130). On the second floor is a Verrocchio *David*, for which his 19-year-old pupil Leonardo da Vinci is believed to have been the model.

Opposite the Bargello you will see the church known as the **Badia Fiorentina** (Florentine Abbey) with its graceful bell tower, which is part Romanesque and part Gothic. Take a brief look inside at Filippino Lippi's delightful *Madonna Appearing to St Bernard*, on the left as you enter.

Casa Buonarroti (Via Ghibellina, 70) was bought by bachelor Michelangelo

*T*he bronze statue of the Porcellino in the Mercato Nuovo. Florentines rub the snout for luck.

for his closest relatives. Decorated by 17th-century artists with paintings commemorating his long life, it displays letters, drawings and portraits of the great man. Most important are two sculptured reliefs of his youth; the *Madonna of the Steps*, done before the artist was 16, and a tumultuous *Battle of the Centaurs*, dating from about the same time but astonishingly different in style.

From Mercato Nuovo to Santa Maria Novella

Start out from the centre, on Via Calimala, the heart of medieval Florence on the street of the drapers' guild taken over today by the colourful **Mercato Nuovo** (the Straw Market). Here, around a 16th-century loggia enclosing the bronze statue of a wild boar known as the *Porcellino*, you can buy a straw hat against the Tuscan sun and a basket to carry off the cheap and not

so cheap jewellery, leather goods and embroidery.

West on Via Porta Rossa is the 14th-century **Palazzo Davanzati**. Its stern, fortress-like exterior is still provided with rings at ground level for tethering horses and on upper storeys to hold torches and lanterns for festive occasions. Inside, on the first floor, is a museum of Florentine domestic life from the 14th to the 16th century, with furniture, utensils and ceramics, at their most attractive in the **Sala dei Pappagalli** (Hall of the Parrots) with its *trompe l'œil* tapestries frescoed on the walls.

The church of **Santa Trinita** has a late 16th-century baroque façade with a Gothic interior. Ghirlandaio decorated the Sassetti Chapel (far right of the high altar) with frescoes of St Francis, and the *Adoration of the Shepherds* on the altar is considered his masterpiece.

Florence's most elegant shops continue Via de' Tornabuoni's centuries-old tradition of aristocratic luxury. On the 15th-century **Palazzo Strozzi**, look out for the intricate wrought-iron lanterns by the much sought-after and expensive craftsman Niccolò Grosso, known as *Caparra* (Mr Down Payment) who coined the philosophy later attributed to Hollywood: "If you want something for nothing, you get what you paid for."

The 13th-century Dominican church of **Santa Maria Novella** is the finest of Florence's monastic churches. Leon Battista Alberti added the graceful white and green marble façade in the 15th century. The church is rich in artistic treasures, but its most prized, and indeed one of the city's greatest

paintings, is the **Masaccio Trinity** (left aisle, third bay). Above a pair of stoic kneeling donors, Mary and St John stand on either side of the crucified Jesus upheld by his Father, while the dove of the Holy Spirit hovers between them, the whole forming an inspiring triangle under the coffered ceiling of a Renaissance chapel. Painted in weird, rather gruesome counterpoint below is a skeleton (perhaps one of the donors) and the inscription in Italian: "I was once that which you are and what I am, you will also be."

The Ghirlandaio **frescoes** of the lives of the Madonna and St John, for the chancel behind the altar, kept the master's whole workshop busy from 1485 to 1490. Among the pupils who perhaps worked on the project was a teenage apprentice named Michelangelo Buonarroti.

The Filippo Strozzi Chapel (right of the altar) is decorated with Filippino Lippi's **frescoes** of Saints Philip and John, rich in colour and anecdotal detail: in the monumental *Exorcism of Demons in the Temple of Mars*, three bystanders hold their nose at the smell.

In the Gondi Chapel (left of the high altar), the Brunelleschi **Crucifixion**, one of his few sculptures (1410), brings to the human body a characteristic idealized harmony, compared with Donatello's more personal piece in Santa Croce (*see* page 138). Of another age, at once austere and serene, is the Giotto **Crucifixion** (1290) in the Sacristy (left transept).

Through an entrance left of the church, escape the bustle of the piazza in the Dominicans' 14th-century **cloister** (*Chiostro Verde*), with Paolo Uccello's frescoes of the *Flood* in the refectory.

ITALIAN PAINTING

Giotto fresco in Padua's Scrovegni Chapel

Medieval Italian art was heavily influenced by centuries of **Byzantine** tradition, but painters injected a native vigour and nervous tension into the languid beauties of Byzantine style. Florence-born **Coppo di Marcovaldo** (active from 1250 to 1275) renewed the Byzantine repertoire with intense emotion, as in his convulsed *Crucifixion* at San Gimignano. The style of **Cimabue** (1240–1302) is more gentle than his nickname,

meaning "dehorner of oxen", and his humanizing of Byzantine formalism in his *Maestà* (Uffizi, Florence) and especially his Assisi frescoes have won him the title of master, even "inventor" of Giotto. In Siena, **Duccio** (1260–1318) paints well within the severe Byzantine tradition, while adding the elegance and sensitivity characteristic of his city's art.

But it is **Giotto** (1266–1337) who achieves the vital

breakthrough in psychological and physical realism, giving bodies a new density, a new depth to space. While his paternity of the Assisi frescoes is disputed, we can unhesitatingly admire his biblical frescoes in the Scrovegni Chapel in Padua or the St. Francis cycle in the Bardi Chapel in Florence's Santa Croce.

Simone Martini (1284–1344) emphasizes the **Siena** school's taste for elegance, pomp, even

a certain luxury in his *Maestà* (in the Palazzo Pubblico) and masterful Gothic altarpieces— *St. Catherine* in the Pisa museum and an *Annunciation* in the Uffizi. Brothers **Pietro** and **Ambrogio Lorenzetti** (active 1305–48) are unique in the scope of detail with which they depict life in Siena and the surrounding countryside, both allegorical and realistic, in the Palazzo Pubblico's *Good and Bad Government* and landscape panels in the Pinacoteca.

In Venice, **Paolo Veneziano** (1300–62) brings east and west together with his use of Gothic line and brilliant colour, especially a most oriental gold, gently combining Byzantine formality and Giottoesque composition: *Madonna in Trono* and *Polyptych* in the Venice Accademia.

If Giotto prepared the ground, it is **Masaccio** (1401–1428) who makes the quantum leap into the visual and psychological world of **Renaissance** painting. In

Florence he draws on Donatello's work for the sculptural quality of his figures and on architect Brunelleschi for innovative geometric relationships, deepening perspectives and heightening drama with a unique source of light. But it is his own personal vision that brings such powerful individual emotion to his frescoes for the Brancacci Chapel of Santa Maria del Carmine.

At a less intense level, **Domenico Ghirlandaio** (1449–94) produces admirably individualized narrative frescoes such as the *Last Supper* in the Ognissanti refectory in Florence and a vivid portrait gallery of his Tornabuoni patrons in the Santa Maria Novella frescoes of the Madonna's life. The inescapably melancholy **Sandro Botticelli** (1445–1510) is more aristocratically light and subtle in line, gentle in colour. He worked for the Medici and included them in his *Adoration of the Magi*. It was they who commissioned

Left: Detail from Botticelli's ALLEGORY OF SPRING

Below: Fra Angelico's ANNUNCIATION *in San Marco museum*

Detail of Leonardo da Vinci's
ANNUNCIATION *in Uffizi Gallery*

his *Birth of Venus* and *Allegory of Spring* (all in the Uffizi).

Amid the progressive secularization of Renaissance art, even when treating religious themes, **Fra Angelico** (1400–55) asserts an intense spirituality. His *Annunciation* in the Museo di San Marco is perhaps the most famous icon of western Christian art, but his subtle perspectives and purity of colour and form are at their best in the Vatican frescoes (Chapel of Nicholas V).

Northern Italy's leading painter at this time is **Andrea Mantegna** (1430–1506), displaying a monumental talent in the altarpiece for Verona's San Zeno. Fascinated by sculpture, he was also a magnificent draughtsman

conducting bold experiments in perspective to achieve dramatic foreshortening of his figures, such as the *Dead Christ* in Milan's Brera Museum. To his tough-minded classicism, brother-in-law **Giovanni Bellini** (1430–1516) brings a warm, humanizing touch. This key figure in Venetian art, brimming over with life, works wonders in colour and light for his altarpieces in Santi Giovanni e Paolo, San Zaccaria and the Frari. He owes a certain debt in the treatment of light and shadow to the passage through Venice of Sicilian **Antonello da Messina** (1430–1479), a brilliant portraitist who introduced into Italy Flemish techniques of painting in oils.

In Umbria, the intelligence and aesthetics of **Piero della Francesca** (1416–92) represent a quintessence of the Renaissance spirit. His work achieves a timeless purity by combining an exquisite sense

of colour with meticulously calculated geometric perspectives to place the human being amid buildings or landscape. An aura of ineffable mystery surrounds his Arezzo *True Cross* frescoes and the *Flagellation* in Urbino's Palazzo Ducale. In comparison, **Perugino** (1448–1523) is touchingly simple in his pious Perugia altarpieces and frescoes for the Sistine Chapel.

At the beginning of the 16th century, a great chance moment in Italian art, indeed in the history of mankind, brought together in one city Leonardo da Vinci, Michelangelo and Raphael—no summit conference, just a concentration in Florence of the age's greatest artistic geniuses. **Leonardo da Vinci** (1452–1519) said: "A painter is not admirable unless he is universal"—easy for a man interested in mathematics, geography, geology, botany, zoology, engineering, aviation, optics, astronomy, town planning, music, athletics, sculpture, architecture and a little painting on the side. But it's only that universality that can begin to explain the man capable of giving his paintings their rich expression of complex composition and subtle intellectual and emotional ambiguities. His celebrated *sfumato* softening of contour, light and shade is just the veil to that mystery. His few works in Italy range from an angel painted in his youth for Verrocchio's *Baptism of Christ* and the great unfinished *Adoration of the Magi* (both in the Uffizi) to the sublime *Last Supper* of Santa Maria delle Grazie, Milan.

With the sheer *terribilità* of his personality, **Michelangelo** (1475–1564) brought to his painting an incomparable heroic dimension in the

Left: Raphael's SELF-PORTRAIT　　*Above: Michelangelo's Sistine Chapel frescoes in Rome*

classical tradition. His earliest painting is the very sculptural *Holy Family* (Uffizi). After sketching the works of Giotto and Masaccio, he learned something of fresco technique with Ghirlandaio. But his immense Sistine Chapel frescoes, the story of Man, are the lonely achievement of ever-striving genius, a creative quest symbolized by that hand of Adam stretched out to God's. He preferred to be thought of as a sculptor, yet no other painter has matched the awesome power of his *Last Judgment* on the Sistine's altar-wall.

After these two giants, the gentleness of **Raphael** (1483–1520) prompts many to dismiss

him as a sentimental painter of pretty Madonnas. Certainly this most accessible of Renaissance artists suffers among critics for his popularity. But the strength is there, in the Vatican's monumental *School of Athens* and *Disputation over the Holy Sacrament*, ambitious imagination in the *Transfiguration* (Vatican Pinacoteca), and acute psychological observation in his portraits—*Pope Leon X* (Uffizi), *Inghirami* (Pitti Palace) and *Maddalena Strozzi* (Borghese Gallery).

The dominant influence on successors was Leonardo—Sodoma in Siena, Andrea Solario and Bernardino Luini in Milan. Brescia's **Vicenzo Foppa**

(1427–1515) asserts a more distinctively steely personality for the Lombard Renaissance: *Crucifixion* in Bergamo's Accademia Carrara and *St. Sebastian* in Milan's Brera.

During the High Renaissance, **Venice** went its own brilliant way. **Vittore Carpaccio** (1465–1525) uses a lively narrative skill to depict everyday Venetian life in his *St. Ursula* cycle (Accademia) and rich luminous colour for interiors like *St. Augustine in his Study* (San Giorgio degli Schiavoni). But even more remarkable is the short dramatic career of Bellini's pupil, **Giorgione** (1478–1510). "Great George", as Renaissance chronicler Vasari nicknamed him (Zorzi in his own lifetime), dazzled contemporaries, above all Titian, with his poetic use of light both in portraits and landscapes, but nowhere more spectacularly than in his mysterious *Tempest* in the Venice Accademia. The melancholy *Enthroned Madonna* in the San Liberale church of his birthplace, Castelfranco Veneto, is his only surviving altarpiece. Among his followers, **Sebastiano del Piombo** (1485–1547) adds a certain monumental quality, while **Palma Vecchio** (1480–1528) applies a Giorgionesque lighting to the landscapes of his numerous *Holy Family* altarpieces. He also shows a penchant for sensual portrayals of courtesans (in Milan's Poldi-Pezzoli museum).

But Giorgione's most illustrious follower, **Titian** (1488–1576), outstripped him in international fame, lending his name to a whole style of sensuous female beauty of which the Uffizi *Venus of Urbino* is perhaps the most celebrated example. His religious works in Venice range from the Frari church's splendid *Assumption of the Madonna* to the more subdued *Presentation of the Madonna* in the Accademia. Among the best of his striking portraits are those of *Pope Paul III* and his family in Naples' Capodimonte.

Outside the Venetian mainstream, **Lorenzo Lotto** (1480–1556) pursued a highly individual career of bizarrely mystical religious painting (*St. Catherine* in Bergamo's Accademia Carrara, *Holy Conversation*, Borghese Gallery, Rome) and profound, often disturbing portraits (*Gentiluomo*, Venice Accademia, *Self-Portrait*, Borghese Gallery).

LA BELLA by Titian, in Florence's Pitti Gallery

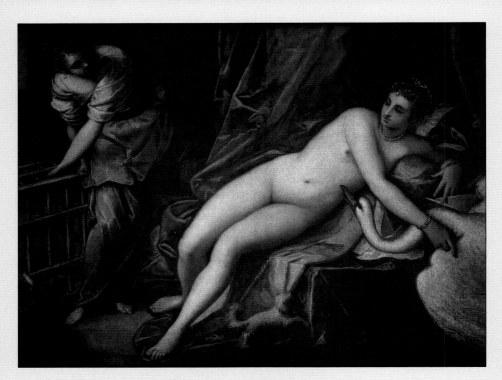

LEDA AND THE SWAN
by Tintoretto, Uffizi Gallery

Averring that he wanted to ally Michelangelo's draughtsmanship to Titian's use of colour, **Jacopo Tintoretto** (1518–94) developed a dynamic, uninhibited narrative style for his dramatic *Last Supper* (San Paolo, Venice) and huge *Crucifixion* (Scuola di San Rocco). **Paolo Veronese** (1528-88) proved a more decorative than emotional successor to Titian, capturing national attention with his controversial *Feast in the House of Levi* (Accademia).

Standing apart from the movements of his time, **Correggio** (1494 –1534) paints with a glorious voluptuousness in his depiction of the *Assumption of the Madonna* for Parma cathedral, more overt paganism in his decoration of the nearby Camera di San Paolo. In the same town, **Parmigianino** (1503–1540) is a prime exponent of the sophisticated forms of **Mannerism**. He demonstrates his total mastery of method in the strange *Madonna with the Long Neck* (Uffizi). The Florentine **Pontormo** (1494–1556) is equally powerful in his skilful

elongations and distortions of the human figure controlled by perfect technique, notably his *Descent from the Cross* (Santa Felicità, Florence).

Bologna's **Annibale Carracci** (1560 –1609) infused religious subjects with sensuous but idealized beauty, just the vehicle with which to woo back stray lambs to the Counter-Reformation flock— *Madonna in Gloria*, Pinacoteca, Bologna, and *Pietà*, Capodimonte, Naples. But his decorative eclecticism was more at home with the pink eroticism of pagan mythology decorating the Farnese Palace in Rome.

Nothing decorative or sophisticated about the revolutionary paintings of **Caravaggio** (1573–1610). This Lombard's saints and Madonnas are peasants and labourers with calloused hands and dirty, bare feet. Stark "photographic" close-cropping enhances the drama of brutally lit scenes of *St. Paul's Conversion* and *St. Peter's Crucifixion* (Santa Maria del Popolo, Rome). Even a still life like the *Bowl of Fruit* in the Milan Ambrosiana has a

Caravaggio's Bacchus, Uffizi Gallery

worrying realism about the rotting apple and withering leaves. His "Caravaggesque" followers were legion—Carlo Saraceni and Orazio Gentileschi in Naples, but also Georges de la Tour in France and even Rembrandt and Rubens.

Baroque painting transforms Renaissance and Mannerist technique into a virtuoso *tour de force*. Luca Giordano and Francesco Solimena in Naples, Giovanni Lanfranco in Parma, Pietro da Cortona in Rome decorated the vaults and ceilings of churches and palaces with extravagant fantasies of pagan and Christian apotheosis, often indistinguishable.

The swan song of 18th-century Venice is celebrated by **Giambattista Tiepolo** (1696–1770), emphatically aristocratic in his *Antony and Cleopatra* frescoes for the Palazzo Labia. The meticulously observed *vedute* (views) of **Antonio Canaletto** (1697–1768) are

Tiepolo: Callisto Surprised by Diana, Accademia in Venice

LE MUSE INQUIETANTI
by Giorgio de Chirico,
Mattioli Collection, Milan

grand, large-scale precursors of the modern picture postcard. But **Francesco Guardi** (1712–93) is more impressionistic, bringing an emotion-laden atmosphere to his *vedute*, a silvery luminosity that seems to presage Venice's twilight (Poldi-Pezzoli, Milan, and Accademia Carrara, Bergamo).

Undistinguished neoclassicists and romantics emphasize the sharp decline of Italian painting in the 19th century. In mid-century, the **Macchiaioli** painters meeting in Florence's Caffè Michelangelo (Giovanni Fattori, Silvestro Lega, Telemaco Signorini) make an interesting stand against the prevailing academicism. Their subdued but lyrical use of splashes *(macchia)* of dark and light colour takes them close to Impressionism.

Twentieth-century **Futurism** exalts the future embodied in the machine—speed and dynamism. A 1909 manifesto proclaims: "Let's kill the moonlight" and waxes lyrical about war. The movement's leading painters were Umberto Boccioni, Giacomo Balla, Gino Severini and Carlo Carrà (modern art museums in Milan, Rome and Florence). Between the wars, **Giorgio de Chirico** (1888–1978) made his mark with the surrealist symbolism of his "metaphysical painting". With the internationalization of contemporary art, Italy has been in the vanguard of **Arte povera** (poor art) which stands against art as a commercial product, choosing ephemeral materials that change and even disintegrate. Exponents include Turin's Mario Merz and Giovannia Anselmo and Rome's Pino Pascali and Gianni Kounellis.

North of Santa Maria Novella, spare a glance for the simple, clean-lined architecture of the **Stazione Centrale** (main railway station). It was built in 1935 in Mussolini's heyday but somehow defies the prevailing monumental bombast of the fascist regime that you can see in Milan's monstrosity.

Heading back down to the river, have a restful drink in the plush neo-Renaissance bar of the Excelsior Hotel (Piazza Ognissanti), even, or particularly, if you are not staying there. Then cross the square to the **Ognissanti** (All Saints Church), 13th-century but with a baroque façade of 1637. In Ghirlandaio's *Madonna of Mercy* (right aisle, 2nd bay), portrayed immediately to the right of Mary, is the Florentine banker-navigator Amerigo Vespucci, who gave his name to the continent of America. Botticelli is buried in a chapel (right transept), his *St Augustine* adorning the church, while in the refectory in the adjoining cloister, you will find Ghirlandaio's *Last Supper*.

South of the Arno

There is nothing very romantic about the muddy green waters of the Arno river, with its broad *lungarni* embankments built in the 19th century to protect from flooding, but it does have two splendid bridges.

The **Ponte Santa Trinita**, destroyed in 1944, has been rebuilt with the original 16th-century masonry scooped from the bottom of the river, including statues of the *Four Seasons*. Bartolomeo Ammanati's three lovely elliptical arches follow drawings by Michelangelo.

The **Ponte Vecchio**, intact since 1345, was Florence's first and for centuries only bridge. The boutiques with their back rooms overhanging the river were built from the 16th to the 19th centuries. Vasari provided a covered corridor for Duke Cosimo to keep out of the rain when crossing from his Pitti Palace to the Uffizi. The duke did not like the smell of the bridge's original butcher shops and had them replaced by the goldsmiths and jewellers whose descendants offer you their high-quality wares today. Their most famous ancestor, Benvenuto Cellini, has his bronze bust (1900) in the middle of the bridge.

In Renaissance times, the quarter south of the Arno was an aristocratic preserve where the Medici held court. Today, their palace is a popular museum and the gardens of their private festivities are a public park.

Cross the Ponte Vecchio to the sprawling **Pitti Palace**, its dauntingly heavy and graceless façade belying the ornate and colourful interior. Duke Cosimo's wife, Eleonora of Toledo, acquired the palace from the Pitti merchant family in 1549 as the Medici's official residence, which passed briefly in the 19th century to the kings of a united Italy.

Its museums take you into the rich world of the Medici, much as they left it. The **Pitti Gallery** (*Galleria Palatina*) is quite simply, quite opulently, the family art collection. The paintings are displayed just as the dukes themselves hung them, two-, three- and four-high, by personal preference rather than in historical sequence. Like any collection of family pictures, there is a preponderance of portraits, although here the

War and Flood

In the 20th century, the Arno river has meant nothing but trouble. To slow the Allied advance in August 1944, the Germans blew up all of Florence's bridges except the Ponte Vecchio. And in case their enemy planned to drive vehicles across this ancient foot-bridge, they blocked approaches by destroying buildings within a radius of 200m.

On 4 November 1966, the river burst its banks and flooded the city, destroying and damaging over 1,000 paintings and 500 sculptures as well as countless precious books and manuscripts in its libraries. In places like the Bargello's Michelangelo Hall (*see* page 138), you can see wall marks recording the flood level: 3m (10ft) and more. However, this was the golden Age of Aquarius and from all over the world, the sixties' art-loving brothers and sisters of the flower children poured into the city to help with the rescue operation spearheaded by Florence's own proud citizenry.

aunts and uncles tend to be princesses and cardinals. Besides, the Medicis' taste and means did permit a considerable number of masterpieces.

The richly decorated halls are named after the themes of their baroque ceiling frescoes: Venus, Hercules, Prometheus, and so on. Painted by Pietro da Cortona for Ferdinand II between 1641 and 1665, the allegorical cycle illustrates the idealized education of the Medici prince.

Titian displays his masterly use of colour and light in *The Concert* (Hall of Venus), a searching portrait of *The Englishman* and bare-breasted *Magdalen* (Hall of Apollo).

Early proponent of "make love, not war," **Rubens** shows Venus restraining Mars in his vivid *Consequences of War* and portrays himself on the far left of his *Four Philosophers* (Hall of Mars).

Raphael is well represented by a stately *Veiled Woman* (Hall of Jupiter), a hauntingly beautiful *Madonna of the Chair* and *Maddalena Doni* (Hall of Saturn), deliberately imitating the pose of Leonardo da Vinci's *Mona Lisa*, and *Pregnant Women* (Hall of the Iliad).

Caravaggio contributes a typically disturbing canvas, an ugly *Sleeping Cupid* with distinct intimations of death (Hall of the Education of Jupiter).

Up on the next floor, the **Modern Art Gallery** is devoted to 19th- and 20th-century Italian art. Most interesting are the *Macchiaioli* school of Tuscan pre-Impressionists who met at Florence's Caffè Michelangelo in the 1860s, seeking a new freedom from academic art that paralleled the political liberation of the *Risorgimento*. Giorgio de Chirico and Filippo de Pisis are among the more important 20th-century painters exhibited.

Left of the main Pitti entrance, the **Silverware Museum** (*Museo degli Argenti*) has 16 profusely ornamented rooms of family treasures, silver, jewels, beautiful 16th- and 17th-century amber and ivory, crystal and porcelain and baroque furniture. The **Carriage Museum** (*Museo delle Carrozze*), in a wing on the far right of the palace, and the **Royal Apartments** (*Appartamenti Monumentali*), upstairs, right of the main entrance, show an opulent, truly palatial life that the Pitti's dour exterior never let you suspect.

Time for a rest in the shade of the cypresses, pines and holm oaks of the palace's **Boboli Gardens**. To the modern eye, they form a Renaissance and baroque theme-park dotted with loggias, cool fountains, grottoes with artificial stalactites, and myriad statues of gods and nymphs.

Directly behind the palace, the **Amphitheatre**, shaped like a Roman circus, was the scene of the Medicis' most extravagant fêtes and masked balls. In the middle of the nearby **Pond of Neptune** (*Vasca del Nettuno*), the burly sea god wields his trident in petrified parody of one of the Boboli's gardeners. Look out too for the amusing **fountain** of a pot-bellied dwarf seated on a turtle (to the left of the entrance arch from the north wing of the palace). It's a statue of Cosimo I's court jester Pietro Barbino, sculpted by Valerio Cioli in 1560.

After the Pitti's riches, the unadorned white façade of the Augustinian church of **Santo Spirito** is sobering. Brunelleschi's design was never completed but the interior preserves the spatial clarity of his Corinthian-capitalled colonnades. In the right transept is a strikingly theatrical *Madonna Enthroned* by Filippino Lippi.

Across the church's tree-shaded piazza, popular for its pleasant market, is the **Cenacolo di Santo Spirito**, formerly the monastery's refectory. This has some 14th-century frescoes of the *Last Supper* and *Crucifixion* by Andrea Orcagna.

The church of **Santa Maria del Carmine** is an essential stop on any artistic pilgrimage to Florence. The church itself is an unprepossessing reconstruction after a devastating fire in 1771, but the Brancacci Chapel with its great **Masaccio frescoes** survived intact. The painter died at 27, after only

*P*ietro Barbino, *Cosimo I's court jester, continues to amuse: seated naked on a turtle in this strange fountain in the Boboli Gardens.*

5 years of known creative activity (1423–28), working with his mild-mannered friend Masolino on scenes from Genesis and the life of St Peter. Compare Masolino's sweet and harmonious Adam and Eve in his *Original Sin* (chapel entrance, upper right) with Masaccio's despairing figures in the *Expulsion from the Garden of Eden* opposite to appreciate one of the early Renaissance's most dramatic statements. Florence's greatest artists, with Michelangelo at their head, came to sketch Masaccio's trail-blazing use of light and visual depth as instruments of emotional impact, particularly striking in the broad sweep of his *St Peter Paying the Tribute Money*. The chapel frescoes were completed in the 1480s by Filippino Lippi, who painted the side walls' lower panels.

*B*enedictine monks stroll past the beautiful Romanesque façade of San Miniato al Monte.

Drive up beautiful winding Viale dei Colli for a wonderful last panoramic view of the city dominated by the cupola of the Duomo from the vast **Piazzale Michelangelo** (with yet another copy of his *David*). While you're there, visit the charming Romanesque church of **San Miniato al Monte** up the hill behind the square. Antonio Rossellino's monumental 15th-century marble **tomb** of the Cardinal of Portugal, in a chapel off the left aisle, is notable for two beautiful genuflecting angels on the sarcophagus which greatly influenced Michelangelo.

Tuscany (*Toscana*)

The original territory of the ancient civilization of the Etruscans has always been independent-minded, even aloof, in its attitude to Rome and the other regions. For the serious Italophile, its beauty and riches deserve weeks, months, even years of attention, but no first visit would be complete without at least one week here.

After an indispensable side-trip from Florence to Fiesole, our itineraries go west to Pisa and Lucca before turning south through the hills to Siena.

Fiesole

Just 8km (5 miles) north-east of Florence (30 minutes on the No. 7 bus from the Duomo), the road winds up a wooded hillside, revealing at each bend ever-changing views of Fiesole's gardens and villas before you and the monuments of the great city below.

Stop on the way at **San Domenico di Fiesole** for its 15th-century church and two important works by Fra Angelico, a *Madonna and Saints* in the first chapel on the left and a *Crucifixion* in the monastery refectory. Just off to the west is the pretty church of **Badia Fiesolana**, originally the town's 10th-century Romanesque cathedral; it was redesigned by Brunelleschi in the 1450s.

Only some wall fragments remain of the former Etruscan stronghold in Fiesole itself, but there are extensive Roman ruins, including a well-preserved **amphitheatre**, still in use, which seats 2,500 spectators.

Car-drivers can negotiate the winding old side-road **Via Vecchia Fiesolana** for glimpses of handsome villas half-hidden among the cypresses and olive trees. The town centre, Piazza Mino da Fiesole, with its austere cathedral, is the starting-point for some exhilarating hill walks, the best being the steep lane leading west to the San Francesco monastery.

Pisa

The town, like the tipsy stubbornness of its Leaning Tower, is one of the world's blessed wonders. In its heyday from the 11th to the 13th century, it created a commercial empire down the Tyrrhenian coast and in Corsica, Sardinia, Sicily, Syria, Palestine and Egypt. Its riches built that gleaming white marble complex of religious edifices known as the *Campo dei Miracoli* (Field of Miracles), left unscathed by the invasions and wars of succeeding centuries.

Conquering a flat, ungrateful landscape with serene, other-worldly harmony, this assembly of buildings in **Piazza del Duomo** celebrates the whole cycle of life from baptistery, cathedral and bell tower to the monumental cemetery of the Campo Santo.

The **Duomo** was built from 1063 to 1118 to honour Pisa's victory over the Saracens in Sicily. With oriental and Byzantine decorative elements reflecting the Pisan Republic's overseas interests, its four-tiered arcaded façade over three porches is a masterpiece of grace and delicacy. Architect Buscheto did not hesitate to write in Latin (in the far left arch) "This marble church has no equal". Inside, there was no reason either for Giovanni Pisano to show false modesty about his superbly sculpted 14th-century **marble pulpit** (left aisle), with its dramatic reliefs depicting the *Life of Christ* and the *Last Judgement*.

The crazy tilt of Pisa's Leaning Tower becomes more pronounced each year—surely one day it must come crashing down?

Work started on the Duomo's campanile, the famous **Leaning Tower** (*Torre Pendente*), in 1173. However, thanks to the unstable subsoil, the structure had begun to list by the time the third storey was reached. The tilting has continued ever since, despite numerous attempts by architects and scientists to put things straight, and the tower is now some 5m (15ft) out of true. Climbing the 294-step spiral staircase to the top is rather like going up a helter-skelter; on the way up one almost expects to be given a mat with which to slide back down again. Sadly, the tower has been closed for structural reinforcement in recent years so you may not get a chance to go up and see the superb view over the Campo dei Miracoli and across the Arno river to the sea.

The lovely circular **baptistery** contains Pisa's greatest work of sculpture,

---

Darkness and Light

Pisa-born Galileo Galilei (1564–1642) switched from medical studies in Pisa to mathematics. At 19, during Mass in Pisa cathedral he timed the oscillation of a swinging lamp against his pulse beats to work out the theory that the timing of a pendulum remains the same however wide the swing. The story that he tested falling weights from the Leaning Tower is apocryphal.

By 1597, he was dabbling in a little Copernican astronomy. On the basis of a Dutch optician's invention, he was able to develop the first astronomical telescope in 1610 and at last observe the distinction between planets (revolving around the Sun) and stars (fixed), the Moon's similar configuration to Earth's, and Jupiter's four moons. He "converted" Jesuit astronomers in Rome to the idea that the Earth moves around the Sun, but in 1616 Copernicanism was condemned. Despite his attempts to convince the pope and cardinals with his telescope that Copernicanism was compatible with the Bible, Galileo was ordered to stop teaching it. After composing a *Dialogue* to show the scientific validity of Copernicanism while acquiescing in the pope's theological dogma, he was brought to trial in 1633. He was forced to abjure his theories, but tradition holds that he muttered under his breath "*Eppure si muove*". ("Nevertheless it does move".) He was sentenced to life imprisonment, which meant house arrest near Florence. The heavens' great observer ended his days in total blindness.

---

a hexagonal **marble pulpit** by Nicola Pisano, father of Giovanni who designed the cathedral pulpit. The 1260 carving of biblical themes has clear links to French Gothic sculpture, while drawing on models from Roman and Etruscan sarcophagi—witness a Herculean Daniel and a Mary inspired by heads of Juno and Phaedra.

The 13th-century cloistered cemetery of the **Campo Santo** (Holy Field), reputedly built on earth brought by Crusaders from the Holy Land, contains remarkable frescoes. Severely damaged by bombs in 1944, the works have undergone extensive restoration. Particularly noteworthy are the remnants of a Renaissance **fresco-cycle** by Benozzo Gozzoli and a haunting fresco of the *Triumph of Death* (1360) showing how commoner and aristocrat face the same destiny.

A short way from the Campo dei Miracoli, **Piazza dei Cavalieri** is a handsome Renaissance square laid out by Giorgio Vasari. Vasari also designed the tower of the church of Santo Stefano dei Cavalieri and created the striking façade to the Palazzo dei Cavalieri.

In a Benedictine monastery down by the Arno, the **San Matteo Museum** houses Pisan Romanesque and Gothic sculpture as well as a gentle Simone Martini *Madonna and Child* and Masaccio's *St Paul* (part of a polyptych split up between London, Naples, Berlin and Liechtenstein).

Back along the Arno, the **Ponte di Mezzo** is the venue for Pisa's *Gioco del Ponte*, a colourful historical pageant held each year on the last Sunday in June. After a 700-strong parade in 16th-century costume through the town, two teams of Pisans engage in a fierce "Push-of-War" across the bridge to the roars of thousands of partisan spectators.

Lucca

The sights of this town take scarcely a day, but the seductive tranquillity within its old ramparts is such that people end up staying for weeks. Peace of mind has always been a priority here. During the stormy 15th and 16th centuries, Lucca's prosperous silk merchants preserved the peace by intercepting enemy armies and paying them to bypass the town. It has been particularly rich in musicians, most notably Boccherini and Puccini, and hosts a series of music festivals throughout the summer.

Begin with a stroll around the nicely preserved 16th-century **ramparts**, along the tree-lined Passeggiata delle Mura, for a good overall view.

The fine 14th-century cathedral, **San Martino**, has a Pisan-style arcaded façade with a *Descent from the Cross* carved by Nicola Pisano over the north porch. Inside, to the right of the entrance, is a 12th-century equestrian sculpture of *St Martin and the Beggar*, with a distinctly ancient Roman flavour. In the left transept, see the graceful 15th-century **tomb** of Ilaria del Carretto by Sienese sculptor Jacopo della Quercia. The cathedral's most venerated work of art is the miracle-working wooden crucifix known as the **Volto Santo** (Holy Face). Legendarily carved with angelic assistance by Nicodemus from a cedar of Lebanon, the sacred effigy is housed in a specially built chapel half-way down the left aisle.

*T*he gleaming gold mosaic of Christ and the Apostles on the façade of San Frediano in Lucca.

North-west of the cathedral, you will find an even more beautiful adaptation of the Pisan Romanesque style in the church of **San Michele in Foro**, less encumbered on its site of the old Roman Forum. The arcaded façade varies the patterns of its columns: sculpted, striped, scrolled, chevroned ink, green, black or white marble. With a pair of binoculars, you can spot up on the third tier of arches (3rd from the right) the heads of *Risorgimento* heroes Garibaldi and Cavour, carved here during a 19th-century restoration.

To capture something of the town's medieval character, explore the tortuous maze of streets west of San Michele.

Make sure you raise your gaze from the elegant shopfronts of Via Fillungo to note the tall thin **Torre dell'Ore** (Tower of the Hours) with its ancient public clock. For a good view of the city and the Apuan Alps beyond, climb the curious tree-topped **Torre Guinigi**, one of several landmarks in the city left by Paolo Guinigi, who ruled Lucca from 1400 to 1430. Note the distinctive elliptical outline of the 2nd-century **Roman amphitheatre**, now the shop-lined Piazza del Mercato. Nearby, the façade of the church of **San Frediano** has a dazzling gold 13th-century mosaic of *Christ and the Apostles*. Inside the church, look for Jacopo della Quercia's marble altar (4th chapel on left aisle) and the mummified remains of St Zita, the patron saint of housemaids.

The countryside around Lucca is scattered with handsome villas, many of them set in large open parks. Most notable are the 16th-century **Villa Mansi** at Segromigno, embellished with an ornate baroque façade by Muzio Oddi in the following century, the equally ostentatious **Villa Torrigani** at Camigliano and the **Villa Reale di Marlia**, country retreat of Napoleon's sister Elisa Baciocchi, who ruled Lucca from 1805 to 1814.

Montecatini Terme

Italy's most elegant spa town is good for people who suffer from skin disorders, digestive ailments and respiratory diseases. It is also popular with filmmakers. Nikita Mikhalkov shot his period film *Oci Ciornie* (*Dark Eyes*) here and you will find many a white-suited Marcello Mastroianni lookalike strolling around the **Parco delle Terme** in search of a lonely dowager. Patients taking the waters can choose between the extravagant Grecian colonnade of the **Tettuccio** or the Art Nouveau **Excelsior**. Mudbathers head for the neoclassical **Terme Leopoldini**. The town's most venerable Belle Epoque monument, the **Grand Hotel e la Pace**, is home from home to dukes, begums and Agnellis. Its orchids are overpowering.

Pistoia

Fight your way through the charmless crowded modern suburbs towards the more spacious nobility of the city centre's **Piazza del Duomo**. Next to the formidable Gothic Palazzo del Comune, a massive campanile dominates the Pisan-Romanesque **cathedral** of San Zeno.

Andrea della Robbia's terracotta *Madonna and the Angels* adorns the portico. Inside, the cathedral's great treasure is in a chapel on the right aisle, the grandiose silver **Dossale di San Jacopo** (Altar of St James). Its 628 bas relief figures from the Bible were wrought by Tuscan craftsmen from the 13th to the 15th century. Brunelleschi, the architect of Florence's great cathedral dome, was one of those to lend a hand.

Across the square, the 14th-century octagonal Gothic **baptistery** in green and white marble was designed by Andrea Pisano.

North of the cathedral, on the 16th-century portico of the **Ospedale del Ceppo**, note the striking multi-coloured terracotta frieze by Giovanni della Robbia (Andrea's son), depicting the charitable works performed by this medieval hospital.

The city's most important work of art is to be found in the 12th-century church of **Sant'Andrea**: the magnificent marble **pulpit** completed in 1301 by Giovanni Pisano. The highly emotional sculpture becomes harrowingly realistic in the *Massacre of the Innocents*. A little light relief (at least for us) is provided by the comic grimace of the caryatid straining to hold up one of the pulpit's pillars on the nape of his neck.

Prato

Sited half-way between Florence and Pistoia, Prato has been prospering from the manufacture of textiles since the Middle Ages. In the 14th century it was home to the wealthy cloth merchant Francesco Marco Datini, the Merchant of Prato of Iris Origo's famous book. Today Prato produces more wool than any other city in the world.

Prato's other main claim to fame is as the home of a legendary relic: the Holy Girdle, traditionally given by the Virgin Mary to Doubting Thomas on her ascension to heaven. The Holy Girdle is housed in a chapel in Prato's cathedral, the **Duomo di Santo Stefano**. Five times a year, the relic is displayed from the **Pulpit of the Holy Girdle**, which projects from the right-hand side of the cathedral's green- and white-striped façade. The 15th-century pulpit was designed by Michelozzo and decorated with reliefs by Donatello (the originals of which are now in the cathedral museum, the Museo dell'Opera del Duomo). Inside the cathedral, look in the apse for Filippo Lippi's frescoes of the *Lives of St John and St Stephen*. More works by the great 15th-century painter can be found in the **Galleria Comunale**, along with several by his son, born in Prato, Filippino Lippi.

Chianti

The best introduction to the Tuscan hill country is a tour of the famous vineyards that grace its southern-oriented slopes. The grapes that qualify as *Chianti Classico*, distinguished by a coveted black rooster label, grow in the region between Florence and Siena, most of them along the N222 Via Chiantigiana. The liveliest, most colourful time is during the autumn grape harvest, *la vendemmia*, but tasting—and buying at the vineyard—goes on all year round.

Start out at **San Casciano** in Val di Pesa, 17km (11 miles) south of Florence, with a bonus for art-lovers of a Simone Martini *Crucifixion* in the church of La Misericordia. South-east across to the N222, you find the characteristic landscape of vineyards interspersed with equally renowned olive groves as you approach **Greve**, a major wine centre on the river of the same name. The town hosts an annual *Chianti Classico* wine fair in September. Local boy Giovanni da Verrazzano, the navigator-explorer of New York Bay, is remembered with a monument in Piazza del Mercatale.

The wine-route continues by way of the fortified hilltop village of **Castellina** with its 15th-century castle and ancient town gate. Then on to **Radda**, where you should peep in at the Piccolo Museo del Chianti, and **Gaiole in Chianti**, one of the best centres for tasting. **Certaldo**, to the west, is linked with Boccaccio, who lived here for the last 13 years of his life and is buried in the church of Santi Michele ed Iacopo.

San Gimignano

The haunting silhouette of this medieval Manhattan, a skyline bristling with rectangular towers, and its lovingly preserved historic centre make it the most magical of Tuscany's hill towns. At a distance, San Gimignano is particularly enchanting when seen from its northern side on the road from Certaldo.

San Gimignano's dizzyingly tall towers were erected as symbols of its medieval merchants' power and prestige.

During the Middle Ages San Gimignano was Florence's most advanced fortress in its wars against Siena. The town prospered and its leading citizens vied with one another by building ever more vertiginous towers. The rivalry continued until there were more than 70 of these symbols of power and prestige. When Siena fell under Florentine domination, San Gimignano lost its strategic importance and went into slow decline. Many of the towers crumbled and fell, or were torn down, and the town itself was frozen in time.

Today, little more than a dozen of the towers remain, their beautiful travertine stone displaying the faintest of pink blushes. The most important are clustered around triangular **Piazza della Cisterna**, named after the city's 13th-century travertine well, and **Piazza del Duomo**, the centre of civic and religious power in San Gimignano.

The 13th-century town hall, **Palazzo del Popolo**, houses the Museo Civico, packed with minor Tuscan masters. Of particular interest are an emotionally intense *Crucifixion* by Coppo di Marcovaldo and a set of paintings by Taddeo di Bartolo depicting the life of St Gimignano, in which you can see what the towers of the medieval city looked like.

The 12th-century Romanesque **Collegiata** was deprived of its cathedral status when the town lost its bishop. Nonetheless, the interior is well worth a visit. Look out for Barna da Siena's dramatic **frescoes** of New Testament scenes along the south aisle. This was the 14th-century master's last work: he fell off the scaffolding and died from his injuries. It's best not to linger long before Taddeo di Bartolo's *Last Judgement*, on the west wall, flanking the church entrance, in which the damned suffer hideous torments of a more than usually explicit nature. In much better taste are the nearby wooden statues of Mary and the Archangel Gabriel by Jacopo della Quercia.

Named after San Gimignano's rather insipid local saint, the **Santa Fina Chapel** is found at the end of the south aisle. When Santa Fina died at the age of fifteen in 1253 (after an uneventful invalid life), violets burst into bloom on her coffin and on the city towers. The beautiful Ghirlandaio **frescoes** here do more than just depict the legend—they are a series of sophisticated social portraits.

Climb up to the ruins of the 14th-century **Rocca** citadel for a fine view of the surrounding country with its olives, cypresses and the vineyards which produce the famous Vernaccia wine. This strong dry white wine was Michelangelo's favourite: it "kisses, licks, bites, thrusts and stings" was the artist's approving verdict.

Volterra

This fortified town perched high in the Tuscan hills can appear bleak and severe to visitors. Some find it strange that a town founded by the pleasure-loving Etruscans some 2,700 years ago should wear such a grim aspect. Put it down to weathered medieval stone and a gaunt location. Signs of the Etruscans abound, from the ancient city walls themselves to the three carved stone heads of Etruscan gods set into the 4th-century BC **Porta all'Arco**, the town's western entrance gate.

The Romans conquered Etruscan *Velathri* in the 3rd century BC and evidence of their presence in the town can be found in the vast **Parco Archeologico** just inside the walls. Volterra's medieval heart is Piazza dei Priori. Here stands the early 13th-century **Palazzo dei Priori**, the oldest of Tuscany's typical town halls, with a two-tiered tower, battlements and fine mullioned windows. Opposite is the massive triple-arched **Palazzo Pretorio**, Volterra's medieval police headquarters. The austere 12th-century cathedral is brightened inside by some fine works of art, including a lovely 15th-century fresco of the *Adoration of Magi* by Benozzo Gozzoli.

The octagonal **baptistery** dates from the 13th century; inside, the font has bas-reliefs sculpted by Andrea Sansovino.

The town's **art gallery** (*Pinacoteca*) is housed in Palazzo Minucci-Solaini in Via dei Sarti and boasts some fine works, including a 16th-century *Deposition* by Rosso Fiorentino. This painting, with its distorted poses and exaggerated foreshortening, is a striking example of early Mannerism.

Away from the centre, you can trace the town's ancient beginnings in the **Etruscan Guarnacci Museum** (Via Don Minzoni, 15). The collection includes sculpted stone, alabaster and terracotta funeral urns dating back to the 6th century BC. "Curiously alive and attractive" is how DH Lawrence found these "ash-chests of Volterra". One gaunt statue, *Ombra della Sera* (Shadow of the Evening), is an uncanny 2,000-year-old precursor of a modern Giacometti. The town's traditions of craftsmanship live on in the many small alabaster workshops, whose artisans turn out everything from tourist gewgaws to genuine works of art.

Siena

A city of rich russet browns and ochres, Siena is as delightfully feminine as grey-stone Florence is imposing in its masculinity. Contrasts with its old rival to the north are striking and inevitable. Whereas the nucleus of Florence was built to a strict Roman city plan of straight streets intersecting at right angles, Siena has all the Tuscan hill town's haphazard organic forms, straggling up and down a forked ridge of not one but three hilltops.

Similarly, while Florentine art developed its formidable intellectual and emotional power, the tone of Sienese painting—Simone Martini, the Lorenzettis, even the Mannerist Sodoma—remained gentle and delicate, bathed in the light and colour of its surrounding countryside. Not that the town lacks vigour. Even after the Florentine conquest of 1555, Siena showed an obstinately independent spirit. This character trait is epitomized today by its lusty summer Palio tournament.

Go easy on those steep streets, rest awhile in the cool courtyard of a great banker's palazzo and enjoy the spicy cuisine with a good local Chianti. Take time out between siestas to see some of Tuscany's most exhilarating monuments. Siena is good for tired blood.

Riding for the Palio

The Palio horse races held on 2 July and 16 August are part of a traditional pageant dating back to the 15th century and beyond. Colourful Renaissance-costumed pages and men-at-arms put on a procession and show of flag-throwing with emblems of the 17 parishes (*contrade*) of the city and surrounding communes such as eagles, snails, porcupines and geese. Ten of them compete in the climactic breakneck bareback horse race round the Campo for which a painted silk standard, the Palio, is the prize.

To get a taste of the intense rivalry that exists between the competing *contrade*, join the throng of supporters crammed into the centre of the piazza. If the crush of bodies seems too much to bear, try to obtain a seat in the stands (available from cafés and hotels near the Campo). But be warned, they are expensive and usually sell out well in advance.

Start at grand sloping fan-shaped **Piazza del Campo**, site of the old Roman forum and arena of the Palio horse race. The piazza's redbrick herring-bone paving is divided by nine marble strips for the nine patrician clans that ruled the city at the end of the 13th century.

Over a late-afternoon coffee on the shady side (next to the Tourist Office), you can appreciate the painterly impact of the "burnt sienna" glowing in the arcaded Gothic **Palazzo Pubblico** opposite, with its splendid 102m- (335ft-) high bell tower, the **Torre del Mangia**. The steep climb up the tower is well worth the effort for a superb view of the city and surrounding countryside. The loggia at the tower's base is a chapel (*Cappella di Piazza*) marking the city's deliverance from the plague of 1348.

The modern town hall offices are on the palazzo's ground floor, but its upstairs chambers, frescoed by the city's foremost artists, have been transformed into a **Museo Civico** (municipal museum). The **Sala del Mappamondo** takes its name from a map of the Sienese world painted here by Ambrogio Lorenzetti to trace the city's international banking interests. Sadly, only the outline of the fresco remains. Still very much visible are two great works by the 14th-century Sienese painter Simone Martini: a stately **Enthroned Madonna** (1315) and an **equestrian portrait** of *condottiere* Guidoriccio da Fogliano (c.1333). The mercenary captain is depicted riding to a historic victory at Montemassi. In the nicely detailed Tuscan landscape, notice the little Chianti vineyard in the military encampment.

The **Sala della Pace** (Hall of Peace) was the council chamber of the Nine Patricians who ruled medieval Siena. The full force of the town's civic pride strikes home in the Ambrogio Lorenzetti **frescoes** (1337–39), which cover three walls of the room. One wall is devoted to *Bad Government*, a gloomy portrait of Tyranny (badly damaged, the work is even more dismal than intended); the other two walls are given over to Siena's own enlightened *Good Government*. The work depicting the *Effects of Good Government* (on the entrance wall) is full of fascinating detail of medieval town life: roof-builders, shoe shop, school, outdoor tavern, ladies dancing in the street, while, beyond the walls, hunters ride out to the surrounding countryside.

*T*he colourful parade of flag-bearers and men-at-arms that winds through the streets of Siena before the Palio horse race is almost as spectacular as the contest itself.

Ascend the stairs to the second floor **Loggia** for another good view of the city. Here too are the battered remnants of Jacopo della Quercia's 15th-century carvings for the city fountain, the Fonte Gaia (of which a poor 19th-century replica stands in the piazza).

South-west of the Campo, the **Duomo**, built from the 12th to the 14th century, is for many the greatest of Italy's Gothic cathedrals. The majestic black- and white-striped façade, with its three intricately carved portals by Giovanni Pisano, presents that quintessential Italian preference for pictorial qualities over mere architecture. The gleaming colour is pure Siena. The interior continues the bands of black and white marble, while **inlaid marble paving** covers the floor with 56 pictures of biblical and allegorical

Siena's Saintly Diplomat
Catherine of Siena (1347–80) is revered in Italy as one of the most beloved and active saints in the Catholic canon. Caterina Benincasa, 24th child of a wealthy dyer, had her first religious visions at the age of six. Fourteen years later she joined the Dominican order and devoted her life to service in hospitals and leper colonies. Steeled by self-flagellation and exalted by recurrent visions of Jesus, Mary and the saints, she embarked on a widespread correspondence with the great spiritual leaders of her day. She received the stigmata of the Crucifixion in 1375, inspiring her to travel a year later to Avignon to persuade the exiled Pope Gregory XI to return to Rome. Thereafter she served as papal envoy to troublesome Florence. It was only at her death that the marks of her stigmata became visible to others than herself.

Statues of prophets, philosophers and patriarchs adorn the richly decorated, polychrome marble façade of Siena's Duomo, a masterpiece of Tuscan Gothic architecture.

themes created over two centuries by some 40 artists, most notably Beccafumi, di Bartolo and Pinturicchio. Off the left aisle is the early 16th-century **Cardinal Piccolomini Library** vividly decorated by Pinturicchio's action-packed frescoes of the life of Enea Silvio Piccolomini—poet, diplomat, scholar and ultimately pope—as Pius II. The frescoes were commissioned in 1495, some three decades after the pope's death, by his nephew, Cardinal Francesco Piccolomini. He himself became pope, Pius III, but lasted only ten days. In the left transept is a magnificent 13th-century octagonal **pulpit** carved by Nicola Pisano, with help

from son Giovanni and Arnolfo di Cambio. Among the fantastic detail of the New Testament scenes, notice the damned being eaten alive in the *Last Judgement*. The 17th-century baroque Madonna del Voto chapel (in the right transept) was designed by Bernini, whose statues of St Jerome and Mary Magdalen flank the entrance.

The Duomo's Gothic **baptistery** has its own share of art treasures, notably the 15th-century marble font by Jacopo della Quercia. Among the reliefs decorating the sides of the font, look for *Herod's Feast* by Donatello and the *Baptism of Christ* and *St John in Prison* by Lorenzo Ghiberti.

In the **cathedral museum** (*Museo dell'Opera Metropòlitana*), Giovanni Pisano's original sculptures of prophets and philosophers for the Duomo's façade have strangely distorted poses because they were meant to be seen from below. Look out, too, for Duccio di Buoninsegna's *Madonna and*

Child Enthroned, Simone Martini's *Miracles of St Agostino Novello* and Pietro Lorenzetti's *Birth of Mary*.

Take a leisurely hour or two for the lovely Sienese paintings in the Palazzo Buonsignori's **Pinacoteca Nazionale**. Besides the works of the 14th-century masters Duccio, Pietro and Ambrogio Lorenzetti and Simone Martini, the gallery has examples of Siena's 16th-century Mannerists. They were painting at a time when the Renaissance teetered on the brink of effete decadence: witness Beccafumi's dreamy *Birth of Mary* and a highly decorative *Christ at the Column* by Sodoma.

Arezzo

Venture east of the Florence–Rome *autostrada* for an artistic pilgrimage to the home of one of the great masterpieces of Italian art.

Beyond the modern suburbs in the town's charming medieval centre, the **San Francesco** basilica cherishes in its chancel the wonderful **Piero della Francesca frescoes** of the medieval *Legend of the Holy Cross*. Out of a tale tracing the wood of the Cross from Old Testament scenes of Sheba and Solomon to the vision that converted Roman Emperor Constantine to Christianity, this most serenely meditative of painters created, between the years 1453 and 1464, a magnetic, even surreal atmosphere. The fresco depicting Constantine's victory over his imperial rival Maxentius, a battle scene in which the Emperor's foes flee before the sign of the Cross, contains what art historian Kenneth Clark called "the most perfect morning light in all Renaissance painting".

The Death of Adam by Quattrocento master Piero della Francesca.

The town's main square, **Piazza Grande**, is host to a bustling antiques fair on the first Sunday of each month. For those who either missed Siena's Palio (*see* page 160) or liked it so much they would like more, it's the scene of a similar, but much less well known tournament on the first Sunday in September—the *Giostra del Saraceno*—the Saracen's Joust. In addition to acrobatics with the gaily coloured banners of Arezzo's historic quarters, horsemen in Renaissance costume ride full tilt at a pivoting statue which threatens to swing and bash them in the back if they're not nimble enough.

The most handsome of Arezzo's churches, the 12th-century **Santa Maria della Pieve** has an intricately colonnaded façade. With binoculars, you can spot one lonely human caryatid sculpted in the middle of the uppermost tier. Inside, the fine Pietro Lorenzetti polyptych has been recently restored.

Up the hill from Piazza Grande, Arezzo's Gothic **Duomo** contains excellent 16th-century stained-glass windows by the great French craftsman Guillaume de Marcillat, as well as a beautiful and strange fresco of *St Mary Magdalen* by Piero della Francesca. Not far from the cathedral, the 13th-century church of **San Domenico** is worth a visit for the Cimabue *Crucifixion* at the high altar.

Sansepolcro

This ancient walled town, 39km (25 miles) east of Arezzo, is famous as the birthplace of Piero della Francesca and contains some of the *Quattrocento* painter's greatest works. Piero's

masterpiece, the *Resurrection*, is housed in the **Museo Civico**. The fresco shows a solemn and impassive Christ rising from the tomb while the four Roman soldiers set to guard it sleep on soundly; on the left is a barren, wintry landscape, but, on Christ's right the trees are beginning to leaf—signs of Spring and of the miracle which has just taken place. Also in the museum is Piero's polyptych of the *Madonna della Misericordia*, painted for a local charitable confraternity.

When he was not away from home fulfilling important commissions, Piero took an active role in the affairs of his native town, serving both on the civic council and in the local militia. He was the registered owner of a crossbow and a watchman who patrolled the city walls at night. Today, Sansepolcro's central **Piazza Torre di Berta** plays host to the pageantry of the *Palio della Balestra*, a crossbow contest in ancient costume with the town's age-old rivals Gubbio.

Art-lovers on the Piero trail must pay a visit to the small town of **Monterchi**, 17km (11 miles) south of Sansepolcro. In the small cemetery chapel which stands on a hill outside the town is found Piero's *Madonna del Parto* (Madonna of Childbirth): the only depiction in Italian art of a heavily pregnant Madonna.

Cortona

On your way up the hill to this walled, largely medieval town of ancient Etruscan origins, stop off to visit the 15th-century Renaissance church of **Santa Maria delle Grazie al Calcinaio**, admirable for the subdued elegance of its interior. Cortona's streets are steep and narrow, but the splendid hillside views of the Chiana valley and Lake Trasimeno, especially in the early morning or at sunset along Via Santa Margherita, make the climb well worth while. **Piazza della Repubblica** is the historic heart of town. The Palazzo Pretorio there houses the **Museo dell'Accademia Etrusca**. Its collections include not only Etruscan bronzes but also notable small paintings by Pinturicchio and Luca Signorelli (who was born and died in Cortona). A separate room is devoted to the works of Cortona-born Gino Severini, a major figure in the modern Futurist movement.

Opposite the much remodelled cathedral, the **Museo Diocesano** has a remarkable collection of Tuscan artists: a Fra Angelico *Annunciation* and *Madonna and Saints*, a characteristically monumental *Descent from the Cross* by Signorelli, and works by Duccio and Pietro Lorenzetti.

Montepulciano

On the route to southern Umbria, this is one of Tuscany's most attractive hill towns, with an excellent local wine. The smooth red *Vino Nobile di Montepulciano* can be tasted in the inviting *cantine*, or wine cellars, scattered about the town's ancient streets. If you are here on the last Sunday in August, you will witness the *Bravio delle Botti*, a fiercely contested race in which teams of locals strive to push stout barrels up the steep main street, Via di Gracciano del Corso.

You can enjoy the town's noble Gothic and Renaissance palazzi all year round. On **Piazza Grande**, the town's highest part, note the 16th-century **Palazzo Contucci**, in front of which stands a graceful well, decorated with griffins and lions. On the other side of the square, the 14th-century **Palazzo Comunale** is a particularly imposing expression of civic dignity. In the austere little **cathedral**, see Taddeo di Bartolo's fine triptych of the *Assumption* on the high altar. Back down the hill, in Piazza Michelozzo, look for the jolly *commedia dell'arte* clown who tolls the hours on top of the **Torre del Pulcinello**.

Antonio da Sangallo, the architect of many of the town's Renaissance palazzi, built his masterpiece, the classically inspired church of the **Madonna di San Biagio**, south-west of town, at the end of an avenue of cypresses overlooking the Chiana valley.

Pienza

This imposing piece of Renaissance urban planning is now a pleasantly tranquil Tuscan backwater. Pope Pius II wanted to do something for his home town of Corsignano, where he was born Enea Silvio Piccolomini in 1405. He called on the Florentine architect Bernardo Rossellino to redesign the town, all in three years from 1459 to 1462. He then renamed it after himself: Pienza. Rossellino's **cathedral**, with the pope's coat of arms high on the façade, has a certain nobility, but is somewhat overpowered by the formidable **Palazzo Piccolomini**, the size of its master's ego. Its square colonnaded courtyard leads to a **hanging garden** with a loggia overlooking the Orcia valley. There is an intriguingly austere bite to the town not unlike its famous tangy *pecorino* cheese.

Monte Argentario

If you're taking the coast road to or from Rome, stop off at the fashionable seaside resorts on this pine-forested peninsula beside the town of Orbetello. The sandy beaches and yachting harbours of Port'Ercole and Porto Santo Stefano are favourite weekend destinations for Romans, but they are much quieter in the week. In 1610 **Port'Ercole** witnessed the tragic end of the great painter Caravaggio: on the run from the authorities after killing a man in a brawl on the streets of Rome, he died from fever in a local tavern. He is buried in the church of Sant'Erasmo. From **Porto Stefano**, on the northern side of the peninsula, take a boat excursion to the pretty island of **Giglio**. The locals are more welcoming of visitors today than in the days when the island was threatened by pirates like the notorious Barbarossa who swooped down on Giglio in 1534 and carried off most of the inhabitants as slaves.

Elba

Not big enough to hold Napoleon for long, the island just off the Tuscan headland of Piombino is the perfect size—27km (16 miles) long and 5km (3 miles) wide in the middle—for some lazy days on the beach, imperial grandeur be damned. Its rugged hills, limpid blue waters and a year-round mild, dry climate might have kept your run-of-the-mill retired emperor happy. However, the little Corsican didn't go in much for the kind of snorkelling, sailing, wind-surfing and fishing that Elba offers around the **Golfo Stella** resort hotels or over at the sheltered beach of **Fetovaia**. His loss.

*E*lba may have become a popular holiday destination in recent years but peace and tranquillity is never hard to find in out-of-the-way corners of the island.

Interlude on Elba

With the English, Prussian and Russian armies at the gates of Paris in 1814, Napoleon abdicated and was sent into exile. After ruling half of Europe, he was assigned tiny Elba as his sole remaining sovereign territory, almost back where he started, within sight of Corsica. He was allowed to keep the title of emperor and allotted an annual subsidy of 2 million francs. With his mother Letizia and sister Pauline came 400 soldiers of his Old Guard, joined by Polish lancers and island volunteers, an army of 1,600 in all. All found plenty to do, Napoleon the first among them, riding over his pocket kingdom on horseback, sailing round the coast on his only warship, the brig *Inconstant*. He set the soldiers to build roads and modernize the town sewers and dictated regulations for agriculture and mining.

But all this was make-work. Napoleon was itching. His fortune was dwindling. He feared assassination. Then news came of French dissatisfaction with the restored monarchy. On 26 February 1815, after barely nine months' exile, he sailed from Portoferraio with six small vessels, 1,000 men and a few guns. Next stop: Waterloo.

Start your tour in the island capital, **Portoferraio**. This "Iron Port" refers to cargo from the now depleted opencast iron mines that provided the high-grade ore with which the Etruscans and Romans forged their mighty swords. The town's promontory looks on one side out to the open sea and on the other along a beautifully curving bay backed by mountains.

Twin forts built by the Medicis guard the port. Between them stands the **Palazzina dei Mulini**, Napoleon Bonaparte's official residence, which had been converted from two windmills. The exiled French emperor's suite of rooms has been restored with period furniture and some of his books.

West of the sandy beaches on the **Bay of Biodola**, edged by shady trees with good camping grounds, is the popular resort of **Procchio** and the old fishing village of **Marciana Marina**, where magnolias, oleanders and palms fringe the shore. From here the road climbs through the chestnut woods to **Marciana** where a cable car will take you to the top of **Monte Capanne**, 1,019m (3,344ft), the highest point on the island. It was here that Napoleon observed: "One must admit, the island is very small."

Umbria

The region has a less spectacular reputation than Tuscany (and is blessedly less crowded), but it is highly appreciated both for its great artistic treasures and the dreamy rolling green landscapes that inspired them.

It was dominated in the past by the papacy, which conquered the Lombard dukes of Spoleto in the Middle Ages, Perugia in the 16th century and held sway until the unification of Italy. Apart from pilgrims streaming to St Francis's Assisi and university students heading for Perugia, it has remained a very happy backwater.

Orvieto

Half the pleasure of this lovely town high on its rocky precipice is a first glimpse of it from afar (not so very different today from Turner's 1828 painting in London's Tate Gallery). For a

*T*he striking façade of Orvieto's Duomo is one of the glories of Italian Gothic architecture. The cathedral was built for Pope Urban VI to commemorate a 13th-century miracle which took place in neighbouring Bolsena.

good view, approach it from the southwest, on the S71 from Lake Bolsena, or look across from the medieval abbey La Badia (now a hotel), immediately south of town.

Connoisseurs come for the great white wine, art-lovers for the magnificent Gothic **cathedral**. Try both at sunset and you'll die happy. Scores of architects worked on the church from the 13th to the 17th century, but its glory remains the gleaming gabled **façade**, with its four slender spired pilasters and rose-window above the beautifully scrolled porches. At the base of the two northern pilasters, look closely at Lorenzo Maitani's marvellous carved marble bas-reliefs of scenes from the Old Testament and the Last Judgement.

Grey and white bands of marble give the interior a spacious simplicity. Off the right transept, the **Chapel of the Madonna di San Brizio** contains an important Renaissance **fresco-cycle** on the theme of the Last Judgement. Begun by Fra Angelico with his pupil Benozzo Gozzoli in around 1447, the frescoes were completed over fifty years later by Luca Signorelli. Contrast the gentle style of Fra Angelico's *Christ in Glory* on the ceiling with the more muscular work of Signorelli on the walls. Note that Signorelli portrays himself and Fra Angelico as bystanders in the vivid *Preaching of the Antichrist* (identified here with Savonarola). The nude figures in the *Resurrection of the Dead* on the right

A Convenient Miracle

It's the 13th century: you're a medieval pope and you're having a hard time getting across the tricky doctrine of transubstantiation: the belief that the consecrated host becomes the body of Christ. Then, lo and behold, your prayers are answered: a miracle happens right on cue and the Church is presented with a useful propaganda tool.

A priest from Bohemia, on his way to Rome, has stopped off at the town of Bolsena, just south of Orvieto. The priest, whose name is Peter, is one of the sceptical fraternity, but his doubts are conquered when, during mass, the host drips blood onto the altar linen.

Peter the priest takes up the blood-stained cloth and hotfoots it to Orvieto, where Pope Urban VI is residing. The pope is no slouch. He immediately institutes the feast day of Corpus Christi (Thomas Aquinas is on hand to write the office) and orders the building of a magnificent cathedral at Orvieto to house the relic, which ever since has been carried through the streets of Orvieto in a solemn procession on the Sunday after Corpus Christi.

wall are less convincing (indeed, they were described by Leonardo da Vinci as "sacks of nuts").

The **cathedral museum** in the Palazzo Soliano includes other works by Signorelli, a Simone Martini polyptych and sculpture by Nino, Andrea and Giovanni Pisano.

If you want to cool off, explore the monumental **Pozzo di San Patrizio**, a 16th-century well dug 63m (206ft) down into the volcanic rock on the north-east edge of the precipice. Well lit by 72 windows, two spiral staircases of 248 steps take you right down to the water level.

Todi

The charm of this town is to wander around its narrow, winding streets, past a little medieval stone well and suddenly spy, perhaps perfectly framed by an ancient arch, a vista of the verdant Umbrian hills beyond. Sober but harmonious **Piazza del Popolo** is the centre of the town's medieval past, where the Romanesque-Gothic **cathedral** at one end faces the fortress-like **Palazzo dei Priori**. Between them, on the east side of the square, the imposing **Palazzo del Capitano** with its Gothic colonnade houses the municipal art museum containing Etruscan and Roman antiquities and a collection of Umbrian paintings, notably Lo Spagna's *Coronation of the Madonna*. The 13th- to 15th-century church of **San Fortunato** graces the top of a staircase on Piazza della Repubblica with a splendid Gothic portal. Inside, in the 4th chapel to the right is a particularly fine **fresco** of the *Madonna Between Two Angels* by Masolino da Panicale, companion artist to Masaccio for the celebrated frescoes in Florence's Brancacci Chapel.

Spoleto

The greatest tourist attractions of this medieval town are the summer music and theatre festivals, but its beautiful natural setting amid densely wooded hills also makes it a base for hikes into the surrounding countryside.

The Festival of Two Worlds, founded by the composer Gian Carlo Menotti in 1958, takes over Spoleto from mid-June to mid-July every year. Many of the town's ancient monuments and historic public spaces are pressed into service as venues, notably the 1st-century AD **Roman Theatre** and **Piazza del Duomo**, with its dramatic approach of steps, Via del Arringo.

Spoleto's medieval atmosphere is perhaps best soaked up when this great arts jamboree isn't taking place. Not that you can ever entirely forget its presence: witness the giant iron sculpture by Alexander Calder outside the railway station, left behind after the 1962 festival.

Santa Maria Assunta, the town's cathedral, was consecrated in 1198, some 40 years after the previous Duomo was sacked by the Holy Roman Emperor Frederick Barbarossa; part of the tussles between papal and imperial forces that dominated much of the town's medieval history. The sober Romanesque façade is alleviated by a graceful Renaissance loggia. Inside, the apse is decorated with Fra Filippo Lippi's luminous **frescoes** of the *Life of the Virgin*. These were the licentious painter-monk's last works: he died in Spoleto in 1469. Lippi's tomb, designed by his son Filippino, is in the left transept.

Spoleto's most spectacular sight is the **Ponte delle Torri**, the Bridge of the Towers. Built in the 14th century over a Roman acqueduct, the bridge spans the deep gorge of the River Tessino and links the town with the green hills of Monteluco.

Montefalco

The region's beautiful mountain greenery deserves a privileged vantage point, and this little fortified hilltop town provides what it proudly claims is the "Balcony of Umbria". Indeed, that's the name of the street, **Via**

Umbria is known as Italy's green heart. Its beautiful landscapes of gently rolling hills and tranquil valleys have provided inspiration for some of Italy's greatest saints and painters.

Ringhiera Umbra, providing a matchless view across the bewitching landscape of the Topino valley on one side and Clitunno on the other. In the church of **San Francesco**, now converted into a museum, you can see fine **frescoes** by Tuscan and Umbrian artists. In the left aisle, the 15th-century Umbrian master Perugino has left an *Annunciation* and *Nativity*, while in the apse is a vivid fresco-cycle by the Florentine Benozzo Gozzoli depicting the *Life of St Francis*.

Assisi

The enduring popular appeal of St Francis (1182–1226) has turned his native town into Italy's major pilgrimage destination, second only to Rome. Its basilica, like the peaceful medieval town-centre, is beautifully preserved, and the centuries-old pilgrim trade manages to avoid most of the crass commercialism that blights other religious shrines.

Park as close as you can to the lower square (Piazza Inferiore) at the west end of town. The basilica of **San Francesco** is in fact two churches, one above the other, built on top of the saint's tomb in the crypt.

The **Lower Church** was begun in 1228, two years after Francis's death, and the frescoes were painted in the 14th century, but a Renaissance porch now precedes the Gothic side-entrance. The subdued light of the low vaulted nave evokes the sober piety of the Franciscan tradition. Simone Martini has decorated the **St Martin Chapel** (first left) with exquisite **frescoes** on the saint's life: note the most aristocratic Jesus appearing in St Martin's dream. Stairs in the nave lead down to the

---

Spoiled Son to Gentle Saint

Francesco di Bernardone was the spoiled son of a rich family well-known for his rumbustious ways. A sojourn in a Perugia jail at 23, followed by a severe illness, sobered him up. After a vision in the Chapel of San Damiano, he vowed a life of poverty in the service of the Church. He nursed lepers and converted bandits. He travelled to Spain, Morocco, Egypt and Palestine, but it was his impact on a troubled Italian population that mattered most to a Church beleaguered by heresy. Thousands responded to the simple eloquence of his preaching. They told how the example of his gentle life had tamed wild wolves and taught swallows to sing a sweeter song. In his religious ecstasy on Monte La Verna (near Arezzo), he was marked with Christ's stigmata: a phenomenon the most sceptical scholars have never placed in doubt. He was canonized St Francis just two years after his death in 1226.

---

crypt and St Francis's **tomb**, rediscovered only in 1818, centuries after it had been concealed from Perugian plunderers.

The superb frescoes of the life of Jesus in the **Mary Magdalen Chapel** (third right) and of St Francis's vows of poverty, chastity and obedience above the elegant Gothic high altar are attributed to Giotto or his pupils.

In the right transept, the famous Cimabue **portrait of St Francis**, believed to be a close physical resemblance, stands to the right of the enthroned Madonna. Over in the left transept, see Pietro Lorenzetti's noble *Descent from the Cross*.

In the **Upper Church**, Cimabue's works in the apse and transepts have turned black, and now look like photo negatives because of the oxydized white lead in his paints, yet you can still feel the intensity of the crowd's anguish in his *Crucifixion*.

In the brilliantly illuminated nave, the faithful are exalted by one of the most grandiose series of **frescoes** in Christendom. The *Life of Francis* is celebrated in 28 scenes along the lower tier (starting from the right transept), while 32 frescoes in the upper tier illustrate scenes from the Old and New Testaments. Giotto's most fervent supporters say he designed the St Francis series and himself painted numbers 2 to 11.

Penetrate the historic heart of Assisi along **Via San Francesco**, with its 15th-century Pilgrims' Hostel (*Oratorio dei Pellegrini*) at number 11. Its frescoes are attributed to Perugino. Noble **Piazza del Comune** is the town centre, grouping medieval palazzi around the old Roman forum. A triumph of Christianity over paganism, the Corinthian-columned church of **Santa Maria sopra Minerva** was a Roman temple under Augustus.

Saint Clare, follower of St Francis and the founder of her own spiritual order, the Poor Clares, is buried in the pretty Gothic basilica of **Santa Chiara**. Her mummified body is contained in the crypt. The **Chapel of the Crucifix** (off the right nave) contains the cross which traditionally spoke to St Francis, instructing him to "rebuild my church".

The little monastery of **San Damiano**, where Francis heard the good word, is 2½km (1½ miles) south of town. In its simple austerity, the church still maintains the purest Franciscan tradition.

Far grander is the baroque church of **Santa Maria degli Angeli**, built over the tiny chapel called the *Porziuncola* used by St Francis and his followers. The cell where the saint died is now the **Cappella del Transito**, an important shrine. The church stands on the plain below Assisi, near the railway station. On the wooded slopes of Monte Subasio, 4km (2½ miles) east of Assisi, lies the **Hermitage of the Carceri**, St Francis's forest retreat.

Perugia

Dominating the Umbrian countryside from its 494m (1,600ft) hill, the town is emphatically more secular and more profane than its Franciscan neighbour. The imposing weight of its past is lightened by the lively cosmopolitan studentry of its two (Italian and international) universities. Constantly at war with Assisi in the Middle Ages, Perugia's belligerence is symbolized on the north side of town by the lovingly preserved **Arco Etrusco** (Etruscan, and partly Roman, triumphal arch) that remained part of the medieval ramparts.

In the town centre, something of the old aggressive civic power is evoked in the formidable **Palazzo dei Priori**, the medieval headquarters of the ruling magistrates, which towers over Piazza 4 Novembre. A note of beauty is provided here by the 13th-century **Fontana Maggiore** (Great Fountain) with its intricately carved reliefs by Nicola and Giovanni Pisano.

The Perugians never finished the façade of the square's Gothic cathedral, the **Duomo of San Lorenzo**. Inside, a chapel in the left aisle contains the town's most treasured relic, the

*T*he Fontana Maggiore
makes a splendid centrepiece for
Perugia's Piazza IV Novembre.
Sculptors Nicola and Giovanni
Pisano supplied the artistry; the
technical know-how came from a
Perugian friar named Bevignate
and a hydraulics expert from
Venice called Boninsegna.

supposed wedding ring of the Virgin
Mary. The onyx ring is securely
housed in a casket with 15 locks and
only displayed to the faithful on one
day of the year.

Perugia's busy pedestrian main
street, **Corso Vannucci**, is named after
the town's most famous native, Pietro
Vannucci, who was better known to us
as Perugino. The painter's works are
given pride of place in the **Galleria
Nazionale dell'Umbria**, which occupies
the third floor of the Palazzo dei Priori (the entrance is on the Corso).
Look out for Perugino's *Adoration of
the Magi* and a *Madonna della Consolazione* as sweet and serene as the
Umbrian landscape of which you'll
catch a glimpse through the museum
windows. The gallery's splendid collection of Umbrian and Tuscan painting also includes a Fra Angelico *Triptych* and Piero della Francesca's
polyptych of the *Madonna and Saints*,
which has a curious *Annunciation* on
top that was much admired by Vasari.
Pinturicchio, the master of narrative
frescoes, is represented here by his
Miracles of the Saints.

Next door to the gallery is the **Collegio del Cambio**, 15th-century hall and
chapel of the bankers' guild. The
vestibule is decorated with 17th-
century baroque walnut-panelling. In
the **Audience Hall** (*Sala dell'Udienza*)
is a delightful series of Perugino frescoes. The left wall is allegorical, devoted to the bankers' widely acknowledged virtues of *Prudence*, *Justice*,
Fortitude and *Temperance*; while religious themes invoke their piety on the
other walls. (*Fortitude* and one of the
Sibyls are attributed to Perugino's 17-
year-old pupil, Raphael.)

If you want to get a real feeling of
the old medieval town, dodge the
chickens scampering across the brick
paving of tiny tunnel-vaulted **Via Volte
della Pace**, which incongruously links

the modern shopping street of Via Alesse to a parking-lot behind the cathedral.

At the south end of Corso Vannucci beyond Piazza Italia, the **Carducci Gardens** provide a restful view of the Umbrian countryside.

Gubbio

Perched on the side of Mount Ingino, some 40km (25 miles) north of Perugia, this venerable fortress-town is not easy to get to and once you're there, it's hard on those who don't like climbing steep cobbled streets. But for anyone who cherishes the tranquillity of a totally unspoiled medieval atmosphere, Gubbio is a delight. **Piazza della Signoria**, paved in brick and stone, is a fine vantage-point for viewing the rest of the city. Its 14th-century battlemented **Palazzo dei Consoli** is one of the grandest civic edifices in all Italy and from the tall arcade that anchors it to the hillside, you have a magnificent panorama of the surrounding country. Climb still higher to the 13th-century cathedral and the Renaissance courtyard of the Palazzo Ducale.

The **Abbey of San Ubaldo** is even further up the slopes of Mount Ingino. It's the destination of the town's annual Candle Race (*Corsa dei Ceri*), a colourful pageant that attracts thousands of spectators. On 15 May three giant wooden candles, topped with statues of saints Ubaldo, Giorgio and Antonio Abate are hauled up the mountain by competing teams in medieval dress. The race is held in honour of St Ubaldo, who saved the town from destruction by beseiging forces under the Holy Roman Emperor Frederick Barbarossa in 1151.

The Marches (*Marche*)

Papal territory until 1860, the region begins just south of San Marino and stretches down between the Apennines and the Adriatic coast to the Tronto river. On the coast, Ancona, the capital, and Pesaro are important commercial ports, but surrounded by pleasant seaside resorts. The interior is heavily dependent on agriculture, but also offers an attractive countryside of rolling hills.

Urbino

The true queen of eastern Italy's hill towns, Urbino has been marked by the tough but enlightened rule of the great Montefeltro family from the 12th to the 16th century. Duke Federico da Montefeltro (1442–82) made his court one of the great humanist centres of Europe. Local artists such as Raphael and architect Bramante achieved international fame, while great talent was attracted from outside. Piero della Francesca played an important role in the Duke's court in the 1450s and 1460s, and Dalmatian architect Luciano Laurana designed most of the ducal palace.

Natural enough, then, that during World War II, Urbino should serve as a repository of art from all over Italy, the old fortifications holding firm throughout the German occupation.

Behind those ramparts, the mighty **Palazzo Ducale** towers over the city and the surrounding hills. This masterpiece of Renaissance architecture was built around two old Gothic palaces. The façade combines redbrick and cream-coloured Dalmatian limestone. The arcaded inner courtyard

*B*ehind its fortress walls, Urbino looks today much as it did during its 15th-century heyday, when Duke Federico da Montefeltro made the city a centre of learning renowned across Europe.

achieves a triumph of Renaissance harmony. Within its walls, the **Galleria Nazionale delle Marche** comprises one of the nation's great collections: among its highlights, the *Flagellation* and *Madonna of Senigallia* by Piero della Francesca, a *Madonna* by Andrea Verrocchio, *Profanation of the Host* by Paolo Uccello, Raphael's intriguing study of a woman known as *The Mute*, and a striking portrait by the Spaniard Pedro Berruguete of Duke Federico himself in full armour reading a book.

The Duke's study or **Studiolo** is decorated beneath its blue and gold coffered ceiling with beautiful *intarsia* (inlaid wood pictorial panels), some designed by Botticelli.

Near the palace, Urbino's **Duomo** is a medieval church that was completely remodelled in the neoclassical style at the end of the 18th century by Giuseppe Valadier. The **diocesan museum** (*Museo Diocesano Albani*) contains a small collection of art connected with the cathedral.

Up steep Via Raffaello on the left is **Raphael's house**, where the great painter lived as a boy. Now preserved as a museum, the house contains a small fresco of the *Madonna* which some attribute to the young Raphael. Others ascribe the fresco to his father, Giovanni Santi, and suggest that Raphael was the model for the infant Jesus.

Raphael: The Reckless Lover

Born Raffaello Sanzio in Urbino in 1483, the painter we know today as Raphael was by far the youngest of the three great creators of the High Renaissance. Yet such was his prodigious talent that while he was still in his twenties he was acknowledged to be the equal of Leonardo da Vinci (born 1452) and Michelangelo (born 1475). In such high esteem was he held that he lived, according to contemporaries, more like a prince than a painter, winning by his art and charm the friendship of cardinals and popes.

In his lifetime Raphael also won renown as a lover. He was always in pursuit of his carnal pleasures, noted his early biographer, Vasari, who soberly recorded that the painter "took great delight in women," and was "ever ready to serve them."

Never one to let work get in the way of his love life, Raphael nearly didn't complete the frescoes which adorn the Villa Farnesina in Rome because of his burning passion for the woman known to posterity as La Fornarina: the baker's daughter. Raphael fell so behind with the work that his patron, the wealthy banker Agostino Chigi, had to resort to extreme measures to get the frescoes finished. One report says that Chigi went so far as to kidnap the painter's mistress. At any rate she was soon installed in the part of the house where Raphael was working and the painting was finished—to Chigi's great relief.

For many years, another of Raphael's eminent patrons, Cardinal Bernardo Dovizi da Bibbiena, urged the painter to marry. Raphael managed to put the cardinal off, saying that he wanted to wait for three or four years. When this period had elapsed the cardinal pressed him to keep his promise. Raphael agreed to marry the cardinal's niece, Maria, but still managed to avoid naming the day—rumour had it that the painter was reluctant to marry because Pope Leo X was dangling before him the prospect of a cardinal's red hat.

Raphael, meanwhile, kept up his secret love affairs and "pursued his pleasures with no sense of moderation," in the words of Vasari. Then, in one amorous encounter, the painter over-exerted himself and returned home in a violent fever. His physicians, not realizing the true cause of his indisposition, rashly bled him. Raphael's condition worsened and he died, aged only 37: killed by over-indulgence in the pleasures of the flesh.

Pesaro

This modern, largely industrial city has an attractive seaside area and a handsome core of Renaissance buildings around **Piazza del Popolo**, still the city centre. The Sforzas of Milan built the grand Palazzo Ducale in the 15th century.

Besides a fine collection of the Bologna school, the Venetian paintings of the **Pinacoteca** (Piazza Toschi Mosca) include a major *Coronation of the Madonna* by Giovanni Bellini. The **ceramics museum** housed in the same building boasts one of the country's best collections of Renaissance and baroque majolica.

Pesaro celebrates its most famous native son, Gioacchino Rossini, with its annual Rossini Opera Festival, held in August and September at the Teatro Rossini. You can visit the composer's birthplace near the cathedral in Via Rossini.

Ancona

Earthquake, war and industrialization have wreaked havoc with this ancient port-city's proud past, but the powerful cathedral of **San Ciriaco** on top of Mount Guasco is worth a visit. Built on the site of a temple of Venus, it incorporates Byzantine, Romanesque and Gothic styles. Its distinctive 12-sided cupola is particularly impressive on the interior. From the cathedral terrace, you overlook the bustling port with its well-preserved **Arch of Trajan**, erected in AD 115 to honour the Roman emperor who "modernized" the harbour.

South of Ancona, the **Riviera del Conero** extends along the rocky coast, a series of inlets, grottoes and pretty little beaches. The sea, ranging in colour from dark green to violet, is one of the best places in the Adriatic for underwater fishing.

Loreto

Pilgrims from all over the world are drawn to this celebrated sanctuary, the site to which angels legendarily transported the house where the Virgin Mary was born. The house was divinely transplanted here in 1294, so the story goes, after first travelling from Nazareth to Istria to escape the Muslim occupation of the Holy Land.

Built to house the shrine, the **Santuario della Santa Casa** is a fortified basilica of vast proportions appropriate to the thousands of worshippers it receives each year. (The most important pilgrimage dates in the calendar are the Annunciation, 25 March; Assumption, 15 August; Mary's Nativity, 8 September; and the Journey of the Santa Casa, 10 December.)

Started in Gothic style in 1468, the church was enlarged and embellished over the next three centuries by many of Italy's leading Renaissance and baroque architects, including Benedetto and Giuliano da Maiano, Sangallo and Sansovino. The great Bramante added the **side chapels** in 1511, Vanvitelli the lofty domed **campanile** in 1750. In the somewhat sombre interior, the **Santa Casa** itself stands under the dome. Its plain brick walls are faced with elegant marble to the design of Bramante and decorated with bas-reliefs and statues by Romano, Sangallo and Sansovino, recounting the life of Mary and the story of the house's miraculous transfer. **St John's Sacristy** in the right transept has some superb frescoes by Luca Signorelli.

Outside the church, Piazza della Madonna is adorned with a 17th-century **fountain** by Carlo Maderno. The nearby **Palazzo Apostolico** was designed by Bramante and contains a small art gallery (*pinacoteca*) exhibiting late works, most notably the *Presentation in the Temple*, of the unique and disturbing Venetian artist Lorenzo Lotto (1480–1556), who served the Santa Casa as oblate (lay attendant) in the last years of his life.

Among the other figures associated with the sanctuary is the English poet and Roman Catholic convert Richard Crashaw, who was a canon at Loreto and died here in 1649 (the result of poisoning, it was rumoured back in England). Galileo and Descartes both visited the shrine, as did the 13-year-old Mozart. He is said to have played the organ in the basilica improvizing preludes and fugues. In 1920, Pope Benedict XV proclaimed the Madonna of Loreto the patroness of aviation, which is why American astronaut Edward McDivitt carried the Madonna's medallion on his flight to the moon.

The Queen of the Adriatic and her Princely Hinterland

Venice, Queen of the Adriatic, still sits enthroned on her hundred isles. Her empire may have vanished, but its glories live on in the sumptuous art and architecture of her palaces and churches. Meanwhile, the cities of the hinterland, once dominated by Venice, have come into their own and are now leading lights of Italy's "economic miracle". Examples of Nature's bounty are provided by the mountains of the Dolomites and the beaches of the Adriatic.

The origins of "La Serenissima" were hardly serene. The city was founded on the islands of the lagoon in the 5th century by refugees from the mainland fleeing the barbarian hordes of Attila the Hun. Yet on these watery foundations Venice rose to become a great maritime empire, her trading might extending beyond the Adriatic to the Aegean and eastern Mediterranean.

*"T*he dear little gondola rests, soothes and consoles the mind, the limbs and the whole body," discovered Tuscan writer Pietro Aretino in the 16th century. Happily it still does.*

"Once did she hold the gorgeous East in fee," wrote Wordsworth, and it was true. The wealth of the Orient poured into the city; Byzantine artists crafted brilliant mosaics in her churches and wealthy merchants built glorious palaces on the banks of the Grand Canal on the proceeds of their mercantile adventures overseas.

Venice won a land empire, too. By bankrolling large mercenary armies she was able to dominate much of northern Italy and ensure her trade routes overland to the west.

Napoleon extinguished the proud Venetian republic in 1797, saying, as he snuffed out the city's liberty, "I shall be an Attila to the state of Venice." But the afterglow of Venice's empire is undimmed. Elegant Palladian villas

179

grace its Veneto mainland from Padua to Vicenza. The glories of Verona extend from its grand Roman arena to the palaces of the medieval and Renaissance princes whose intrigues inspired Shakespeare. In Emilia-Romagna, the pride and creativity of the great city-states is still very much in evidence in the monuments and museums of Bologna, Ferrara and Parma. Stretch your muscles in the Dolomites, with its first-class winter sports and summer hiking, or soak up sun and sea in the Adriatic resorts around Rimini.

Venice (*Venezia*)

These palaces, canals and lagoons claim a place apart in our collective imagination. As our 20th century ends, Venice remains a dreamworld, its myth more powerful than harsh reality. Even

*N*orth-east Italy (below).

*C*ity plan of Venice (opposite).

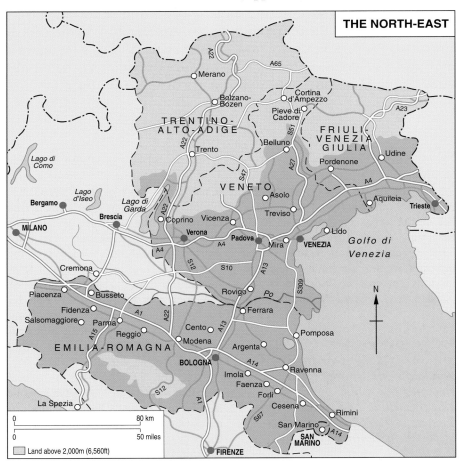

180

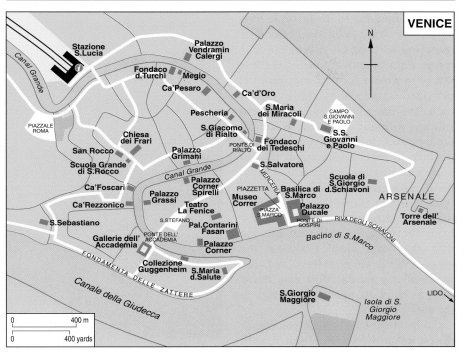

VENICE

N

Canal Grande

Stazione
S.Lucia

Palazzo
Vendramin
Calergi

Fondaco
d.Turchi   Megio

Ca'Pesaro

Ca'd'Oro

PIAZZALE
ROMA

Pescheria

S.Maria
dei Miracoli

CAMPO
S.GIOVANNI
E PAOLO

Chiesa
dei Frari

S.Giacomo
di Rialto

S.S.
Giovanni
e Paolo

San Rocco

Palazzo
Grimani

PONTE DI
RIALTO

Fondaco
dei Tedeschi

Scuola Grande
di S.Rocco

Canal Grande

S.Salvatore

Ca'Foscari

Palazzo
Corner
Spirelli

Palazzo
Grassi

PIAZZETTA

Museo
Correr

MERCERIA

Basilica di
S.Marco

Scuola di
S.Giorgio
d.Schiavoni

ARSENALE

Ca'Rezzonico

Teatro
La Fenice

PIAZZA
S.MARCO

Palazzo
Ducale

S.Sebastiano

S.STEFANO

Pal.Contarini
Fasan

PONTE DI
SOSPIRI

RIVA DEGLI SCHIAVONI

Torre dell'
Arsenale

Gallerie dell'
Accademia

PONTE DELL'
ACCADEMIA

Palazzo
Corner

Bacino di S.Marco

FONDAMENTA DELLE ZATTERE

Collezione
Guggenheim

S.Maria
d.Salute

Canale della Giudecca

S.Giorgio
Maggiore

Isola di S.
Giorgio
Maggiore

LIDO

0   400 m
0   400 yards

Grand Canal: Left Bank

The superb Renaissance Palazzo Vendramin-Calergi, where Richard Wagner died in 1883, is today the winter casino. The gilt has gone from the façade of the 15th-century Ca' d'Oro (Golden House), but it's still the town's most beautiful Gothic palace. Italy's most impressive post office, Fondaco dei Tedeschi, was once the trading-centre of Czechs, Hungarians and Austrians as well as the Germans of its name. Just beyond, the shop-lined Rialto Bridge arches over the canal at its narrowest point. The 18th-century Palazzo Grassi was recently restored for modern art exhibitions. The prefecture puts its bureaucrats in the fine Renaissance Palazzo Corner (or Ca' Grande), while gondoliers claim Othello's Desdemona lived in the lovely late-Gothic Palazzo Contarini-Fasan.

Grand Canal: Right Bank

The 700-year-old Fondaco dei Turchi was a warehouse in the 17th century for the merchants of Constantinople, now the Natural History Museum. It stands next to the plain brick 15th-century Megio wheat granary, decorated by the city seal of St Mark's lion. The imposing 17th-century baroque Ca' Pesaro houses the Modern Art Museum. Come back early in the morning to the Pescheria (fish market), 20th-century neo-Gothic, but nicely done. The university has a department in the handsome 15th-century Gothic Ca' Foscari. The Ca' Rezzonico is itself a fine specimen of the 18th-century Venetian art for which it is now a museum. Beyond the wooden Accademia Bridge, the perspective is completed by the magnificent baroque church of Santa Maria della Salute.

when it threatens to disintegrate into nightmare at times of winter flood or overcrowded summer, visitors can take refuge on a boardwalk across the waters or in a quiet corner away from the mob, and continue their dream. One of the city's many blessings is that there still are so many quiet and beautiful corners. Another, so obvious, but impossible to over-emphasize, is the *absence of cars*—the simple joy of wandering around a town relieved of our built-in urban traffic-stress, of standing on a little humpback bridge far from the Grand Canal and hearing only the water lapping against the moss-covered walls or the occasional swish of a gondola. You may never want to break the spell and go back to the real world.

Go in May or October if you can as the crowds at Easter and from June to September can be truly horrendous. Venice at Christmas has become fashionable and the February Carnival is very commercial. Whenever you go, don't try to do Venice in a day. Without the time to explore those hidden corners, you risk hating it for the rest of your life. Give yourself a minimum of three days, time to get lost: ultimately, but perhaps regretfully, you'll get back to the main landmarks signposted with bright yellow arrows. The town has more than enough sights to see, but you can taste many of its pleasures before you even set foot inside the museums, churches and monuments. The only "must" is Venice itself, your own Venice.

Grand Canal

From the railway station or the car park of Piazzale Roma, you begin with a *vaporetto* water bus along the Canal Grande, the most stunning main street in the world. Use this wonderful first contact with the city as your introductory tour. Vaporetto No. 1 takes you to the historic centre of town, Piazza San Marco, but beware of the faster No. 2; it takes a short-cut across a loop in the inverted S-shaped canal, missing out three-quarters of the sights.

If you arrive by air, airport motor launches cross directly to San Marco from the Lido. Just drop your bags off at the hotel and take the Grand Canal in the opposite direction, round-trip. (Save your gondola ride for when you have settled in.)

The Grand Canal winds for more than 2 miles through the city, varying in width from 30–70m (100–230ft) and lined with the old trading offices and

warehouses of its commercial heyday. Known locally as *ca'* (short for *casa*) as well as *palazzo*, the marble, brick and white limestone palaces range over 600 years from Venetian-Byzantine to baroque and neoclassical, but most of them are 14th- and 15th-century Flamboyant Gothic, Venice's trademark in architectural styles. Their sea-resistant limestone foundations stand on massive pinewood stilts driven 8m (26ft) into the lagoon bed.

Around San Marco

Building-space on the water being what it is, Venice has only one real piazza, but in comparison, any other would have died of shame anyway. Gloriously open to skies and sea, **Piazza San Marco**—to locals, just "the Piazza"—embodies the whole Venetian adventure. Its airy arcades reach out to

There can be few city prospects anywhere on earth as romantic as the view across the Bacino di San Marco at dusk.

the 900-year-old basilica and turn a corner past the soaring campanile to the piazzetta and landing stage of St Mark's basin (*bacino*), gateway to the Adriatic. The odysseys of victorious commanders began and ended here.

Here, too, the republic fell in 1797, at the hands of Napoleon. While he was removing the four bronze horses from the basilica along with other art treasures to ship back to Paris, he was said to remark that the Piazza San Marco was "the finest drawing-room in Europe". He closed off the piazza's west end with an Ala Napoleonica

(Napoleonic Wing), through which you enter the **Museo Correr**. If not in a nutshell then at least under one roof around two sides of the piazza, the museum tells the story of Venice past and present in vividly visual form. Exhibits include the crimson robes of the doges, rare old maps of the city along with Jacopo de Barbari's fascinating wood engraving of Venice in 1500 (near the entrance), election documents and portraits of the doges, coins minted over the centuries, a library of ancient tomes and manuscripts, spears and armour both Venetian and oriental, naval cannon and models of the galleys that scouted the empire.

The upper level's art gallery includes a Lotto portrait, a *Crucifixion* by Giovanni Bellini, *The Courtesans* by Carpaccio and northern European works by Cranach, Van der Goes and Dieric Bouts. One of the Correr's most intriguing features is a series of large colour photographs of the city's major attractions side by side with paintings by the masters depicting the same scenes of past centuries. It is astonishing how little Venice has changed.

The north and south arms of the square, the 16th-century **Procuratie Vecchie** and **Procuratie Nuove**, were the residences of the republic's most senior officials. They are now lined with fashionable boutiques, jewellery shops and, most important for breakfast *cappuccino* and afternoon tea, two elegant 18th-century cafés. During the Austrian occupation, the enemy frequented Quadri on the north side, while Italian patriots met only at Florian, opposite. To this day, the latter has the favour of Venetians, but also of foreigners who want to avoid foreigners, which complicates things for Venetians. Out in the square, orchestras play Palm Court music. The pigeons chase seed-vendors chasing tourists chasing their children chasing pigeons. This is no drawing-room, Bonaparte, it's another great piece of Italian theatre.

The glittering façade of the **Basilica di San Marco** forms an exotic backdrop, illuminating Venice's role at the crossroads of eastern and western culture. What began in around 830 as a chapel to house the remains of the evangelist Mark, the city's patron saint, was rebuilt in the 11th century as a grandiose Byzantine-oriental basilica. Greek mosaicists were brought in to decorate the arches and domes. Five Romanesque portals correspond to the five Islamic-style domes covering the church's Greek cross ground-plan. Spired Gothic tabernacles enhance the teeming richness.

The mosaics which adorn the basilica's façade are mostly 17th–19th-century reconstructions; the **San Alipio**

Going, Going Gondola

The proud fleet of 10,000 gondolas of a century ago has dwindled to a few hundred, while the prices have gone in the opposite direction. Apart from commuters taking the cross-canal ferry gondolas, Venetians leave the sleek and slender black craft to the tourists. Still handing on the business from father to son, the gondoliers in their straw hats and sailor's jumpers or striped T-shirts are as cheerful and witty as, say, any other taxi-driver, but they don't sing as often or as well as they used to. Exorbitant they may be, but how could you explain to grandchildren, after the last gondolas have disappeared, that you visited Venice and never went in one?

The dazzling mosaics of the Basilica di San Marco have earned it the name of Chiesa d'Oro—the Church of Gold.

Reflections on the Water
The water explains almost everything. When the Lombards swept east across the Po valley, the Venetians found their salvation literally in the sea: perched on an archipelago of isles and shoals. Ruled by an energetic oligarchy under an elected doge or duke, the Serenissima or Most Serene Republic of St Mark turned its back on the hostile mainland and made a fabulous fortune with an empire stretching across the eastern Mediterranean and beyond to the silk and spice routes of Asia opened up by Marco Polo. Italy had no vital importance for Venice until overseas trade declined and new sources of wealth had to be sought in agriculture on the mainland.

Protected by the lagoons, Venice needed no ramparts and its palaces could be light and decorative rather than the solid fortress-like residences of Florence. Fronting canals instead of streets, the façades are designed to take their colour from the water's reflection as well as the sunlight. While Florentine art impresses us with its mastery of form and line, the most striking qualities of Venetian painting, with the added influence of Byzantium and the Orient, remain that colour and light.

portal, first on the left, is the only one decorated with an original 13th-century mosaic. It depicts the *Transfer of St Mark's Body* and shows how the basilica looked at the time the mosaic was created. Featured in the scene are the famous bronze horses brought from Constantinople after the Crusade of 1204. The ones you see today over the triple-arched main entrance are copies. (Now restored, the originals are kept in the basilica museum.)

Just inside the church entrance, to the right, is the tomb of Doge Vitale Falier, who consecrated the basilica in 1094. In the six small cupolas of the narthex (vestibule), 13th-century **mosaics** portray Old Testament scenes of Abel's murder, Noah, Abraham and Moses.

The glow in the interior from the mosaics, gently illuminated by high windows, and the soft brown patina of the once-white marble fully earn the basilica the name of "church of gold". The original **mosaics** on the five domes and the great barrel vaults separating them date from the 11th to the 15th centuries. Among the best are the 12th-century *Pentecost* dome in the nave

185

Invasion of the Body Snatchers

Here's the story. It's 828 or thereabouts. A couple of merchants (Venice is full of them) hear that the doge needs a prestigious holy relic to bolster his position *vis à vis* the pope. "How about the evangelist Mark?" they ask. "We can get you the whole body." "Go for it," says the doge.

They go to Alexandria, where Mark had been bishop, and sneak the body out of the mausoleum, after carefully refilling the evangelist's shroud with the remains of Claudian, a minor saint lying near by. Clever, but not clever enough to fool the Egyptians, who search their ship. "Hallo, hallo, what's in that basket?" they ask. "See for yourselves," say the merchants, uncovering some slabs of meat. "*Kanzir, Kanzir!*" ("pork, pork"), cry the Muslim soldiers and flee in horror, leaving Mark's bones safely concealed beneath.

and the central dome's 13th-century *Ascension*. Others have been heavily restored or replaced, not with true mosaics, but reproductions in coloured stone of drawings by such artists as Bellini, Mantegna and Tintoretto.

The **high altar** stands over St Mark's tomb. Scholars can't decide whether the altar's carved alabaster-columned canopy is 6th-century Byzantine or 13th-century Venetian. They agree it's fine work. Beyond it is the **Pala d'Oro**; a great golden altarpiece dating back 1,000 years and bejewelled in its present form in the 14th century. Guides will tell you that there were once 2,486 precious stones, including 1,300 pearls, 400 garnets, 300 sapphires, 300 emeralds, 90 amethysts and 15 rubies. Give or take the few pilfered by Napoleon, it is still precious enough that crowds

have to be kept down by charging an entrance fee.

On your way out, stairs to the right of the main entrance lead to the **museum**, in which you can see the original four **bronze horses**, probably imperial Roman, and to the loggia where they once stood overlooking the square.

North of the basilica, the 15th-century **Torre dell'Orologio** is one of those busy little clock-towers, all gilt and polychrome enamel, that activate statues, in this case two green bronze Moors, to clang out the hour. On Epiphany (6 January) and in Ascension week in May, the Moors are joined by the three Magi and a trumpeting angel revolving around a gilded Madonna. You can watch the Moors from the roof terrace.

The beloved **Campanile** towers 98.6m (324ft) over the city, for 10 centuries its belfry, lighthouse, weathervane and gun turret. Emperor Frederick III rode his horse up its spiral ramp. Galileo demonstrated his telescope to the doge from the top. Criminals were suspended from it in wooden cages. In 1902, it cracked, crumbled and collapsed slowly into the piazza. Ten years later, on its 1,000th anniversary, it was rebuilt a few tons lighter but much the same as before: "*com'era, dov'era*" ("as it was, where it was"). Its collapse hurt no one, but did crush Jacopo Sansovino's beautiful 16th-century **Loggetta**, equally lovingly restored as the entrance to the campanile's elevator. The ride to the top, or climb if you're feeling energetic, is well worthwhile for a view high over the Adriatic and all the way north, on clear days, to the Dolomites.

*O*n the Torre dell'Orologio, the Lion of St Mark clearly prefers to ignore these Moors frivolously clanging their bell. They have been bashing away for nearly 500 years but have left only a small dent in the bell.

Flanking the **Piazzetta** that leads to the Bacino San Marco, opposite the Doges' Palace, Sansovino's exquisite white limestone **Libreria Sansoviniana** is the city's most perfectly realized Renaissance structure, fulfilling all the classical ideals of harmonious proportions. Its Doric-columned arcade, inspired by the Roman Colosseum, supports an Ionic gallery carrying the eye up to the beautiful roof balustrade with its obelisks and statues of Greek divinities. Inside, the **Marciana Library** contains some 750,000 volumes and manuscripts, including the poetry of Petrarch in his own hand, and Marco Polo's testament.

The two tall **columns** facing out over St Mark's basin were booty from the Orient (Constantinople or Syria), brought to Venice in the 12th century. They are topped by statues of St Mark's winged lion and the city's first patron saint, Theodore, with his crocodile. Criminals were publicly executed between the columns until the middle of the 18th century.

The **Doges' Palace** (*Palazzo Ducale*) was for 900 years the focus of Venice's power and pomp, evoked in the imposing elegance of its pink marble and white limestone façades with their airy arcades, loggias and balconies fronting the piazzetta and the basin. Erected over an older Byzantine-style castle, the present 14th–15th-century Flamboyant Gothic building has three fine sculptural groups at its corners, the *Drunkenness of Noah* by the Paglia Bridge, *Adam and Eve* at the Piazzetta, and the *Judgement of Solomon* by the basilica.

The **Porta della Carta** (Gate of the Paper, where the doge posted his

---

It's a Doge's Life

The doges saw their authority wax and wane between that of absolute monarch and pathetic figurehead. Subject to the changing powers of the republic's oligarchic council, many were murdered, executed for treason or ritually blinded— traditional punishment for a disgraced ruler. Though elected by the council, many created virtual dynasties. When the revered Giustiniani family were reduced by battle and plague in the 12th century to one last male, a monk, he was hauled out of his monastery on the Lido and persuaded to sire nine boys and three girls to continue the line before being allowed to return to his vows of chastity.

---

decrees) makes a magnificent entrance. The Gothic sculpture shows the doge kneeling before St Mark's lion, flanked by *Prudence* above *Temperance* in niches on the left and *Fortitude* above *Charity* on the right.

(That book in the lion's paw seen all over Venice is inscribed: *Pax tibi, Marce evangelista meus*, "Peace unto you, my evangelist Mark".)

In the inner courtyard, the **Scala dei Giganti** staircase is so named for Sansovino's giant statues of Neptune and Mars. Visitors take the golden **Scala d'Oro** past the doges' opulent private apartments to the spectacularly decorated council chambers on the third floor. Here, as in most of the city's palaces and churches, the walls are decorated with painted panels and canvases rather than frescoes, too easily damaged by the Venetian climate.

Look out for Veronese's *Rape of Europa* and Tintoretto's *Bacchus and Ariadne* and *Vulcan's Forge* in the **Anticollegio**; a masterly allegorical series by Veronese glorifying Venice in the **Sala del Collegio**, where foreign ambassadors were received; weapons and suits of armour in the **Armoury** (*Sala d'Armi*).

The highlight of the palace tour, back down on the second floor, is the huge **Sala del Maggior Consiglio** (Great Council Hall), in which Venice's ruling oligarchy of patricians met to discuss matters of state. On 12 May 1797 the Maggior Consiglio assembled here for the last time. Submitting to Napoleon's demands, the Council agreed to dissolve the Republic's constitution and voted itself out of existence.

Covering the wall behind the doge's throne is the largest oil painting in the world, Tintoretto's *Paradise*. Measuring 22m by 7m (72ft by 23ft), it was done, with the help of son Domenico, when the artist was 70. Look, too, for the brilliant colours of Veronese's oval ceiling painting of *Venice Crowned by Victory*, the forerunner of the baroque *tours de force* in perspective. Lining the cornice beneath the ceiling are the portraits of 76 doges. One, however, is blackened out, that of Marino Faliero, beheaded for treason in 1355.

The romantic **Bridge of Sighs** connects the ducal palace with the State prisons across a narrow canal. Built in 1603, the baroque covered bridge supposedly takes its name from the sighs of the prisoners on their way to incarceration. In actual fact, it was a worse fate to be imprisoned in the older cells of the Palazzo Ducale itself, either in the *Pozzi*, the wells, or in the *Piombi*, "under the leads": beneath the lead roof of the palace.

Stretch your legs along the **Riva degli Schiavoni** (Quay of the Slavs), named after the Dalmatian merchants who unloaded their goods here. The ghosts of Dickens, Wagner and Proust wander around the venerable Danieli Hotel; you may bump into any number of flesh-and-blood celebrities here, too.

"Inland" from the quay, in the little **Scuola di San Giorgio degli Schiavoni** which served as the Dalmatian merchants' guildhall, is a splendid cycle of paintings by Vittore Carpaccio. Rich in fanciful landscape details and bathed in

A pair of gondoliers prepare to guide their craft beneath the romantically named Bridge of Sighs.

In a symbolic wedding ceremony on Ascension Day that celebrated the Venetian Republic's dominion over the sea, the Doge sailed out in a magnificent gilded barge (depicted here by Francesco Guardi) to cast a golden ring into the waters of the lagoon.

the amber light of an oriental fairytale, the paintings in the ground-floor chapel tell the stories of Dalmatia's three patron saints, George, Tryphon and Jerome. It may come as a blow to the English to have to share George with the Dalmatians, but they can enjoy the particularly gruesome version of George slaying the Dragon amid the rotting corpses of the beast's recent victims.

The **Arsenale**, another of those Venetian words, like ghetto and gondola, that has passed into the world's languages, was once the mightiest of Europe's shipyards. (Incidentally, the word derives from the Arabic *darsin'a*, meaning house of industry.) The Arsenale drove 16,000 master-craftsmen to toil amid vapours of boiling pitch, a sight which much impressed the visiting Dante and inspired a celebrated passage of his *Inferno*. For greater speed and efficiency, the yard evolved the conveyor-belt system: fitting out newly built galleys by towing them one after the other in a continuous line past supply storehouses. In order to impress France's Henri III, the Arsenale turned out one completely equipped galley while the king was eating his dinner.

Today, the Arsenale is just another sleepy yard for the Italian navy. The

No. 5 *vaporetto* sails right through, but pedestrians have to settle for a peep through the handsome Renaissance triumphal arch.

Just four minutes by *vaporetto* from the Schiavoni, on its own little island, is the church of **San Giorgio Maggiore**; its campanile offers the most photogenic view of the city and its lagoon. The 16th-century church is a rare ecclesiastical building by Andrea Palladio, the man whose classic designs became the blueprint for aristocratic residential architecture throughout Europe and North America. His customary Corinthian-columned elegance prevails here, extended from the façade to an airy interior. Two superb Tintoretto paintings decorate the chancel, *Gathering of the Manna* and an otherworldly *Last Supper* in which Jesus administers communion while servants bustle to clear up the dishes.

Around the Accademia

With that egocentrism that Venice's admirers find so charming, and justified, the rambling **Gallerie dell'Accademia** is devoted almost exclusively to Venetian painting, from the 14th century of its emerging glory to the 18th century of its gentle decadence. We propose here only some of the collection's most representative highlights:

Room 1: the 14th-century *Coronation of the Madonna* of Paolo Veneziano, the first of the city's great masters, already glows with characteristic Venetian colour and texture.

Room 2: Giovanni Bellini, youngest and most gifted member of the celebrated family of painters, brings gentle humanity to his *Enthroned Madonna with Job and St Sebastian* (1485).

Room 4: Andrea Mantegna makes his *St George* a very cool dragon-killer, a most appropriate patron saint for England; Giovanni Bellini's *Madonna with St Catherine and the Magdalen* gives further proof that he was the greatest of the Venetian *Madonnieri* (Madonna painters).

Room 5: Giorgione's great *Tempest* (1505) is one of the museum's most cherished, most mysterious treasures, a girl calmly nursing her child in a landscape prickling with the electricity of the approaching storm.

Room 7: Lorenzo Lotto, a troubled loner among Venice's 16th-century artists, portrays a *Gentleman in his Study* with subtle, sombre psychology.

Room 10: most important of Renaissance rooms. Titian's *Pietà*, a vibrant last work completed by pupil Palma il Giovane, was originally intended for his tomb in the Frari church (*see* page 193); Veronese's *Feast in the House of Levi* was meant to be the Last Supper, until the Holy Inquisition complained about its "buffoons, drunkards, dwarfs, Germans, and similar vulgarities"; Tintoretto gives full play to his dark sense of drama in the *Miracle of St Mark Freeing a Slave.*

Room 17: Canaletto's hugely popular 18th-century *vedute* (views) of Venice were aristocratic precursors of modern postcards. Like postcards, most of his works went abroad; the Accademia only has one. In such works as *Island of San Giorgio Maggiore*, Francesco Guardi sought more poetry and melancholy and died a pauper.

Room 20: Gentile Bellini breathes little life into the grand pageant of his *Procession on San Marco* (1496), but it remains a fascinating "photograph" of Renaissance Venice.

Room 21: Vittore Carpaccio depicts in six canvases the bizarre *Story of St Ursula*, a British princess said to have led 11,000 virgins on a pilgrimage to Rome, all of whom were raped and slaughtered on their way back.

East along the Grand Canal, a breath of the 20th century awaits you at the **Peggy Guggenheim Collection** of modern art in the Palazzo Venier dei Leoni. Home of the American heiress until her death in 1979, this unfinished 18th-century palace provides a delightful setting for Picasso, Marcel Duchamp, Magritte, Kandinsky and Klee, but above all for her compatriots Jackson Pollock, Mark Rothko and Robert Motherwell. In the overgrown garden there are sculptures by Giacometti, Henry Moore, and the collector's husband, Max Ernst. She herself is buried there.

Almost as familiar a silhouette as the San Marco campanile is the lovely octagonal domed church of **Santa Maria della Salute**: just Salute to its friends. It's the masterpiece of Baldassare Longhena and was built to mark the city's deliverance from a plague in 1630. For a baroque edifice, the interior is remarkably sober, even chaste. Tintoretto's *Marriage at Cana* is on the wall opposite the entrance, while three of Titian's most vivid canvases decorate the chancel: *Cain and Abel, Abraham Sacrificing Isaac* and *David and Goliath*, whose drama is heightened by the perspective *di sotto in su* (looking up from below).

The **Zattere**, along the Giudecca canal, are quays where heavy goods coming into Venice were once unloaded from rafts or *zattere*. Now they make a pleasant, uncrowded promenade. Behind the Stazione Marittima, where the big cruise-liners dock, seek out the church of **San Sebastiano**. This is a veritable monument to the genius of Veronese, whose home was nearby and who is buried in its left aisle. See his magnificent ceiling paintings of the *Story of Esther*, especially the great oval *Triumph of Mordecai*, and the *Apotheosis of the Madonna* in the choir.

Over on the Grand Canal, the **Ca' Rezzonico** is a grand baroque palace completed in the 18th century and now a museum dedicated to those sunset years of the Venetian Republic. When the last of the Rezzonico family disappeared, Elizabeth Barrett and Robert Browning bought the palazzo, and the poet died in a first-floor apartment in

1889. Soaring allegorical frescoes like Giambattista Tiepolo's *Merit between Virtue and Nobility* in the "Throne Room" (actually for Rezzonico weddings) and others, more wistful, by Guardi, all catch the tone of a declining Venice enraptured by its own legend.

All over the city, you'll find *scuole* that are not schools but old confraternities similar, but for their religious affiliation, to the Freemasons, Rotarians, Elks or Lions. North of Ca' Rezzonico, the **Scuola Grande di San Rocco** is Venice's richest confraternity, in a fine 16th-century chapter house next to its own church. Happily, Tintoretto was a member and created for the house some 50 paintings over a period of 23 years. This series is comparable in grandeur to Giotto's frescoes in Padua or Masaccio's for the Brancacci chapel in Florence. In the Sala Grande, see the high drama of *Moses Striking Water from the Rock* and a fascinating *Temptation of Christ*, with Satan portrayed as a beautiful youth. Titian is something of an interloper here with a remarkable easel-painting of the *Annunciation*. Tintoretto's masterpiece in chiaroscuro effects, is the grandiose *Crucifixion* in the Sala dell'Albergo. You will find a self-portrait just right of the room's entrance.

The nearby brick and white marble Gothic church of the **Frari** (full name Santa Maria Gloriosa dei Frari) is above all celebrated for the high altar adorned with Titian's jubilant *Assumption of the Madonna*. The master's only painting on such a massive scale is a triumph of primary reds, blues and yellows that irresistibly draw you up to the altar. Drag yourself away to see his other work here, the *Madonna di Ca' Pesaro* (left aisle), in which St Peter presents the Pesaro family to Mary. The Venetian composer Monteverdi's tomb is in a chapel left of the altar, but Titian's own monumental tomb (in the right aisle) is a cold and ponderous 19th-century monstrosity. Donatello has sculpted a fine polychrome wood *John the Baptist* for his compatriots' **Florentine Chapel**, right of the altar.

Back on the Grand Canal again, Longhena's exuberant baroque **Ca' Pesaro** is now the town's Modern Art Gallery, devoted principally to purchases from the Venice Biennale exhibitions. Italian artists such as the Futurists Giovanni Fattori and Telemaco Signorini and the Ferrara trio of Filippo de Pisis, Carlo Carrà and Giorgio de Chirico, are better represented than other Europeans, of whom Matisse, Klee and Ernst are the most notable.

Around the Rialto

The ancient commercial heart of the city, named after the 9th-century settlement on *Rivo Alto* (high bank), the **Rialto** spread over both sides of the Grand Canal. Here the oriental spices and silks were unloaded. The merchants went to the banks and the sailors to the brothels. Today, the action is in the food markets and the boutiques. On the west bank, the **pescheria** (fish market) bustles early in the morning, but the **erberia** (fruit and vegetables market) is worth a return visit in the late afternoon when the barges are unloading their fresh produce at the *Fabbriche Vecchie* warehouses. Nobody knows for sure, but nobody dares to dispute the locals'

claim that the little church of **San Giacomo di Rialto**—San Giacometto to them—is the town's oldest. It was consecrated in the 5th century, around the time Venice itself was founded, and rebuilt in the 11th century (decipher the Byzantine interior under its baroque incrustations).

Coming from San Marco, follow the **Merceria** on the east bank, an ever-busy shopping street, past the 16th-century church of **San Salvatore** (Titian fans pop inside for his *Transfiguration* over the silver reredos on the high altar and *Annunciation*, right aisle).

The 16th-century **Rialto Bridge** is no architectural gem—Antonio da Ponte wangled the contract over the likes of Michelangelo, Palladio and Sansovino—but it is still one of the liveliest spots in town. Until 1854, it was the Grand Canal's only bridge. Along the double row of shops with three lanes of pedestrian traffic, you'll find perfumes and jewellery, clothing and shoes, a few treasures, but a lot of junk, too.

North-east of the bridge, past the Fondaco dei Tedeschi post office, seek out the little 15th-century church of **Santa Maria dei Miracoli**. Its refined façade of delicate inlaid coloured marble and intricately carved friezes has won it the name of "golden jewel box" (*scrigno d'oro*), its designer Pietro Lombardo more sculptor than architect.

It is worth carefully mapping out your visit to the **Campo Santi Giovanni e Paolo**. Follow the calle Larga Giacinto Gallina to the Ponte del Cavallo humpbacked bridge for the all-important first view of the magnificent **equestrian statue** of Bartolomeo

Colleoni dominating the square. With his last and greatest piece of sculpture brilliantly evoking all the fierce resolution of a *condottiere* riding into battle, Andrea Verrocchio need not regret abandoning painting to his pupil Leonardo da Vinci. (Verrocchio's clay model was cast in bronze shortly after his death by Alessandro Leopardi.) Colleoni willed his huge fortune to Venice on the understanding his monument would be on Piazza San Marco, but once dead, he had to settle for this spot, in front of the *scuola* of San Marco, a very Venetian solution.

The 13th-century Gothic church of **Santi Giovanni e Paolo**, compressed by Venetians into San Zanipolo, was the doges' funeral church. Some 25 are buried here, many in masterpieces of monumental tombs. On the west wall, left of the entrance, is a fine Renaissance monument for Doge Pietro Mocenigo. In the choir is the 14th-century Gothic tomb of Doge Michele Morosini.

Returning to the Grand Canal, you'll find in the glorious **Ca' d'Oro** the quintessential decorative tradition of Venetian architecture. It is more successful in its compact form here than in the beautiful but sprawling Doges' Palace. Completed in 1440, its Flamboyant Gothic design has a flair and grace that bewitch you into imagining the long-gone gilt of its façade. Take another, more leisurely, boat-ride for the view from the canal. The treasures of Renaissance art of its **Galleria Franchetti** include Andrea Mantegna's *St Sebastian* and fragments of the Titian and Giorgione frescoes that once adorned the Fondaco dei Tedeschi.

FILM IN ITALY

Above: Francesca Bertini, on the right, was one of Italy's stars of the silent movies

Below: A scene from "Cabiria" by Giovanni Pastrone

Italian cinema was born in Turin in 1904 with short comic features and newsreels known as *scene dal vero* (scenes from true life). The first full-length feature was Giovanni Vitrotti's *Hell's Cavalry* which won instant international success. Milan and Rome jumped into the act and 25 production companies sprang up to turn out documentaries and comedies, but above all historic epics that were to be the distinctive mark of the Italian film industry long before Hollywood had dreamt up the Italianate word extravaganza for its own super-productions. Director **Mario Caserini** was the true father of popular Italian cinema, both with his melodramas, *L'Adultera* (The Adulteress) and *Infamia Araba* (Infamy in Araby), and costume spectaculars, *Lucrezia Borgia* and *Nero and Agrippina*. Rome, ancient or Renaissance, was a natural box office attraction.

It was the monumental *Quo Vadis?* directed by **Enrico Guazzoni** in 1912 which really set the world on fire with its extravagant sets and brilliant crowd scenes. This and the three-hour *Cabiria* by **Giovanni Pastrone** in 1914 had enormous influence on the Hollywood epics of D.W. Griffith. Indeed, film historians now acknowledge that many of the American director's editing and lighting techniques originated with the Italian pioneers. Written by poet Gabriele d'Annunzio, *Cabiria* tells the story of a passionate Roman damsel saved from sacrifice to pagan gods by strong-man Maciste, who was to continue his Tarzan-like career throughout the 1950s.

At the same time, another distinctive feature of Italian cinema crept in almost unnoticed with **Nino Martoglio's** *Sperduti nel Buio* (Lost in the Shadows), precursor of the great Neo-Realist movement with its story of a Neapolitan working-class girl seduced and abandoned by a marquis.

But in the shadow of World War I, the public preferred the escapist fantasies dominated by fascinatingly insufferable vamps like **Francesca Bertini** in *I Setti Peccati Capitali* (Seven Deadly Sins) or **Pina Menichelli** in Pastrone's *Tigre Reale* (Royal Tigress). These screen divas tyrannized directors and their exorbitant salaries drove the studios to bankruptcy— from 1923 to 1930 production dropped from 80 to 7 or 8 films a year.

Benito Mussolini took the industry in hand when he realized what a potent propaganda weapon cinema could be. In the 1930s he launched university film courses and set up the Cinematographic Experimental Centre, where directors Rossellini and Antonioni both started their careers, as well as producer Dino de Laurentis and actress Alida Valli. The Fascist dictator opened Rome's great Cinecittà studios in 1937 and launched the world's first film festival at the Venice Biennale.

Director **Alessandro Blasetti** performed an ideological tightrope act with the populist patriotic *1860* extolling Garibaldi and a Neo-Realist forerunner in *Quattro Passi Fra le Nuvole* (Four Steps in the Clouds), while turning out straight Fascist propaganda in *Vecchia Guardia* (Old Guard). Finally, he played it safe with cloak-and-dagger adventure films. **Mario Camerini** carved himself a niche with harmless "white telephone" comedies (so-called because of the then extraordinary white telephone adorning the living room), one of them, *Gli Uomini Che Mascalzoni* (What Scoundrels Men Are), starring the young Vittorio de Sica, epitome of the debonair Latin lover.

In World War II, **Roberto Rossellini** was directing officially approved vehicles like *Un Pilota Ritorna* (A Pilot Returns) and the much-criticized *L'Uomo della Croce* (Man of the Cross), about an Italian padre fighting in Russia.

But he retrieved his honour at the war's end with the magnificent *Roma Città Aperta* (Open City), shot just two months after the liberation of the capital, in the rubble-strewn streets where the last fighting had taken place. Starring Anna Magnani, till then a music-hall performer, with comic actor Aldo Fabrizi

portraying the heroic priest, the film spearheaded the post-war Neo-Realist movement, together with its successor, *Paisà*, depicting Italy's liberation in six episodes.

Vittorio de Sica turned from acting to directing to join the new movement with three poignant studies of Italian street-life: *Sciuscia* (Italianized

Above: "Bicycle Thief"

Left: Anna Magnani in "Roma Città Aperta" (Open City)

version of "shoe shine" hopefully offered by street-urchins to passing G.I. soldiers); *Bicycle Thief* and *Umberto D*, a lonely retired functionary holding onto life.

Luchino Visconti had made his first stab at Neo-Realism back in 1942 with *Ossessione* (Obsession). His setting of James M. Cain's murder story, *The Postman Always Rings Twice*, among the labourers of the Po Valley was promptly censored by the Fascists for its uncompromising view of the proletariat. They might have expected something different from this wealthy aesthete, member of an ancient aristocratic Lombard family, but he continued on his Marxist path in 1948 with *La Terra Trema* (The Earth Trembles), grim story of Sicilian fishermen. He later turned to grander subjects on a truly operatic scale from *Senso* and *The Leopard* to *Death in Venice* and *Ludwig II*.

Collaborating on the screenplay for Rossellini's *Roma Città Aperta* was **Federico Fellini**, probably the most imaginative of all Italian directors. *I Vitelloni* (Useless Louts) and *La Strada* (The Street), featuring Anthony Quinn as a fairground performer, were his personal contributions to Neo-Realism

before he moved on to that examination of his own life and dreamworlds stretching from *La Dolce Vita* and *8 1/2* to *Amarcord* (I Remember) and *E la Nave Va* (And the Ship Sails On).

Michelangelo Antonioni is considerably less heroic in posture than his first name suggests, but no less

Above: Federico Fellini on set

Michelangelo Antonioni behind the camera

introspective. His works in the 1960s, *L'Avventura* (The Adventure), *La Notte* (Night) and *Deserto Rosso* (Red Desert) were often obscure and difficult, but hypnotic. His *Blow Up* was a brighter but still mysterious investigation of Swinging London, while the more recent *Identification of a Woman* returns to the meditation mode.

In a world of his own, **Pier Paolo Pasolini** brought the piercing insight of a ruthless poet to the slums of *Accatone*, the prostitute's world of *Mamma Roma* or the harsh spirituality of the *Gospel According to Matthew*.

Below: Claudia Cardinale in "The Leopard"

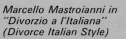
Marcello Mastroianni in "Divorzio a l'Italiana" (Divorce Italian Style)

Right: Vittorio Gassman in "Profuno di Donna"

Below: Sergio Leone's "Once Upon a Time in the West"

Above: Sophia Loren

And where are the laughs? In **Pietro Germi**, with his *Divorzio all'Italiana* (Divorce Italian Style) and *Sedotta e Abbandonata* (Seduced and Abandoned). In **Dino Risi**, with his *I Mostri* (The Monsters), and **Mario Monicelli**, with his *Amici Miei* (My Friends) and *Un Borghese Piccolo Piccolo* (A Petty Petty Bourgeois).

Laughs of a different kind come from **Sergio Leone**, long scorned for his "spaghetti westerns", *A Fistful of Dollars* and *Once Upon a Time in the West*, until people took a second look at his high stylizations, the American myth viewed with Italian irony.

The stars of Italian cinema have become true icons. Among the actresses, the passionate **Anna Magnani** stands out as the queen, **Alida Valli** and **Monica Vitti** seem both to pursue a disturbing inner vision, while **Sophia Loren** and **Silvana Mangano** have each brought a more mature dignity to their earlier commercial sex-appeal. In the male pantheon, let's mention first the great comics: outrageous **Alberto Sordi**, wistful **Nino Manfredi**, ever-puzzled **Ugo Tognazzi**, and end triumphantly with actors whose charm goes beyond mere seduction with **Marcello Mastroianni** or the prodigious **Vittorio Gassman**.

Off the Beaten Track

Among the corners of town far from the madding crowd, the old Jewish **Ghetto** (north-east of the railway station) is particularly peaceful and reveals a fascinating page of Venetian history. It was probably a local iron foundry, *ghetto* in Venetian dialect, which lent its name to this and scores of other enclaves for the forced isolation of Jewish communities through out Europe. In 1516, some 900 Jews (rising to a peak of nearly 5,000 by the mid-17th century) were confined to what was then an island beyond the Cannaregio canal.

In the cramped quarters of the Ghetto, the Jews had to build the six- and eight-storey tenements you see today, twice as high as those permitted elsewhere. Since Jews were forbiden to own land, the community was forced to rent the entire Ghetto on a long lease. Napoleon threw open the gates to the Ghetto in 1797 but Jewish families still live in the neighbourhood.

On the island of the **Giudecca**, you will find another of Palladio's great Venetian churches, the **Redentore**. The grace of its overall form can best be viewed from across the canal, because, like St Peter's in Rome, the dome disappears at closer quarters behind its elongated nave. The Giudecca takes its name either from the Jews (*Giudei*), who lived here in the 12th century, or from the *Giudicati*, nobles who were banished here by ducal judgment. It's now a quiet refuge for fishermen, artists—and tourists seeking to escape the mob. The strange neo-Gothic fortress at the west end of the island is in fact an abandoned grain mill from the 19th-century, the **Mulino Stucky**.

Out in the lagoon, they have been manufacturing glass on the island of **Murano** since 1292, when the hazardous furnaces were moved away from the city centre. In the Middle Ages, Venice had a monopoly on the techniques of making crystal glass. It was jealously protected by hired killers who did away with any craftsman venturing outside Venice with the manufacturing secret. Today, Murano's furnaces and shops are an undeniable tourist-trap, but the **museum** (*Museo Vetrario*) tracing the glass industry back to Roman times is worth a look. Many enjoy watching burly fellows blowing molten globules into cute little green giraffes. The island's quiet spot is the 12th-century Venetian-Byzantine church of **Santa Maria e San Donato**, with a good mosaic in the apse.

The island of **Burano** is a simple fishing village, a true haven of tranquillity where old ladies sit making lace on the doorsteps of their brightly coloured houses. A centuries-old tradition lies behind the islanders' lace-making skills: you can learn the secrets of their craft at the **Scuola dei Merletti**, with its museum and shop, in Piazza Galuppi, the island's main square.

Beyond Burano, the romantically overgrown island of **Torcello**, Hemingway's favourite hang-out, is one of the lagoon's oldest inhabited spots, and was very prosperous until emptied by malaria. The mosquitoes have gone but its superb **cathedral** remains. Founded in the 7th century and reconstructed in 1008, it is probably the finest of the Venetian-Byzantine churches. In the apse there is a moving mosaic of the Madonna above a frieze of the 12 Apostles. Notice, too, the fine Corinthian capitals on the slender Greek marble columns.

With its fine sandy beaches and smart hotels, the **Lido** is as restful as any fashionable seaside resort, but after a couple of days in Venice, its *cars* come as something of a shock. Nostalgics take tea in the Grand Hôtel des Bains to recall the melancholy atmosphere of Thomas Mann's novella (and Luchino Visconti's movie), *Death in Venice.*

From the 16th to the 18th century, Venetian aristocrats travelled down the Brenta canal in summer to their rural country estates to escape the heat of the city.

Veneto

The Venetian mainland reflects some of the *Serenissima's* artistic glories, but the cities that came under its domination in the 15th century retain their individuality.

An *autostrada* links Venice to Padua, Vicenza and Verona for those in a hurry, but others should take the charming backroads.

The Brenta

When Venetian aristocrats gave up the high seas for a more leisurely life on the land, they built Palladian Renaissance villas and extravagantly frescoed baroque country houses on the banks of the Brenta Canal between Venice and Padua. A romantic way to visit some of the best is on the *burchiello*, a modern version of the rowing barge that took the gentry, Casanova and Lord Byron to their trysts and parties

*G*iotto's frescoes in the *Scrovegni Chapel, Padua, are important landmarks in the development of Western art.*

in the country. (Get details from the region's tourist offices of the day trips by *burchiello* between Venice and Padua, in either direction three times a week, optional return by bus, from May to October.)

Otherwise, follow the canal along the pretty S11 country road to Padua. First stop, off a side-road to Fusina, is Palladio's **La Malcontenta** (1571), to which a too-flighty Venetian countess was sent to pine, malcontent, in exquisite isolation on the canal. The villa with its classical portico to catch the summer breezes was the architect's visiting card for scores of commissions. His style would be copied worldwide, particularly in the English country houses of the 18th century and the *ante-bellum* mansions of America's Deep South, where elegant porch-living became an article of faith.

At nearby Oriago, the Palladian style can be seen in **Villa Gradenigo** and, at Mira, in the 18th-century **Villa Widmann**. The influence is clear even in the most spectacular of the Brenta villas, at Stra, the opulent **Villa Pisani** (or Villa Nazionale). It was built for the Pisani doges in 1756, with 200 rooms, Tiepolo frescoes in the ballroom, and vast park with pond, labyrinth and stables. It was bought by Napoleon in 1807 and subsequently hosted Tsars, Habsburg emperors and, for their first meeting in 1934, Hitler and Mussolini.

Padua (*Padova*)

This proud university town was a major centre of the *Risorgimento*, the 19th-century movement to unify Italy. Galileo taught physics here from 1592 to 1610. Something of the old spirit remains at the handsome neo-

classical **Caffè Pedrocchi**, the activists' meeting place on a little square off bustling Piazza Cavour.

North along the Corso Garibaldi is the 14th-century **Scrovegni Chapel**, also known, because of its site among ruins of a Roman amphitheatre, as the Arena Chapel. As a penance for his father's usury, the patrician Enrico Scrovegni built the simple little hall in 1303 and immediately engaged Giotto to decorate its interior. In 38 pictures arranged in three rows under a starry heavenly blue vault, Giotto tells the stories of Mary and Jesus. Among the most moving, look for the *Kiss of Judas*, the *Crucifixion* and the *Lamentation*. A monumental *Last Judgement* covers the entrance wall. The fresco-cycle is beautifully preserved and represents a critical point in the development of Western art. Giotto gave a solidity and naturalism to the human figure that marked a decisive move away from the stiff formalism of Byzantine painting.

*B*uilt to house the tomb of St Anthony, the Basilica di Sant'Antonio is one of the most revered shrines in Italy.

The nearby church of the **Eremitani** was damaged by bombs during the Second World War and its great 15th-century fresco-cycle by Mantegna, the artist's first recorded work, was almost completely destroyed. The fragments which survived and those which have been restored can be seen in the **Orvetari Chapel** (right of the high altar), including the *Martyrdom of St Christopher* and an *Assumption*.

The entrance to Piazza del Santo south of the city centre is guarded by Donatello's grand **statue of Gattamelata**, the 15th-century *condottiere* Erasmo da Narni, the perfect ideal of a Renaissance hero, whose "honeyed" or "speckled" cat nickname still mystifies historians. Donatello's monument was the first great equestrian statue to be cast in bronze since Roman times. Behind Gattamelata looms the 13th-

and 14th-century **Basilica of Sant' Antonio**, the Portuguese-born Franciscan monk, known more popularly as *il Santo*, who died in Padua. The Romanesque façade makes a striking contrast with the eight Byzantine cupolas and four minaret-like towers around a central Gothic cone-shaped dome. In the lofty Gothic interior, Donatello's sculptures at the **high altar** include a stoical *Crucifixion* and large bronze reliefs narrating St Antony's miracles, notably the *Mule Adoring the Eucharist* and the healing of the *Irascible Son*, who cut off his foot in remorse at kicking his mother. The **Scuola di Sant'Antonio**, right of the church, has Titian frescoes of the saint.

Vicenza

This is Andrea Palladio's home town and he has made of it a place in many ways more serene than the often more lively Venice. At the centre, **Piazza dei Signori** is graced by his **Basilica**, not a church, but the old Roman concept of a civic hall. Here Palladio encased an existing building, the Gothic Palazzo della Ragione, with a colonnade and loggia. If you wonder what to think of it, Palladio's modest opinion was that it "ranked among the most noble and most beautiful edifices since ancient times, not only for its grandeur and ornaments, but also its materials" (hard white limestone). Inside is a museum of his designs and models.

The main commercial street is, inevitably, **Corso Palladio**, lined with elegant town houses by the master and his disciples. The 15th-century **Palazzo da Schio** (No. 147) is also known as Ca' d'Oro, after the famous Venetian Gothic palace. You'll find Palladio's best town palace where the Corso widens out into the Piazza Matteotti to give him more freedom for the wonderfully airy **Palazzo Chiericati**. Its Museo Civico houses works by Tintoretto, Veronese, Hans Memling and Van Dyck.

Set in a little garden, the audacious **Teatro Olimpico** is Palladio's last work (completed by Vincenzo Scamozzi in 1584). Facing an amphitheatre auditorium is a fixed décor of classical Roman statuary and columns with what look like three long streets leading away from the stage. It's quite a shock when you go through the archways and find the streets go back only a few feet, a simple illusion of perspective.

Two of the region's most interesting villas lie just outside Vicenza on the slopes of **Monte Berico**. Little more than a mile south-east of the town, off the road to Este, is the 18th-century **Villa Valmarana**, also known as the Villa dei Nani after the figures of dwarfs (*nani*) sculpted on its garden walls. The villa's architecture is undistinguished but its interior easily makes amends, decorated as it is with lavish rococo **frescoes** by the father-and-son team of Giambattista and Giandomenico Tiepolo.

A short distance from the Villa Valamarana is Palladio's most celebrated building, the hilltop **Villa Rotonda**. Designed as a belvedere for Cardinal Capra in 1551, it's an exquisite piece of applied geometry, a domed rotonda set in a square surrounded on all four sides by simple Ionic-columned porticoes, offering different views of town and countryside as the light changes. Film-director Joseph Losey used the villa for his *Don Giovanni*, in which Leporello unrolls down the long staircase the list of his master's mistresses: 1,003, *mill'e tre*.

Verona

A favourite of Roman emperors and the "barbarian" rulers that followed, the city likes to be known as *la Degna*, the Dignified but it also has a very lively atmosphere, stimulated by the Adige river flowing swiftly down from the Dolomites. And perhaps by a memory of its fierce medieval history. The family feuds that inspired Shakespeare's *Romeo and Juliet* ended only with the ascendancy of the tough Scaliger dynasty in the 13th century. They, in turn, were overthrown by Gian Galeazzo Visconti of Milan in 1387 before the city fell under Venetian rule in 1405.

The hub of city life is vast Piazza Bra, with the town hall on its south side and the great **Roman Arena** dating back to AD 100. Only four of its outer arches survived an 1183 earthquake undamaged, but the inner arcade of 74 arches is intact. Today it is the venue for Verona's famous summer opera festival. With thousands of spectators holding lighted candles, a tremendous atmosphere is created for the performances. The Arena seats as many as 25,000 but the acoustics are such that the music carries to all parts of the amphitheatre. People in the top rows get a terrific view of the surrounding city.

Along the north side of the piazza, the **Liston**, a people-watcher's delight lined with smart cafés and restaurants, is the street for the Veronese bourgeoisie's evening stroll (*passeggiata*). It leads to the boutiques, galleries and

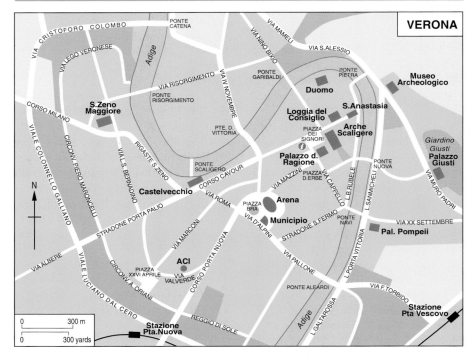

City plan of Verona.

antique shops of equally fashionable **Via Mazzini**.

Turn right at the end down Via Cappello for the 13th-century tavern that the local tourist industry understandably insists was **Juliet's House** (*Casa di Giulietta Cappelletti*), complete with balcony. Romantics arriving after closing time (6.45 p.m.) "with love's light wings o'erperch these walls; for stony limits cannot hold love out."

Piazza delle Erbe along the ancient elongated Roman forum makes the prettiest of market-places. Its medieval houses and old umbrella-covered stalls surround a 14th-century fountain and a line of columns, one of which bears the lion of St Mark, in old allegiance to Venice.

Neighbouring **Piazza dei Signori**, formerly the city's main square, is

bounded by medieval and Renaissance palaces. The late 15th-century **Loggia del Consiglio**, built to house meetings of the city council, is the best example of early Renaissance architecture in the city. At the east end of the square is the residence of the Scaligeri, the della Scala family who ruled Verona in the 13th and 14th centuries. The family's elaborate canopied tombs, the **Arche Scaligere**, stand in front of the nearby Romanesque church of Santa Maria Antica. On the wrought-iron fence that encloses the tombs note the family's ladder emblem, ubiquitous in Verona (*scala* means ladder).

West of Piazza Bra, the massive brick 14th-century **Castelvecchio** fortress on the Adige river houses an art museum. Its collections are mainly of the Venetian school, notably Mantegna's *Holy Family*, a Giovanni Bellini *Madonna*, and Lorenzo Lotto's *Portrait of a Man*.

The austerely handsome 12th-century church of **San Zeno Maggiore** with superb bronze doors and imposing free-standing brick campanile is a rare jewel of Italian Romanesque architecture. (The 14th-century battlemented tower to the left is the remnant of an old abbey.) The dignity to which the town aspires is there in the simple interior, illuminated by the magnificent Mantegna **triptych** on the high altar.

Open-air opera seasons have been held in Verona's spectacular Roman Arena since 1913—with intermissions during the two World Wars.

Treviso

In recent years Treviso has been busily prospering from manufacturing and commerce, with textiles a particular success: both Benetton and Stefanel are based nearby. But the town's antique charm attests to a long and dignified history. Enclosed within the town's 16th-century ramparts is a stately old quarter of arcaded streets bordering tree-lined canals.

The golden age of Treviso's independence was the 13th century, under the powerful Da Camino family. However, along **Via Canova** and the **Calmaggiore**, the many fine houses adorned with late Gothic carvings and Renaissance frescoes bear witness to the prosperity enjoyed under Venetian rule after 1389. The Calmaggiore leads into **Piazza dei Signori**, the hub of municipal life enclosed by three fine buildings: the Romanesque **Palazzo del Podestà** (rebuilt in the 19th century); the 15th-century **Palazzo Pretorio** and,

above all, the venerable **Palazzo dei Trecento** (1217), embellished by a Renaissance arcaded loggia.

A couple of stone lions supporting pillars on the north wall are among the few Romanesque vestiges of the now largely neoclassical **Duomo**. The elegant interior remains remarkable for its seven cupolas and a Titian *Annunciation* on the chapel altar at the end of the right aisle.

More impressive is the Gothic redbrick church of **San Nicolò**. Note the slender vaulting of its chancel. Next door, see the series of lively portraits of Dominican friars by Tommaso da Modena in the chapter-house of the church's old convent, now a **seminary**. More of Tommaso's works are in the **Museo Civico** (Borgo Cavour, 22) with Venetian artists Giovanni Bellini, Titian, Lotto and Jacopo Bassano.

Friuli-Venezia Giulia

Italy's far north-eastern corner borders on Austria and Slovenia. Like the Veneto, this attractive region is characterized by lagoons formed by rivers coursing down to the sea from the Alps. But the countryside is more varied—both softer and more rugged—with a sprawling limestone plateau, the Carso or Karst, along its eastern frontier. The farming is rich here and the wines are some of the best in the country, but many towns are still only slowly recovering from the terrible earthquakes of 1976.

Trieste

The grand old port-city remains an enigmatic mixture of patriotic Italian feeling, sober memories of the Austrians for whom it was the major maritime outlet until 1918 and even a certain wistful affinity with the Slovenes just over the border. The coffee-houses have a decidedly *Mitteleuropa* air about them, their pastries suspiciously, deliciously Viennese in flavour. Naming the airy neoclassical square at the hub of city life **Piazza dell'Unità d'Italia** doesn't hide the fact that the imposing city hall, government palace and head offices of the Lloyd Triestino shipping line would not be out of place on the Austrian capital's Ringstrasse.

This was all part of the building boom when the Habsburgs' port at last began achieving big profits, after the opening of the Suez Canal in 1869. This made it all the more attractive to Italian nationalists. At the end of World War I, the town was seized by Italian forces, led by the writer Gabriele d'Annunzio. After World War II it was the turn of Yugoslavia, but Trieste reverted to the international status of a free port until a 1954 plebiscite won it for Italy.

The trade goes on. Walk along the **harbour** to observe the movement of freighters and tankers from around the world. Cruise liners dock at the Molo dei Bersaglieri. Beyond that is the fish market (*pescheria*) and the Porto Sacchetta for private yachts.

For a great overall view of the city and waterfront, walk up to the **Cattedrale di San Giusto**. The present 14th-century building with its beautiful Gothic rose-window combines two adjacent Romanesque churches, built on the site of a Roman temple. Parts of the latter's propylaeum are incorporated into the campanile. Inside the

*U*ntil 1918, Trieste
was the chief port of the
Habsburg Empire. Today,
visitors still detect an Austro-
Hungarian air to the city.

church, Venetian **mosaics** of the 13th century in the left apse depict the Madonna with Archangels Michael and Gabriel.

Above the cathedral, at the top of a pleasant green park, the **Castello** was built by the Austrians in 1470 on the site of an older Venetian fortress. It now houses several **museum** collections, including some vicious-looking antique weaponry.

Downhill again, the **Museo di Storia ed Arte** on Via della Cattedrale, traces the city's prehistoric and Roman past in artefacts, bronzes, glasses and vases. It also houses a superb collection of 274 Tiepolo drawings.

The town's own Roman remains are meagre: at the bottom of the hill, an Augustan arch renamed **Arco di Riccardo** in the mistaken belief that England's Richard the Lionheart had been imprisoned in Trieste; and the restored remains of a **Roman theatre**.

In Via San Francesco is a monumental **synagogue** built in 1910 for the city's large Jewish community, of whom the most famous member was the great novelist of Trieste bourgeois society, Italo Svevo. Epitomizing the town's cultural ambiguity, his pen-name means, roughly, Germanic Italian—just as aptly illustrated by his real name, Ettore Schmitz. His great friend was James Joyce, who taught English at the Berlitz school in nearby Pula (now just over the Slovenian border).

A popular excursion into the hills north-west of town is to the **Grotta Gigante**, a vast underground cave with fantastic formations of stalactites.

Aquileia

Set back from the coastal lagoons, this serene and lovely town is deeply imbued with a feeling for its illustrious past. Founded in 181 BC as part of the Empire's defences against the Germanic tribes, this frontier fort was as important to ancient Rome as Trieste was to the Austrians and Italians. In 452, the town was ravaged by Attila's Huns, but rose to greatness again in the Middle Ages as a seat of the Eastern Orthodox patriarchate.

That role is recalled in the **basilica**, set among pine, cypress and linden trees. With its noble **campanile** characteristic of Friulian architecture, the great 11th-century Romanesque church of Patriarch Poppo was built on an early Christian sanctuary. The simple interior, transformed with a graceful Gothic arcade and Renaissance coffered ceiling, has a superb 4th-century **mosaic pavement** from the original church, which mixes pagan and Christian imagery (including the story of Jonah and the Whale). The **crypt** under the chancel has medieval frescoes of the life of Christ, while another, the **Cripta degli Scavi** (entrance outside the church), contains excellent Roman and early Christian mosaics.

Most of the local Roman remains have been collected in the **Museo Archeologico**. The cypress-lined Via Sacra from behind the church leads you to the excavated **Roman harbour** (Porto Fluviale) and warehouses on the river.

Grado

Set on an island between lagoon and sea, this ancient fishing port once provided sanctuary for the people of Aquileia fleeing the barbarian hordes. Today, it is a popular resort with two **beaches** where immersion-therapy in the sun-heated fine crystalline sands or seawater provides relief for aching joints. A long jetty bridges the lagoon and 5km (3 miles) away from the mainland, Grado also enjoys exceptionally pure air. The mild climate gives it a long beach season, from May to October. Dominated by a 15th-century bell tower, the church of **Sant'Eufemia** dates in part back to the 6th century, notably the mosaic pavement. See, too, the finely sculpted Romanesque capitals and **pulpit**, carved with emblems of the Evangelists, under an Arab-style cupola.

Udine

The region's capital is an enchanting town, graced with the familiar Gothic-Renaissance architecture of the Venetians who ruled here from 1420 to 1797. There is, however, a bonus of easy-going tranquillity you won't find in Venice itself. The epitome of this harmonious urban décor, at the heart of the city, is **Piazza della Libertà** with its pink-and-white-stone Palazzo del Comune (also known as the Loggia del Lionello, after the architect). Opposite is the elegant 16th-century **Porticato di San Giovanni**, surmounted by a clock tower (*torre dell'Orologio*) complete with Venice's Lion of St Mark and two Moors to ring the bell.

Pass through **Arco Bollani**, designed by Palladio, to reach the Venetian governor's castle housing the **Museo Civico**, with works by Carpaccio, Ghirlandaio and Tiepolo. Udine boasts some of Tiepolo's finest baroque paintings: in the cathedral, a *Holy Trinity* on the first altar to the right and a *Resurrection*, fourth right; in the **Oratorio** across from the cathedral, a celebrated *Assumption*; and in the **Palazzo Arcivescovile** (Archbishop's Palace) on the Piazza del Patriarcato, an admirable series of biblical frescoes.

To appreciate fully the town's serenity, wander through the arcaded streets to **Piazza Matteotti**, where a colourful market takes place by Giovanni da Udine's 16th-century fountain. For your picnic, sample the region's famous sweet ham, *prosciutto di San Daniele*, and spicy Friuli salami.

*F*rom the corner of the Palazzo del Commune, Bartolomeo Bon's statue of the Madonna commands a view of Udine's Piazza della Libertà.

The Dolomites

The mountain landscape of Italy's eastern Alps is an exhilarating mixture of rich green Alpine meadows with jagged white limestone and rose-coloured granite peaks. Summer hiking in the largely German-speaking region of Alto Adige (Austrian South Tyrol till 1918) is a delight. Well-marked paths lead to farmhouses and rustic mountain-restaurants where you can try the local bacon (*speck*) or spinach dumplings (*spinatknödl*) as a change from spaghetti. It saves you carrying a picnic.

Merano (*Meran*)

Good clean mountain air makes this elegant resort a bracing haven of peace and a gateway for winter sports and summer hiking. It has come a long way. After losing its Tyrolean supremacy to Innsbruck in 1420, Merano fell into oblivion. By the 18th century, cattle roamed the city centre. In 1836, a Viennese court physician, Josef Huber, informed his royal patients that Merano's climate and its table grapes had great healing properties, turning the dilapidated town almost overnight into a thriving spa frequented by the proverbial crowned heads of Europe.

Even if you don't share their liver problems, you'll enjoy a stroll along the **Summer** and **Winter Promenades** (*Passeggiate d'Estate* and *d'Inverno*) on the banks of the swiftly flowing Passirio river. Copper beeches, chestnuts and fir trees cast their shade, along with a first hint of Tuscan cypresses. The Habsburgs are still present on the Summer Promenade with a statue of "Sissy", the wife of Austrian Emperor

T he Queen of Italian winter sports resorts, Cortina d'Ampezzo won international renown when it hosted the Winter Olympics in 1956.

Franz Joseph. Open-air concerts of Strauss waltzes are held in front of the gleaming yellow-and-white **Kursaal**. Chic boutiques line arcaded **Via dei Portici** (*Laubengasse*) in the medieval heart of the town. The imposing late Gothic **cathedral** is now largely baroque inside.

equipment on the old arcaded shopping street, Via dei Portici (*Laubengasse*). Then head north-east of town to the **Renon** (*Ritten*) plateau for wonderful views of the Dolomite peaks, which are reached by both cableway and rack railway.

To the east, Ortisei and Selva are the main ski resorts of the beautiful **Val Gardena**. Here, in isolated communities, you will no doubt come across locals speaking an obscure language known as Ladin. Originally derived from Latin, this ancient tongue is kept alive by some 15,000 people.

Trento

The town's historic centre has much of the dignified severity associated with the famous Council of Trent, which was convened here from 1545 to 1563 to counter the Reformation movement led by Martin Luther. With apt symbolism, a weighty 16th-century bell tower has been added to the already formidable mass of the Romanesque-Gothic **cathedral** completed 300 years earlier. Handsome Renaissance mansions line **Via Belenzani**. Turn left on Via Colico to the church of **Santa Maria Maggiore** in which most of the Council's meetings were held: a contemporary painting shows the princes of the Church sitting in semi-circular debate.

The mighty **Castello del Buonconsiglio** was the stronghold of the prince-bishops who ruled Trento from the early 11th century until the beginning of the 19th century. The castle has three sections—the Venetian-Gothic **Castelvecchio** (Old Castle) to the north, linked to the 17th-century **Giunta Albertina** (Albertina Wing) in the centre,

Bolzano (*Bozen*)

South Tyrol's historic capital makes a good base for hikes. It has a 14th-century Gothic **Duomo** with a characteristically Austrian polychrome tiled roof. Inside there is a fine 16th-century sculpted sandstone pulpit and a marble high altar. Get your hiking with the Renaissance **Magno Palazzo** (Great Palace) to the south. The provincial **art museum** now housed there includes some notable 16th-century frescoes by Dosso Dossi and Romanino.

Cortina d'Ampezzo

The queen of Italian winter sports resorts has elegant hotels, smart boutiques and a bouncing nightlife. In its sunny sheltered basin high in the Boite valley of the eastern Dolomites, it provides excellent skiing facilities as well as good opportunities for skating and bobsleigh. It, too, is a favourite with summer hikers. Take the cable car to **Tofana di Mezzo** for an awesome view clear down to the Venetian lagoon. Equally spectacular are the panoramas from the **Belvedere di Pocol** and **Tondi di Faloria**. North of town, drive out to the pretty **Lake Ghedina**, which is particularly popular for its excellent trout-fishing.

Emilia-Romagna

The two regions were united at the time of the *Risorgimento*, with Emilia following the Apennines from Bologna to Piacenza while Romagna covers the eastern area of Ravenna and the Adriatic resorts from Rimini down to Cattolica.

Rimini

The Adriatic coast, of which Rimini is the chief resort, has wide sandy beaches, at some points stretching 300m (1,000ft) from the water's edge back to the dunes. Its lively hotels, beach clubs and myriad discos make Rimini a favourite playground for the sun-soakers, while the fishing port remains surprisingly peaceful.

Inland, on the other side of the railway, is the old city that was Ariminum to the Romans. The 27 BC **triumphal arch** (Arco d'Augusto), anachronistically ornamented with medieval battlements, stands at the junction of the imperial highways from Rome, Via Flaminia and Via Aemilia (which gave the region its name). The **Ponte di Tiberio** bridge built over the Marecchia river in AD 21 is still in use.

The unfinished 15th-century **Tempio Malatesta** is one of the greatest achievements of architect Leon Battista Alberti, who transformed an existing Gothic church into a Renaissance masterpiece, borrowing ideas from the Arco d'Augusto for the classical façade.

More pagan temple than church, the building served as a mausoleum for the cultivated but cruel tyrant, Sigismondo Malatesta, and his mistress, Isotta degli Atti. The Tempio's interior decoration is by Matteo de' Pasti and Agostino di Duccio: note the recurring motifs of elephant and rose (symbols of the Malatesta family) and the entwined initials *S* and *I* (for Sigismondo and Isotta), which resemble the US dollar sign.

In the Chapel of the Relics is a damaged **fresco** by Piero della Francesca showing Sigismondo kneeling before his patron saint, but looking far from penitent.

To the south of Rimini are the resorts of **Riccione**, which is very popular, and the quieter **Cattolica**. **Cesenatico**, to the north, with its colourful fishing port.

San Marino

Tucked in between Emilia-Romagna and the Marches, this anachronistic mountain state provides a natural excursion from Rimini, just half an hour's drive away. The world's oldest and smallest republic, a mere 62km² (23 square-mile) patch founded more than 1,500 years ago—is also, if we are to believe all the shop-signs in English and German—the home of the "best booze", "cheapest brandy" and all kinds of other duty-free watches, cameras and souvenir junk.

With its capital perched on the three-peaked pinnacle of Monte Titano, the country was for centuries safe from Italy's wars and invasions until the bombs of World War II made bitter nonsense of its neutrality. Today the republic has a population of about 20,000, with its own army, coins, stamps and licence plates. It maintains diplomatic relations with some 35 countries. The government is headed by two "regent captains" ruling jointly for six months. The investiture every 1 April and 1 October is a colourful public ceremony. The Grand Council meets in the Gothic **Palazzo Pubblico** on Piazza della Libertà. In the 14th-century church of **San Francesco** is a small art gallery noteworthy for Guercino's *St Francis* and a *Madonna and Child* attributed to Raphael.

But the three peaks of **Monte Titano** remain San Marino's greatest asset, for the wonderful view of the Adriatic, Apennines and Po Valley.

Ravenna

For those who find it rather difficult to appreciate mosaics as we usually see them, in fading indecipherable

San Marino's rocky perch on Monte Titano has enabled the ancient republic to preserve its independence for more than 1,500 years.

fragments, the beautifully preserved mosaic decoration of Ravenna's churches come as an exciting revelation. Up to 1,500 years old, they stand at the summit of the art as originally practised by the Greeks and Romans.

Now some 10km (6 miles) from the sea, the ancient capital of the western half of the Byzantine Empire was once a flourishing port on the Adriatic. Emperor Honorius made it his capital in 402, followed by his sister Galla Placidia. Ruled in the early 6th century by Theodoric, king of the Ostrogoths, it was recaptured for Emperor Justinian and Byzantine culture left its mark for another two centuries.

You can see something of the town's Venetian-dominated era (1441–1509) on graceful **Piazza del Popolo**, bordered by the 17th-century Palazzo Comunale. The Venetian insignia on the piazza's two columns have been replaced by local saints Apollinaris and Vitalis.

The oldest of the Byzantine monuments, in the northern corner of the city centre, is the 5th-century **Mausoleum of Galla Placidia**. Three sarcophagi stand in the cross-shaped chapel, but no one knows if her remains are in one of them. The deep blue, gold and crimson **mosaics** on the vaults and arches depict St Laurence, the Apostles and the *Good Shepherd Feeding His Sheep* (over the entrance).

In the same grounds is the octagonal redbrick church of **San Vitale**, consecrated in 547. The basilica's plain exterior gives little indication of the treasures inside, for the magnificent green and gold **mosaics** in the choir and apse are unrivalled. Try to come on a bright morning when the sun provides natural illumination.

The Old Testament scenes in the lunettes, such as *Abraham Sacrificing Isaac*, are more lively and naturalistic than the panels on the side walls of the apse with their brilliantly colourful but rigidly formal portraits of the Emperor Justinian (left wall) and the Empress Theodora (right wall), accompanied by their splendid court retinues. Another fine mosaic, in the dome of the apse, shows Christ between two angels, with St Vitalis and Bishop Ecclesius, who, as the basilica's founder, holds a model of the church.

Next to the church, the cloisters of a former Benedictine monastery house Ravenna's **Museo Nazionale**. The museum contains a large and well-arranged collection of Roman, early Christian and Byzantine art and artefacts.

Ravenna's Duomo is undistinguished—the original 5th-century basilica having been almost completely rebuilt in the 1730s. Far more rewarding is the adjoining **Battistero Neoniano** (Baptistery of Bishop Neon). The domed octagonal building, once a Roman bath house, is crowned by mosaics from about 450 of the Baptism of Christ surrounded by an evocative procession of the Apostles.

A short walk away, next to the church of San Francesco, is a neoclassical monument housing the **tomb of Dante**, who died here, in exile, in 1321, with a fellow poet's epitaph: "Here I lie buried, Dante, exile from my birthplace, son of Florence, that loveless mother."

East of the city centre, the early 6th-century church of **Sant'Apollinare**

*E*mpress Theodora, the powerful consort of the 6th-century Byzantine emperor Justinian, is portrayed with her court retinue in this mosaic in Ravenna's San Vitale.

Dante and Beatrice

If Dante Alighieri (1265–1321) is now known as the father of Italy, it is largely due to his being banished from Florence, at 36, for backing the wrong side in the interminable political squabbles between Guelfs and Ghibellines (*see* page 51). Forced to travel to Verona, to Lucca, to Ravenna, he sensed that, in the absence of one unifying royal court, it was itinerant intellectuals like himself who represented the scattered national identity. On his wanderings, he wrote in the noble Tuscan vernacular that was to become the basis of the national language the *Divine Comedy*, the symbol of Italian nationhood and civilization.

The Beatrice to whom he dedicates his poetic masterpiece is believed to be the Florentine lady Beatrice Portinari whom he first saw when he was just nine. She died when he was 25. He idealized her ever after as the inspiration of all his work, though he married another, Gemma Donata, with whom he had several children. In the *Divine Comedy*, after fellow poet Virgil leads him through the Inferno and Purgatory, Beatrice takes over in Paradise. Not an easy trip: "Beatrice looked at me with eyes so full of the sparkling of love and so divine that my power, overcome, took flight and, with eyes cast down, I was almost lost."

"Beatrice mi guardò con li occhi pieni
di faville d'amor, così divini,
che, vinta, mia virtue diè le reni,
e quasi mi perdei con li occhi chini."

Nuovo was built by the Christianized Ostrogoth king Theodoric. In the nave, classic Byzantine **mosaics** show on the left Ravenna's fortified port of Classe, from which a procession of 22 virgins follow the three Magi with gifts for Jesus on his mother's lap; on the right, from Theodoric's palace, 26 martyrs carry jewelled crowns.

Five kilometres (3 miles) south of the town, protected only by a couple of cypresses from an incongruous wilderness of highways and bleak urban development, stands the lovely church of **Sant'Apollinare in Classe** (549), next to it, a splendid cylindrical 11th-century Romanesque campanile. In the apse of the Greek-columned interior is a delightful **mosaic** of St Apollinaris, Ravenna's first bishop and martyr, surrounded by sheep (the faithful), with Moses and Elijah in the clouds above him.

Bologna

The capital of Emilia-Romagna is a thriving town with a certain patrician atmosphere to its elegantly arcaded historic centre. It is the home of Europe's oldest university, established in the 11th century on the foundation of a distinguished law school dating back even earlier, to the end of the Roman empire. Dante, Petrarch and Boccaccio all studied here. Mozart was awarded a diploma by the Philharmonic Academy in 1770. Marconi conducted early experiments in the physics department. As well as the soubriquet *Bologna la dotta* or Bologna the learned, the city has earned the nickname *Bologna la grassa*, Bologna the fat, for its world-renowned cuisine.

The heart of Bologna is large and handsome **Piazza Maggiore** and adjoining **Piazza del Nettuno**, both of which are surrounded by important public buildings. Overlooking both squares, the massive medieval **Palazzo Comunale** is a striking expression of Bologna's civic power. The façade on the west flank of Piazza Maggiore has a Renaissance **porch** by Galeazzo Alessi, topped by a bronze statue of Pope Gregory XIII. He was a native of Bologna, principally remembered today as the reformer of the calendar. In the neighbouring square, the 16th-century **Neptune Fountain** is one of the town's most popular symbols, for which Giambologna sculpted the bronze sea god surrounded by nymphs and cherubs.

The 14th-century basilica of **San Petronio** ranks among the most imposing of Italy's Gothic churches. It has a fine **central portal** with reliefs of Old Testament scenes on its pilasters sculpted with great dignity and power by Jacopo della Quercia. Adam's pose in the *Creation* scene (top left) inspired the Michelangelo figure reaching out to God on the Sistine Chapel ceiling. The soaring vaults of the sober interior have the monumentality of French or German Gothic.

The **Palazzo dell'Archiginnasio** was built in 1563 to bring together the various schools of the University which until then had been scattered throughout the city. It now houses the municipal library. Inside, the walls are decorated with the coats of arms of former rectors and professors. The 17th-century **Anatomy Theatre** (in the same building) has two remarkable wooden anatomical figures supporting the professor's chair.

A medieval atmosphere clings to the old houses in the tiny streets behind the **Metropolitana cathedral** to the north. At the end of busy Via Rizzoli, the two **leaning towers** are all that remain of a whole forest of medieval status-symbols—like those of San Gimignano in Tuscany (*see* page 158). The 12th-century Torre degli Asinelli, 97.6m (200ft), is the taller, with 500 steps to its rooftop view.

You will find the city's characteristic arcaded **palazzi** along Via Zamboni leading past the university to the

*B*ologna *may be a thriving, go-ahead city of business and industry but it has one of the best preserved historic centres in Italy.*

Pinacoteca Nazionale. The Pinacoteca's fine collection is devoted in large part to the Bologna school, most notably the baroque paintings of the Carracci family, of whom Annibale was the most gifted: see his *Annunciation* and *Madonna in Glory*. Guido Reni was strongly influenced by the Carracci; he's represented here by a number of fine paintings, including a dramatic *Massacre of the Innocents* and a powerful *Samson Victorious*. Look out, too, for Raphael's important *Ecstasy of St Cecilia,* commissioned for the local church of San Giovanni in Monte, and Parmigianino's *Madonna di Santa Margherita.*

South of the city centre, the founder of the Dominican order is buried in the church of **San Domenico**, mostly 13th-century but with many 18th-century baroque modifications. His marble **tomb**, (*Arca di San Domenico*, 6th chapel, right aisle) was designed by Nicola Pisano with additional works by Nicolo dell'Arca and the 20-year-old Michelangelo. He did the saints Petronius and Proculus, and the angel on the right. It was the first and last time he ever put wings on an angel.

Ferrara

Half an hour's drive from Bologna on the *autostrada* takes you to this

---

The Borgias

Before she became Duchess of Ferrara at 25, Lucrezia Borgia (1480–1519) was accused of sharing the bed of her father Pope Alexander VI (formerly Rodrigo Borgia), and of her brother Cesare, quite apart from making her own poisonous contribution to their myriad assassination plots. Being of Aragonese origin, the family was subject to the heated anti-Spanish propaganda of the times, so the facts are less lurid. But still pretty lurid.

Hoisted to the pinnacle of the Catholic church by uncle Alfonso (Pope Calixtus III), Alexander VI was indeed a great sensualist and had four children by his mistress Vannozza Catanei, but there is no evidence he had an incestuous relationship with Lucrezia.

The apparent extent of Lucrezia's involvement in her father's and brother's political plots is her acquiescence in three marriages: to Giovanni Sforza of Pesaro (annulled by her father); to Duke Alfonso of Bisceglie (in Puglia), murdered by Cesare's agents; and to Alfonso d'Este, heir to the duchy of Ferrara, an ancient papal territory. This marriage was allowed to last, even producing seven children. Perhaps relieved to be left in peace, Lucrezia acquired a reputation for charity and generosity. She presided over a brilliant court, attracting great artists and poets such as Ariosto and Pietro Bembo, with whom she conducted a passionate but platonic correspondence.

Cesare (1475–1507) may not have slept with his sister but he did justice to every other sin in the book. Cardinal at 17, he is said to have engineered the murder of his brother and handed in his red hat so as to devote himself full time to the business. His service as papal legate to France won him French support to seize Romagna, Elba, Urbino, Rimini, Pesaro and Faenza. In 1502, several of his own officers plotting to stop him were invited to his Sinigaglia castle and strangled. He in turn was poisoned but survived: it was in his blood, they said. However, Pope Julius II proved too tough for him, forcing him to flee to Spain, where he died fighting for the king of Navarre.

stronghold of the high-living d'Este dukes, archetypal scheming, murderous, lovable Renaissance villains. In their formidable **Castello Estense**, a 14th-century moated fortress, guides tell delightfully dubious tales of what went on in the dungeons.

You get a sense of the dukes' grandeur among the Renaissance palazzi of **Corso Ercole I d'Este**, part of a 15th-century urban expansion, *Addizione Erculea*, that was one of the most ambitious pieces of town planning of its age. The d'Estes' **Palazzo dei Diamanti** (12,600 pieces of diamond-shaped marble on its walls) houses the Pinacoteca Nazionale, with works of the Ferrara masters Cosmè Tura, Ercole de' Roberti, Garofalo and Dosso Dossi.

The triple-gabled 13th-century **cathedral** still has its loggia of shops attached to the south wall. The cathedral museum exhibits two major works by Cosmè Tura, *St George* and the *Annunciation*, and fine sculptures by Jacopo della Quercia of the *Madonna of the Pomegranate* and *St Maurelius*.

The **Palazzo Schifanoia**, south-east of the cathedral, was the summer retreat of Duke Borso d'Este (1450–71). Inside, the **Salone dei Mesi** (Room of the Months) has a delightful Renaissance fresco cycle (sadly much damaged) by Francesco Cossa and Ercole de' Roberti. The frescoes give a charming impression of daily life at the d'Este court.

Not that it was all fun for the painter. Cossa was so dissatisfied with his pay that he left Ferrara without completing the job and moved to Bologna.

An easy excursion 50km (30 miles) east of town takes you out to the lovely Benedictine **Abbey of Pomposa**, which was founded in the 7th century but abandoned in the 17th century when the monks were driven out—not by doctrinal or political enemies, but by the malarial mosquitoes (long gone, too). Built in the long-arcaded Romanesque style of Ravenna's Sant' Apollinare in Classe (*see* page 216), the abbey-church is dominated now by its soaring campanile added in the 11th century. The 14th-century **frescoes** in the chapter-house and refectory are worth a look.

Modena

Another Renaissance bastion of the d'Este dynasty, the town has much of the charm and sparkle of its Lambrusco wines. And the infectious dynamism of the nearby Ferrari and Maserati works.

Wide avenues have replaced the medieval ramparts that once surrounded the city centre. The d'Este **Palazzo Ducale**, begun in 1634, is one of the biggest buildings in all Italy and now houses the Military Academy. On Piazza Grande, the **Torre Ghirlandina** bell tower makes a magnificent landmark towering over the Romanesque **cathedral** begun in 1099. Notice the splendid biblical reliefs sculpted over the portals. Inside, look out for the sculptures on the pulpit and rood screen, telling the story of Christ's Passion. North of the bell tower is the cathedral's **Museo Lapidario** with exceptional Romanesque sculpted friezes from the buttresses.

The city's art collections are housed in the 18th-century Palazzo dei Musei, with the great **Galleria Estense** on the top floor. In the vestibule is a Bernini bust of Francesco I d'Este, the founder of the collection. The works are principally north Italian, from Emilia-Romagna: Tommaso da Modena, Cosmè Tura, Cima del Conegliano and Correggio; and from Venice: Veronese, Tintoretto and Jacopo Bassano. The foreign works include a small El Greco triptych and a Velázquez portrait of Francesco I d'Este. The **Biblioteca Estense**, on the first floor, has a large collection of illuminated books, including the 15th-century *Bible of Borso d'Este*.

Parma

As home of two famous painters, Correggio and Parmigianino, Parma has more to offer than just great cheese and ham. **Piazza del Duomo** forms a wonderfully harmonious space for the graceful octagonal baptistery and the austere nobility of the 12th-century Romanesque **cathedral** and its 13th-century campanile. Inside the Duomo, on the ceiling of the central octagonal dome, is Correggio's grandiose fresco of the *Assumption of the Virgin* (1530). In this, his masterpiece, Correggio has achieved, in the truest sense, exalted emotion without the sentimentality of Mannerist imitators.

The lovely 13th-century pink Verona marble **baptistery** has superbly sculpted doors by Benedetto Antelami, who also carved most of the 12 statues of the months in the interior.

Behind the cathedral, the 16th-century Renaissance church of **San Giovanni Evangelista** also has in its dome a fine Correggio fresco of the *Vision of St John on Patmos*. Look out,

too, for the **Parmigianino frescoes** in the 1st, 2nd and 4th chapels on the left aisle. The old pharmacy next door to the church was founded by the Benedictines in 1298 and displays some handsome ceramic jars and giant mortars and pestles from the 15th to the 18th century.

In the 16th-century Renaissance church of the **Madonna della Steccata** (Via Garibaldi), Parmigianino painted the frescoes of the *Wise and Foolish Virgins* on the arch above the high altar. The artist spent the last ten years of his life working on frescoes in the church but made such slow progress that in 1539 he was sacked and imprisoned for breach of contract. He died the following year.

In the charming **Camera di San Paolo** (Via Melloni), you'll find the Benedictine convent's private dining room for the highly unconventional abbess, Giovanna da Piacenza. She commissioned Correggio to decorate it in 1518 (his first work) with mischievous *putti* angels and a very pagan view of Chastity as symbolized by the goddess Diana.

The **Galleria Nazionale** is housed in the austere Renaissance Palazzo della Pilotta on Piazzale Marconi. The picture gallery exhibits more excellent works by Correggio and Parmigianino, and a sketch of a young girl, *Testa di Fanciulla*, by Leonardo da Vinci.

The splendid High Renaissance façade to the church of San Giovanni Evangelista in Parma.

Big Business and a Wealth of Art and Natural Beauty

Lombardy and Piedmont and their greatest cities, Milan and Turin, may be the economic powerhouses of the nation, but they have a rich heritage of art and architecture, too. They also boast the fertile Po Valley, the source of much of Italy's agricultural wealth. Liguria is smaller in size and importance but it is home to Italy's largest port, Genoa, and to a coastline of rugged cliffs and fine sandy beaches.

Prosperous and cosmopolitan, industrious and smart, Milan is indisputably the country's economic and cultural capital. It plays host to Italy's main stock exchange and to a high fashion industry which, some say, puts that of Paris in the shade. The icing on the commercial cake is provided by major Romanesque and Gothic churches and some splendid galleries and museums.

Turin is home to Gianni Agnelli's mighty Fiat group—Europe's largest automobile producer—and to the two great football teams of Torino and Juventus. It also has stately arcades, baroque palaces and that mysterious Shroud.

For relaxation, the Italian Riviera east and west of Genoa alternates dramatic stretches of rocky coastline with sandy beaches. Hugging the slopes of Mont Blanc (*Monte Bianco*), Courmayeur is Italy's senior ski resort. To the south, Gran Paradiso is the country's oldest national park. North and east of Milan are the romantic lakes Como, Maggiore and Garda.

The Flamboyant Gothic façade of Milan's great cathedral took centuries to complete.

Milan (*Milano*)

This is clearly the country's economic and cultural capital. Despite its prestigious museums and magnificent

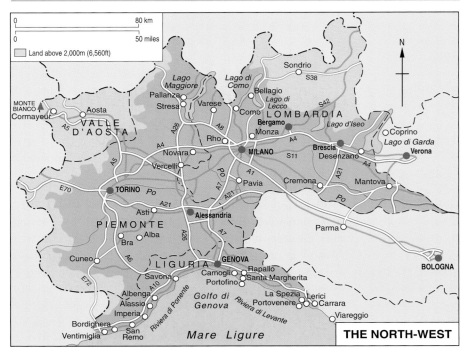

THE NORTH-WEST

North-west Italy.

cathedral, tourists do not think of Milan as an obvious holiday destination (though some do make the pilgrimage just for Leonardo da Vinci's *Last Supper*). But anyone interested in contemporary Italian life will want to hang out a few days in its cafés and restaurants, elegant shopping avenues and side-street art galleries. If the main railway station in Piazza Duca d'Aosta is a monstrous reminder of Mussolini, the Pirelli skyscraper opposite is a more graceful symbol of the new era. With its vivacious residents, fashion-conscious and self-assured to the point of pushy, this is *the* modern city of Italy.

Around the Duomo

Nowhere does a cathedral more dominate a major city centre. Almost non-stop throughout the day, but especially at that magic moment of the *passeggiata*, **Piazza del Duomo** is one of the liveliest squares in all Europe. People gather around the cafés, kiosks and shopping arcades, the young discussing music and clothes, their fathers arguing politics and business, and everybody talking football.

It all happens in the shadow of the **Duomo**, the most grandiose of Italy's Flamboyant Gothic cathedrals. Teams of Italian, French, Flemish and German architects and sculptors contributed to this astonishing edifice, begun in 1386 under Duke Gian Galeazzo Visconti but completed centuries later. The awesomely rich façade

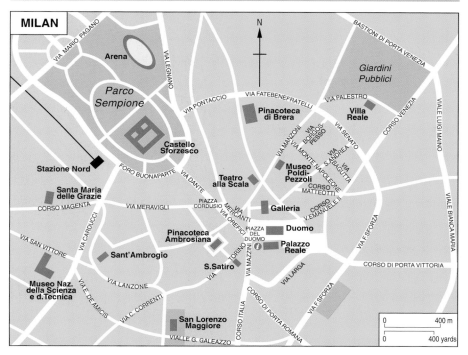

MILAN

Arena

Parco Sempione

Castello Sforzesco

VIA MARIO PAGANO

VIA LEGNANO

FORO BUONAPARTE

VIA DANTE

VIA PONTACCIO

VIA FATEBENEFRATELLI

VIA PALESTRO

Giardini Pubblici

BASTIONI DI PORTA VENEZIA

N

Pinacoteca di Brera

Villa Reale

CORSO VENEZIA

VIALE LUIGI MAINO

VIA MANZONI

VIA BORGOS-PESSO

VIA SENATO

VIA MONTE NAPOLEONE

VIA S. ANDREA

VIA S. SPIRITO

Stazione Nord

Santa Maria delle Grazie

CORSO MAGENTA

VIA MERAVIGLI

Teatro alla Scala

Museo Poldi-Pezzoli

CORSO MATTEOTTI

VIA MANZONI

VIALE BIANCA MARIA

Pinacoteca Ambrosiana

PIAZZA CORDUSIO

VIA MERCANTI

VIA OREFICI

Galleria

CORSO V.EMANUELE II

Duomo

PIAZZA DEL DUOMO

Palazzo Reale

VIA F. SFORZA

VIA CARDUCCI

VIA SAN VITTORE

Sant'Ambrogio

S.Satiro

VIA TORINO

VIA MAZZINI

CORSO DI PORTA VITTORIA

Museo Naz. della Scienza e d.Tecnica

VIA LANZONE

VIA E. DE AMICIS

VIA C. CORRENTI

San Lorenzo Maggiore

CORSO ITALIA

CORSO DI PORTA ROMANA

VIA LARGA

CORSO DI PORTA ROMANA

VIA F. SFORZA

VIALLE G. GALEAZZO

| 0 | 400 m |
| 0 | 400 yards |

City plan of Milan.

was only finished in 1813 on the orders of Napoleon. For the best view of the cathedral's bristling silhouette of marble pinnacles and statues, stand in the courtyard of the Palazzo Reale south of the cathedral. (It houses the Cathedral Museum, which displays fine examples of Gothic sculpture from the façade.) The cathedral's interior is a vast and noble space, showing its north European influence in the soaring columns and a decoration of **stained-glass windows**, from the 15th century to the present day. In the right transept is the **tomb** of Gian Giacomo Medici with bronze Michelangelesque statues by Leone Leoni; opposite is Marco d'Agrate's gruesome **statue** of St Bartholomew displaying his flayed skin.

Give yourself plenty of time for a spectacular walk out on the **roof**. The elevator entrance (clearly signposted outside the cathedral) is in the right transept. Wander high above the city turmoil under the flying buttresses and around the statues (2,245 in all) and pinnacles (135), up to the roof-ridge for an unbeatable view of the city. To go down, take the staircase (158 steps) for some fascinating close-ups of the cathedral's construction.

West of Piazza del Duomo, tucked away between busy Via Orefici and Via Mercanti, is the last vestige of the medieval city, **Piazza Mercanti**. The 13th-century seat of communal government on its south side, Palazzo della Ragione,

Visitors to the rooftop of Milan's cathedral will find themselves in the midst of a forest of pinnacles—135 in all.

has a fine Romanesque equestrian relief of a *podestà* (chief magistrate). It stands opposite the elegant porticoed Palazzo dei Giureconsulti (1564).

Leading north from Piazza del Duomo, the huge cross-shaped shopping arcade of the **Galleria Vittorio Emanuele** is a splendid monument in steel and glass to the expansive commercial spirit of the 19th century. (In a tragic accident, the architect, Giuseppe Mengoni, fell to his death from the top of the Galleria only days before its opening in 1878.) Today, cafés, restaurants, bookshops, boutiques and a department store bathe in its unabashed neo-Renaissance décor.

In the winter, the Galleria provides a sheltered, albeit draughty, passage from the Duomo to another holy of holies, the 18th-century **La Scala** theatre, the high temple of opera. Even if you cannot be there for an opera (opening with a gala to end all galas every sacrosanct 7 December), attend a concert there, or at least visit the little museum (left of the theatre), if only for a chance to see the sumptuous neoclassical auditorium with its six tiers of balconies and galleries.

Milan's most prestigious thoroughfare is **Via Monte Napoleone**, an august parade of neoclassical palazzi and luxury shops. Narrow side streets such as Via Borgospesso, Via Sant'Andrea and Via Bagutta take you into a more tranquil 18th-century world, now graced by art galleries, antique shops and the town's smarter *trattorie*.

Around Castello Sforzesco

The massive brick fortress, **Castello Sforzesco**, north-west of the city centre, was rebuilt in its present form in the 15th century by Duke Francesco

Sforza. The bulk of the solid square structure stands around a vast courtyard, Piazza d'Armi. Beyond, in the handsome old residential quarters of the Corte Ducale, is the entrance to the Castello Sforzesco **art museums**, devoted to sculpture, painting (*pinacoteca*), ceramics, furniture and archaeology. In collections that include important works by Giovanni Bellini, Mantegna, Titian, Correggio and Tintoretto, pride of place goes to Michelangelo's last work, the unfinished *Rondanini Pietà* (1564). Working on it until six days before his death, the sculptor chiselled a pathetic Mary struggling to hold up the dead

*M*usical cognoscenti reckon that a diva has not truly attained divine status until she has won the approbation of the audience at La Scala: the world's most famous opera house.

Autopsy of a Masterpiece
The great culprit in the disintegration of the *Last Supper* was not so much Milan's infamous humidity or modern pollution as Leonardo himself, or at least the understandable demands of his genius.

For this summit of his life's work, Leonardo did not want to suffer the restrictions of fresco (painting onto damp plaster). A fresco was painted section by section without modifying once dry, thus denying him the chance to add that overall shadowy *sfumato* effect that gave his paintings their psychological depth and subtlety. Nor would the sustained effort demanded by a fresco's damp plaster permit him, as was his habit, to leave the painting when inspiration deserted him, to go and work on something else.

So Leonardo preferred a tempera with oil and varnish on an ideally dry surface, in fact a disastrous choice for the damp climate. Deterioration was already noted in 1517, when Leonardo was still alive. By the time fellow artist Giorgio Vasari saw it a generation later, there was "nothing visible but a muddle of blots". It is a miracle that 400 more years of dust and smog have left anything at all.

Jesus, a strange throwback to medieval sculpture for his last tussle with recalcitrant stone.

Behind the castle is a delightful English-style **park** for a rest away from the city and even a dream of tropical lands among the exotic fish of the municipal Aquarium in the right-hand corner.

Even without Leonardo da Vinci's masterpiece in the adjoining refectory, the church of **Santa Maria delle Grazie** (Corso Magenta, south-west of the Castello) would be well worth a visit as a jewel of Renaissance architecture. Adding to an earlier late Gothic design, Donato Bramante, who was Pope Julius II's chief architect in Rome, fashioned in 1492 a magnificent red-brick and white stone chancel (*tribuna*). The graceful lines of the rectangular choir and 16-sided cupola are best viewed from the little cloister that Bramante built on the north side. Inside the church, stand in the choir to appreciate the full majesty of the dome.

Leonardo da Vinci's **Last Supper** (*Cenacolo*) is being lovingly resuscitated in the little Dominican refectory to the left of the church. Despite centuries of deterioration and clumsy restoration since it was completed in 1497, there is enormous psychological impact in Leonardo's depiction of the trauma for each of the disciples when Jesus declares: "One of you will betray me." Almost as awe-inspiring as the painting itself is a glimpse of the immense effort going since 1979 into the painstaking centimetre-by-centimetre recovery of the fragmentary but powerful traces of the "real Leonardo". We can now see, for example, that Philip (leaning over towards Jesus, third to the right) has an expression of acute grief rather than the simpering pathos left by "restorers" who presumed to improve on the original.

For another aspect of Leonardo da Vinci's talents, visit the **Science Museum** (*Museo della Scienza e della Tecnica*) in nearby Via San Vittore. Among the rooms devoted to the history of science and technology, one gallery is reserved for Leonardo's inventions, displayed as models constructed from his notebooks. You will see his aircraft, a machine for making screws, a hydraulic timber-cutter, a revolving bridge, various machine-tools and a system of map-making by aerial views long before any aircraft, even his, was operational.

At the eastern end of Via San Vittore, beyond a noble atrium courtyard, the church of **Sant'Ambrogio** is the city's most revered sanctuary, built from the 9th to the 12th century. It stands on a foundation that dates back to the time of St Ambrose (340–397), the first bishop of Milan and one of the Church's four founding fathers (with Peter, Paul and Jerome). Its sober five-bayed façade is characteristic Lombard Romanesque, flanked by a 9th-century campanile and taller 12th-century tower topped by a modern loggia. In the interior, left of the centre nave, notice an 11th-century **pulpit** standing on a Christian sarcophagus of the Roman era. Under a canopy carved with Romanesque-Byzantine reliefs is the **high altar**, richly encased in bejewelled and enamelled plates of gold and silver.

The Brera and Other Museums

The handsome 17th-century palace of the Jesuits is now the **Pinacoteca di Brera**, one of the country's foremost art museums. In its fine arcaded courtyard, notice a bronze statue of Napoleon, a remarkable, rare example of the emperor with no clothes. (It was he who turned the Brera into a national gallery with confiscations from the Church and recalcitrant nobles.)

Among the highlights: two paintings by Giovanni Bellini of the *Madonna and Child* and a highly personal *Pietà*; Veronese's *Jesus in the Garden*; Tintoretto's dramatic *Discovery of St Mark's Body*; and an impressive *Christ at the Column* by Donato Bramante.

Mantegna has a touching *Madonna*, but his masterpiece here is the *Dead Christ*, achieving a gripping emotional effect with its foreshortened perspective. Piero della Francesca's celebrated *Montefeltro Altarpiece* (1474) is his last work.

The gentle beauty of Correggio's *Nativity* and *Adoration of the Magi* and Raphael's stately *Betrothal of the Virgin* contrast with the earthier inspiration of Caravaggio's *Supper at Emmaus* (a second version of the painting in London's National Gallery).

The non-Italian artists include El Greco, Rubens, Van Dyck and Rembrandt. In the modern collection, look out for Modigliani, Boccioni, de Chirico, Carrà and de Pisis.

The **Pinacoteca Ambrosiana** (Piazza Pio XI, 2) was the 17th-century palace and library of Cardinal Federigo Borromeo. Its principal treasure is Leonardo da Vinci's luminous *Portrait of a Musician* (1485), unfinished but at the same time the best preserved of the master's few surviving works. You can see his pervasive influence on Milanese artists in the decorative paintings of Bernardino Luini and a fine *Portrait of a Young Woman* by Ambrogio de Predis. There is nothing sweet about Caravaggio's *Bowl of Fruit*: the worm is in the apple and the leaves are withering. Travellers on their way to or from Rome will be especially interested in Raphael's cartoon (preparatory drawing) for his *School of Athens* fresco in the Vatican. The Cardinal's own favourite among his collection was Titian's *Adoration of the Magi*, the highlight of a number of good Venetian paintings in the gallery, including Jacopo Bassano's *Rest on the Flight into Egypt*.

The **Poldi-Pezzoli Museum** (Via Manzoni, 12) is a small, formerly private collection displayed in the lavishly decorated rooms of a 19th-century Milanese nobleman's home. Both house and collection were bequeathed to the city by their owner, Gian Giacomo Poldi-Pezzoli, in 1879. Its prize pieces include Piero della Francesca's *San Nicola da Tolentino*, Mantegna's *Madonna and Child*, a Botticelli *Madonna* and Antonio Pollaiuolo's lovely *Portrait of a Young Woman*.

Milan's **Modern Art Gallery** is housed in the 18th-century Villa Reale (Via Palestro, 16), once occupied by Napoleon. The heart of the collection is the work of northern Italian painters of the 19th century including some masterly portraits by Francesco Hayez and Pellizza da Volpedo's monumental *Fourth Estate*. The French Impressionists are well represented on the second floor with works by, among others, Gauguin, Manet, Van Gogh and Cézanne. A special section of the gallery is devoted to the work of the leading Italian sculptor Marino Marini, donated by the artist in 1974. The rooms at the back of the villa, many of them dripping with chandeliers, look out upon an attractive English-style garden.

Lombardy

This central part of the Po Valley is only a fraction of the Italian lands conquered by the Lombards when they crossed the Alps from eastern Europe in the early Middle Ages. Yet it has proved the most fruitful, and all too tempting to the acquisitive appetites of France, Spain and the rival Italian duchies and city-states such as Venice, which pushed its Republic as far west as Bergamo. Natural fertility was enhanced by Europe's most advanced systems of irrigation, still operating in the medieval canals that you'll see on your way south to Pavia. Lombardy's rice, wheat and maize are the main basis of the nation's *risotto*, *pasta* and *polenta*.

The extravagant polychrome marble façade of the Certosa di Pavia is one of the wonders of northern Italy.

On a more sentimental note, the three major lakes at the foot of the Lombardy Alps, Garda, Como, and Maggiore, are perfect settings for mending broken hearts, breaking mended hearts and all romantic conditions in between.

Pavia

The Lombards' first capital, before Milan, is now a sleepy redbrick university town. Its principal attraction, the spectacular charterhouse or **Certosa di Pavia**, is in fact some 8km (5 miles) north of the city, a 30-minute drive from Milan. Built by Gian Galeazzo Visconti, Duke of Milan, for his family mausoleum, the monastery's 15th-century church is a high point in the transition from Flamboyant Gothic to Renaissance. Even without the originally designed crowning gable, the sculpted marble **façade** makes a dazzling impact, with its statues of prophets, saints and apostles above the medallion reliefs of Roman emperors.

The Gothic interior is lightened by the brightly coloured paving and groin-vaulting. Among the chapels, which were given baroque finishings in the late 16th century, notice an exquisite Perugino altarpiece of *God the Father*. Right of the triumphant baroque high altar is a beautifully carved 15th-century lavabo (ritual basin) and a charming *Madonna and Child* by Bernardino Luini. In the right transept is the Visconti tomb, and a door leading to the lovely small cloister of russet terracotta, with a fine view of the church's galleried octagonal tower. Since 1947, Cistercians have taken over from the Carthusian monks, but they continue the manufacture of herbal liqueurs.

Bergamo

Rising out of the plain of the Po Valley on its own steep little hill, 47km (30 miles) east of Milan, the delightful town of Bergamo makes a welcome break in the monotony of the *autostrada*. Those rustic dances known as Bergamasques, which originated here, led outsiders to regard the people of Bergamo as clowns, but the city has a proud soldiering history. It gave the Venetian Republic a famous *condottiere*, Bartolomeo Colleoni (*see* page 194), and the largest contingent in Garibaldi's 1,000 Red Shirts.

The Città Bassa (Lower City) at the foot of the hill, is the modern town of shops, hotels and restaurants serving a savoury *risotto* they insist is superior to Milan's. **Piazza Matteotti** is the hub of the town's lively café scene, with pleasant arcades along the Sentierone promenade. Opposite is the Teatro Donizetti and a monument showing the Bergamo-born opera composer accompanied by the naked lady he is said always to have needed for inspiration.

Venetian ramparts still protect the historic **Città Alta** (Upper City) up on the hill. Gracious **Piazza Vecchia** is surrounded by Renaissance public buildings, notably the **Palazzo della Ragione** with a medieval Torre del Comune—take the lift to the rooftop view over the Po Valley to the Alps. The town's most venerable edifice is the 12th-century Romanesque church of **Santa Maria Maggiore**. Notice the finely carved monumental north porch and slender campanile. The baroque interior has some impressive 16th-century tapestries and inlaid wooden choir stalls and beautiful intarsia work at the altar rail. Adjacent to the church is the Renaissance **Colleoni Chapel**, an ostentatious mausoleum in red, white and green marble.

A short walk from the Città Alta's Porta Sant'Agostino, the **Galleria dell'Accademia Carrara**, founded by an 18th-century count, has one of the most important collections of paintings in northern Italy. Among its highlights are several Bellini *Madonnas*, including the exquisite *Madonna of the Pear*; a solemn Mantegna *Madonna and Child*; Lotto's haunting *Mystic Marriage of St Catherine* and interesting works by Raphael, Cariani and Titian.

T his stone lion of St Mark in Bergamo's Piazza Vecchia is a reminder of centuries of Venetian rule over the city.

Brescia

Famous past and present for its weapons manufacture (Beretta guns), Brescia suffered as a natural target in World War II, but rebounded as an ebullient modern city. It has preserved and restored a historic core around **Piazza del Duomo**. The more interesting of the two churches there is not the present cathedral, a rather ponderous affair of the 17th century, but its Romanesque predecessor, the Duomo Vecchio, usually known as the **Rotonda**. The large round 12th-century building contains in the choir some fine paintings by local Brescia artist Moretto.

Valiantly resisting the brutal modern office blocks in neighbouring Piazza della Vittoria is delightful **Piazza della Loggia**. The handsome 16th-century **Loggia** by Palladio and Sansovino (now occupied by civic offices) stands at the west end of the square, with the early Renaissance **Palazzo del Monte di Pietà**, on the south side.

The ruins of the **Capitoline Temple** erected by Vespasian in AD 73 are on Via dei Musei; the town's Roman past is well illustrated in the **Museo Romano**, housed in a modern building behind the temple. The museum's most important exhibit is the famous 1st-century bronze *Winged Victory*, discovered here in 1826.

The art collection of the **Pinacoteca Tosio-Martinengo** (Via Martinengo da Barco) is devoted principally to Brescia's own Renaissance masters: Vicenzo Foppa, Moretto, Romanino and Moroni. The gallery also boasts fine works by Raphael, Lotto (a fine *Adorration of the Shepherds*), Tiepolo and Tintoretto.

Cremona

Splendid medieval **Piazza del Comune** is certainly worth a tour with the old town-hall (*Palazzo del Comune*) opposite the Romanesque **cathedral** and great **Torrazzo** bell tower 111m (364ft) high. But the town is remembered above all as the home of Europe's most illustrious manufacturers of musical instruments: the Stradivarius, Guarneri and Amati families.

Next to the municipal museum, the **Museo Stradivariano** (Via Palestro, 17) has a fine collection of instruments and documents with original signed drawings and models of the masters' matchless craft from the 16th to the 18th century. The king of them all, Stradivarius Cremonensis, to give him his formal Latin name, is said to have made more than 1,100 instruments, the last when he was 93 years old. The **International School of Violin-Making** on Piazza Marconi trains new craftsmen, but nobody knows now how to duplicate the varnish and handiwork of the golden era.

Mantua (*Mantova*)

This wistful, almost melancholy city's venerable past, illuminated by the rule of the powerful Gonzaga family of dukes and cardinals, makes it well worth a visit for some fine Renaissance monuments and the 15th-century paintings of the great Andrea Mantegna. Lakes formed by the Mincio river, once mosquito-infested but now bringing a certain serenity, surround the town on three sides, while the lively market on **Piazza delle Erbe** adds a lighter touch.

The **Sant'Andrea** basilica is an important Renaissance work of Leon Battista Alberti, with a dome added by baroque master Filippo Juvarra in the 18th century. In the first chapel on the north aisle is the tomb of Mantegna, whose pupils, including Correggio, carried out his designs for the church's wall paintings.

Some of the master's most celebrated frescoes are to be seen in Gonzaga's gigantic **Palazzo Ducale**, a sprawling fortress built from 1290 to 1707. The most notable room, in a corner of the palace's Castello San Giorgio, is the **Camera degli Sposi** (Bridal Chamber) decorated by Mantegna for Ludovico Gonzaga and his wife Barbara. His frescoes and brilliant *trompe l'œil* ceiling depict all the colour and pomp of the Gonzaga court. The Gonzagas' more harmonious summer residence, the **Palazzo del Tè**, amid pleasant gardens, was designed by Giulio Romano on the southern edge of the city centre.

Lake Garda

On the west shore, the people of Salò, where native son Gaspare Bertolotti is regarded as the originator of the violin, suggest his design was inspired by the contours of the lake. But Italy's largest lake is shaped more like a banjo, 52km (32 miles) from the ruggedly romantic cliffs of the neck down to its broad "sound box", 18km (10 miles) across, and surrounded by rolling green hills. Graced with vineyards (notably Bardolino), lemon trees, olives and noble cedars, the lake enjoys mild winters and mellow summers.

At the south end, boat cruises start out from Peschiera, Sirmione and Desenzano, particularly recommended for dramatic views of the east shore's mountains and the beautiful **Punta di San Vigilio**, with its little church and 16th-century Villa Guarienti. Darting in and out of some 80 tunnels, the road which circles the lake, **La Gardesana**, represents a magnificent feat of Italian engineering and affords breathtaking views.

Begin your road tour out on the narrow **Sirmione** promontory. A popular summer retreat for the Romans, this fishing village and renowned spa resort continues to draw leisure-seekers. The sensual Roman poet Catallus had a villa here. No-one knows exactly where, but locals have given the name **Grotte di Catullo** to the remains of a large Roman villa overlooking the lake. Another splendid view of the lake is offered by the tower of the 13th-century castle, **Rocca Scaligera**, the stronghold of the della Scala or Scaliger family, medieval rulers of Verona.

Continuing round Lake Garda, the drive along the winding **Gardesana Occidentale**, cut through the cliffs of the west shore, is one of the most spectacular in all Italy.

The resort-town of **Gardone Riviera** is much appreciated for its parks and botanical gardens and as a base for hikes back into the hills. Above the resort, in Gardone di Sopra, is a 20th-century "folly", **Il Vittoriale**. This was the bizarre and disturbing residence of Gabriele d'Annunzio—poet, adventurer, fascist. Melancholy gardens of dense shrubbery, dark laurel and parades of cypresses lead up to a mausoleum containing the writer's sarcophagus flanked by those of his disciples.

It overlooks the prow of a World War I warship, the *Puglia*, hauled up the hillside as the crowning piece of his relics, for which the villa is a museum. Among the exhibits are two cars in which the poet drove to his war exploits and the aircraft from which he dropped propaganda leaflets over Vienna in World War I.

Lake Como

Embraced by green wooded escarpments, the lake favoured by some of England's most romantic 19th-century poets—Wordsworth, Shelley and Byron—retains a certain wistful atmosphere for the leisure hours of the Milanese. As at Garda, a mild climate nurtures luxuriant vegetation in the villa gardens and parks.

The lake divides into two arms on either side of the tranquil resort town of **Bellagio**, which juts out on a hilly promontory. Up on the heights above the town, the elegant 18th-century **Villa Serbelloni** stands in the middle of a beautiful park of rose trees, camellias, magnolias and pomegranates. (This should not be confused with the Villa Serbelloni luxury hotel down near the lake front.) You can take a bracing swim at the lido at the southern end of town. Lake cruises and carferries leave from the Lungolario Marconi.

The lake's south-west arm is the most attractive. From Lezzeno, take a boat cruise to see the colourful **Grotta dei Bulberi**, and look out for the waterfall at Nesso. **Como** itself is a factory town, but it has a handsome Gothic-Renaissance cathedral crowned by a superb baroque dome, completed in 1770, by Turin's great architect, Filippo Juvarra. It stands next to the arcaded Broletto, the 13th-century seat of municipal government.

The western shores of the lake are lined with gracious villas nestling in perfumed gardens. At **Cernobbio**, the 16th-century Villa d'Este was once the home of Caroline of Brunswick, the estranged wife of England's Prince Regent (later George IV). It is now a hotel where you can at least take tea as an excuse to stroll among the cypresses and magnolias. Between the genteel resort towns of Tremezzo and Cadenabbia is one of the lake's most beautiful residences (open to the public), the 18th-century **Villa Carlotta**. There is a marvellous view of the lake from its terraced gardens, famous for the display of camellias, rhododendrons and azaleas in late April and May. Inside, the ground floor of the villa has a collection of painting and sculpture, including a number of frigid neoclassical works by Canova. Stendhal, a guest in 1818, made the villa the setting for the opening scenes of his great novel *The Charterhouse of Parma*. In the novel, Lake Como is described as *"le plus beau site du monde"*.

Lake Maggiore

The northern end of the lake lies in Switzerland, the southern in Italy. The whole area shares the other lakes' mellow climate. The resort towns offer excellent opportunities for relaxation and sports on longer stays, but for short visits, you will get a better idea of the lake on a boat cruise (3–4 hours, with a meal on board, from Stresa, Baveno or Pallanza) than by road.

Close to the western shore, the **Borromean Islands** (*Isole Borromee*) are celebrated for their baroque palazzi and magnificent gardens. They are still the property of the Borromeo family that provided Milan with its greatest cardinals. **Isola Bella**, the best known of the islands, is named after Isabella, wife of the 17th-century Count Carlo Borromeo, who planned the island haven for her. The Count's heirs continued the island's transformation from rocky outcrop to paradisal retreat. The Palace, erected by Vitaliano Borromeo, is decorated with admirable paintings by Annibale Carracci, Tiepolo, Zuccarelli and Giordano. The terraced gardens constitute one of the finest ensembles of the Italian formal style: all the more astonishing when you consider that the soil had to be brought by barge from the mainland. View the lake from the uppermost of the 10 terraces, by the unicorn statue that is the Borromeo family emblem. **Isola dei Pescatori** is a delightfully peaceful fishing village with tiny narrow streets. **Isola Madre**, further out in the lake, is the largest of the islands and almost deserted, except for its palazzo and botanical garden inhabited by peacocks and pheasants.

Stresa has been Lake Maggiore's principal resort since the 19th century when it was a favourite *Belle Epoque* retreat. Frederick Henry, the hero of Hemingway's *Farewell to Arms*, stayed at the elegant Grand Hotel et des Iles Borromees. The lakeside promenade, Lungolago, is famous for its flowers and bewitching view of the islands. Take the cable car to the peak of the **Mottarone** at 1,491m (4,892ft) for its exhilarating view of the Lombardy lakes, the Alps and Po Valley. A toll road will also take you there via the Giardino Alpinia (Alpine Garden), displaying over 2,000 varieties of mountain plants.

Piedmont (*Piemonte*)

As its name suggests, this region of the upper basin of the Po river lies in the foothills of the Alps.

From the fall of the Roman Empire to the 19th century, it stood outside the mainstream of Italian history. Its royal House of Savoy walked a diplomatic tightrope between the rivalries of France, Switzerland, Spain and the German emperors until the fall of Napoleon. The new nationalism led Piedmont into the Italian orbit at the head of the *Risorgimento* unification movement, and the House of Savoy provided the first king of united Italy, Vittorio Emanuele.

Close links with France have left their mark. A French *patois* is still spoken in hill villages and you will notice bilingual street signs in the Aosta

Isola Bella is the most romantic of the Borromean islands; an island paradise created by Count Carlo Borromeo for his wife, Isabella.

Valley (geographically part of Piedmont, but administratively separate). The country's most venerable ski resort, lying on the Italian side of Mont Blanc, is known as Courmayeur, not Cortemaggiore. The classical palaces and squares of Turin, Piedmont's royal capital, are in many ways closer in spirit to France than the rest of Italy. Yet whatever cooler Gallic ambience this may have created has been thoroughly Italianized by the steady influx of workers from the south for the steel, chemical, automobile and communications industries.

Turin (*Torino*)

Best known for its industry, most notably the giant Fiat automobile works, the proud Piedmontese capital is far from being a dull, dismal factory town. It has retained the checker-board layout of its origins as a Roman *castrum*. Its rise to prominence in the 17th and 18th centuries was accompanied by Italy's first coherent urban planning and the classical and baroque palaces and monuments give its main streets and squares a great dignity and panache.

The tone is set by the formal elegance of **Piazza Castello**, dominated by Filippo Juvarra's richly articulated baroque façade for the **Palazzo Madama**. The original medieval castle received its new name when transformed in the 17th century into the royal residence of Vittorio Amedeo I's widow, Maria Cristina. It now houses the **Civic Museum** (*Museo Civico d'Arte Antica*) beside a splendid ceremonial staircase, also designed by Juvarra. The paintings include Jan van Eyck's 14th-century miniatures for the *Book of Hours of the Duc de Berry*, Pontormo's *St Michael* and a particularly handsome *Portrait of a Young Man* by Sicilian master Antonello da Messina. On upper floors are royal collections of furniture, ceramics and carved ivories.

Across the square is the former royal chapel, the 17th-century church of **San Lorenzo**, designed by Turin's other great baroque architect, Fra Guarino Guarini. Philosopher and mathematician as well as priest, he has created a marvellously intricate interior surrounding the octagonal space with 16 red marble columns. Arches rise to hold the central lanterned cupola formed by an 8-pointed star.

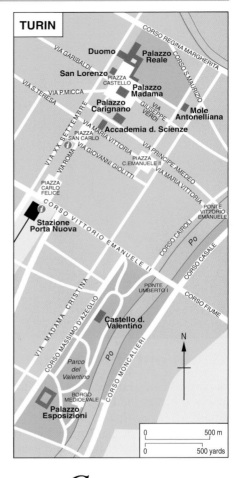

*C*ity plan of Turin.

At the **Armoury** (*Armeria Reale*), housed in a wing of the Palazzo Reale, take a look at the interesting collection of Asian and European weapons and armour dating back to Roman and Etruscan times. Then relax a while behind the palace in its **Royal Gardens**, designed by Louis XIV's Versailles landscape-architect, André Le Nôtre.

The late 15th-century **cathedral** cherishes one of Italy's most celebrated relics, the shroud said to have enveloped Jesus on his descent from the cross, taking the imprint of his face and body. Kept in the **Chapel of the Holy Shroud**, (*Cappella della Sacra Sindone*), it was brought to Turin in the 17th century after a journey 200 years earlier from Jerusalem to France via Cyprus. Measuring 4.1m by 1.4m (13ft by 5ft), the sheet is kept in an iron-boxed silver casket placed in a marble urn on the altar. Modern scientific tests have proved it is a medieval forgery, but crowds still visit its black marble chapel, a masterpiece of Guarini's High Baroque, with its cone-shaped dome formed by a web of intersecting arches that rise to a 12-pointed star.

The pride of Turin, as in so many Italian cities, is not in one monument but in a glorious square, **Piazza San Carlo**, one of the most beautiful in Europe. The 17th-century palazzi make an exquisite setting for your late afternoon *passeggiata* along the arcades of shops and cafés, culminating in the graceful symmetry of two baroque churches: Juvarra's Santa Cristina and its twin, San Carlo. Stretching north and south of the square is the town's most elegant shopping street, Via Roma.

North-east of the piazza, in the Palazzo dell'Accademia delle Scienze, stands the **Egyptian Museum** (*Museo Egizio*) second in importance only to the one in Cairo. Its treasures include statues of the Pharaohs of 1500 BC, of Tutankhamen and the god Amen-Ra, as well as a mummified crocodile, and artefacts of everyday life, clothes, kitchen utensils, even food.

On the second floor is the **Galleria Sabauda** (Savoy Gallery), with an important collection of Italian and European art. The Italian works include a Fra Angelico *Madonna and Angels*, Veronese's *Supper at Simon's House* and Pollaiuolo's *Tobias and the Archangel*. Among the European paintings are Jan van Eyck's *St Francis Receiving the Stigmata* and works by Roger van der Weyden, Van Dyck, Rembrandt, Hans Memling and François Clouet.

One of the city's more bizarre monuments is the **Mole Antonelliana**, with its swordfish-like 167m- (547ft-) high granite spire, named after its engineer-designer Alessandro Antonelli. Planned originally in 1863 as a synagogue, it is now a beloved city symbol used for exhibitions and elevator trips to its panoramic terrace.

On the left bank of the Po stand the beautiful gardens of the **Parco del Valentino**, opened in 1856. The park contains a Botanic Garden dating back to 1729 and the curious Castello del Valentino, a 17th-century castle built in the style of a French chateau. Further south lies the **Borgo Medioevale**, a mock-medieval village built for the international exhibition hosted by Turin in 1884.

The designing talents of Fiat, Alfa Romeo, Bugatti and Ferrari (but also Benz, Peugeot and Ford) are celebrated out at the **Museo dell'Automobile** (Corso Unità d'Italia, 40), south of the city centre beside the Po river.

Take the pretty excursion across the river to Sassi, 10km (6 miles) east of Turin, to see Juvarra's baroque masterpiece, the splendid domed **Basilica di Superga** and the hilltop view of the Alps and the Po Valley. Kings of the House of Savoy are buried in the basilica's crypt.

Courmayeur

The 4,810m (15,781ft) peak of Mont Blanc (*Monte Bianco*) may be in France, but the Italian side of the mountain gets the better weather. The Aosta Valley's Courmayeur is as pleasant a base for hiking, and more strenuous mountain-climbing, in summer as it is for skiing in winter. Adepts recommend the mineral waters for whatever ails you, and a shot of *grappa* for whatever doesn't.

This is Italy's oldest ski resort, and an Alpine museum traces its history in the Casa delle Guide (*Maison des Guides*). One of the most spectacular excursions in the whole country is the 90-minute **cable-car ride** from La Palud, north of Courmayeur, to the Colle del Gigante, 3,354m (11,004ft) and the Aiguille du Midi, 3,842m (12,606ft), just across the border in France. This gives you a wonderful view across to the peak of Mont Blanc and the whole roof of the western Alps.

Italian Riviera

The Ligurian coast that holiday-makers have dubbed the Italian Riviera has an ancient history of piracy and commerce, not always easily distinguishable. The great port-city of Genoa made the Mediterranean more or less safe for respectable traders and the rest of the coast settled down to some quiet fishing, sailing and harmless traffic in postcards and sun-tan lotion.

The picturesque, more rugged coast east of Genoa is known as the Riviera di Levante (Riviera of the Rising Sun), while the coast west to the French border at Ventimiglia is the Riviera di Ponente (Riviera of the Setting Sun), better known for the sandy beaches of its family resorts.

Genoa (*Genova*)

Hemmed in between the Apennine mountains and the sea, Genoa has tended, like its historic rival Venice on the east coast, to turn its back on Italy to seek its fortune on the high seas. This may account for a cool reserve, almost aloofness, that some read even into the architecture of the tall houses in the narrow streets behind the port.

With 28km (17 miles) of docks, Italy's biggest port remains the key to the city's identity. For a close-up of the giant oil-tankers that have replaced the schooners of old, start your city tour with a motor-launch **harbour cruise** from the Calata degli Zingari quay between the passenger and cargo terminals.

Genoa's historic centre is a maze of steep, twisting lanes (known as *caruggi*) and precipitous flights of steps rising up from the port. **Piazza San Matteo** was the medieval home of the august Doria family, navigators and merchants who helped build the city's great commercial empire. Their arcaded houses, with grey- and white-striped façades (Nos 15–17) were built from the 13th to the 15th century. The Romanesque-Gothic church of **San Matteo** has the same grey and white façade. In the crypt, you'll find the tomb of Andrea Doria, the 16th-century admiral who took Genoa into the Spanish camp against the French and became the city's virtual dictator.

A fairy-tale castle looks out over the lovely Valle d'Aosta.

240

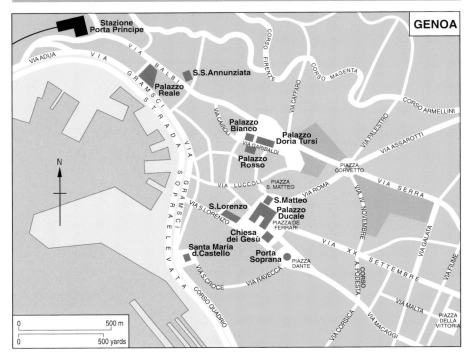

City plan of Genoa.

Genoa's cathedral, **San Lorenzo**, was consecrated in 1118 but work continued over the centuries to come leaving the building a blend of Romanesque, Gothic and Renaissance styles. The cathedral's **Treasury** is reached from the sacristy, at the end of the left nave. Among the exhibits of religious art and artefacts, the most fascinating relics are a 1st-century Roman green glass chalice supposedly used by Christ at the Last Supper and a 1st-century BC chalcedony dish said to be the platter on which St John the Baptist's head was presented to Salome (the saint's image was added in the 15th century).

The Renaissance and baroque palaces of **Via Garibaldi** are a unique testimony to the town's historic prosperity. Many of them are now banks or museums. The **Palazzo Bianco** (No. 11) makes a handsome setting for its collection of Genoese painters, Cambiaso, Strozzi and Magnasco, as well as works by Pontormo and Palma il Vecchio, and the Flemish school: Rubens, Gérard David and Van Dyck. The 17th-century baroque **Palazzo Rosso** (No. 18), taking its name from the red façade, displays works by Veronese, Titian, Dürer, Rubens and Van Dyck. The 16th-century **Palazzo Doria Tursi** (No. 9) is the city's town hall but visitors are allowed in to see some of the lavishly decorated rooms including the **Sala della Giunta** in which is displayed the Guarnerius violin of Nicolò Paganini, born in Genoa in 1784.

The Garibaldi Obsession

The surprising thing about Giuseppe Garibaldi (1807–82) in the unification of Italy is that he found time to be around at the crucial moment. In 1836, he was waging his first guerrilla warfare in Brazil. Six years later he moved on to some more freedom-fighting in Uruguay, but got back to Europe in time for the 1848 combat in Sardinia against Austria. After a quick round-trip to the United States, he settled in for the serious business of *Risorgimento*. Once the loose ends were tied up after the Expedition of 1,000 (*see* page 59), he was to be seen fighting for the Prussians in the Austro-Prussian War of 1866 and then for the French in the Franco-Prussian War of 1871. His son Ricciotti continued the good work for the Greeks against the Turks in 1897 and 1912. His grandson Peppino turned up on the British side in the Boer War, in a Venezuelan revolution, on the Greek side in the Balkan Wars and, for old times' sake, with an Italian regiment of volunteers in World War I. His opposition to Mussolini obliged him to emigrate to the United States in 1924.

It is appropriate, given the city's great maritime heritage, that Genoa's most famous native son should be a navigator: Christopher Columbus. In **Piazza Dante**, near the medieval turreted gate of Porta Soprana, is the house where the explorer is said to have spent his childhood. On the other side of town in **Piazza Acquaverde**, outside the Porta Principe Station, stands a statue to Columbus, erected in 1862. This proud, civic monument conveniently disregards the fact that the discoverer of the Americas had to look elsewhere to find funding for his visionary voyage.

Riviera Resorts

Quite apart from its superb beaches, the coast is rich in colour and fragrancy—almond, peach and apricot blossoms in spring, groves of orange, lemon and eucalyptus trees, exquisite gardens of mimosa, roses and carnations.

Along the mostly rugged Riviera di Levante east of Genoa, by far the prettiest spot is **Portofino**, where you are likely to come across as many millionaire's yachts as fishing boats moored in the harbour. Unless you are also arriving by sea, you will have to walk the last stretch to get to the heart of Portofino as cars have been banned from the

Genoa celebrates its most famous son in this majestic 19th-century monument to Christopher Columbus in Piazza Acquaverde.

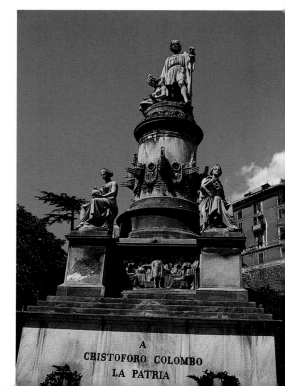

A
CRISTOFORO COLOMBO
LA PATRIA

waterfront area. Above the colourfully painted houses clustered around the harbour, take a cliff walk past the church of San Giorgio (containing relics of the saint brought by Crusaders from the Holy Land) to the **lighthouse** (*faro*) at the end of the promontory for a superb view along the coast. The cliffs are clothed in a profusion of exotic vegetation, with occasional glimpses of imposing villas.

Boat excursions will take you to other beautifully secluded fishing villages, such as **Camogli** and **San Fruttuoso**, whose 13th-century abbey, with its magnificent cloister and church, holds the tombs of the noble Doria family. By road, you can visit the charming little town of **San Rocco** and take a 40-

Charles Dickens described the seaport of Camogli as "the saltiest, roughest, most piratical little place". The town has apparently quietened down somewhat since then.

minute walk over to Punta Chiappa, looking out over the whole Riviera.

Santa Margherita Ligure is a jolly resort town with lively cafés, discos and *trattorie*. **Rapallo** is the region's most popular resort. Its beautiful natural setting at the head of the Tigullio gulf has been somewhat marred in recent years by unbridled development but it continues to draw visitors with a range of diversions, from golf and horse riding to scuba-diving and boat trips. Further down the coast, past the shipbuilding town of **Chiavari**, the family resort of **Sestri Levante** has fine sandy beaches.

To the south lies the fascinating region of the **Cinque Terre**, made up of five historically remote villages: Monterosso al Mare, Vernazza, Corniglia, Manarola and Riomaggiore. They are simple and starkly beautiful places on a little-visited, rugged part of the coast. Vineyards producing the white wine *Sciacchetrà* rise to seemingly unworkable heights up almost vertical mountainsides. Five castles stand on peaks above, five fishing harbours lie below.

The Explorers

The Polo brothers travelling by camel caravan, from the Catalan Atlas of 1375

Italy has contributed many of the world's greatest explorers. But without the national unity that might have nurtured a true empire as opposed to the overseas trading networks of maritime republics like Venice or Genoa, they travelled either on their own account or in the service of a foreign ruler.

Marco Polo (1254–1324) was a very patriotic Venetian but his epic journey to China was strictly a family enterprise. His merchant father Niccolò and uncle Maffeo first visited the court of Kublai Khan in Kaifeng in 1266. Impressed by their talk of Christianity, the emperor Kublai Khan, son of Genghis Khan, asked them to come again with "one hundred intelligent men acquainted with the arts".

For their second trip in 1271, they took 17-year-old Marco along. The two Dominican friars soon dropped out of the party, but Marco loved the four-year trek through Persia,

Title page of first edition of "The Book of Marco Polo", printed in 1477

the Afghan mountains, Mongolia and the Gobi desert to Cambuluc (Beijing). And Kublai loved the tale of his adventures, making him a personal emissary to trade throughout China, South-East Asia and India. For three years, Marco was governor of Yangchow.

He finally left China with his father and uncle in 1292, but back in Venice at the family home (its Byzantine archway still stands behind the church of San Giovanni Crisostomo) nobody recognized these fellows in shabby oriental robes. It was only when they cut open their linings to shower forth emeralds, rubies and pearls that people began to believe their stories of the fabled wealth of the East. Marco's account of his adventures was entitled "Il Milione", the word he repeatedly used to describe the masses of riches he had seen wherever he went.

Christopher Columbus

(1451–1506), the man who discovered America without knowing it, was born in Genoa into a family of woollen weavers. The Spanish, French, English, Irish, Greeks, Polish and Russians have claimed him as their own, but none so brazen as the Scandinavians suggesting he was an American-born Norseman from an 11th-century Viking colony who first sailed *back* to Europe and then returned to "re-discover" America! In fact, after sailing the Mediterranean in his twenties, he was shipwrecked off the Portuguese coast in 1476. He took on as a sugar merchant sailing out to Madeira, Cape Verde and the Azores where he heard his first tales of lands even further west. The kings of Portugal, France and England all turned down his plan to find a westward passage to the Indies: China, Japan, India and the spice islands. Finally, Spain's Ferdinand and Isabella backed the expedition of 1492.

Left: Portrait of Columbus, by Ridolfo del Ghirlandaio

On that and three further voyages, Columbus discovered the Bahamas, Cuba, Puerto Rico, Jamaica, the mouth of Venezuela's Orinoco river and, in 1502, the mainland coast of Central America. But no sign of Japan. The "Admiral of the Ocean Sea" returned to die in obscurity, believing his *Otro Mundo* (Other World) was an extension of the Malayan peninsula.

Below: The Spanish view of the American Indians, an illustration from the first edition (1493) of Columbus's letter telling of his discovery

John Cabot

(1450–1499), who crossed the Atlantic for England's Henry VII, was originally named something like Giovanni Caboto—as the Spanish envoy in London said, "another Genoese like Columbus," but a naturalized Venetian citizen. In 1497, he set sail from Bristol and in 35 days (two days longer than Columbus), he was raising St. George's banner to claim Newfoundland for England, plus one of St. Mark's to honour Venice. Good winds took him back to England in 15 days, the king gave him £10 and, with great Italian bravado, Cabot blew it on silk clothes and a binge on London's Lombard Street. A few months later he was America-bound again, but this time disappeared without a trace.

John Cabot leaving Bristol in 1497 on the voyage that took him to Newfoundland

*Recreation of Amerigo
Vespucci's ship of discovery*

*Portrait of Amerigo Vespucci,
Uffizi Gallery*

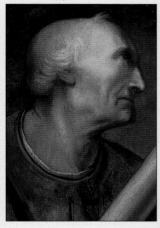

Amerigo Vespucci (1454–
1512) was not without merit in
having his name attached to
the continents of the New
World. A Florentine merchant
seaman originally in the service
of the Medici, he joined the
expedition from Seville of
Alonso de Ojeda in 1499. They
separated in the Caribbean and
Vespucci sailed south to
explore the mouth of the
Amazon river and the north
shore of South America. He
perfected a scientific method to
compute exact longitude and
had no doubt that he was
charting a new continent, not a
part of Asia. German scholar
Martin Waldseemüller credited
this insight in his
Cosmographiae Introductio of
1507 by naming the land mass
America.

Giovanni da Verrazzano
(1485–1528) was another
Florentine, of landed gentry
originally from Greve in the
Chianti country. French king
François I, patron of Leonardo
da Vinci and Benvenuto Cellini,
happily welcomed another
Italian, especially if Florentine
bankers in Lyon were prepared
to foot the bill. So Verrazzano
sailed from Dieppe in 1523 to
explore the American coast
from North Carolina to Maine.
In the Bay of New York, he
anchored in the narrows now
spanned by the Verrazzano
Bridge, but passed up an
invitation from cheerful,
feather-clad natives to explore
Manhattan Island. Five years
later, less friendly fellows in
Guadeloupe slaughtered him
and ate him on the beach.

The origins of the hardy people of Cinque Terre are unknown. Some say they are descended from the Etruscans of 2,500 years ago and that they were given shelter in these craggy cliff spaces in return for creating and nurturing the precipitous vineyards.

The Gulf of La Spezia gets its alternative name of the **Golfo dei Poeti** from its associations with the English Romantic poets Byron and Shelley. The redoubtable Byron swam across the gulf in 1822 from **Portovenere**, a charming village of brightly coloured houses perched on the rocky coastline, to visit Shelley at the Casa Magni in San Terenzo near Lerici. Later the same year, Shelley drowned in the gulf when his boat the Don Juan went down in heavy seas.

Down the coast, beyond the naval city of La Spezia, the beaches of **Viareggio** are the favourite resort of the Tuscans, if not to everone's taste. The monotony of regimented lines of *stabilmenti balneari* (corridors of private beaches where you must rent your patch of sand by the day or week) is relieved by striking Art Nouveau architecture and shady umbrella pines. Nearby **Forte dei Marmi**, once a centre for shipping marble, is the most fashionable resort on this stretch of coast, the Versilian Riviera. Here the beaches are less crowded, the discotheques more elegant and the Apuan mountains provide a beautiful backdrop.

Cool off with an excursion inland to **Carrara**, where the marble quarries provided the raw material of Italy's greatest achievements, the monuments of the Roman Empire and the Renaissance. The town is still full of sculptors, and Piazza Alberica is the scene of a summer sculpture competition which allows 14 days to produce a masterpiece. Visit the still active **quarries** of Fantiscritti and Colonnata. The marble that Michelangelo chose for his *Moses* and *Pietà* is now hewn for replicas at Caesar's Palace, Las Vegas, and tombstones in the Los Angeles Forest Lawn cemetery.

Between Carrara and the coast, the lower slopes of the Apuans produce a delicious sweet white wine known as *Candia*. The vines cling to the slopes in lines of terraces, a system of cultivation which probably dates from the Lombard invasions of the 6th and 7th centuries when the people of the old Roman settlement of Luni were forced to flee the plains. In the early 14th century the local feudal lord, Malaspina della Lunigiana, played host in his **Castello di Fosdinovo** to Dante, who was acting as ambassador for the archbishop of Luni, but also found time to write part of his *Divine Comedy*.

The Riviera di Ponente west of Genoa is an almost continuous chain of family resorts with broad stretches of fine sandy beaches.

The area around **Finale Ligure** is honeycombed by scores of deep limestone caves, some of them the dwellings of the region's prehistoric inhabitants. There are interesting paleolithic remains in the **museum** attached to the convent of Santa Caterina at Finalborgo. Those more interested in soaking up the sun should head for the beaches at Finale Marina and Finale Pia.

The quiet medieval town of **Albenga** was once a thriving Roman port but now lies almost a mile inland, thanks to a shifting coastline. In the town centre Romanesque-Gothic houses cluster around the 11th- to 14th-century cathedral and early Christian (5th-century) baptistery. A short way along the coast, **Alassio**'s long sandy beach makes it one of the region's most popular holiday destinations. The resort is justifiably proud of its gardens nurtured by a particularly mild winter.

San Remo, with its Art Nouveau casino and elegant promenade along the Corso Imperatrice, is the most glamorous of the Riviera's resorts. The town's Russian Orthodox church of San Basilio is a reminder of the period when San Remo was home to a colony of exiled Russian aristocrats after the Bolshevik revolution. An earlier Russian visitor was the composer

San Remo's glamorous heyday was between the World Wars, when exiled Russian aristocrats made it their home. The resort may no longer have quite the same cachet but it's still the smartest place on the Riviera di Ponente

Tchaikovsky, who finished his 4th Symphony and the opera *Eugene Onegin* while staying at the resort in 1878. Today, San Remo plays host to a highly popular International Song Contest.

If you can bear to drag yourself away from the beach, find time to explore the narrow winding medieval streets of the **La Pigna** quarter, leading up to the 17th-century sanctuary of the Madonna della Costa. From its terrace, you have a splendid view of the coast.

Nearby **Bordighera** is particularly proud of the palm trees along the Lungomare Argentina promenade. Since the 16th century, the town has had the exclusive privilege of providing Rome with its palm fronds for the Sunday before Easter.

Just inside the French border, 6km (4 miles) west of Ventimiglia, the village of Mortola Inferiore is location of the renowned **Giardino Hanbury**, a large botanic garden founded in 1867 by English merchant Sir Thomas Hanbury. The garden contains some 3,000 varieties of plants and trees from around the world and offers splendid views of the sea.

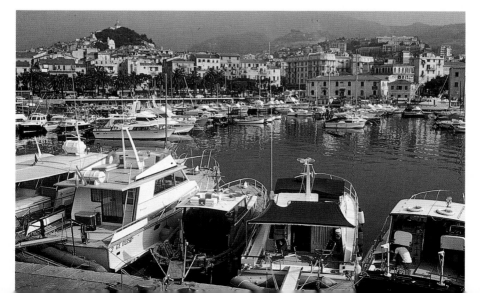

Italy's Mezzogiorno: a Sun-baked Land of Contrasts

The sun which beats down on Italy's *Mezzogiorno* illuminates a land of contrasts. There is undeniably poverty, backwardness and crime, but they co-exist with a wealth of natural and artistic treasures: the islands of Capri and Ischia; the Amalfi coast; the ruins of Pompeii in the shadow of Vesuvius. "See Naples and die," goes the famous saying. Such is the heart-stopping beauty of the city's magnificent bay it might well prove true.

The chief pleasure of the south or *Mezzogiorno* is the people. If the warm-hearted, outgoing, gregarious Italian in love with the music and sun of life is a delightful legend, then the nearest the myth meets reality is in the south. Despite dilapidation, cultural treasures survive: the Greek temples of Paestum; Puglia's intriguing stone *trulli* houses, of prehistoric design; the baroque riches of Naples. And beyond the ugly suburbs of the south's modern building speculation, hardly worse than in the north, is a countryside largely unspoiled: the Lattari Hills behind Amalfi, Puglia's Gargano peninsula, and a landscape dotted with *trulli*, feudal castles and Romanesque churches.

Over the centuries Italy's south has suffered more than its share of disasters—both natural and man-made. The ruins of Pompeii are testimony to the region's most famous catastrophe: the eruption of Vesuvius in AD 79.

Naples (*Napoli*)

The very idea of this teeming, undisciplined town (population over 1,200,000) may intimidate the faint-hearted, but for those as enterprising and cheerful as the Neapolitans themselves, the rewards are rich. Indeed, two of its museums are among the most important in Europe, but they

THE SOUTH

ROMA

Isole
Tremiti

Vieste

Monte Sant'Angelo   Testa del Gargano

Manfredonia

Lucera   PUGLIA

Troia   Foggia

Barletta   Trani

Benevento   Molfetta

Caserta   Castel   Bitonto   Bari

del Monte   Polignano a Mare

NAPOLI   Castellana

VESUVIO   A16   Alberobello   S613

Cuma   Matera   Brindisi

Pozzuoli   Pompei   S94   Potenza   Massafra

Ischia   Ercolano   Castellaneta   S106   Lecce

Sorrento   Salerno   Táranto

Capri   Amalfi   BASILICATA   Metaponto   Otranto

Paestum   Golfo di   Gallipoli

CAMPANIA   Táranto

Maratea   Capo Santa
Maria di Leuca

Mare
Tirreno

N

Rossano

Cosenza   San Giovanni
in Fiore

Crotone

Golfo di   S106
Sant'Eufémia   Pizzo   Catanzaro

Tropea   CALABRIA
Capo Vaticano

G.di Gioia

Palmi

Scilla   Locri

PALERMO   Reggio di   Mare
Calabria   Ionio

Melito di
Porto Salvo

Sicilia

0   80 km
0   50 miles
Land above 2,000m (6,560ft)

and the monuments play second fiddle
to the street-life. In the outdoor theatre
that is Italy, Naples is unabashed
melodrama. Around the port, in the
popular quarters of Spaccanapoli, even
in the more bourgeois neighbourhoods
of Vomero and Posillipo, the everyday
drama of Neapolitan life presents a
fascinating spectacle. Spend hours in
the restaurants. Whether the Chinese
or the Italians invented noodles,
Naples is where real spaghetti began
and where the Spaniards brought
Italy's first tomato.

*S*outhern Italy.

Driving in the seething cauldron that
is Naples traffic is a nerve-shattering
experience for the uninitiated. Neapolitan drivers ignore traffic signals, drive
in the wrong direction down one-way
streets, overtake on the inside, make illegal turns with impunity and park
wherever they please. The best course
is to leave driving to the locals and
stick to walking or the bus. But you
can still admire the skill and audacity

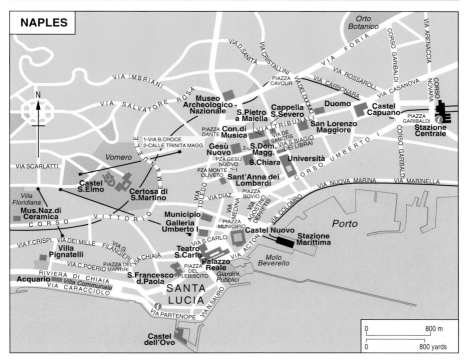

City plan of Naples.

with which Neapolitan drivers shunt and slalom their way out of a traffic jam without hurting a flea.

The face of Naples has been made and remade by its many earthquakes, permitting, even imposing transitions from Gothic to Renaissance and baroque. Remember that today many of the city's churches, palaces and museums may be closed for ongoing reconstruction and restoration after the devastating earthquake of 1980.

The Port and Spaccanapoli

Traffic roars down broad Corso Umberto I to pivotal **Piazza Municipio** to serve the docks or spin off into the commercial district behind Santa Lucia, the teeming historic centre of Spaccanapoli or the residential districts of Vomero and Posillipo.

Towering over the long rectangular square on its south side is the massive dry-moated **Castel Nuovo**. Originally the 13th-century fortress of Naples' French ruler Charles d'Anjou, it was rebuilt in the 15th century as a palace for the Spanish kings of Aragon. The entrance to what is now administrative offices and a communal library is between two towers on the west side, away from the harbour, through a fine two-storey Renaissance **triumphal arch** crowned by a statue of St Michael. Francesco Laurana's sculpted reliefs celebrate the ceremonial entry of Alfonso I of Aragon in 1443.

The **port** is a vast enterprise of civil, commercial and military activities.

Thriving and Surviving

Two attitudes to this town are fatal. One is to see all Neapolitans as lovable fellows evicted from their tenements singing *O Sole Mio*. The other is to imagine them all cut-throats waiting in doorways just for you.

Romantics are inevitably disillusioned by a town where the major art is the art of survival, overcoming the hardships of a chronically depressed economy with a maximum of ingenuity and optimism that leaves little room for sentimentality. The people will sell you anything you want and a lot that you don't. Sing *O Sole Mio*, Okay, but for money.

If paranoiacs, as social psychologists in Naples have observed, find their suspicions "satisfied" by becoming easy prey for pickpockets or purse-snatchers, it is because their whole nervous demeanour almost begs the thieves to act. Some people, say the criminologists, are born victims.

Without waving your jewels in dark alleys, stay cool and self-assured and no harm will come. When you have finished raging over the Gucci bag or Cartier watch you thought you'd haggled for so brilliantly, only to discover it's a fake, you may doff your hat to the hustler's diabolical talent and the back-street industry behind him.

Ocean liners dock at the great Stazione Marittima, ferries to the islands of Capri and Ischia (*see* pages 264-6) leave from the Molo Beverello, while out in the bay you will see huge oil tankers and ships of the United States Navy. Naples is an important base for American NATO forces and their white-uniformed sailors are a fixture of the city's night life.

Celebrated in song, the old popular harbour district of **Santa Lucia** is lined with elegant hotels and restaurants now, contrasting with the formidable medieval **Castel dell'Ovo** out on the promontory. The fortress was built in the 12th century over the ruins of a Roman villa and gets its strange name, Castle of the Egg, from a medieval legend that the poet-enchanter Virgil magically secured the foundations by building on an egg placed in a jar under the sea. A more prosaic theory holds that the castle is named for its oval shape. The sunset walk along the headland gives you a great view of the bay and Mount Vesuvius.

Via Caracciolo continues the bay promenade alongside the pretty gardens of the **Villa Comunale**, a respite from the city traffic among holm oaks and palms and the welcome fragrancy of pines and eucalyptus. The **Aquarium** in the middle keeps its 200 species of flora and marine life from the Bay of Naples in water coming in directly from the sea, thus avoiding the environmental shock of a habitat purified of Naples' famous pollution. Beyond the gardens, on Piazza della Repubblica, is a monument to Neapolitan resistance to the Nazi occupation. Early in the morning, you can watch the fishermen of **Mergellina** bringing their catch into Porto Sannazaro at the western end of the harbour.

Return to the centre, south of Piazza Municipio, where Via San Carlo curves round to the 19th-century steel and glass shopping arcade of **Galleria Umberto I**, opposite the great neoclassical temple of Neapolitan *bel canto*, the **Teatro San Carlo**. Dating back to 1737, the San Carlo is one of the oldest, and largest, opera houses in the world and continues to attract an extremely vocal and partisan audience.

*I*ntrigue behind the scenes at Naples' Teatro San Carlo has at times rivalled the drama on stage. In the early 1820s, the soprano Isabella Colbran was the mistress of both the theatre's manager and the King of Naples, until the composer Rossini stole her away to become his wife.

The sumptuous gilt stucco interior was created when the theatre was reconstructed after a fire in 1816. The solemnly monumental colonnaded hemicycle of **Piazza del Plebiscito** was laid out by Napoleon's marshal Joachim Murat when, as King of Naples, he occupied the Spaniards' **Palazzo Reale** on the east side of the piazza. The rooms are still decorated and furnished with the baroque pomp of the 17th and 18th century.

From the north-west corner of the palace, a lively shopping district extends along Via Chiaia, growing more elegant around **Piazza dei Martiri**, with its fashionable cafés and boutiques of Italy's major designers.

Leading north from the palace, the Neapolitans' favourite shopping street of **Via Toledo** is named after Viceroy Dom Pedro Alvarez de Toledo (but confusingly on some maps it goes by the name of Via Roma). It separates the Town Hall (*Municipio*) and broad commercial streets going down to the harbour from a checker-board of narrow alleys to the west, a neighbourhood favoured by Naples' Spanish rulers in the 16th century that is now a mass of tall crowded tenements badly hit by the 1980 earthquake.

East of Via Toledo, behind an unprepossessing façade on Piazza Monteoliveto, the church of **Sant'Anna dei Lombardi** contains in its chapels a magnificent collection of Renaissance sculpture. Immediately to the right of the entrance, through a finely carved Renaissance arch, is Benedetto da

Maiano's marble altarpiece of the *Annunciation* (1489). Equally impressive is Guido Mazzoni's *Pietà* (1492), a dramatic group of eight life-size terracotta figures in the Holy Sepulchre Oratory (off the right aisle beyond the 5th chapel). In the **Piccolomini Chapel** left of the entrance, look for the monumental marble tomb of Maria of Aragon, with bas-reliefs carved by Antonio Rossellino that recall his work in Florence's San Miniato.

Via Toledo takes you into the city's historic heart, **Spaccanapoli** (around a Roman road that splits Naples into upper and lower districts). In an area stretching from the permanently traffic-jammed Piazza Dante, between Via San Biagio dei Librai and Via Tribunali and over to the porta Capuana, the popular image of old Naples survives. Children and dogs splash each other in the ornate fountains. Jewellers, second-hand bookshops, fishmongers and teeming tenements jostle decaying Spanish baroque palazzi commandeered as workshops for carpentry, leather craft and more clandestine manufacture. A permanent festival of laundry hangs across the narrow streets. Gossip, business and vendettas fly between balconies, while ropes haul up baskets of vegetables, letters and pet cats.

For a sense of the neighbourhood's old splendour, start on **Piazza Gesù Nuovo**, with its characteristically extravagant baroque Immacolata column (*guglia*) in the centre. Behind an embossed façade, the same architectural exuberance continues inside the Jesuit church. The jewel here, on the south corner of the square, is the 14th-century church of **Santa Chiara**, built for the wife of Robert d'Anjou and retrieved from its 18th-century baroque additions and 20th-century fire-bombing. The original rose-window and elegant porch survive and the French Gothic interior is beautifully restored. In the choir are the sculpted **tombs** of Marie de Valois (on the right) and Robert d'Anjou (behind the high altar). Through an entrance between the church and campanile, visit the lovely 14th-century **cloister** (*Chiostro delle Clarisse*), converted in 1742 into a country garden by the rococo architect Domenico Vaccaro. Avenues of columns and benches, beautifully decorated with majolica tiles, create a delightful and vitally necessary haven of tranquillity.

Despite the many baroque transformations of the 13th-century church of **San Domenico Maggiore** (just north of Via Benedetto Croce), the French spirit remains very much present in its Gothic arcades. The medieval theologian Thomas Aquinas taught in the Dominican monastery here and the Renaissance philosopher Giordano Bruno was a pupil. In the little Capellone del Crocifisso beyond the 6th chapel off the right aisle, is the 13th-century Crucifixion painting which is said to have spoken to Thomas Aquinas. Francesco Solimena's baroque frescoes embellish the sacristy. East of the church, in Via De Sanctis, the **Cappella Sansevero**, 16th-century funeral chapel of the princely del Sangro family, is now a museum of allegorical baroque sculptures. Outstanding pieces are Francesco Queirolo's *Disillusion*, an amazing *tour de force* of a man entangled in a net meticulously chiselled out of marble; Giuseppe Sammartino's moving *Dead Christ*; and Antonio

Corradini's rather immodest representation of *Modesty* as a veiled nude.

Take Via Tribunali to the Franciscan church of **San Lorenzo Maggiore**, with its 14th-century marble porch incorporated into a baroque façade and added after the earthquake of 1731. Inside, the French Gothic chancel, exceptional in Naples for its ambulatory around the nine chapels, contrasts with the baroque chapel left of the choir.

The **Cattedrale di San Gennaro** was built by Naples' Angevin kings in the 13th and 14th centuries on the site of an early Christian basilica. The cathedral owes its present appearance to several earthquakes and subsequent reconstructions and restorations. The three handsome 15th-century portals by Antonio Baboccio are somewhat overpowered by the ugly 19th-century neo-Gothic façade. Inside, to the right of the baroque nave, the **chapel of San Gennaro** contains relics of Naples' martyred patron saint, Januarius, beheaded by the Romans in 305. In a tabernacle behind Solimena's grandiose silver altar are kept the saint's head enclosed in a 14th-century silver reliquary and two phials of his congealed blood. Three times a year (on the first Saturday in May and on 19 September and 16 December) crowds gather to watch the miraculous liquefaction of the saint's blood. Tradition holds that if the congealed blood fails to liquefy, disaster lies in store for the city.

Go down to Naples' earliest known Christian sanctuary—to the left of the nave—the 4th-century basilica of **Santa Restituta**, founded on the site of a temple of Apollo. The original Roman columns have survived. At the end of the right nave is the 5th-century domed baptistery with remnants of some fine mosaics in the dome.

Hidden away behind the cathedral, **Santa Maria Donnaregina** is in fact two churches. The baroque edifice by Turin architect Giovanni Guarini with some Solimena frescoes in the choir, stands in front of the Gothic church built early in the 14th century by Queen Mary of Hungary, after whom it is named. Enter via the 18th-century cloister to see, to the left, the queen's monumental tomb by Sienese sculptor Tino di Camaino. Up in the nun's choir-gallery are frescoes by Pietro Cavallini and pupils depicting the *Last Judgement*, the *Passion* and the legends of St Catherine, St Agnes and St Elizabeth of Hungary.

The eastern end of Spaccanapoli is dominated by the Hohenstaufen emperors' medieval **Castel Capuano** (law courts since the 16th century) and a Renaissance city gate, **Porta Capuana**, flanked by massive towers from the Spanish ramparts. Between the gate and the fortress, a boisterous market offers a veritable open-air museum of counterfeit luxury brands of luggage, wristwatches, polo shirts and tennis shoes.

The Museums

The roguish image of the city's present might make it easy to forget the city's glorious past. Luckily, two truly magnificent museums preserve the region's treasures from the ravages of earthquake and theft. Inquire at one of the city's Tourist Information offices (at the main railway station or Via Partenope 10a in Santa Lucia, for example) about the ever-changing details of opening times.

Originally a 16th-century cavalry barracks, the **Archaeological Museum**

(*Museo Archeologico Nazionale*) is in no way a dry bundle of old bones and stones, but sheer pleasure for anyone even remotely interested in southern Italy's Greek, Etruscan and Roman past. All visits to Pompeii and Herculaneum should begin or end here. The collections display, beautifully, not only the paintings and mosaics buried there nearly 2,000 years ago by Mount Vesuvius, but a host of other sculptures from the region's villas and temples.

(As the collection is subject to frequent rearrangement and the works are poorly labelled, you may want to identify those on display with the museum guide cataloguing them by number.)

The ground floor is devoted to **sculpture**, including many Roman copies of classics from Greece's Golden Age in the 5th century BC. Imperfect as they are, these copies are our only link to many of the lost masterpieces of antiquity. The most famous of these is the *Doryphorus* (Spear-carrier) of Polycleitus, second in fame only to Pheidias among Greek sculptors. The Roman writer Pliny records that the statue was taken as the model of the ideal male form by later artists. Other highlights include two works discovered in the Baths of Caracalla in Rome: the *Farnese Hercules*, a copy of a 4th-century BC work by Lysippus, the court sculptor to Alexander the Great, that was much

*T*he Farnese Hercules, *an impressive copy of a 4th-century BC work by the celebrated Greek sculptor Lysippus, was discovered among the ruins of the Baths of Caracalla in Rome.*

admired for its muscular realism by artists of the baroque; and the *Farnese Bull*, which shows the terrible punishment inflicted on the Theban queen Dirce. She was tied to the horns of a bull and trampled underfoot.

The **Pompeii mosaics** are on the mezzanine floor. The lively secular and pagan mosaics from Pompeii's patrician villas make a striking contrast with the rigid formality of church mosaics that we see elsewhere in Italy. They include *Clients Consulting a Sorceress* and *Strolling Musicians*, vivid little friezes of an octopus, a cat catching a quail and the huge exciting mural of *Alexander* driving Darius of Persia from the battlefield at Issus in 333 BC.

Upstairs, on the first floor, you will find the renowned collection of **bronzes** that were discovered at the Villa of the Papyri in Herculaneum, including a number of strikingly realistic portrait

busts. A series of rooms on this floor display everyday household objects: lamps, mirrors, combs, kitchen utensils and such like. But the ancient world comes most vividly alive in the **wall paintings**, the best preserved of any from Roman antiquity—frescoes in brilliant blues, greens and the inimitable Pompeii reds. The most celebrated is the sophisticated portrait of *Pasquius Proculus and his Wife*, but look out, too, for the powerful *Hercules and Telephus* from Herculaneum and four delicate portraits of women, including *Diana* and the *Flower Gatherer*, from the town of Stabiae, also destroyed in the eruption of Vesuvius in AD 79.

The **Capodimonte Museum** is housed, as its name suggests, in an 18th-century hilltop palace. Built for the Bourbons, it was originally intended as a majestic hunting-lodge. The large park offers a welcome rest before and after a visit to the rich collections of Italian and European painting.

The wall paintings discovered at Pompeii give revealing insights into Roman life. However, it is unlikely that this scene depicts an everyday occurrence.

The **National Gallery of Naples** is housed on the museum's second floor. Highlights include: Simone Martini's *St Louis of Toulouse Crowning the King of Naples*; a Masaccio *Crucifixion*; an early Botticelli *Madonna and Child with Saints*; a Perugino *Madonna and Child*; a fine Lorenzo Lotto portrait of *Cardinal Bernardo de' Rossi*; Giovanni Bellini's gentle *Transfiguration of Christ* standing serenely between Moses and Elijah; Mantegna's *Portrait of a Boy*; Michelangelo's drawing of *Three Soldiers* for his Vatican fresco of *St Peter's Crucifixion*; Parmigianino portraits of *Lucrezia* and the celebrated Roman courtesan *Antea*;

an Annibale Carracci *Pietà* and *Mystic Marriage of St Catherine*.

The Titian room contains half a dozen of his great works, among them the revealing portrait of *Pope Paul III with his Farnese Nephews*; *Danaë*, a piece of mythological eroticism painted for Ottavio Farnese; the artist's daughter *Lavinia Vecellio*; and *Philip II* of Spain. The stark realism in Caravaggio's *Flagellation* and the *Seven Works of Mercy* launched a whole Neapolitan school of "Caravaggeschi". Among his followers displayed here are Caracciolo, Stanzione, Ribera and Artemisia Gentileschi, whose violent and gory *Judith killing Holofernes* has almost become a feminist icon.

Most notable among the museum's non-Italian painters are El Greco, Breughel (*Blind Leading the Blind* and the *Misanthrope*), Cranach, Holbein, Dürer and a Van Dyck *Crucifixion*.

Downstairs, on the first floor, a series of rooms displays the museum's collection of 19th-century Italian painting. Here too are the sumptuously furnished **Royal Apartments** with their outstanding collections of majolica and porcelain. These include works from the celebrated Capodimonte porcelain factory, established in the grounds of the palace by Charles Bourbon in 1739. The apotheosis of the porcelain maker's craft is the famous **Salottino di Porcellana**, a small room decorated entirely in Capodimonte ware.

Vomero and Posillipo

Much of Naples' middle class looks out over the city from the hilltop **Vomero** neighbourhood, an area of geometrically laid out, tree-shaded streets respectably named after artists and musicians of the Renaissance and baroque periods: Michelangelo, Giordano, Scarlatti and Cimarosa. On the south-east edge of the Vomero hill just below the massive Castel Santomo, the elegant baroque charterhouse, **Certosa di San Martino**, offers a haven of tranquillity in its white cloisters and monastery gardens. The 16th-century church is rich in Neapolitan baroque paintings, notably by Caracciolo, Stanzione and Giordano. The monastery houses the **Museo Nazionale di San Martino**, which traces the kingdom of Naples' long history in costumes, sculpture, paintings and prints. Children adore the collections of ship models and rococo Christmas cribs (*presepi*), a Neapolitan speciality presenting the characters of the Nativity accompanied by peasants and artisans. The most elaborate of these is the monumental *Presepe Cucimiello*, which has 177 painted terracotta figures, each clothed in hand-sewn period costume.

The 19th-century **Villa Floridiana** houses a fine museum of ceramics from all over Europe and Asia. From its delightful gardens, famous for their camellias amid the pines, oaks and cedars, you have a superb view of the Bay of Naples.

The genteel **Posillipo** neighbourhood enjoys a privileged position on a promontory at the western edge of town. Drive around its gardens and villas, some of them romantically dilapidated but still graceful, such as the 17th-century Palazzo di Donn'Anna on the bay front.

At the southern edge of Posillipo lies the little fishing hamlet of **Marechiaro**, celebrated by another popular Neapolitan song and equally appreciated for its great seafood restaurants.

Campania

The green and fertile region around Naples, between the Tyrrhenian coast and the western slopes of the Apennines, was originally colonized by the Etruscans and Greeks. The volcanic soil has produced a profusion of tomatoes, olives, walnuts, grapes, oranges, lemons and figs.

The succession of authoritarian rulers from the Middle Ages to the 18th century—Norman and Angevin French, German emperors and Spaniards—kept in place a feudal system that has left the region to this day socially backward compared with the north. Village festivals and processions bear witness to the heavy rural attachment to religion and even pagan superstition harking back to Roman times.

Holiday-makers favour the islands in the Bay of Naples and the resorts of the Amalfi coast. All are in easy reach of the remains of Pompeii and Herculaneum, the Vesuvius volcano and, further down the coast, the Greek temple of Paestum.

Caserta

The Bourbon kings of Naples created this royal residence amid good hunting country 28km (18 miles) north of the capital as a conscious counterpart to Louis XIV's Versailles. The giant **Palazzo Reale** and its vast gardens offer a fascinating glimpse of vanished splendour. To build his palace in 1752, Charles III called on Luigi Vanvitelli (Neapolitan-born son of a Dutchman, Gaspar van Wittel). His work has been described as a baroque swansong of quite overwhelming impact, but the classic harmony is somewhat marred by the sheer gigantic scale, with austere façades unrelieved by the dome and corner towers originally projected. The travertine and brick structure (now partially housing an air force academy opposite the railway station) forms a massive five-storey rectangular block 250m (820ft) long and 185m (607ft) wide, with crossing wings to enclose four large inner courtyards. The masterpiece of the interior design is the **grand vestibule** with its staircase dividing and leading majestically up to a magnificent octagonal arcaded hall of marble columns, a triumph of Italian theatricality. Visit the little chapel and **throne room** with its medallions celebrating 44 kings of Naples from the Normans to the last of the Bourbons in 1859. The Germans signed their unconditional surrender here on 29 April 1945.

Vanvitelli also designed the great baroque **park**, a climax of monumental French-style landscaping before tastes changed to the romanticism of English gardens. Walk (or drive part of the way to Via Ponte) around the fishponds and fountains of formal gardens that stretch 3km (2 miles) to the grandiose **Cascata di Diana**. Water plunges 76m (249ft) from the Carolino aqueduct onto a sculptural group of Actaeon transformed into a stag and devoured by his dogs for watching the goddess at her bath. To the right of the cascade are English gardens added by Vanvitelli's son Carlo, complete with swan lake and fake ruins.

Campi Flegrei

The volcanic Phlegrean (literally Burning) Fields between Naples and

Cuma no longer erupt, but the subterranean ovens still cook up hot springs at the spa resorts. At **Agnano Terme**, you can sweat it out in steaming caves beside the crater of an extinct volcano and then cool off with a stroll in the **Bosco degli Astroni**, a lovely wooded parkland of poplars, elms, chestnuts and oaks. Or watch horseracing at the **Ippodromo** in the middle of the crater.

The hot springs and mud-baths of Pozzuoli's spa come from the big elliptical crater of **Solfatara** east of town. Take a guided tour along the crater bed for a close-up view of the mudpits

In the gardens of the Royal Palace at Caserta, Actaeon is transformed into a stag and attacked by his own hounds for having stumbled upon the goddess Diana at her bath.

and fumaroles puffing out jets of sulphurous steam at over 160°C (320°F). It's hot underfoot but jump up and down and you can sense the hollow volcanic caverns underneath. Founded as the Greek trading post of Puteoli in the 6th century BC, **Pozzuoli** sits on a precarious promontory constantly subject to powerful, but usually slow-moving earthquakes. Heaving up the ground most recently in 1970 and 1983, the quakes toppled the old living quarters in the south-west corner of town.

The **Cattedrale di San Procolo** was built on the site of the Greco-Roman acropolis and a marble temple was revealed when a 1964 fire destroyed its baroque façade. The Italian composer Giovanni Pergolesi, who died in Pozzuoli in 1736 just after his 26th birthday, lies buried inside. In a seaside park north of the city centre is the so-called **Serapeum** (temple to the Egyptian god Serapis). In reality, this is a

Roman marketplace of 35 shops built around an arcaded courtyard of Corinthian columns (now partly submerged by the sea). From bread to circuses, visit the **Anfiteatro Flavio**, seating 40,000 spectators, and imagine the vast arena, 72m (236ft) long and 42m (138ft) wide, at times flooded with water for mock naval battles.

Off the coast road west past the sandy beach of Lido di Napoli is the entrance to hell. That is the age-old reputation of **Lake Averno**, where the dense dark forests once completely surrounded a swampy malarial volcanic crater in which dignitaries made

*T*he romantic ruins of ancient Cumae, one of the earliest Greek colonies in southern Italy. The transplanted Hellenistic civilization became known as the Magna Graecia.

propitiatory sacrifices to the masters of the underworld. The visiting Hannibal went through the motions here as a blind to his real purpose of military reconnaissance. The modern cemented lake shore makes it less ominous now, but visitors can still be seen tossing in a hopeful coin or two.

Baia is an altogether more cheerful seaside village, once the playground of Roman high society where Tiberius, Caligula and company built sumptuous palaces and villas. The area was the setting for the decadent goings-on described in Petronius's *Satyricon*. Baia's most infamous moment came when Nero had his mother put to death here in AD 59 after she had survived a staged boating accident. Many of the ancient villas are now under the sea thanks to bradyseism: the slow rising and sinking of the earth's crust. In the **Parco Archeologico**, visit the remains of the Imperial Palace and its spa "temples" of Mercury, Venus and

Diana, named after statues found on the hillside terraces. Above the village stands the **Castello di Baia**, a sturdy 16th-century fort built by Spanish viceroy Pedro de Toledo as a defence against pirates.

Down the coast, **Bacoli** is a little seaside resort and fishing village with vestiges of its Roman past. The huge reservoir, **Piscina Mirabile**, built in the form of a five-aisled basilica with 48 pillars, was designed to supply water to the nearby Roman naval base of Misenum, built by Agrippa in 41 BC. The steep path to the promontory of **Capo Miseno** rewards climbers with a splendid view of Ischia and the whole Bay of Naples.

Cuma (ancient Cumae) was the northernmost Greek colony on the Tyrrhenian coast. There are few more romantic ruins than its Greek acropolis, Roman forum and amphitheatre disappearing among the vines and olive trees on and around the Monte di Cuma. For an overall view clear across to the sea, stop at the **Arco Felice**, a brick viaduct-arch built in the 1st century AD by Emperor Domitian. At the famous **Cave of the Cumaean Sibyl** (*Antro della Sibilla Cumana*), see where Virgil's Aeneas, among others, went for advice. A long corridor lit by six galleries from the seaward side leads to the oracle's sanctuary, later a Christian cemetery. In this rectangular chamber marked by three niches, the Sybil dispensed her mystic wisdom from a throne. "Thus from her sanctuary," said Virgil, "does the Cumaean Sibyl spread the sacred horror of her ambiguous oracles and moans in her cave, where truth is shrouded in shadow."

> **Three for the Price of Nine**
> Rome eventually got hold of the Sybil's books, but at a price. The historian Livy relates that King Tarquin came to the cave at Cumae to buy all nine volumes. The oracle named her price. "Too much," said Tarquin. The oracle threw three of the books into the fire and offered the remaining six for the same price. Again Tarquin refused. The Sybil threw three more on the fire and offered the last three still at the same price. This time Tarquin accepted. Thereafter, for 600 years, the Sybilline books guided the destinies of Rome. They were kept in a temple on the Palatine and consulted by the Senate in times of emergency and disaster. Finally, they perished in the great fire during the reign of Nero in AD 64.

Capri

With its fragrant subtropical vegetation, mountainous terrain and dramatic craggy coast, this beautiful island manages to cater to the boisterous fun of the package tours while providing quiet hideaways for that blessed, cursed race we like to call the idle rich. Winters here are marvellously mild and deserted, but even in summer you can seek out the island's many enchanted corners away from the mob.

Ferries or hydrofoils leave from Naples, Sorrento and Positano. Look out for the dolphins accompanying the ships across the Bay of Naples. Cars are not allowed on to the island from the beginning of April to the end of October. At the harbour of Marina Grande, take a minibus or the funicular railway up to the main town of **Capri**. The bustling piazzetta is the town's heart, with souvenir shops and pizzerias clustered around the pretty 17th-century domed church of Santo

Stefano. It remains quite easy to get away from the madding crowds: pick up maps and brochures detailing out-of-the-way walks from the piazzetta's Tourist Information office.

Escape down the little paved road south of town to the peace of the shady Romanesque and Renaissance cloisters of the **Certosa di San Giacomo**. Take your siesta with a view over the cliffs of the south coast and port of **Marina Piccola**. Celebrated in song by Noel Coward, this is the prime bathing spot on the island.

Dominating the western half of the island, the quieter resort town of **Anacapri** derives a sleepy charm from its white villas along narrow flowery lanes. A short walk from Piazza della Vittoria is the Swedish doctor-writer Axel Munthe's famous **Villa San Michele**. The house is an intriguing mixture of baroque furniture and Roman antiquities, but the main attraction is the charming garden with its trellised arches and terraces looking out over the bay. Back at the piazza, take the chairlift for a soaring view of the whole island on your way up to the terraced gardens and chestnut trees of **Monte Solaro**, 589m (1,933ft).

The island's most popular excursion, prettiest by boat from Marina Grande, but also possible by road north-west of Anacapri, is to the celebrated cave, the **Blue Grotto** (*Grotta Azzurra*). Most effective at noon, the sun shining through the water turns the light inside the cave a brilliant blue, and objects on the white-sand sea bed gleam like silver. Duck your head as the rowing-boat takes you through the one-metre- (3ft-) high cave entrance. The cave, 57m (187ft) long, 15m (49ft)

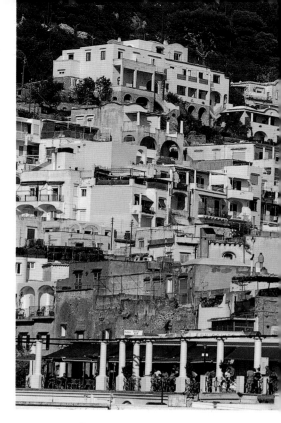

A place in the sun: gleaming white houses cling to the hillside above Capri's main square, Piazza Umberto I, better known as the Piazzetta.

high and 30m (98ft) wide, is believed from the man-made niches to have been a *nymphaeum*, a kind of watery boudoir for the Emperor Tiberius, who retired to Capri in the 1st century AD.

Of the dozen villas that Tiberius built on Capri, the best preserved are the ruins of **Villa Jovis**, sprawling across an eastern promontory opposite the mainland. The spectacular view from the 297m- (974ft-) high Salto di Tiberio precipice is said to be the last pleasure enjoyed by the emperor's enemies before they were hurled over the edge.

Ischia

Augustus may have exchanged it with the Neapolitans for the smaller Capri but that does not mean you should pass up a trip to Ischia. Lying at the western end of the Bay of Naples, it is reached by ferries or hydrofoils from Naples and Pozzuoli. The island boasts thermal springs, fine sandy beaches and good facilities for watersports. **Casamicciola Terme** and **Lacco Ameno** are among the smarter spa resorts.

One of the best beaches, pock-marked with volcanic steam spouts, is the **Lido dei Maronti** on the south coast near the pretty little fishing village of Sant'Angelo. The island interior has a rich vegetation of vines, olive trees and exotic plants. Nature-lovers can hike up the extinct volcano of **Mount Epomeo** 788m (2,585ft), starting from Fontana.

Near Forio, a popular resort (especially with German tourists) on the western side of Ischia, the English composer Sir William Walton and his wife Susana took advantage of the island's fertile volcanic soil to create a splendidly lush and colourful garden, **La Mortella**. The garden's outstanding plants include aloes, palms, yuccas and gingers; bougainvillea, camellias and almost a dozen species of magnolia. La Mortella is open on Tuesdays, Thursdays and Saturdays from Easter until the end of October.

Pompeii

More than in any of the empire's colossal arenas, soaring aqueducts or triumphal arches, you'll find the reality of daily Roman life in the bakeries, wine shops, groceries and brothels of Pompeii. The town that Vesuvius blotted out along with Herculaneum on 24 August AD 79 is still being meticulously excavated from its ashes. It was rediscovered in 1594 by an architect cutting a new channel for the Sarno river, but excavation did not begin until 1748.

To enjoy Pompeii to the full, try to divide your visit into two, early morning and late afternoon (there is practically no shade), with a siesta in between. Good rubber-soled shoes are essential. On-site guides will tell you some jolly but highly fanciful stories; more serious guides are available by advance arrangement through the museum (*Antiquarium*). Start at the Porta Marina entrance on the south of the site, near the Villa dei Misteri railway station.

We can point out the some of the site's most interesting features, but the magic is, as always, in the serendipity of making your own discoveries, both moving and frivolous. The tragic dimension remains, 19 centuries later, in the shapes of human victims or a pet dog in huddled or contorted postures found preserved under the cinders and reconstituted in plaster or transparent resin. Even stronger is a sense of the everyday life of a moment earlier in the curbed streets with their smooth paving stones rutted by chariot wheels and pedestrian crossings on stepping stones.

The road from the main gate passes on the right the basilica law courts and stock exchange to reach the **Forum**, the town's main public meeting place directly facing Mount Vesuvius. Imagine a square looking originally something like Venice's Piazza San Marco, with two-storey porticoes running along

266

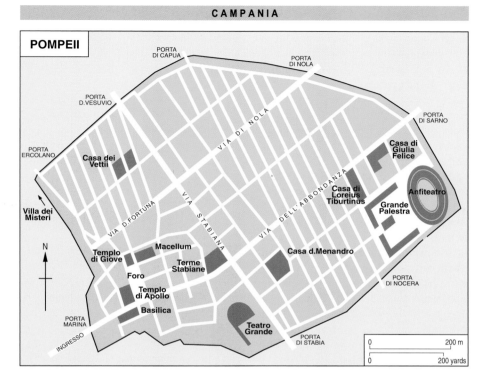

POMPEII

PORTA DI CAPUA
PORTA DI NOLA
PORTA D.VESUVIO
PORTA DI SARNO
VIA DI NOLA
PORTA ERCOLANO
Casa di Giulia Felice
Casa dei Vettii
VIA D.FORTUNA
VIA DELL'ABBONDANZA
Casa di Loreius Tiburtinus
Anfiteatro
Villa dei Misteri
VIA STABIANA
Grande Palestra
N
Macellum
Templo di Giove
Casa d.Menandro
Foro
Terme Stabiane
PORTA DI NOCERA
Templo di Apollo
Basilica
PORTA MARINA
Teatro Grande
PORTA DI STABIA
INGRESSO

0   200 m
0   200 yards

three sides and the six-columned Temple to Jupiter flanked by ceremonial arches at the north end. (After earlier earthquake damage, the temple was used as the *Capitolium* and city treasury.) You can still see plinths from the square's statues of local and national celebrities and the white base of the orator's platform. In the north-east corner is the market (*macellum*).

On **Via dell'Abbondanza** running east from the Forum, those are ancient, not modern graffiti you find scratched and daubed in red on the walls of the houses and shops. Election slogans, insults, obscene drawings—our subway kids continue a venerable tradition. Prominent phallus signs often indicate a brothel, with an arrow pointing upstairs to where the action is, but sometimes they are just a shop-

The excavated ruins of Pompeii.

House and Garden

Unlike the predominantly aristocratic Herculaneum, Pompeii's population of 20,000 was a mixture of patricians, nouveau riche merchants, small shopkeepers, artisans and slaves. They made their money from commerce in wool and wine.

The typical patrician house had two storeys, with servants and lodgers living upstairs. The family's living and sleeping quarters surrounded a first courtyard or atrium. Opposite the entrance was a main living room (*tablinum*) backing onto the dining room (*triclinium*). This looked onto another courtyard or Greek-style porticoed garden (*peristylium*).

keeper's good-luck sign. Notice the oil and wine jars in the shops, the bakers' ovens and flour-grinding mills shaped like giant cotton-reels (excavators found a donkey lying by one he had been turning when Vesuvius erupted).

At the **Stabian Baths** (*Thermae Stabianae*), you can see the separate men's and women's facilities, changing room, with clothes-locker niches, and three baths: cold, lukewarm and hot (*frigidarium*, *tepidarium* and *caldarium*). The **Teatro Grande** seated 5,000 spectators. Behind the stage was the gladiators' barracks, where 63 skeletons were found. Their weapons, along with Pompeii's more fragile works of art, are exhibited at Naples' Archaeological Museum (*see* pages 257–9), which provides an invaluable adjunct to your visit here.

At the far end of Via della Abbondanza, visit two of the town's best villas: the **House of Loreius Tiburtinus**, for its beautiful peristyle garden of fountains, water channels and cascades, one of them with paintings of *Narcissus* and *Pyramus and Thisbe*; and the **House of Julia Felix**, big enough to have been perhaps a luxury hotel, with its own bath-house and a handsome portico of slender marble columns around the peristyle. At the great **Amphitheatre** just to the south, you get a fine view back over the town from its upper tiers.

Mount Vesuvius looms on the horizon across the Forum of ancient Pompeii. The town was buried in gigantic showers of ashes, cinders and pumice pebbles when the volcano erupted on 24 August AD 79.

If you have time and stamina remaining, try to visit the **House of the Vettii** on the corner of Vicolo di Mercurio and Vicolo dei Vettii on the other side of town. The carefully restored house of two wealthy merchants, it contains fascinating wall paintings. Just inside the entrance is an unabashedly lewd fresco of Priapus, the god of fertility. Paintings of mythological subjects abound throughout the house, among them *Hero and Leander*, *Bacchus and Ariadne*, and *Leda and the Swan*. One of Pompeii's most famous images is found on the threshold of the **House of the Tragic Poet** in Via delle Terme: the mosaic of a dog and the inscription *Cave Canem*, "Beware of the Dog".

A short walk outside the main site to the north, the **Villa of Mysteries** (*Villa dei Misteri*) is Pompeii's most cherished artistic treasure. The "mysteries" are those depicted in frescoes of a woman's initiation into the Dionysiac cult. Archaeologists suggest that the scenes of dancing satyrs, flagellation and a woman kneeling before a sacred phallus indicate rites that the town preferred to keep at a decorous distance in this splendid suburban villa.

Vesuvius

The old Roman name of Europe's most famous volcano means "unextinguished" and there is still no reason to change it. Over the centuries, long periods of inactivity have alternated with times when there have been eruptions every few years. When Vesuvius blows its top, molten lava at a temperature of 1400°C (2552°F) bursts from the volcano's magma chamber some 5,000m (14,000ft) down in the earth's bowels.

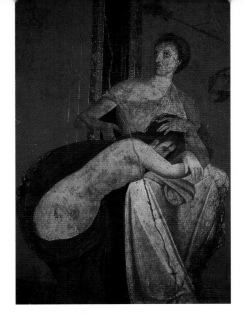

*T*his wall painting from the Villa of the Mysteries in Pompeii shows one of the orgiastic rites that accompanied initiation into the cult of Dionysus, the Greek god of wine and ecstasy.

Succesive eruptions have altered the volcano's size and shape. In the 1980s, it was 1,281m (4,203ft) high, having added 79m (259ft) with the big eruption of 1944 and subsequent smaller ones.

Barring risks from "unscheduled activity", you can peek inside the crater. From the Ercolano *autostrada* exit, take the winding mountain-road's right fork for a short chair-lift ride to the summit. Exploiting the fertile volcanic soil, some vineyards still produce the esteemed *Lacryma Christi* white wine. The **Eremo Observatory** half-way up the mountain has been studying eruptions since 1845 and has an impressive display of relief plans, seismographs and geological specimens spewed out of the volcano. Inside the crater, look for the fumarole phut-phutting steam and hot gases. You also have a grand view, if the mist allows, back over Naples and its bay.

Herculaneum (*Ercolano*)

You can combine your Vesuvius trip with a tour of one of the volcano's victims near what is now Ercolano. Herculaneum is smaller and perhaps less spectacular than Pompeii, but its very compactness and better preservation give a more immediate sense of the shape and ambience of a whole Roman town. While Pompeii was burned out by volcanic cinders, the mud swamping Herculaneum covered the houses in a protective crust that kept upper stories and even some of the woodwork still intact. The gardens have been lovingly replanted.

Rediscovered by well-diggers in the 18th century, the town is still being excavated; a delicate business as much of it is covered by modern buildings.

The entrance off Corso Ercolano takes you around the site for a striking view across the town of terraced villas from which wealthy Roman landowners looked out to sea towards Ischia on the horizon. The streets (Cardine III, IV and V) have curbed pavements, lined with two-storey houses with balconies and overhanging roofs for shade.

At the southern end of Cardo V, the spacious **House of the Stags** (*Casa dei Cervi*) is named after its two marble sculptures of stags attacked by hounds. In one of the rooms off the garden is a statue of a shockingly drunken Hercules. In the middle of Cardo IV, the **House of Charred Furniture** (*Casa del Mobilio Carbonizzato*)

has a marvellously preserved latticed divan bed and small table. Next door, the **House of Neptune** has lost its upstairs façade but the ground-floor wine shop with its narrow-necked amphoras on the shelves looks open for business. The inner courtyard has a lovely green and blue mosaic of Neptune with his wife Amphitrite.

The grandest of the villas, the **House of the Bicentenary** (excavated 200 years after the first dig in 1738) stands on the avenue Decumanus Maximus on the north-east edge of town. It has splendid marble paving and, etched in the wall of one of the smaller rooms, a controversial cross regarded by some as evidence of a Christian chapel, although others insist that the emblem was not adopted until the conversion of Constantine three centuries later.

Sorrento and the Amalfi Coast
The coast curving along the southern arm of the Bay of Naples round the Sorrento Peninsula to Salerno is one of the most romantic in Italy. Clinging to the side of rugged cliffs, with a steep drop into the sea, the sinuous coast road—the famous **Amalfi Drive**—tames the most audacious Italian driver. In olden days, only brigands and pirates ventured out here, their ruined redoubts still dotting the hillsides. Now, wild roses and camellias tempt lovers out onto jutting crags high above terraces of orange and lemon groves, vineyards, walnut and almond trees.

From the mermaids that tried in vain to tempt Ulysses and his sailors onto its rocks to the sentimental songs of latter-day minstrels, the town of **Sorrento** has lost none of its popular enchantment. Surrounded on three sides

by ravines above the sea, the pretty tree-shaded resort makes a perfect base for excursions along the coast. Its artisans are famous for their inlaid walnut woodwork. Compare their modern wares with their ancestors' baroque furniture exhibited at the **Museo Correale di Terranova**, in an 18th-century palazzo at the east end of town.

Positano spills down its hillside in a spectacular cascade of gleaming white houses dotted with gardens of oranges and lemons. Take the **cliff-walk** from the town's main beach, the broad Spiaggia Grande, to the long and narrower Spiaggia Fornillo. In the little church of Santa Maria Assunta, with the region's characteristic majolica-tiled dome, see the 13th-century Byzantine-style altar-painting.

The most charming and lively of the coast's resorts, **Amalfi** was once a powerful rival to the maritime republics of Pisa and Genoa, with trading posts in the 10th and 11th centuries in Palestine, Egypt, Cyprus, Byzantium and Tunis. Its two destinies combine in Piazza del Duomo where open-air cafés and ice-cream parlours look up along staircase to the Arab-Norman **campanile** and polychrome mosaic façade of the Romanesque **cathedral**. It was built in the 9th century, with the façade added in the 13th, when the remains of St Andrew the Apostle were brought to its crypt from Con-

Six spiral columns, encrusted with mosaics and borne by lions, support the magnificent 13th-century pulpit in the cathedral of Ravello.

Life is much quieter now for this picturesque village on the Amalfi coast than in the days when Saracen pirates raided the seaboard. Today it is only tourists who swoop down on the region.

stantinople. The cathedral's striking **bronze doors** were made for Amalfi's colony in Constantinople in the 11th century. The interlacing Arab-Norman arches of the 13th-century cloister, **Chiostro del Paradiso**, make a handsome setting for the summer recitals of chamber music. Amalfi has excellent facilities for sailing and other water sports. Take a trip to nearby Conca dei Marini to visit the stalactites and stalagmites of the **Grotta di Smeraldo**, where the waters are as brilliantly emerald green as those of Capri's Grotta Azzurra are blue.

Set back on a high ridge behind Amalfi, the peaceful village of **Ravello** was once a hide-out for Romans fleeing the Huns and Visigoths. Today, it is a delightful resort of modest but elegant hotels and villas, most notably the **Villa Cimbrone**, where the fragrant gardens command a marvellous view of the Gulf of Salerno. The exotic flowers and palm trees of the **Villa Rufolo**, with its mysterious polychrome arcaded cloister, gave Richard Wagner inspiration for his last opera, *Parsifal*. "I've found the magic garden of Klingsor," he wrote, "the garden in which diabolically beautiful women bewitched the knights seeking the Holy Grail."

Salerno

This busy industrial port, where the Allied army landed in September 1943, is also a university town revered for its School of Medicine dating back to the 11th century. Badly hit by both war and earthquake, the city preserves an attractive medieval quarter of narrow winding streets around Via dei Mercanti.

The **cathedral**, built in 1076–85 by Duke Robert Guiscard, is a typical, intriguing Norman mixture of Greek, Romanesque, Byzantine and Arab architectural elements. At the top of a stairway, the **Porta dei Leoni** has oriental sculpted palms in its entablature leading to an atrium in which Arab-style arches span Greek columns from Paestum. The church portal's distinctly Byzantine columns frame a beautifully

black-patterned **bronze door** brought from Constantinople in 1099. In the overall Romanesque plan of the interior, note the **mosaic of St Matthew** over the entrance and, at the end of the nave, two 12th- and 13th-century **pulpits** and a **paschal candlestick**, combining Arab and Byzantine ornament in their gold enamel and red, blue and green mosaic. The baroque **crypt** claims the remains of St Matthew, brought to Salerno in 954.

Stroll along the palms and laurel trees of the splendid **Lungomare Trieste** sea-promenade and, for a last panoramic view of the town, climb up to the old Lombard **Castello di Arechi**.

Paestum

Italy has no more magnificent testimony of its Greek colonies than this complex of wonderfully preserved Doric temples dating back to the 5th and 6th century BC. Standing alone in fields leading to the sea, their buff-stone columns take on a wonderful

M istakenly dubbed the Temple of Neptune in the 18th century, this magnificently preserved Greek temple at Paestum is now known to have been dedicated to the goddess Hera.

golden glow at sunset. Four temples loom over the forum and residential quarters of Poseidonia (as it was known before the Roman era).

Founded in around 600 BC, the port-town was settled by merchants from Sybaris (on the Gulf of Taranto) whose fame for luxury living has given us the word *sybarite*. The colony came under Roman rule in 273 BC and enjoyed considerable prosperity. It was particularly favoured by Rome after showing its resistance to Hannibal at a time when other Greek colonies preferred to collaborate with the Carthaginian invader. In the Middle Ages, the town fell into decline and was finally abandoned to malaria and Arab invaders in the 9th century. Its monuments disappeared under wild vegetation until the building of a road across the plain by the Bourbon king Charles III led to their rediscovery 900 years later.

The most spectacular of the ruins, directly opposite the entrance to the site, is the 5th-century **Temple of Neptune**. The roof has gone, but with its entablature and 36 columns still standing, it is, with Athens' Theseion, the best preserved of all Greek temples. To the south, the more dilapidated **Temple of Hera** (also known, mistakenly, as the Basilica) is a hundred years older. The **Temple of Ceres** was used as a church in the early Middle Ages, as is attested by Christian tombs.

Opposite the temples, the **Museo di Paestum** contains art and artefacts excavated from the site. The museum's most treasured exhibits are the wall paintings from the famous 5th-century BC **Tomb of the Diver**, rare and charming examples of Greek mural painting.

Puglia

Known to many under its Roman name of Apulia, the region stretches from the spur of the Gargano peninsula to the heel of Italy's boot. It is endowed with a wild and unspoiled beauty over the gently undulating stony plateaus grazed by sheep and goats. Massive fortresses and fortress-like churches testify to the passage of the Normans and then the German emperors in the Middle Ages. In among the groves of olive, almond and fig trees, the stones have been gathered up from time immemorial to build the smaller, but equally sturdy corbelled *trulli*.

Gargano

The peninsula's seaside resorts have good beaches among the pine groves, first-class camping and water-sports facilities with excursions and hikes into an attractive hinterland of rolling hills. Before starting out on the coastal circuit from Manfredonia, visit the 12th-century church of **Santa Maria di Siponto** (south-west of town), built over a 5th-century crypt.

Pugnochiuso is among the best of the beach resorts, along with **Vieste**, where Emperor Frederick II left a castle from which you can view the Adriatic, and the pretty fishing village of **Peschici** climbing up its rocky promontory.

Go inland through Vico to join the wild deer for picnics in the **Foresta Umbra**, densely wooded with beech, oak and chestnut. Perched on the Gargano heights south of the forest, **Monte Sant'Angelo** was a major medieval pilgrimage town, celebrated for its **Sanctuary of St Michael**. This is a mountain cave in which the archangel appeared to the Bishop of Siponto in the 5th century. The sanctuary itself inspired the building of the great French island-monastery of Le Mont Saint-Michel after Bishop Aubert travelled to Gargano to collect a piece of St Michael's red cloak. From a Gothic portico in the middle of town, beside the massive 13th-century **campanile**, a staircase of 90 steps takes you down to the sanctuary's 11th-century bronze doors. Notice to the left of the altar the beautifully carved stone episcopal throne.

From the north coast resort of Rodi Garganico, you can take a 90-minute boat trip out to the pine-tree-covered **Tremiti Islands**. The Insulae Diomediae of Greek mythology, they were the dwelling place of the companions of Diomedes when transformed into herons by the goddess Aphrodite. Later exiles include political prisoners of Mussolini's regime, held in the fortified convent of Santa Maria a Mare on the island of San Nicola. Today, tourists flock to the biggest island of the group, **San Domino**, which offers good camping and a holiday village organizing underwater diving and snorkelling.

Around Foggia

Lying inland from the Gargano peninsula, the provincial capital of **Foggia** is a comfortable stopover for day tours of the surrounding Tavoliere plain before you go down the Adriatic coast to Bari. Earthquake and wartime bombing have made way for a totally modern town with good hotels and first-rate restaurants: try the local mussel pie or stuffed squid.

Head out west along highway 17 to **Lucera**, a hilltop fortress-town guarding the plain. In 1224, German Emperor Frederick II resettled 20,000 Arabs here from his Sicilian lands. After 80 precarious years, the whole population was forcibly converted, expelled or massacred by Frederick's Angevin successors, who built their Gothic **cathedral** on the site of the principal mosque. Note the use of Roman columns in the austere façade's main portal, but most impressive is the formidable buttressed chancel. This epitome of medieval siege mentality is reinforced by the Angevin expansion of Frederick's great **castle** at the western edge of town. The massive ramparts, with 24 towers, enclose remains of the German palace and the French dwellings which housed the Provençal families brought in to repopulate Lucera. Today, everybody is Italian.

Turn south some 20km (12 miles) to **Troia**, another little fortified hill town, which once attracted emperors and popes to worship and hold ecumenical councils in its handsome Romanesque **cathedral**, which was begun in the 11th century. The façade's fine stone ornament is the work of Sicilian Arabs. Above the graceful blind arcades, note especially the rose-window's superb stone tracery. On the **central portal**, the sculpture of the lintel has the delicacy of carved ivory, portraying Christ enthroned between Mary and Peter. Inside, the capitals on the nave's columns have sculpted masks of wild animals and birds, while the 12th-century **pulpit** shows a vivid, characteristically Persian scene of a lion harassed by a dog while slaughtering a lamb. Inserted in the apse's rose-window are two lions, figures seen by scholars as gibes at Troia's local rivals. One lion holds down an Arab, referring to repressive Lucera; the other grasps a demon, which represents evil Foggia.

Bari

This bustling, bumptious city is a keen commercial and industrial rival to Naples, with an equally proud history. Its vital port for trade with the eastern Mediterranean has attracted an endless procession of foreign invaders: Illyrians, Greeks, Romans, Ostrogoths, Lombards, Arabs, Byzantines, Normans, German Swabians, French Angevins, Spanish Aragonese, Austrians and, today, thousands of tourists taking the car-ferries to Greece.

The historic nucleus of the town huddles on a promontory at the east end of the main port (where the ferries dock). The modern city has been spreading rapidly inland since Napoleon's King of Naples, Joachim Murat, first laid out its gridiron street pattern in 1813. If the maze of the old town deliberately blunted the attack of invaders snared in its dead-end streets, the more rational plan of the modern city is foiled by dense traffic entangled in an equally diabolical system of one-way streets. Park your car and walk.

The broad and airy **Corso Vittorio Emanuele II** that divides the old town from the new is a good place to start. This is the scene of the late afternoon *passeggiata*, when the good people of Bari stroll past the prefecture, town hall and municipal theatre and take a look at the city's most elegant boutiques on **Via Sparano**.

To visit the **Città Vecchia** (Old Town), head off from Piazza della Libertà to the **castle**. Two of its four towers still survive from Frederick II's 13th-century fortifications. Once inside the old town' street-maze, keep an eye on the tower identifying the proud but somewhat dilapidated Romanesque **cathedral**, only slowly recovering from the assault of invaders, the sea's humidity and a clumsy baroque transformation.

From here, the little Strada del Carmine leads north through an arch to the most famous of Bari's monuments, the **Basilica San Nicola**. It was built by the Normans in 1087 to house the relics of the original Santa Claus, Bishop Nicholas of Myra (Demre in modern Turkey). Like St Mark's for Venice (*see* page 196), the bishop's body was stolen from its Turkish tomb by Bari sailors with three priests, to boost the city's prestige and the pilgrimage trade. It proved a huge success, making the basilica's crypt a "must" for northern European pilgrims and crusaders on their way to Constantinople and Palestine and for others from the eastern Mediterranean heading for Rome and Santiago de Compostela. It took on political importance, too, as the Norman dukes and later kings of Naples all sought to be consecrated at St Nicholas's tomb.

But the church is of great architectural importance, too. It set the style for Puglia's Romanesque churches. With mullioned windows and blind arcades along the eaves, the façade is divided by pilasters into three parts, corresponding to the interior's nave and side-aisles. At the rear, rather than a cluster of articulated chapels, the chancel is enclosed by a rectangular wall.

Cone-shaped trulli *dot the Puglia landscape. On the horizon stands Castel del Monte, hilltop fortress of 13th-century German emperor Frederick II.*

The columns of the **central portal** rest on two patient, worn-out bulls, symbols of Christ's sacrifice. In the doorway's sculpted frame, you can make out the symbols of the Eucharist—peacocks and doves picking at wine-grapes and angels bearing bread—along with Norman warriors. The interior's unity is broken by three huge transverse arches added in the 15th century. Notice the fine *Madonna and Four Saints* by the Venetian painter Bartolommeo Vivarini, dating from 1476, in the left aisle. The columns of the **canopy** over the high altar have finely carved capitals of eagle-headed oxen and floral motifs, while behind the altar, **Elijah's throne** (for the bishop) is held up by lions and rather rebellious-looking slaves. Down in the **crypt**, with fine Romanesque capitals on its 26 columns, Santa Claus's relics are still there under the altar.

The town's art museum, the **Pinacoteca Provinciale**, is currently housed in the Palazzo della Provincia along the Lungomare Sauro sea promenade. It includes works by Giovanni Bellini, Veronese and Tintoretto. A short walk away, in Piazza Umberto I, the **Museo Archeologico** contains some fascinating Greek and Roman coins, vases, jewellery, bronzes and other treasures excavated in the region.

Bari's Coast and Hinterland

A looping tour on either side of the A14 *autostrada* west of Bari will take you through an attractive variety of fishing villages, cathedral towns and medieval fortifications.

Start inland at **Bitonto**, an agricultural town renowned for its olive oil, as is proclaimed by the extensive olive groves surrounding it and the olive tree in its coat of arms. Within its ramparts, the town's labyrinthine medieval quarter forms a tranquil, secluded island amid a bustling modern

278

conglomeration. The 12th-century **cathedral** is one of the best preserved of Puglia's Romanesque churches, and one of the few to have avoided later architectural embellishments and transformations. Like Bari's San Nicola, it has a tripartite façade, but with a more elaborate rose-window high in the gable. The south wall's graceful arcade beneath a slender-columned gallery brings an impressive elegance to the massive structure—watched over now by a baroque *guglia* (column) *dell' Immacolata*. The finely carved floral motifs of the **central portal** show Arab influence. In the white limestone tympanum, Jesus is flanked on his right by Abraham leading Adam and Eve, and on his left by David playing a triangular harp. Equally elaborate carvings grace the capitals of the solemn interior, the first being to the left of the nave, as a symbol of humility, showing Alexander carried to heaven by two griffins, then, losing his crown, returning precipitously to earth.

The charming little town of **Ruvo di Puglia** produces an estimable wine along with its delicious table grapes and almonds. Pottery in terracotta continues a 2,500-year-old tradition and, in the **Museo Jatta** on Piazza Bovio, you can compare the earliest local production of the region's Greek colonies. Its late 12th-century **cathedral** remains in the main Puglia Romanesque tradition, but is more emphatically triangular in silhouette, with a free-standing belfry that served as a look-out tower.

Wariness was the region's medieval watchword, achieving its most handsome architectural expression in Frederick II's magnificent Gothic **Castel del Monte**. Built in 1240 during the emperor's wars against the forces of the pope, this octagonal fortress with octagonal towers at each angle sits atop a pine-wooded hill like a shining white limestone crown.

The entrance is a Gothic version of a Roman triumphal arch leading to what was, belying the formidable and austere exterior, a luxurious palace. Eight sturdy ground-floor rooms surround the courtyard leading by spiral staircase up to eight more elegant chambers formerly decorated with Arab mosaics and columns of pink marble and cipolin (green- and white-grained marble) with finely sculpted capitals. It was here, between battles, that Frederick received his poets, philosophers and scientists. Fans of Umberto Eco will recognize the castle as the model for the grim library building in his novel *The Name of the Rose*.

Head over to the coast via Andria to the pleasantly relaxed seaside town of **Barletta**, a centre of the region's wine trade. Sandy beaches stretch west of the port along the Litoranea di

The Challenge of Barletta

Barletta was the scene of an epic fight of which Italian children learn with pride at school. During the struggles between French and Spaniards for domination of southern Italy, a French captain was brought as prisoner to Barletta. He was unwise enough to disparage the courage of the Italians, who promptly challenged 13 French knights to meet an equal number of Italian knights in combat. In the ensuing battle on 13 February 1503, the French were totally defeated. The names of the 13 valiant knights are recorded in Piazza della Sfida in the city centre.

Ponente. It was here in the 13th century that a gigantic piece of jetsam was washed up from a Venetian ship wrecked on its way home from Constantinople: the huge bronze **Colosso** now dominating the north flank of the Gothic church of San Sepolcro. This 4th- or 5th-century statue, probably of Roman Emperor Valentinian I, stands over 5m (16ft) tall, "converted" for the occasion with a cross thrust into his right hand. Only the head and torso are of the original cast, as the arms and legs were melted down by Dominican friars to make a bell. In the local **museum** (*Museo e Pinacoteca Comunale*, Via Cavour) is an equally heroic and much better sculpted Roman-style bust of Frederick II, as well as a Benvenuto Cellini *Bacchus* and paintings by Neapolitan artists Luca Giordano, de Mura and Solimena. The **cathedral** is an interesting hodgepodge of 12th-century Romanesque with later Gothic additions and a 16th-century Renaissance portal. An 18th-century spire and belfry top the Romanesque tower. An inscription above the side-entrance on the north flank notes Richard the Lionheart's contribution to the building, on his way to the Crusades.

Much of the magic of **Trani** derives from the location of its 12th-century **cathedral**, San Nicola Pellegrino, dominating a promontory with the Adriatic as its backdrop. The beautifully weathered limestone glows pink in the morning, white at noon and golden in late afternoon. The reconstructed 14th-century **campanile** has served quite deliberately as a landmark for seafarers and, if you stand by the lighthouse at the east end of the harbour, you can share the viewpoint of

*F*ew churches can boast quite so dramatic a setting as the cathedral of Trani, anchored to a spit of land overlooking the sea.

pilgrims returning from Palestine. The powerful fortress-like chancel faces the sea with three towering apsidal chapels. The façade's **central portal** has superb bronze doors and fine marble sculpture in the French manner, portraying in particular Jacob asleep and then fighting with the angel. This entrance at the top of a staircase leads to the uppermost of three superimposed churches. Visitors enter through a south entrance to what was the old church of **Santa Maria della Scala**, which now serves as a crypt to the new church of **St Nicholas the Pilgrim**. Not to be confused with Bari's (Santa Claus) Nicholas, this saint was a zealous Corfu pilgrim who ran with the Cross from the Holy Land across Greece to end up dying of exhaustion in Trani. Below the crypt is the pre-Romanesque **St Leucius chapel** (*ipogeo*) with recently discovered mosaics. Stairs lead from the St Nicholas crypt to the brightly lit upper church, with modern furnishings and organ, but note the fine **mosaic fragments** rediscovered around the high altar. They depict Adam and Eve, a dog confronting a stag and Alexander rising to heaven. The nearby **diocesan museum** exhibits the church's past treasures of Romanesque, Renaissance and baroque sculpture. Walk back round the harbour to picnic in the pretty seafront **city park** (*Villa Comunale*).

Once a popular rest-and-recreation centre for Crusaders, the historic but now very modern town of **Molfetta** is still a major fishing port. On the harbour promontory, the **old quarter** has a street-pattern like the bones of a plump Dover sole. Fishermen and sailors gather to consecrate the sea in an annual ceremony on 8 September. Craftsmen and wine shops make a pleasant enough living in the medieval arcades and houses with Renaissance and baroque portals. Sadly, most worshippers have deserted the imposing port-side 12th-century **Duomo Vecchio** in white stone for the more exuberant baroque cathedral at the southern edge of the old quarter. Unlike at Trani, neighbouring buildings crowd in on Molfetta's seafront church, leaving it no room for a real façade. But from the water, its two towers and three pyramidal domes (a Sicilian Arab touch) make a graceful silhouette, a view well worth a boat-trip around the harbour.

In the baroque cathedral, be sure to see Corrado Giaquinto's altar-painting of the Assumption in the right transept. Among the baroque paintings in the nearby little episcopal museum is Bernardo Cavallino's masterly *Pietà*.

Alberobello

This agricultural town is the centre of the region of Puglia famous for *trulli*, the whitewashed houses with ruddy or grey dry-stone roofs, cone-shaped, which dot the landscape like giant spinning tops turned upside down. The cone is formed by small limestone slabs set in a spiral without mortar to bind them. Though the region's oldest surviving *trulli* date back only to the 16th century, the construction technique is prehistoric, brought here perhaps from Greece or the Middle East. Many roofs are daubed with an ancient religious symbol, pagan, Christian, even Jewish (for example the menorah candlestick).

In Alberobello, two neighbourhoods of *trulli* houses, shops and churches, **Rioni Monti** and **Aia Piccola**, are protected as a *zona monumentale*. Shopkeepers are happy to let you climb up to their roof-terraces for a striking view across a whole forest of *trulli* domes. In the country in and around the beautiful hilltop town of **Locorotondo** and the wooded hills of **Selva di Fasano**, you will find *trulli* farms, barns, grain-silos, even filling stations.

North-west of Alberobello, a *Strada panoramica* along a ridge overlooking the Adriatic coast leads to the **Grotte di Castellana**, a group of spectacular caves 65m (210ft) underground. Take a guided tour of the translucent stalactites reaching down to fuse with stalagmites in glowing columns of red, green and pink. Besides the usual comparisons with temples, cathedrals and church organs, the strange formations remind people of old relatives and new lovers.

East to Brindisi

The coast between the two great port-cities of Bari and Brindisi varies between dramatic rocky cliffs, fishing coves and sandy beachaes. The port of **Mola di Bari** serves both the local fishermen and tourist vessels. The old town out on the promontory boasts a glowering Angevin castle and a more cheerful Renaissance cathedral.

Polignano a Mare is a charming resort of bright whitewashed houses, offering good sailing, deep-sea fishing and cruises around the many **caves** along the craggy coastline. Glide through the green-blue waters of the Grotta dei Colombi or della Foca. At the Grotta Palazzese, you can have a meal in the hotel restaurant built into the cave.

The cold mineral waters and mud-baths at the spa resort of **Torre Canne** will nurse your digestion, liver or gynaecological problems. Dunes shelter the quiet sandy beaches.

If you are looking for good camping sites near the beach, try the well-equipped holiday villages of **Pilone** and **Rosa Marina**. These are part of the long Marina di Ostuni coastline divided up by the rocks into small sandy coves.

Inland, amid the olive groves, the gleaming white city of **Ostuni** sprawls dramatically across three hills, fortified by medieval ramparts and towers. When the heat of the day has gone, join the *passeggiata* around lively **Piazza della Libertà**. The impeccable whiteness of the houses, illuminated at night, is a point of pride for the local townspeople. The oldest quarters are perched on the highest of the hills, dominated by a Flamboyant Gothic 15th-century **cathedral** adorned with a spectacular rose-window.

The ancient Roman port of **Brindisi** is now a modern industrial city, familiar to holiday-makers taking the ferry to Greece. (From the Stazione Marittima at the end of busy Corso Garibaldi, you can also take a **boat-cruise** around the harbour). Two **Roman columns** mark the eastern terminus of the old Appian Way extending nearly 600km (370 miles) from Rome. Erected at the tip of the promontory that separates the two arms of the city's inner harbour, one column is 19m (62ft) high, with a finely carved capital. Only the base and a stump of the other remains, the rest having been carried off to Lecce when it collapsed in the 16th century (*see* below).

Lecce

This airy, sophisticated town has a place apart in the life of Puglia. It is famous not only for its highly decorative baroque architecture, but also for its bright and witty population. The city centre is elegant, with an atmosphere that is at once lively and relaxed. It was an important cultural centre for the Romans and a favoured residential town for the Norman nobility. Its university is renowned for its historians, lawyers and economists.

Baroque ornament found its ideal medium in the local fine-grained golden sandstone known as *pietra di Lecce*, easily worked for intricate carving and then hardening when exposed to the elements. As you stroll around town, notice even on the private houses along **Via Palmieri** and **Via Libertini** the plethora of ornate doorways, colonnades, balconies and window-arches, alive with nymphs, gods, goddesses and fanciful monsters among the carved fruit and vines.

A more orderly visit begins in the historic centre, bustling **Piazza Sant' Oronzo**, named after the city's first bishop and patron saint Orontius, martyred by Nero. His 18th-century **statue** stands nearby on the Roman column brought from Brindisi (*see* above), near the entrance to the **Roman amphitheatre**. In an arena seating 25,000 spectators, a few bas-reliefs of gladiators and wild animals are still visible, but the best preserved are in the local museum.

Take Via Umberto I to the grand 16th- and 17th-century church of **Santa Croce**, a true masterpiece of baroque decoration. The façade is dominated by the extravagant **rose-window** of Giuseppe Zimbalo (more familiarly known as Zingarello, or little gypsy). The 13 creatures supporting the entablature below the window are characteristic of the town's wry humour—men grimly struggling to bear the weight while various monsters have a good chuckle. The spacious, more subdued interior is the work of Gabriele Riccardi. The adjacent **Palazzo del Governo** was originally the church's very elegant monastery.

Many of the town's most fashionable boutiques are on and around **Via Vittorio Emanuele**, which curves around to the magnificent baroque theatre-set of **Piazza del Duomo**. To your right is the **Seminary** with its splendid windows designed by Giuseppe Cino, Zingarello's pupil. Look, too, at his exquisite well in the courtyard. In the corner of the square stands the **bishop's palace** with its graceful loggia. Zingarello himself gave the **cathedral** its grandiose baroque transformation, adding a remarkable five-storey campanile with a balustrade at each level. It is hard to believe that the exuberant ornament of the baroque altars inside is not stucco but carved in Lecce sandstone.

Zingarello's most elaborately decorated façade can be seen on the **Chiesa del Rosario** at the end of Via Libertini. This contains an astonishing and elaborate profusion of birds and cherubim and interlacing spiral columns. For two more intimate churches there are Cino's classical **Santa Chiara**, off Piazza Vittorio Emanuele, and a little further south, Achille Carducci's bizarre **San Matteo**, with the convex lower and concave upper tiers of its façade covered entirely in scales.

Besides the Roman amphitheatre's bas-reliefs and other ancient sculpture, the **provincial museum** (Viale Gallipoli) has a collection of paintings that includes baroque works by Andrea Vaccaro, Corrado Giaquinto and Oronzo Tiso.

Around the Tip of the Heel

Italy's easternmost town, **Otranto** is still very much turned towards the ancient Greece and Byzantium of its origins: Greek dialects can still be heard in isolated parts of Otranto's hinterland. This popular resort has first-class water-sports facilities and easily accessible sandy beaches, rocky fishing coves and grottoes that were once prehistoric dwellings.

The 11th-century **cathedral** was built after the Norman conquest of Otranto as a deliberate act of rupture with the Greek Orthodox tradition that had prevailed here. But the great treasures of the Romanesque church (much transformed by a Gothic rose-window, a baroque façade and a Renaissance portal) are the wonderful **mosaics**, a supremely Byzantine art. Created in 1166 with a delightful spontaneity, they literally carpet the whole nave, transept and chancel with dozens of biblical, historical and legendary characters: Adam and Eve, Noah and the Flood, a particularly vivid Tower of Babel, but also King Arthur chasing a fabled cat that finally gets him by the throat. In lugubrious contrast is the **Martyrs' Chapel** along the south wall displaying the bones of hundreds of victims of the Turkish invasion in 1480.

Many of the 42 pillars of the **crypt** originated from ancient Greek and Roman temples, their Romanesque capitals sculpted with moustachioed lions, harpies, eagles and parrots.

The formidable ruin of an old Aragonese **castle** guarding the port is being transformed in part into an archaeological museum to study the region's prehistoric cave-paintings.

The coast to the north is dotted with popular seaside resorts and lively holiday villages. You will find two fishing lakes at **Pineta Alimini**, while the sandy beach at **Torre dell'Orso** is nicely sheltered by pine trees. The landmark at **Rocca Vecchia** is its medieval look-out towers.

South of Otranto, on the rocky coast of **Porto Badisco** you will find caves with prehistoric paintings, most notably the **Grotta dei Cervi**.

At the old-fashioned spa resort of **Santa Cesarea Terme**, where mineral waters and mud-baths work wonders for respiration and tired bones, take a cliff-walk among prickly pear cacti and look across towards the Albanian coast. Further south, guided tours are organized down to the pretty **caves** of Romanelli and Zinzulusa, prehistoric dwellings with striking iridescent light effects.

Capo Santa Maria di Leuca marks the heel-tip of the Italian boot. This white limestone cliff, with the sanctuary of **Santa Maria Finibus Terrae** (at

*B*eyond the sanctuary of Santa Maria di Leuca, one last spur of land marks the very tip of the heel of Italy's boot.

land's end) is built on the ruins of a pagan temple to Minerva. (Actually, Puglia's southernmost point is a little to the west at Punta Ristola).

In Greek, Kallipolis means beautiful city and this is certainly true for the ancient fishing port of **Gallipoli**. The attractive medieval town on its own island is now joined by bridge to a more modern city on the mainland. Guarded by the formidable mass of an old Angevin fortress, the narrow streets winding around the old town's white houses and little baroque churches make a charming, cool and shady haven of tranquillity. At the centre, the richly decorated baroque façade of the 17th-century **cathedral** offers a distinct echo of Lecce. The link is reaffirmed inside with local artist Giovanni Andrea Coppola's fine painting of Lecce's patron saint Orontius. At sunset, take the Riviera promenade around the water's edge. Besides the good fishing and sailing facilities around the harbour, there is a fine beach just down the coast at **Lido San Giovanni**.

Taranto

Founded by the Spartans in 706 BC, Taranto became one of the richest of Italy's ancient Greek colonies. Practically all vestiges of this great seaport's proud civilization were subsequently laid low by 19th-century industrial and urban development. Today, Taranto (with the accent on the first syllable) is a military naval base and centre of heavy industry (steel, oil and cement), but masterpieces of the region's Greek and Roman art are preserved in the great **Museo Nazionale** (Piazza Architta). Among the highlights of Greek sculpture are an *Eros* and *Aphrodite*

from the celebrated school of Praxiteles (4th century BC) and a 6th-century bronze of *Poseidon*. The Greek **ceramics** include the small but highly decorative Corinthian (yellow and green) as well as the larger, more

familiar black and red Attic vases. Look, too, for the exquisite collection of **gold jewellery**. Oustanding in the Roman collection are the **mosaics** depicting a hunting scene and a lion fighting a wild pig.

A deep gorge runs through the centre of Massafra, leaving these houses clinging to the rocks, suspended over the abyss.

Bitten by the Dancing Bug

These days, any big hairy spider gets called a tarantula, but up to 300 years ago it was reserved for the hairy wolf spider found around Taranto, with a bite believed to cause melancholy madness: tarantism. This disease was believed curable only by passionate music and wild dancing, a hysteria that reached its height in southern Italy in the 17th century. In fact, the tarantula bite is only slightly poisonous and has no more harmful lasting effects than the tarantella dances composed by Chopin, Liszt and Weber.

As at Gallipoli, Taranto's medieval quarter is preserved on an island now joined to the mainland by a bridge. Here, the 15th-century castle is Spanish. The 11th-century **Duomo** has a magnificent baroque façade. Inside, notice the fine Roman and Byzantine capitals on the recycled Greek temple-columns. Right of the high altar, some remarkable inlaid marble adorns the baroque **chapel of San Cataldo**.

Massafra

A gaping ravine dramatically divides the town's historic neighbourhood of **Terra**, to the west, from the more modern **Borgo Santa Caterina**. Two viaducts, Ponte Nuovo and Ponte Vecchio, offer a superb view of the phenomenal abyss. The **Gravina di San Marco** was populated in the 9th and 10th centuries by fugitive monks of the Orthodox order of St Basil and later inhabited by local peasants seeking a haven from Arab invaders. The monks carved sanctuaries out of the ravine's caves, forerunners of the **crypt-churches** that you can visit on a guided tour (details at the police station on Piazza Garibaldi). The troglodytes' frescoes have disappeared, but you can see the continuation of the tradition with Romanesque and baroque cave-wall frescoes in the churches of **San Marco**, **La Candelora** and **San Leonardo**. One kilometre north of town by highway 581, surrounded by old cliff-dwellings, the 18th-century sanctuary of the **Madonna della Scala** is built over one of the oldest of Massafra's crypt-churches, **Madonna della Buona Nuova**.

Nearby **Castellaneta**, also perched on the edge of a ravine, is the birthplace of Rodolfo Guglielmo di Valentino d'Antonguolla (1895–1926), better known to his fans as silent-movie heart-throb Rudolph Valentino. The family house on the main highway, at 114 Via Roma, displays a bronze plaque of the Latin Lover kissing a nude beauty above the inscription (in Italian): "Rudolph Valentino— a name which in a far-off land signified art and Italian beauty. Placed here by the fans of the Rudolph Valentino Club of Cincinnati, Ohio."

Basilicata

The region bounded by the western plain of Puglia, the Tyrrhenian Sea and the Gulf of Taranto is economically one of Italy's poorest. With the advantage of being almost virgin

At Matera in Basilicata you will find centuries-old houses and chapels cut into the sides of a deep ravine.

territory for tourists, the countryside is predominantly mountainous, broken up in places by sudden, dramatic ravines. Isolated communities conserve their old traditions and costumes, but new seaside resorts are springing up along the south coast.

Matera

One of the most spectacularly situated cities in southern Italy, this old provincial capital is built not just around a vast ravine scooped out of its hillside, but right down in the ravine-bed itself. The houses are set in the rocky cliffs (*sassi*), often terraced one above the other around crypt-churches built in the more spacious caves. After years of an increasingly wretched troglodyte existence, dramatically portrayed in Carlo Levi's novel *Christ Stopped at Eboli*, most of the *sassi*-dwellers have been moved out of the ravine to modern housing on the hill. Yet many chose to stay and, with progressive restoration of the houses and churches as a tourist attraction, the *sassi* are even becoming a chic residential quarter for local artists and architects.

The local Tourist Office, on the upper town's Piazza Vittorio Veneto, organizes guided tours of the ravine, recommended for reliable information about the town's history and culture. The more fanciful unofficial guides down in the *sassi* give you colourful information about what it's like to live there.

From Piazza San Francesca, take Via Duomo for a first view over the two halves of the ravine, **Sasso Barisano** to the north and **Sasso Caveoso** to the south. The **cathedral** itself is an attractive 13th-century Romanesque edifice in the Puglian style with handsome belfry and rose-window. The interior is baroque. At the eastern edge of the Sasso Caveoso, you will find two crypt-churches carved out of the rock: **Santa Maria d'Idris** and **Santa Lucia**, with 13th-century frescoes, most notably one of St Michael in the latter chapel. Two free-standing churches, as their belfries indicate, are the 17th-century baroque **San Pietro Caveoso** and its 11th-century counterpart on the northern slope, **San Pietro Barisano**.

The **Museo Ridola** (Via Ridola) has interesting prehistoric remains from the region's so-called trench-villages, but is above all useful if you want a know ledgeable guide to the surrounding countryside's many cave-crypts, some of which contain superb Byzantine frescoes.

South to the Coast

On highway 7, **Miglionico** is worth a brief stop for its massive castle and for Cima da Conegliano's splendid altar-painting in the church of San Francesco. The enchanting hilltop village of **Pisticci** gives you a superb panorama of the rolling landscape of southern Basilicata. People in the older quarter of spotless white houses favour the region's traditional black costume just as their baroque church **Chiesa Madre** has retained its Romanesque portal and campanile.

Metaponto is an ancient Greek colony transformed today into a modern seaside resort. Take time off from the beach to visit the nearby remains of a 6th-century BC Doric temple known as the **Tavole Palatine** and the **Antiquarium**, a fine modern museum of Greek antiquities.

Calabria

This ruggedly beautiful mountain country, of which barely 10 per cent is arable flatland, has not had it easy. Repeated earthquakes have destroyed much of its proud Greek heritage (happily motivating a great museum in Reggio di Calabria). Chronic feudal violence has lived on in modern form in the 'Ndrangheta, Calabria's equivalent of the Sicilian Mafia or Neapolitan Camorra. The region is only now beginning to reverse unbridled industrial development of the coast to encourage additions to the delightful Tyrrhenian seaside resorts. The toe of the Italian boot deserves attention.

Reggio di Calabria

The region's largest city, with a bustling community of 175,000, has recovered over and over again from earthquakes throughout its history, none more devastating than the most recent, in 1908. After this and wartime bombardment in 1943, a completely modernized town has emerged with a gridiron network of arrow-straight streets spreading out from the coast.

Even if you are only passing through town on your way to or from Sicily, the **Museo Nazionale** is an obligatory and memorable reason for stopping. The museum has assembled an astonishing collection of Greek art from all over southern Italy dating back to the 7th-century BC. Exhibits include marble sculpture, terracottas and jewellery. But the great attraction, comparable in popularity to the Louvre's *Mona Lisa* or the Uffizi's Botticellis, is down in the basement: the **Riace bronzes**. These matchlessly beautiful statues of two Athenian warriors from the golden era of Greek creativity were found on the seabed off the coast of the Calabrian fishing port of Riace in 1972. Only three other original Greek bronzes of Athens' 5th century BC exist, all of them inside Greece. Identifiable only as Statue A and Statue B, they each stand around 2m (6½ft) tall, weighing some 250kg (550lbs). Scholars have estimated that **Statue A** was created around 450 BC, perhaps by the greatest of all Greek sculptors, Pheidias himself. The young man has lost his shield and spear, but he stands, stunningly handsome, strong and ready for combat. Probably created some 20 years later, **Statue B** (missing his weapon, shield and a helmet) is of an older man but equally impressive in his mature strength and elegance. You should also spare time for a third, less celebrated but no less magnificent bronze, the **Head of a Philosopher**, found in a Greek shipwreck in the Straits of Messina in 1969. The moving details of its furrowed brow, aquiline nose and flowing beard make it the only known truly personal facial portrait in Greek sculpture.

Stretch your legs on **Lungomare Matteotti**, a superb promenade at night facing the lights of Sicily across the Straits of Messina. The main thoroughfare through the city-centre is **Corso Garibaldi**, scene of a boisterous evening *passeggiata* when, closed to traffic, it becomes an open-air club for the young.

L'Aspromonte

The last kick of the Apennines, this mountain plateau stretches from the Straits of Messina down to the Ionian Sea. It makes a pleasant day's excursion out of Reggio. Drive south along

291

the coast-road past groves of peach, fig trees and bergamot, the sour citrus fruit whose rind is used for perfume, barleysugar and suntan oil. Just before the sleepy beach-resort of **Melito di Porto Salvo**, the southernmost town on the Italian mainland, make a short detour inland to the mysterious abandoned village of **Pentedattilo**, hugging a dramatic arid backdrop of five finger-like peaks (*pentadaktylos*) of Monte Calvario.

Highway 183 takes you north via Bagaladi into the Aspromonte. The winding road rises high above the Melito valley and the coastal orchards give way to forests of chestnut, beech and oak and then fir trees. A signposted road just before Gambarie leads to the Aspromonte's highest peak, **Montalto**, 1,955m (6,416ft) with a giant bronze statue of Christ the Saviour at the top. **Gambarie** is a popular ski-resort but also a great base for summer hikes into the surrounding forests. Take the chair lift up to **Puntone di Scirocco**, 1,660m (5,448ft), for a great view clear across the peninsula west to the Tyrrhenian Sea and Mount Etna on Sicily and east to the Ionian Sea. Drive west on highway 184 to the beach at **Gallico Marina** and back to Reggio.

The Calabrian Seaside

Standing on a cliff overlooking the Gulf of Sant'Eufemia, the fishing village of **Pizzo** makes its living from its tunny and swordfish catch, but is also a charming little beach resort. In its 15th-century **castle**, Napoleon's King of Naples, Joachim Murat, was executed by firing squad by his Bourbon successor, Ferdinand IV, in 1815.

Head west on the beautiful winding coast road past sea-pines and craggy cliffs plunging down to the brilliant blue and emerald Tyrrhenian Sea. Another fishing port, **Briatico**, is flanked by two fine sandy beaches, La Rochetta and Galera. Down the coast at **Parghelia**, you'll find comfortable modern beach-hotels with ample sports facilities.

The jewel of the region is **Tropea**, a fortified cliff-top fishing town boasting luxury hotels and immaculate sandy beaches. It was a popular resort for the Roman nobility and refuge for feudal

*T*he Calabrian countryside, too rugged for easy access, is an ideal hideaway for anyone seeking a quiet holiday—and for bandits.

knights. Notice the sculpted sandstone balconies and doorways on the handsome old houses from the Spanish era. The 12th-century **cathedral** has been restored to its original Sicilian Norman form with a fine Gothic arcade. The interior has a sober Renaissance décor, an impressive black Crucifix and, at the high altar, the 12th-century Byzantine-style silver-framed *Madonna of Romania*, a miraculous image supposedly painted by St Luke.

The beaches at **Capo Vaticano** are on a promontory around the lighthouse. **Nicotera** is an attractive old hill town overlooking a sandy beach. From the square in front of the baroque cathedral, you get a great view of the Gulf of Gioia.

The 1908 earthquake devastated the so-called Calabrian Riviera, but the rebuilt modern town of **Palmi** commands a lovely position among olive groves on Monte Sant'Elia. Drive to the summit (579m/1,900ft) for a view over the Straits of Messina to Sicily's Mount Etna. Palmi's ultra-modern **museum**, devoted to Calabrian folklore.

Fans of Homer's *Odysseus* will recognize **Scilla** as the notorious death-trap of Scylla which the hero's ship had to confront to avoid the treacherous whirlpools of Charybdis. Scholars identify the rocky home of the voracious female monster as the site where now an old castle houses a youth hostel. According to the poet, Scylla sat on her rock with "twelve feet, all dangling in the air, and six long necks, each ending in a grisly head with triple rows of teeth, set thick and close, and darkly menacing death."

Lands of Ancient Civilizations and Untamed Nature

Sicily has been described as the most Italian part of Italy: a place where all the nation's faults and virtues are somehow magnified. Sardinia has always been a world and law unto itself. Italians from the mainland may descend en masse every summer to bask on its beaches but few outsiders bother to explore the island's wild and rugged interior.

Sicily (*Sicilia*)

"It's impossible to understand Italy without knowing Sicily," wrote Goethe, "for Sicily is the key to it all." To unlock the mystery you must first understand something of the foreign influences that have left their mark on this, the Mediterranean's largest island. Take note of the striking remains of the ancient Greek settlements at Syracuse, Agrigento and Selinunte; admire Palermo's handsome Arab-Norman architecture and the Spanish baroque of

*P*retty majolica tiles decorate a steep flight of steps in the inland Sicilian town of Caltagirone.

Catania. You won't be able to avoid Mount Etna, Europe's largest volcano, but try to find time for some of the towns of the interior and the offshore islands.

Palermo

This bustling capital deserves the necessary effort to get at its colourful past. Cleverly integrating designs of Arab and Byzantine predecessors, the Norman palaces and churches join the crumbling grandeur of Spanish baroque façades in momentary triumph over the chaos of the modern port-city.

The intersection of Corso Vittorio Emanuele and Via Maqueda is the town's historic centre, **Quattro Canti** (Four Corners), in a characteristic

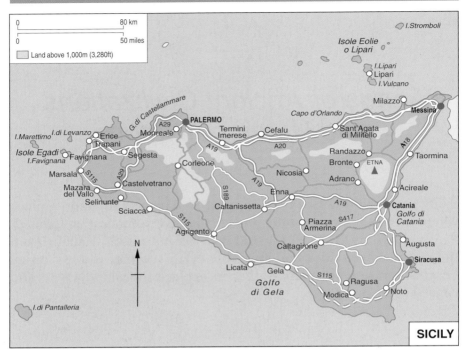

Sicily.

setting of baroque palaces, fountains and statues. Two nearby churches illustrate different aspects of the Sicilian baroque: contrast the simple and harmonious façade of San Giuseppe with the exuberant decoration of the interior of Santa Caterina. **Piazza Pretoria** is distinguished by a monumental 16th-century **fountain** whose riot of nude statues won it the nickname of "the fountain of shame". Behind the town hall, **Piazza Bellini** evokes Palermo's cosmopolitan history. The 12th-century church of **San Cataldo** with its three little red domes and Arabic inscriptions was originally built as a synagogue. Beside it, the Norman Gothic church of **La Martorana**, partly

remodelled with a baroque façade and porch, has a fine campanile of four storeys of slender mullioned windows. Inside the porch, 12th-century **mosaics** show, to the right, Jesus crowning Norman ruler, Roger II, and to the left, the king's admiral and chief minister, George of Antioch, kneeling at the feet of the Madonna. In the nave are mosaics of Christ Pantocrator (Almighty Lord) with angels.

West along Via Vittorio Emanuele, the **Palace of the Normans** (Palazzo dei Normanni), converted from the Arabs' 9th-century fortress into a royal residence, made an appropriate setting for the later brilliance and luxury of Emperor Frederick II's 13th-century Sicilian court. In the royal apartments, see the hunting mosaics in **King Roger's room** (*Sala di Re Ruggero*), but

296

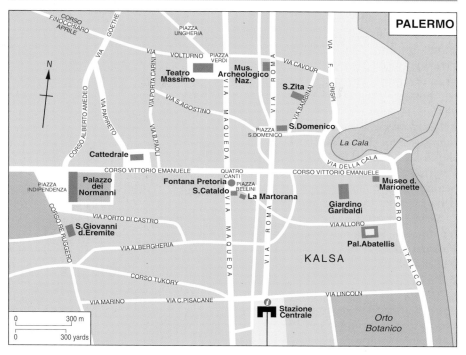

Town plan of Palermo.

the jewel of the palace, indeed one of Norman architecture's greatest achievements in Italy, is the 12th-century **Palatine Chapel** up on the first floor. The noble Romanesque interior has a magnificent painted wooden ceiling with Arabic honeycomb motifs and stalactite pendentives. The **mosaics** of the dome and apse depict Christ Pantocrator with the Evangelists and Jesus blessing Peter and Paul. The combination of figurative and intricate geometric designs was a collaborative effort by Syrian Muslim craftsmen and Byzantine Christians. To the right of the sanctuary is a pulpit on chevron-patterned Corinthian columns next to a tall, carved Easter candelabrum.

Built on the site of a mosque, the pink-domed church of **San Giovanni degli Eremiti** (Via dei Benedettini) is another intriguing example of 12th-century Arab-Norman design. Its exotic character is enhanced by the twin-columned **cloister** overgrown with tropical plants, orange, lemon and palm trees.

With colours and smells redolent of an Arab souk, Palermo's lively outdoor food market, the **Vucciria**, occupies the streets around Piazza San Domenico. Particularly delightful are the seafood stalls selling the freshest of swordfish, tuna, squid and octopus.

Housed in a 17th-century monastery, the town's **Archaeological Museum** (Piazza Olivella) displays superb statues and sculpted *metopes* (friezes) from the Greek temples of Selinunte

297

(600–500 BC), on Sicily's south coast. Another aspect of Sicily's past is on show in the **Marionette Museum** (*Museo delle Marionette*) in Via Butera near the port. The island's tradition of puppet theatre stretches back centuries—tales of heroic Christian knights battling Saracen foes still prove mainstays of the repertory. Puppet shows take place at the museum and at Palermo's **Museo Pitrè** a museum of Sicilian folklore and craft in the Parco della Favorita in the north of the city.

Near the port in the old Arab quarter of La Kalsa, the 15th-century **Palazzo Abatelli** houses the **National Gallery of Sicily**. The collection includes a gripping fresco of the *Triumph of Death* by an anonymous 15th-century artist, Antonello da Messina's exquisite *Annunciation* and Francesco Laurana's sculpture of *Eleonora of Aragon*.

Sun-worshippers head north of the city to **Mondello**, Palermo's liveliest beach resort and, in summer, the site of its most fashionable nightlife. A very different experience is in store at the **Catacombe dei Cappuccini** in the west of the city. The underground passages store around 8,000 mummified corpses, some dating back 500 years. Dressed in their Sunday best and occupying their own individual niches, the corpses provide a gruesome *memento mori*.

Monreale

This hilltop suburb south-west of Palermo boasts Sicily's finest **cathedral**, a masterpiece of Romanesque architecture. The cathedral was founded on royal lands by Norman king William II to counter the ecclesiastical power

T he tranquil cloister of San Giovanni degli Eremiti. Arab influence is apparent in the lush vegetation and exotic red dome.

base being created in Palermo by Walter of the Mill, the city's English archbishop. Go round to the back of the church to see its wonderful russet and brown stone chancel of interlacing arches, Gothic rose-windows and Arab windows with pointed arches. In the grandiose interior, the 12th- and 13th-century **mosaics** of the nave and apse depict Old Testament scenes and Christ Pantocrator with saints, while the aisle mosaics narrate the miracles of Jesus. The more warmly human figures are believed to be the work of Venetian mosaicists, as opposed to the more rigidly formal Byzantine figures of Palermo's Palatine Chapel.

The beautiful **cloister** offers strangely mixed sensations: spiritual meditation along the arcades of delicate chevron-fluted columns and an almost sensual pleasure among the exotic flowers and trees and Arab fountain of its garden.

Cefalù

One of Sicily's oldest settlements, dating back to the 9th century BC, the town exerts a magnetic charm both with its majestic site up on a promontory and the intimacy of its indigo and ochre houses. Its beaches are inviting and the fishing harbour hospitable to summer yachts. Its pride and joy is the Romanesque **cathedral**, one of the finest and best preserved examples of Norman church architecture in Italy. Begun by King Roger II in 1131, its massive but elegant forms, with golden façade and twin bell towers, dominate the old town. Inside, be sure to see the brilliant gold **mosaics** of Byzantine design, most poignant of all a glowing-eyed Christ Pantocrator in the apse.

Messina

Strategically located on the north-eastern tip of Sicily, this modern port is the island's main gateway to mainland Italy, with frequent car and passenger ferries. Down in the straits, the legendary whirlpools of Charybdis (*see* page 293) still churn up a harvest of more than 100 different species of fish. Devastated by the earthquake of 1908 and Allied air raids of 1943, the **Duomo** has been lovingly reconstructed in its original Romanesque-Gothic form.

The free-standing **campanile** houses a gigantic **astronomical clock**. Each day at noon, a cannon heralds its fantastic movements: the lion roars, the rooster crows, the angel hovers, the Madonna blesses, Christ appears and the dove of the Holy Spirit soars. Death comes with a scythe, the days pass and the moon turns.

Artistically more satisfying is the **Museo Nazionale** (Viale della Libertà), which includes works by the town's most famous son, Renaissance master Antonello da Messina, a *Madonna* and the polyptych of *St Gregory*; and by

---

Chiaroscuro

Sicily is a fascinating study in light and shade. It may surprise visitors expecting in a sun-drenched island an equally sunny, happy-go-lucky disposition among its people. Somehow the experience of successive waves of Greek, Arab, Norman, German and Spanish rulers before entering the national Italian orbit has left its people more withdrawn than, say, the Neapolitans on the mainland. Like the thick, almost windowless walls that shield their dwellings against the summer heat, a cool, even sombre reserve protects the people from the visitor's probing curiosity in the too-dazzling light of a Sicilian day. The joy is there, but private.

Evolving during the rule of the Spanish, in place of official justice, the Mafia exploited the Sicilian custom of settling personal wrongs among themselves and administered its own law and order, pocketing fines, punishing obstreperous enemies and rewarding obedient friends. But recent Mafia outrages, including the murder of two top judges in 1992, have provoked a wave of revulsion amongst ordinary Sicilians. One day, perhaps soon, *l'onorata società* (the honourable society) may be unable to command the respect and loyalty it needs to maintain a stranglehold on the island.

Caravaggio, while a fugitive in Sicily, the *Adoration of the Shepherds* and the *Resurrection of Lazarus*.

Aeolian Islands (*Isole Eolie*)

Named after Aeolus, the god of the winds of Greek mythology, who kept the winds in a cave here, this archipelago is remarkable for its stark volcanic beauty. A world apart, the islands (also known as the *Isole Lipari*) appear much more remote than the few kilometres that separate them by ferry from Messina (or *Milazzo*). To the eternal fascination of smoking volcanoes, add the bizarre lunar landscapes, secluded coves and grottoes, and great underwater exploring and fishing. Seven of the islands are populated: Vulcano, Lipari, Salina, Filicudi, Alicudi, Panarea and Stromboli.

Much of **Vulcano**, the island which is closest to Sicily, is a smoking mass of lava, though the last serious eruption was in 1890. Steam and gases puff through the fumaroles and a hellish whiff of sulphur hangs in the air. If you like such things, sulphur and mudbaths in the hot pools here are good for whatever ails you. Aesthetically more pleasant is a swim in the warm waters of the Baia di Levante, at the north end of the island, where underwater hot springs heat the sea close to the beach.

Lipari is the largest of the islands and worth a drive around the characteristic volcanic formations that have left deposits of glassy black obsidian rock and white pumice stone, the island's chief export. The stuff at the side of the road is free for all. The town of Lipari boasts a **museum** of the island's prehistoric and classical culture in a Spanish-built castle that incorporates a Greek tower of the 4th century BC. The local seafood restaurants are excellent.

The volcano on **Stromboli** spouts an ever-present plume of smoke from its crater. It is accessible on a three-hour hike. More relaxed is a boat trip to watch the lava run down a fissure known as **Sciara del Fuoco** (Pit of Fire), especially spectacular if you see it at night. The rich volcanic soil produces fine Malvasia grapes and a delicious dessert wine. The island has a distinctive architecture of whitewashed Arab-style houses with outside staircases among citrus, olive and palm trees.

Sparks fly from the crater of Stromboli's volcano around the clock, but the spectacle is most impressive at night.

Taormina

This attractive resort town, very popular in antiquity as a vacation spot for the Greek bourgeoisie from Syracuse, commands a splendid view of the Mediterranean from its hillside villas and hotels. No Sicilian *passeggiata* is more celebrated than a promenade on the elegant shopping street of **Corso Umberto** and out along the **Via Roma** past the subtropical vegetation of the terraced gardens. With great views south along the coast and to the volcano of Mount Etna to the west, the **Greek Theatre** (3rd century BC) provides a wonderful setting for drama, dance and music in the summer and a slightly surreal one for the Taormina International Film Festival in July. Excursions further up the mountain take you to two medieval fortresses, on foot to **Castello di Taormina** and, by car along a winding road, to the hill village of **Castelmola**, for grand panoramic views.

Mount Etna

Europe's tallest volcano is still very active, as you will see from tell-tale yellow sulphur stains of mini-eruptions as you approach the crater. The summit currently stands at around 3,330m (10,925ft) above sea level, but varies according to the destruction wreaked by the latest eruptions and the lava deposits left behind. Because of the erratic nature of the eruptions, approaching the crater is no easy business. The routes by bus, special Land Rover and cable car from Taormina or Catania change from year to year, lava permitting. Enquire at local tourist offices and travel agencies before setting out. In any case, the last stretch to the crater itself is on foot, so take sturdy shoes and warm clothing since it is cool and windy up there, even in summer. From October to May, the summit is covered in snow.

The volcanic soil produces a rich crop of citrus fruits—oranges, tangerines and lemons—as well as figs, almonds, grapes and olives. The slopes are remarkably sweet-smelling for a volcano, with forests of eucalyptus and umbrella pine among the oak and pistachio. Higher up, you get a whiff of sulphurous gases hissing from the small craters pock-marking the barren moonscape of the summit. When the Rifugio Sapienza, 1,881m (6,172ft), is in use, an overnight stay on the volcano makes it possible to reach the summit at sunrise for a spectacular view both into the crater and back over the Sicilian coast to the Italian mainland. Otherwise, try to be there at sunset.

Catania

Sicily's second city (population 360,000) has suffered over the centuries from Etna's eruptions, earthquakes and World War II bombs in 1943. The result is a busy, thoroughly modern town with only a few vestiges of its past. Characteristic of old Catania is the baroque ensemble of **Piazza del Duomo**, with its reconstructed cathedral and city hall (*Municipio*), and in the centre a charming **fountain** of a lava-stone elephant bearing an Egyptian granite obelisk. More baroque villas and churches line **Via Crociferi**, leading to the **Roman Theatre** rebuilt over a Greek one where orator Alcibiades sought to win Catanians to the cause of Athens in 415 BC.

Catania's most famous native son, the composer Vincenzo Bellini, has a park, a piazza and a theatre named after him, while his greatest opera is celebrated by local dish, *spaghetti Norma*. In Via Crociferi, the house where Bellini was born in 1801 is now a **museum** containing memorabilia of the composer's life.

Syracuse (*Siracusa*)

The east-coast Corinthian settlement founded in 734 BC was the most powerful of Greece's overseas colonies and, under Dionysius (405–367 BC), a direct rival to Athens. In its heyday, its population was nearly three times the size of today's 125,000. It was here in the 3rd century BC that mathematician Archimedes worked out his water displacement theory in the bath and ran naked into the street crying "Eureka!".

Syracuse's original settlement was the port-island of **Ortygia**, joined by two bridges to the mainland. Two pillars surviving from the Greek Temple of Apollo stand like a gateway, but the Spanish era has given it a charming 17th-century ambience of baroque houses with balconies supported by floral carvings and an occasional stone nymph. Graceful, crescent-shaped **Piazza del Duomo** is the perfect place for breakfast surrounded by 17th- and 18th-century palazzi and the **cathedral**. The church is in fact a baroque elaboration of the Greeks' Temple of Athena (5th century BC), with its columns incorporated into the masonry of the outside walls. South of the cathedral in Via Capodieci, the **Palazzo Bellomo** houses Syracuse's **Museo Regionale**. The highlights of the collection are Antonella da Messina's celebrated *Annunciation* and Caravaggio's sombre and dramatic *Burial of St Lucy*. On the island's west side, the **Fontana Aretusa** is a freshwater spring with black and white ducks swimming in its semi-circular papyrus pond.

The principal excavated site, **Parco Archeologico**, is located on the northwest corner of the modern city. Rebuilt by the Romans to hold 15,000 spectators for their games, the **Greek Theatre** dates back to the 5th century BC when Aeschylus personally came over from his south-coast home at Gela to supervise productions of his tragedies. A classical drama festival is

*P*indar described ancient Syracuse as "the queen of all towns". The splendour of its classical civilization is apparent in the impressive collections of the National Archaeological Museum.

held there in May and June, every other year.

Rather than tragic drama, in which all the violence happened offstage, Roman tastes ran more towards bloody gladiatorial combat. Note the entrance for gladiators and wild beasts at the nearby **Roman amphitheatre**, one of the largest ever built.

The neighbouring **Paradise Quarry** (*Latomia del Paradiso*) provided the city's building materials and is now a pleasant garden of oleander and orange trees. Its popular attraction is the cave known as the **Orecchio di Dionisio** (Dionysius's Ear), a huge cavern carved from the rock which acts like an echo chamber. Legend holds that Dionysius kept his prisoners in this cave and used its remarkable acoustics to eavesdrop on their conversations.

Classical drama in the setting of Syracuse's ancient Greek theatre dates back to Aeschylus, who directed the world premieres of several of his plays here in the 5th century.

The **Museo Archeologico Nazionale**, housed in the grounds of the Villa Landolina, boasts a fine collection of 5th and 4th century Greek vases, sculptures and friezes. Its greatest treasure is the *Landolina Venus*, a headless statue showing the goddess rising from the sea. Over the road from the museum is the **Santuario delle Lacrime**, a modern church in the shape of a teardrop built to house a miraculous statue of the Madonna which supposedly shed tears for five days in 1953.

Agrigento

Of all the pilgrimages to be made to the great Greek sanctuaries of Sicily, the most compelling is to Agrigento's **Temple Valley** (*Valle dei Templi*) dating right back to the 5th century BC. Founded by colonists from the nearby Greek city of Gela in 582 BC, Akragas (as the Greeks called it) was described by the poet Pindar as "the most beautiful of all mortal cities".

The prosperity enjoyed by Akragas in its heyday is evident in the splendour of its sacred buildings. The **Temple of Juno** with its sacrificial altar stands in majestic isolation high on a ledge at the eastern end of the Via Sacra. The **Temple of Concord** is the best preserved, thanks to its subsequent use as a church in the 6th century AD. The golden glow of the temples' Doric columns and the idyllic setting amid acacia and almond trees on a precipice overlooking the Mediterranean are enough to start you worshipping a whole pantheon of Greek gods.

The **Temple of Hercules** is the oldest of the temples; eight of its original columns have been re-erected, the rest lie scattered on the ground. Over the road are the remains of the **Temple of Zeus**, the largest Doric temple ever built (albeit never completed), and the **Temple of Castor and Pollux**, whose striking four columns are actually the result of a 19th-century reconstruction.

North of Temple Valley, next to the 12th-century Norman church of San Nicola, the **Archaeological Museum** has a fine marble sculpture of a youth, known as the *Ephebus of Agrigento* (5th century BC), and a gigantic *telamon*, a male figure used to hold up a temple roof's entablature, and some superb Greek wine vessels.

The nearby town of **Caos** (now effectively a suburb of modern Agrigento) is remembered as the birthplace of the great Sicilian playwright and novelist Luigi Pirandello (1867–1936). The house where the writer was born is now a **museum**, packed with memorabilia; Pirandello's ashes lie beneath a pine tree in the grounds of the house.

Selinunte

The few romantic remains of these **Greek temples**, standing on a gentle rise between what were once two harbours, are a veritable allegory in stone of the violence of man and the elements. Nothing survives from the town itself, twice sacked by the Carthaginians; the second time (250 BC) left it in total ruin. Earthquake completed man's devastation and what you see today is a painstaking reconstruction of the pillars and stones found strewn among the wild celery (Greek: *selinón*) that gave the settlement its name.

The ruins, in two major groups on either side of a dried-up river gorge, can be designated only by letters. In the eastern group, **Temple E** is a splendid Doric structure with at least its columns and a part of the entablature resurrected. You can see parts of its beautifully carved friezes in Palermo's Archaeological Museum (*see* page 298). To the north, the slightly smaller **Temple F** lies in eloquent rubble, while of the northernmost, **Temple G**, originally one of the biggest in Sicily, only a single column remains upright. West of the gorge is the acropolis that contained other smaller temples. The north colonnade of **Temple C** has been reconstructed, bearing part of the entablature.

In late afternoon, when the scattered stones glow golden in the sun, take one last walk around the ruins and then go off for a dip in the sea at the beach of **Marinella**.

The West Coast

The ancient port of **Marsala** was founded by the Carthaginians, but it was an Englishman, John Woodhouse, who in 1773 spread its name and sweet golden dessert wine around the world. You can taste (and buy) at a local wine-warehouse (*enoteca*). Every five years, the old wine is partially drained off for bottling and a new wine added.

So when you sip a Marsala Stravecchio you may be sampling some drops of the same wine that Garibaldi's thousand men drank to celebrate their successful landing here on 11 May 1860— the start of their campaign to liberate Sicily from Bourbon rule.

On the north-west coast, **Trapani** is a tunny-fishing port that served as an important communications link with

When the sun in Sicily is directly overhead you'll understand why Italy's south is known as the mezzogiorno *(midday). Your best course is to seek refuge in the shade.*

Spain during the rule of the House of Aragon. On the outskirts of town, the graceful 14th-century Gothic **Santuario dell'Annunziata** has a fine marble Madonna from the workshop of the Tuscan sculptor Nino Pisano. In the 16th-century Gothic-Renaissance church of **Santa Maria del Gesù**, see Andrea della Robbia's beautiful glazed terracotta *Madonna of the Angels* (in the chapel at the far right of the nave). North of Corso Italia in the old Jewish ghetto is an ornate Spanish-style **Palazzo della Giudecca** (Palace of Jewry) of the 16th century.

Some 14km (9 miles) inland from Trapani is one of the most charming, unspoiled villages in Sicily, the medieval **Erice** perched on top of a 750m- (2,460ft-) high mountain. In Greek times, it was revered by sailors for its temple to Aphrodite and her sacred courtesans. Today, a calmer clientele is attracted by the town's old Norman houses on cobbled streets, the charming 14th-century **Chiesa Matrice** with its free-standing campanile, and the **fortress** that the Normans built on the site of the temple. The sanctuary's sacred well is still there. There's a grand view of the surrounding countryside and west to the offshore Egadi Islands.

Between Erice and Palermo, the beautifully preserved, but probably unfinished **Temple of Segesta** reigns over one of the most bewitching sites in the Mediterranean. Built in the 5th century BC, the solitary sanctuary looks out across pine-covered hillsides to the Gulf of Castellammare beyond. Standing among wild fennel, its peace disturbed only by the occasional goat bell tinkling from afar, the temple seems still very much impregnated with the Earth Mother cult to which its sacrifices were originally offered. Further up the Monte Barbara, past a few remains of the ancient city's fortifications, is a **Greek theatre** (3rd century BC) cut out of the granite.

Sardinia (*Sardegna*)

Like Sicily, the island of Sardinia is worth a holiday all to itself—ideally in a sailing boat—and much more detailed treatment than we give it here. But for those who want in a few days to get just a feel for its atmosphere as part of a first-time visit to Italy, we suggest some seaside resorts, trips along the coast and a couple of excursions into the hinterland.

The island's prehistoric inhabitants dotted the island with mysterious cone-shaped *nuraghi* dwellings and watch-towers before it was colonized by Cretans, Phoenicians, Carthaginians and Romans. Later, the island became part of the commercial empires of Pisa, Genoa and the Spanish and was annexed in 1718 by the dukes of Savoy. Malarial mosquitoes and repressive feudalism restrained the island's development until the 19th century, since when it has undergone a rapid industrialization balanced today by renewal of its cattle farming.

Cagliari

The island's capital and main port is a largely modern city, but with a Spanish flavour to its older quarters up on

*S*ardinia.

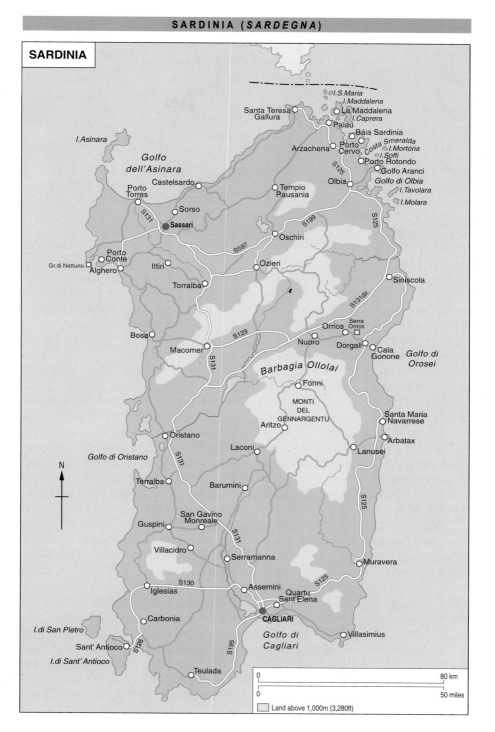

SARDINIA

I.Asinara

Golfo
dell'Asinara

I.S.Maria
I.Maddalena
Santa Teresa
Gallura
La Maddalena
I.Caprera
Palau
Báia Sardinia
Arzachena
Porto
Cervo
Costa Smeralda
I.Mortória
I.Soffi
Porto Rotondo
Golfo Aranci
Olbia
Golfo di Olbia
I.Tavolara
I.Molara

Castelsardo
Porto
Torres
Sorso
Tempio
Pausania

Sassari
Oschiri
S199
S125

Porto
Conte
Gr.di Nettuno
Alghero
Ittiri
Ozieri
S597

Torralba
Siniscola
S131dir.

Bosa
Orrios
Serra
Orrios

Macomer
Nuoro
Dorgali
Cala
Gonone
Golfo di
Orosei

Barbagia Ollolai
Fonni

MONTI
DEL
GENNARGENTU
Aritzo
Santa Maria
Navarrese
Arbatax

Oristano
Laconi
Lanusei

Golfo di Oristano
N

Terralba
Barumini
S125

San Gavino
Monreale
Guspini

Villacidro
Serramanna
Muravera
S131

Iglesias
S130
Assemini
S125

Carbonia
Quartu
Sant'Elena
CAGLIARI

I.di San Pietro
Villasimius

Sant' Antioco
S126
Golfo di
Cagliari
S195

I.di Sant' Antioco
Teulada

| 0 | 80 km |
| 0 | 50 miles |

☐ Land above 1,000m (3,280ft)

the hill. Housed within the walls of a medieval castle built by the Pisans, the **Archaeological Museum** includes important bronze statues of warriors and priests found in prehistoric tombs. The much renovated **cathedral** has two superbly carved 12th-century pulpits, originally commissioned for the cathedral in Pisa. Before heading for the open road, try the savoury local cuisine, combining Spanish-style fish stews and Genoese pasta dishes.

The winding Cagliari–Muravera road across the plunging ravines of the Sarrabus mountains to the east coast is one of the most spectacular drives on the whole island.

Continue up the coast to Lanusei and head inland across the rugged **Gennargentu** mountains, covered with dense forests of cork oak and chestnut trees. Another regional delicacy are *sebadas*: golden pancakes filled with cheese and covered with honey and sugar.

Or take the more easterly route up to Dorgali from the attractive port and beach resort of **Arbatax** with its purple rocks. Stop off at the pretty village of **Santa Maria Navarrese** facing the

A nuraghe near Alghero. Distinctive features of the landscape, these mysterious conical towers of stone are vestiges of the island's Bronze Age past.

ruddy-hued little island of Ogliastra. Further north, from the resort of **Cala Gonone**, you can take boat cruises around grottoes inhabited in prehistoric times by humans but now only by the occasional seal, the most famous being the **Grotta del Bue Marino** (Sea-ox Grotto).

Just off the Nuoro–Dorgali road is the secluded site of **Serra Orrios**, a well-preserved prehistoric village (signposted *Villaggio Nuragico*). A short walk along a marked path through the fields takes you to a group of dry-stone houses with two arched temples and circular ramparts in a lovely setting of eucalyptus and olive trees. Built over 3,000 years ago by the island's Bronze Age inhabitants, the *nuraghi* are as enigmatic as the Etruscan tombs on mainland Italy or the monoliths of

Stonehenge. Archaeologists have located some 7,000 of these structures around the island, most of them flattened cone towers believed to be parts of fortified citadels.

Costa Smeralda

The glittering Emerald Coast on the north-east tip of the island is one of Italy's smartest resort areas, with beautiful beaches, grand hotels, sports complexes and marinas for yachts and motor launches. Developed as a playground for the super rich by a consortium headed by the Aga Khan, the Costa Smeralda stretches north of Olbia round bays and rocky inlets to the promontory of La Maddalena.

Olbia serves as the airport and sailing gateway to the northern part of the island. It has some of the best seafood restaurants in Sardinia and the busy harbour area is the place to do your last-minute gift-shopping: it is particularly good for rugs and ceramics.

Porto Cervo is the coast's fashionable centre, but **Baia Sardinia** competes with its craggy coastline. Off the beaten track is the little luxury resort island and fishing village of **La Maddalena**, a 15-minute ferry-ride from Palau. It is the principal island of an archipelago of 14, most of them little more than a pile of rocks.

Linked to La Maddalena by a 7km (4-mile) causeway, the isle of **Caprera** was the last home of Giuseppe Garibaldi, the military leader of the *Risorgimento* movement for Italian unity (*see* page 57). The house where he died in 1882 (his tomb is nearby) is now a **museum**, practically a sanctuary, where devout patriots refer to him not by name, but as "the Hero", *l'Eroe*.

Sardinia's northern coast is notable for its weather-worn rocks, massive boulders beaten and chiselled by the elements into fantastic shapes. The north-coast road makes an enjoyable excursion along the dunes and pine groves lining the Gulf of Asinara. The fortress-town of **Castelsardo** stands high on a spectacular promontory overlooking the gulf. Inside its 16th-century cathedral, you hear the sea crashing on the rocks directly below its foundations.

At **Porto Torres**, visit the important 11th-century Pisan Romanesque church of San Gavino. It has no façade, but its interior has a noble simplicity. Some of the pillars come from an ancient Roman temple, with two Corinthian capitals serving as a lectern.

Alghero

This quiet little seaside resort on the north-west coast has a pleasant Catalan flavour to its older quarters around the cathedral. Take a sunset stroll along the 16th-century Spanish ramparts.

There is good fishing to be had in the nearby bay of Porto Conte, and the Palmavera *nuraghe* citadel is well worth a visit. On the bay's south-western promontory is the fascinating **Grotta di Nettuno** (Neptune's Grotto). Guided tours of these subterranean caverns with their dramatic stalactites and stalagmites are organized by boat from Alghero or on foot directly at the site, down a rather steep stairway in the cliffs. It's a freshwater grotto fed by an underground river. The stalactites grow down at the rate of one centimetre every 100 years, faster than the stalagmites rising to meet them from the cave floor.

Pastime Pursuits Performed with Panache

Italy may have given the world the phrase *dolce far niente*, "how sweet to do nothing", but there is no need to stand idle when you take time off from all that church-going and museum visiting. Italians may have a reputation for being laid-back but that doesn't mean they don't throw themselves energetically into all manner of activities. The choice is immense: from sport to shopping, folk music to discos, grand opera in the open-air to age-old festivals in the country. But wherever you go, one thing is constant: whatever the pursuit, you can be sure the Italians will be doing it with style.

Sports

It would be an understatement to describe the Italians as sport-crazy, at least as far as spectator sports are concerned. For millions, Sundays are less sacred for mass in the morning than football in the afternoon. In a country with just a century of national unity and the scalding experience of Mussolini's fascism, sport seems almost the only activity which can inspire in Italians any semblance of patriotic fervour.

There are many things to do and see the length and breadth of Italy throughout the year—as you will find if you join the Italians in their own pastimes.

Witness the crowd's ferocious, unashamedly chauvinistic partisanship at Rome's international open tennis championships or the Davis Cup. On a day when Italy is involved in an international football match, streets all over the country are deserted until the cars come out honking for a frenetic victory parade or the men shuffle on foot to Piazza del Duomo for a funereal post-defeat commiseration and recrimination.

You can observe the **football** (soccer) phenomenon, with the *tifosi* (fans) in full cry, in all the major cities. The most celebrated teams, studded with top foreign stars, are in Turin (Juventus and Torino), Milan (AC and Inter), Florence (Fiorentina), Genoa (Sampdoria), Rome and Naples.

T he Dolomites have an extensive network of hiking trails. Mountain huts, known as rifugi, *provide accommodation for overnight stops.*

Cycling races are still popular, especially the round-Italy *Giro d'Italia* in June. You can watch World Cup **skiing** at Cortina d'Ampezzo and Val Gardena. **Bocce**, the bowls game similar to French *boules* or *pétanque*, is played wherever there is a patch of tree-shaded sandy gravel and a bar (*osteria*) close enough at hand to serve a glass of wine or *grappa*.

Motor racing fans can watch the Grand Prix of Italy at Monza, near Milan, or at Imola, near Bologna.

On the beaches of the Adriatic coast, the Italian Riviera, Sardinia and Sicily, the pleasure of **swimming** needs a few words of warning. Conditions of water pollution change every year, but observe the general rule of thumb of avoiding a dip in the immediate vicinity of major industrialized port-cities like Genoa, Naples and Palermo. Look out for red flags warning of dangerous undercurrents and for small children check that beaches are patrolled by life-guards. Remember, for many resorts like the Venice Lido or Tuscany's Forte dei Marmi, to budget for umbrellas, deck-chairs and mattresses.

For water sports at the resorts, you can usually hire equipment on the spot for **snorkelling** and **wind-surfing** (particularly good on the lakes). The Italians are great experts at **scuba-diving** and have skilful (and handsome) instructors. You may well come across archaeological finds: ancient anchors, wine-jars, even sculpture. All *must* be reported to local municipal authorities. It's not difficult to get hitched up to a motorboat for **water-skiing**.

Sailing is great sport around Sardinia and Sicily, but also on the Argentario peninsula.

Offshore **fishing** is popular all along the coasts, notably for tunny (tuna) off western Sicily, for swordfish on the east coast and spear-fishing at Bordighera. For freshwater fishing in the inland lakes and rivers, you should get a permit from the local municipality.

Hiking is the simplest and most exhilarating way of seeing the countryside, up in the Dolomites or the Alps, around the lakes and the Abruzzo National Park. Remember good shoes, light but solid, and some warm clothing. You can hire horses for **riding** at resorts like Sestri Levante, Alassio, San Remo. To explore the back country on horseback, inquire at the ANTE (National Association of Equestrian Tourism), Largo Messico 13, Rome.

Golf players can usually play on local private courses with proof of their home club membership. Venice has an 18-hole course at the Lido's Alberoni. On the Riviera, try Rapallo, San Remo or Garlenda (near Alassio). **Tennis** is less widespread than in other major western European countries, but growing in popularity. Your hotel can help you find a hard or clay court.

Skiing is first-class in the established resorts of Cortina d'Ampezzo and Courmayeur, with a perhaps more explosive thrill on Mount Etna.

Entertainment

From time to time, the Italians move the melodrama of their lives indoors and call it **opera**. Most famous of the high temples of this art is, of course, Milan's La Scala (*see* page 226), privileging the works of Verdi, Bellini, Rossini and Puccini. The taste for the grandiose musical spectacle has spread all across the western world, but the greatest stars and divas need a triumph at La Scala for true consecration. Its season is from December till mid-May. For good tickets, you should plan well in advance through a travel agency, but your hotel may be able to help with seats from last-minute cancellations.

The other great opera houses are La Fenice in Venice, Florence's Teatro Comunale and the great Teatro San Carlo of Naples. However, Bologna, Parma, Perugia, Rome and Palermo also have fine regional houses, beginning around December or January and going on till late spring or early summer.

In the summer, **open-air opera** is the great attraction in Rome's ancient Baths of Caracalla (though concerns for the monument's condition have recently halted performaces) and Verona's Roman Arena, when *Aida* and other lavish productions may include horses, camels or even elephants on stage.

Torre del Lago Puccini situated near Viareggio in Tuscany has a summer opera festival dedicated to Puccini. Trieste hosts an open-air operetta festival in July and August.

Orchestral concerts of symphonic and chamber **music**, for which it is usually easier to get tickets, are held in the opera houses outside and sometimes concurrently with the opera season, but also in Milan's Conservatorio and Rome's Accademia Filarmonica Romana. Florence's spring Maggio Musicale Fiorentina and Spoleto's summer Festival of Two Worlds attract leading international artists. Perugia, Ravenna,

Rimini and Stresa all hold important music festivals. In Tuscany San Gimignano and Lucca stage open-air concerts, while Amalfi's are given in the cathedral cloisters.

Classical music and ballet are performed on summer evenings in the outdoor theatres of Pompeii.

A great open-air festival of **jazz, pop** and **rock** music is held in the parks and gardens of Rome for the *Estate Romana* (Roman Summer). Perugia hosts the Jazz Festival of Umbria in July. Alassio's jazz festival is in September. Milan has the best discos and night-clubs, while others are attached to hotels at the seaside resorts. Most Italians go over the border to France to gamble, but Venice has a winter **casino** in the Palazzo Vendramin-Calergi.

*I*talians are famously adept at making music, from grand opera to the humbler variety practised here in the village of Bussana Vecchia in Liguria.

Theatre requires a good knowledge of Italian. The best productions are in Rome and Milan, the latter famous for the internationally acclaimed Piccolo Teatro founded by Giorgio Strehler.

One of the most entertaining ways to polish your Italian is at the **cinema**, where all foreign films are dubbed into Italian (though a minor revolution is taking place in a few movie-houses playing original versions in Milan and Rome). International film festivals are held at Venice and Taormina.

Shopping

The inspired vanity of the Italians has turned their country into a delightful bazaar of style and elegance for the foreign visitor. Of stupefying junk, too. The luxury goods of Milan, Venice, Rome and Florence, jewellery, clothes, especially shoes, but also luggage and household goods of impeccable modern design, are second-to-none in the world. Not inexpensive, but then the bargain here is not in the price, but in the meticulous workmanship.

The souvenirs also merit a homage to endless invention in the realm of the cheap—and not-so-cheap—and nasty: Leaning Tower of Pisa pencil-sharpeners, Trevi Fountain water-squirters, musical gondolas, fluorescent volcanos, priapic Pompeians, Colosseum with plaster Christians fed to plastic lions, glass balls of the pope blessing the faithful in a snow storm, and a do-it-yourself *Last Supper* colouring-book. Maybe the sublime looks even more sublime when it hangs around the plainly ridiculous.

Some souvenirs are, or course, more tasteful. Save such purchases as gourmet delicacies for the end, to get them home as fresh as possible. These include cheeses, salami, Parma ham, Milanese sweet *panettone brioche*, Lucca's olive oil, Siena's cakes, biscuits and famous *panforte*, a spicy fruit-and-nut concoction, and the better Chianti and Orvieto wines that you may not find back home.

If you have fallen in love with Italian coffee, why not buy a compact version of the *espresso* machine or a streamlined coffee pot that does practically the same job on the stove? Italian kitchenware is in general beautifully styled with a great sense of colour and line.

In a country where civilizations have come and gone like commuter-trains, there is a considerable traffic in archaeological antiquities. When anybody at an ancient site in Rome, Pompeii or Sicily offers you a Roman coin, Greek pot or statue, you can be fairly sure it's a fake.

For quality goods, Italians prefer shopping in small boutiques with a long tradition, very often a family business that guarantees generations of good craftsmanship. As a result, you won't find upmarket department stores, but popular, lower-price chainstores: Coin, Standa, Upim or Rinascente. These are useful for your extra T-shirts, suntan lotion or throw-away beach sandals.

Even when sales people do not speak English, they will bend over backwards to be helpful. If you want friendly treatment in the more expensive stores, you must dress decently. Even the warmest-hearted Italian can, perhaps understandably, be snooty towards people dressed like slobs. Credit cards work almost everywhere these days, apart from a few Sardinian basket-weavers and Apulian potters. Shops in the big cities are only too happy to take your foreign currency, at larcenous rates of exchange, so stock up at the bank on shopping days (*see* page 28).

Haggling is a thing of the past. You can get an occasional small *sconto* (discount) for bulk purchases, but the spread of foreign travel has taught shopkeepers in the remotest province the going international price for everything. Except among antique, art and secondhand dealers, where negotiation is part of the business, you may get a very cool response if you question the marked price.

Many cities are renowned for products of their traditional crafts: Naples' costumed terracotta figures for its Christmas cribs; Sorrento's inlaid walnut furniture and music boxes; Ravenna's mosaics; Pisa's alabaster and Gubbio's ceramics. For the rest, the widest range of products will be found in the big cities. (Unless you are buying things you want to use during your vacation, such as clothes or sports equipment, save your shopping till the end, so as to avoid lugging the stuff all around the country.)

Rome

The capital's smartest and most expensive boutiques (even if you are not buying, it is worth window-shopping just for the superb displays) are conveniently concentrated in a four-by-four-block area around Via Condotti. Closed to cars, it is bounded by Piazza di Spagna to the east and Via del Corso to the west. Here you will find the finest leather goods (Gucci, Fendi, Ferragamo). Women's fashions include the major French designers as well as the natives (Valentino, Armani, Gianni Versace, Gianfranco Ferrè and Missoni). Almost as expensive are the two children's clothing shops of Tablò. Among the men's clothes meccas are Davide Cenci, Testa and Battistoni.

In **jewellery**, for sheer exclusivity, there is nothing like the imposing marble façade of Bulgari (Via Condotti), the ultimate monument to Roman luxury.

Two streets dominate the market in **art** and **antiques**, Via Margutta and Via del Babuino.

On the outskirts of this high-class shopping district, you will find mass-produced sweaters, jeans and other casual wear, as well as more moderately priced leather goods, on bustling Via Tritone and Via del Corso.

If you are looking for second-hand bric-à-brac, try the shops around the Campo dei Fiori and Piazza Navona. The Sunday morning **flea market** at Porta Portese in Trastevere is as much

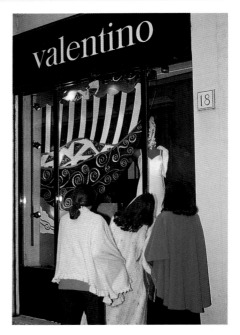

*T*he Valentino boutique in Rome's Via Bocca di Leone. Alta moda *may be beyond the reach of many, but window-shopping is free to all.*

fun for the street-musicians as for the chance of picking up bargains. Keep your own valuables safe: pickpockets love this place.

Florence

If it has ceded to Milan its place as Italy's fashion capital, the old Renaissance city is still a centre of exquisite, if somewhat conservative elegance. The principal thoroughfares for the smarter **fashion** boutiques, for men and women, are Via de' Tornabuoni and Via de' Calzaiuoli.

Florentine **leather goods** remain unequalled. You can smell out the country's, indeed Europe's, finest craftsmen at work in leather factories around San Lorenzo and Santa Croce. Watch the making of handbags, wallets, gloves, belts and desk-equipment without any obligation to buy. Look out, too, for the leather school tucked away behind Santa Croce's sacristy in what were once Franciscan monk's cells.

Ponte Vecchio is the most picturesque place to shop for very reasonably priced **gold, silver** and **jewellery**, designed with centuries of tradition behind them.

Multicoloured glass mosaic jewellery such as brooches, pendants, bracelets and rings can be found all over town. Handmade in local cottage-industry, they are amazingly cheap and very attractive.

Inlaid wood or *intarsia* is a venerated craft here, perfected in the 16th century with the inlay of semi-precious stones. Using the same techniques, **furniture** is likely to be expensive, but framed pictures of Tuscan landscapes or views of Florence are more moderately priced and, as souvenirs go, tastefully done. The town also specializes in **bookbinding** and stunningly beautiful **stationery**.

Antique shops are centred mainly around Borgo Ognissanti and San Jacopo, Via della Vigna Nuova and della Spada. Even if you cannot afford the mostly prohibitive prices, they are worth visiting as veritable little museums of Renaissance and Baroque sculpture and furniture. If the creative geniuses are long dead, master craftsmen continue the tradition of superb reproductions, at negotiable prices.

Venice

One of the many great adventures here is separating the treasure-house from the tourist-trap, distinguishing priceless gems from pricey junk. By and large, the better, but more expensive shops are around Piazza San Marco. The busy shopping streets of the Mercerie have good quality boutiques growing progressively moderate in price as they approach the Rialto. For cheap purchases, head for the Strada Nuova leading behind the Ca' d'Oro to the railway station.

The bargains, or at least more authentic and tasteful products, are to be found, like the havens of tranquillity, far from these main tourist-centres. Artisans' workshops on the Giudecca, in the Dorsoduro behind the Zattere and over by the Ghetto, should be hunted down individually and guarded as precious secrets.

Two true institutions stand out among the **jewellery** shops: Missiaglia on Piazza San Marco and Sfriso on Campo San Tomà near the church of the Frari. For a cross-section of Venetian craftsmanship in more moderately priced jewellery, as well as **ceramics** and **glass mosaics**, take a look at Veneziartigiana, just off San Marco in Calle Larga.

The famous **glassware** poses a problem of quality and price. Much of the stuff is unspeakably ugly, but there is also an admirable renewal in both classical and modern design. Just hunt carefully. Necklaces of crystal or coloured beads are popular. Prices in the Murano island factories are marginally better than "downtown". When choosing gifts to be packed, remember: if real giraffes are fragile enough as it is, glass ones will never make it home; go for a rhinoceros.

Visit the island of Burano to see intricate **laceware** being made in the time-honoured manner, on the doorstep. Modern reproductions of traditional patterns can be bought on and around Piazza San Marco, along with beautifully embroidered tablecloths and napkins.

The venerable Legatoria Piazzesi (in Campiello della Feltrina, near Santa Maria Zobenigo) is the last of the great Venetian printing presses, still producing exquisite handmade **paper goods**, stationery and bookbindings. You can give your fancy dress balls a touch of Renaissance class with the finely crafted papier-mâché **masks** produced for the great Mardi Gras Carnival by workshops also turning out delightful toys, dolls and funny hats.

The range of **fashion** boutiques around San Marco is small but select, with a special emphasis on top-class **shoes** and other **leather goods**.

Milan

With the commercial leadership of the country, Milan has also taken over as **fashion** capital. For women's and men's clothes, you will find all the great Italian designers: Valentino, Gianni Versace, Fendi, Krizia, Armani, Missoni and Gianfranco Ferré, on and around Via Monte Napoleone. Here, too, are the leading **jewellery** shops.

The Galleria Vittorio Emanuele has plenty of smart, bright and more moderately priced boutiques for younger tastes. Bargain-hunters in jeans, shoes and cheaper fashions head for the popular stores along Via Torino and Via Manzoni.

You will find the **modern art** galleries and **antique** shops in the neighbourhood of the Brera Gallery and the side streets of Via Monte Napoleone: Via Borgospesso, Via della Spiga and Via Sant'Andrea.

The town offers by far the best range of **household goods**. This is the place to find the very latest design in *espresso* machines and other kitchen gadgets.

Themes and Variations

Virtually every little town in Italy has some sort of museum. Usually it is a civic museum (*museo civico*), with exhibits of local history, traditions and culture. If the town is associated with a particular product, there is often a museum, or at least a wing of the civic museum, dedicated to this speciality.

You will have ample opportunity to admire Italy's great art works in its galleries and churches, but you may also want to pursue a special interest or hobby. Given the vagaries of museum opening hours, check in advance with the local tourist office or the museum itself to avoid disappointment.

Botanical Gardens

With such a wide variety of flora, from Alpine plants in the north to subtropical species in Sicily, Italy can boast some outstanding botanical gardens and museums.

Florence: Museo Botanico, Via Pira 4. Considered one of the finest botanical museums in the world. Next door is the Giardino dei Semplici, site of a botanical garden laid out in the 16th century for Cosimo I.

Ischia: La Mortella, Forio. Mediterranean garden created by English composer Sir William Walton and his wife, Susana.

Mortola Inferiore (near Bordighera): Giardino Hanbury. Botanical garden with plants from around the world, founded in 1857 by Sir Thomas Hanbury.

Padua: Orto Botanico, Via Orto Botanico 15. Dating back to 1545, the oldest botanical garden in Europe, preserving its original layout in four sectors. Exotic and local species.

The Giardino Hanbury at Mortola Inferiore, founded by English merchant Sir Thomas Hanbury in 1857, contains some 3,000 varieties of plants and trees from around the world.

Rome: Collezione dell'Istituto di Botanica, Università, Piazzale A. Moro; and Orto Botanico, Largo Cristina di Svezia 24.

Siena: Istituto ed Orto Botanico, Via Pier Andrea Mattioli 4.

Turin, Orto Botanico dell'Università, Viale Mattioli 25. Founded in 1729, the gardens specialize in plants used for medicinal or industrial purposes.

Trento: Giardino Botanico Alpino, Viotte di Monte Bondone.

Ceramics

The people of Italy have excelled in the art of ceramics, especially majolica, since ancient times, and there are still several centres of local production.

Albisola (near Savona): Museo Manlio Trucco, Centro Ligure per la Storia della Ceramica, Viale Matteotti.

Ascoli Piceno: Museo della Ceramica, Palazzo Malaspina, Corso Mazzini 79.

Caltagirone (Sicily): Museo Statale della Ceramica, Via Roma.

Deruta (near Perugia): Museo delle Ceramiche, Palazzo del Comune, Piazza dei Consoli. Ancient and modern decorated ceramics. Visit on request.

Faenza: Museo Internazionale delle Ceramiche, Viale Baccarini. History of ceramic production in Faenza, as well as works from other Italian centres and around the world.

Florence: Museo delle Porcellane, Casino del Cavaliere, Giardino di Boboli. Some 2,000 pieces from the greatest manufacturers in Europe.

Laveno-Mombello (Lake Maggiore): Museo Civico Raccolta di Terraglia, Palazzo Giulizzoni-Perabò. Local pottery through the ages.

Naples: Museo Nazionale della Ceramica, Villa Floridiana. Porcelain collection of over 6,000 pieces begun by the Duca di Martina; and De Ciccio Collection in the Royal Apartments of Palazzo Reale di Capodimonte.

Pesaro: Musei Civici, Palazzo Toschi-Mosca, Via Toschi 29. Section devoted to ceramics of the Renaissance and Baroque periods.

Tolentino: Museo delle Ceramiche, Basilica di San Nicola da Tolentino. Documenting important Italian schools from 15th century up to today.

Vietri sul Mare (near Salerno): Museo della Ceramica, Villa Guariglia, Raito.

*A*ncient craft traditions are upheld in this small workshop in Florence's Piazza Santa Croce.

Crafts and Trades

You won't necessarily have to go to a museum to see Italian craftsmanship. Nonetheless, the museums do house some excellent examples of a variety of Italian specialities.

Carrara: Mostra Nazionale del Marmo, Via XX Settembre, Stadio. Museum of the famous marble quarried in the area.

Florence: Museo delle Pietre Dure, Via degli Alfani 78; works of art in precious stones, "Florentine mosaic" and cameo. Museo degli Argenti, Palazzo Pitti. Precious metals, gems and stones, ivories, textiles and tapestries.

Prato (near Florence): Museo del Tessuto, 5 Viale della Repubblica. Textiles from the 5th century AD to the present day.

Sorrento: Museo Correale di Terranova. Campanian decorative art of the 15–18th century, including inlaid furniture and porcelain.

Curiosities

Some museums are devoted to unusual or intriguing subjects.

Alessandria (between Turin and Genoa): Museo del Cappello, Corso Cento Cannoni 23. Traces the history of a local felt-hat factory founded in 1857.

Capo di Ponte (in Dolomites, north of Brescia): Parco Nazionale delle Incisioni Rupestri. Prehistoric rock engravings from Bronze Age to Roman times.

Florence: Museo di Storia della Fotografia Fratelli Alinari, Palazzo Rucellai, Via della Vigna Nuova. Museum illustrating history of the Alinari firm of photographers.

Gignese (near Stresa): Museo dell' Ombrella e del Parasole. Umbrellas from the 16th century to the present day.

Pontedassio (near Imperia): Museo Storico degli Spaghetti, Via Garibaldi 96. History of pasta.

Rome: Museo del Fonografo, Palazzo dei Antici Mattei, Via Caetani 32. Old phonograph museum.

Santa Maria Maggiore: Museo dello Spazzacamino. Chimney Sweep's Museum.

Tolentino: Museo Internazionale della Caricatura, Via della Pace (or Piazza Mauruzdi). Originals and reproductions of famous caricatures.

Famous Italians

Many of the great names in Italy's history, more often in the realms of art, architecture, literature and music than politics, have museums or collections devoted to them. A few have already been dealt with in LEISURE ROUTES AND THEMES, *see* pages 66–81.

Angelico, Fra (d.1455), Florentine painter and Dominican monk: *Florence*, Museo di San Marco, Piazza San Marco. Former Dominican monastery, with monks' cells decorated with frescoes by the "blessed" Angelico. *Vicchio* (near Florence), Museo del Beato Angelico, Palazzo Comunale, Via Garibaldi.

Bellini, Giovanni (c.1430–1516), Venetian artist: *Catania* (Sicily), Museo Belliniano, Piazza San Francesco 3.

Boccaccio, Giovanni (1313–1375), novelist and author of the Decameron: *Certaldo* (near Florence), Casa del Boccaccio, Via Boccaccio, tomb nearby in church of Santi Michele e Jacopo.

Dante Alighieri (1265–1321), poet, author of *The Divine Comedy*: *Ravenna*, Tomba di Dante, Via Dante Alighieri; and Museo Dantesco, Via Guido da Polenta. *Florence*, Casa e Museo di Dante, Via Santa Margherita 1, supposed to be Dante's birthplace.

Donizetti, Gaetano (1797–1848), operatic composer: *Bergamo*, Casa di Donizetti, Via Borgo Canale 14. Museo Donizettiano, Palazzo della Misericordia, Via Arena 9.

Garibaldi, Giuseppe (1807–1882), Italian patriot and hero of *Risorgimento*: *Como*, Museo Civico Storico G. Garibaldi, Piazza Medaglie d'Oro 1. *La Maddalena* (Sardinia), Museo Nazionale Garibaldino. *Mentana* (near Rome), Museo dei Garibaldini, Ara dei Caduti.

Manzoni, Alessandro (1785–1873), novelist, author of *I Promessi Sposi*: *Lecco* (near Como), Villa di Manzoni, Via Amendola. *Milan*, Museo Nazionale Casa di Manzoni, Via Morone 1.

Puccini, Giacomo (1858–1924), operatic composer: *Lucca*, Museo Pucciniano, Via del Poggia. *Viareggio*, Villa Puccini, Torre del Lago Puccini.

Raphael (Raffaello Sanzio) (1483–1520), painter and architect: *Urbino*, Casa Natale di Raffaello, Via Raffaello.

Rossini, Gioacchino (1792–1868), operatic composer: *Pesaro*, Museo Rossiniano, Via Rossini 34; and Conservatorio Rossini, Piazza Olivieri.

Titian (Tiziano Vecellio) (1487–1576), Venetian painter: *Pieve di Cadore*, Casa di Tiziano, Via Arsenale.

Toscanini, Arturo (1867–1957), conductor: *Parma*, Casa Natale di Toscanini, Borgo Rodolfo Tanzi 3.

Verdi, Giuseppe (1813–1901), operatic composer: *Busseto* (near Parma), Villa Verdi, Sant'Agata di Villanova.

... and One Non-Italian

Napoleon Bonaparte (1769–1821): *Portoferraio* (Elba), Museo Napoleonico, Villa San Martino; and Palazzina Napoleonica dei Mulini. *Rome*, Museo Napoleonico, Via Zanardelli 1. Tolentino, Museo Napoleonico, Palazzo Parisani-Bezzi, Via della Pace.

Music and Theatre Museums

Music and theatre is in the Italian blood, so it is no coincidence that an Italian invented the scale and that Italy is the home of opera. (*See* also FAMOUS ITALIANS for specific musicians).

Bologna: Museo Bibliografico Musicale, Piazza Rossini 2. One of the most important museums of music in Italy, with over 20,000 items.

Cremona: Saletta dei Violini, Palazzo del Comune; and Museo Stradivariano, Via Palestro 17. Violin-making.

Florence: Museo degli strumenti musicali antichi, Conservatorio Musicale Luigi Cherubini, Palazzo Vecchio. Precious collection of musical instruments begun by Ferdinand de Medici. Raccolte del Teatro Comunale, Via Italia 12/c.

Forlì: Museo Romagnolo del Teatro, Corso Garibaldi 96. In particular musical instruments belonging to famous musicians of the last two centuries.

Milan: Museo Teatrale alla Scala, Piazza Scala. Paintings, sculpture, porcelain, autographs, scenery related to La Scala productions.

Piacenza: Museo del Teatro, Via Verdi 41. Original librettos, autographs of famous singers, musical instruments.

Pisa: Museo Teatrale, Teatro Verdi, Via Palistro.

Rome: Museo Nazionale degli strumenti musicali, Piazza San Croce 9/a; and Raccolta Teatrale del Bucardo, Via del Sudario 44.

Spoleto: Museo del Teatro, Teatro Nuovo, Via Filitterria 1; and Raccolta di Disegni Teatrali, Convento di San Nicolò, Via Gregorio Elladio.

Transport Museums

Getting around on wheels, and as fast as possible, has always been a major Italian preoccupation, from the state carriages of days gone by to the sleek Ferraris of today.

Florence: Museo delle Carrozze, Palazzo Pitti. Carriages belonging to the grand dukes of Lorraine.

Macerata: Museo delle Carrozza, Piazza Vittorio Veneto. Carriage museum.

Naples: Museo delle Carrozze, Villa Pignatello, Riviera di Chiaia 200.

Piacenza: Museo delle Carrozze, Piazza Cittadella. Carriages from the 18th–19th centuries.

Rho (near Milan): Museo Storico Alfa Romeo.

Turin: Museo dell'Automobile Carlo Biscaretti di Ruffia, Corso Unità d'Italia 40. History of the automobile and other means of locomotion. Centro Storico Fiat, Via Chiabrera 20. History of Fiat from its founding in 1899 till the present day.

Italy with Children

If you take yours, it won't take long to realize that in Italy children merit special attention. Italian families adore and pamper their own and take them everywhere, even to restaurants in the evening, and yours too will receive regal treatment. Depending on their age, they will be able to appreciate such sights as the Leaning Tower of Pisa and Rome's Colosseum, but you may need to space your cultural tour with a little light relief. Here are some ideas:

A stall of colourful puppets on Rome's Janiculum Hill.

Bergamo (on autoroute halfway between Bergamo and Milan): Mini Italia. Italy in miniature, with some 200 models of monuments.

Bomarzo (near Viterbo): Parco dei Mostri. "Monster Park", created by Vicino Orsini in 1557, with gigantic rock sculptures of weird and wonderful creatures.

Camogli (near Genoa): Acquario Tirreno, Torre del Castello Dragone; marine life of the Tyrrhenian sea.

Collodi (near Lucca): Pinocchio Park and the Kingdom of Toys.

Milan, Museo del Cinema-Cineteca Italiana, Palazzo Dognani, Via Manin 2/b. From pre-cinema to the present day.

Naples: Edenlandia, Viale Kennedy 76; amusement park. Acquario e Stazione Zoologica, Villa Comunale, Via Caracciolo; aquarium and zoo.

Palermo: Museo Internazionale delle Marionette, Palazzo Buteira, Via Buteira; puppet museum.

Perugia: Città della Domenica, amusement park.

Peschiera del Garda (near Verona): Gardaland Amusement Park.

Rome: Giardino Zoologico, Villa

Borghese gardens, entrance on Via Aldrovandi. Luna Park fairground at EUR. Punch and Judy shows on Pincio and Janiculum. Museo delle Cere, Piazza Venezia 67. Waxworks museum. **Trieste**: Acquario Marino, Riva Sairo 1. Examples of the marine population of the Adriatic as well as of tropical waters.

Turin, Museo della Marionetta Piemontese, Teatro Gianduia, Via Santa Teresa 5. Regional museum devoted to puppets and puppet-making. Museo Nazionale del Cinema, Piazza San Giovanni 2. History of cinematography. Projections from November to May.

Language Guide

Standard Italian is understood by most Italians, though many different dialects are spoken. Some, like Venetian, show Slavic and Illyrian influences, while others have affinities with French. Sardinian is so different that it is virtually a separate language.

Staff at the major hotels and shops in the big cities and resort areas usually speak some English. Most Italians appreciate foreigners making an effort to communicate in their language, even if it's only a few words.

Just bear in mind the following tips on pronunciation:

c is pronounced like *ch* in change when it is followed by an *e* or an *i*

ch together sounds like the *c* in cat

g followed by an *e* or an *i* is pronounced like *j* in jet

gh together sounds like the *g* in gap

gl together sounds like *lli* in million

gn is pronounced like *ni* in onion.

The Berlitz phrase book *Italian for Travellers* covers almost all the situations you are likely to encounter in your travels in Italy. Also useful is the Berlitz Italian–English/English–Italian pocket dictionary, which contains the basic vocabulary a tourist will need, plus a menu-reader supplement.

Useful Words and Phrases

yes/no	**si/no**
please/thank you	**per favore/grazie**
excuse me/you're welcome	**mi scusi/prego**
How are you?	**Come sta?**
Very well, thanks.	**Molto bene, grazie.**
Goodbye.	**Arrivederci.**
Good morning.	**Buon giorno.**
Good evening.	**Buona sera.**
Good night.	**Buona notte.**
Hello/Bye	**Ciao**
where/when/how	**dove/quando/come**
how long/how far	**quanto tempo/quanto dista**
what/why/who	**che (che cosa)/perchè**
yesterday/today /tomorrow	**ieri/oggi/domani**
day/week/month/ year	**giorno/settimana/mese/ anno**
(to the) right/left/ straight ahead	**(a) destra/(a) sinistra/ sempre diritto**
near/far	**vicino/lontano**
up/down	**su/giù**
good/bad	**buono/cattivo**
big/small	**grande/piccolo**
more/less	**più/meno**
full/empty	**pieno/vuoto**
cheap/expensive	**buon mercato/caro**
hot/cold	**caldo/freddo**

open/closed	aperto/chiuso
free (vacant)/ occupied	libero/occupato
old/new	vecchio/nuovo
here/there	qui/là
early/late	presto/tardi
easy/difficult	facile/difficile
right/wrong	giusto/sbagliato
I don't understand	Non capisco
Do you speak English?	Parla Inglese?
Does anyone here speak English?	C'è qualcuno qui che parla inglese?
I don't speak (much) Italian.	Non parlo (bene) l'italiano.
Could you speak more slowly?	Può parlare più lentamente?
Can you tell me...?	Può dirmi...?
Can you help me?	Può aiutarmi?
Where is/are...?	Dov'è/Dove sono...?
I'd like...	Vorrei...
How much does this cost?	Quanto costa questo?
Monday	lunedì
Tuesday	martedì
Wednesday	mercoledì
Thursday	giovedì
Friday	venerdì
Saturday	sabato
Sunday	domenica

In the Restaurant

To help you order...

Waiter!/Waitress!	Cameriere!/Cameriera!
May I have the menu, please?	Potrei avere il menù, per favore?
Do you have a set menu?	Avete un menù a prezzo fisso?
I'd like to pay.	Vorrei pagare.

I'd like a/an/some...	Vorrei...
beer	una birra
bread	del pane
butter	del burro
coffee	un caffè
black/with milk/with cream	nero/macchiato/ con panna
dessert	un dessert, un dolce
fish	del pesce
fruit	della frutta
ice-cream	un gelato
meat	della carne
milk	del latte
pepper	del pepe
potatoes	delle patate
salad	un'insalata
salt	del sale
soup	una minestra
sugar	dello zucchero
tea	un tè
(mineral) water	dell'acqua (minerale)
wine	del vino

...and read the menu

anchovies	acciughe
garlic	aglio
lamb	agnello
sour	agro
apricots	albicocche
pineapple	ananas
eel	anguilla
watermelon	anguria, cocomeroa
duck	anarta
spiny lobster	aragosta
orange	arancia
herrings	aringhe

roast	**arrosto**	shrimps	**gamberetti**
(rib) steak	**bistecca (di filetto)**	prawns	**gamberi**
mixed boiled meat	**bolliti misti**	crab	**granchio**
chop	**braciola**	raspberries	**lamponi**
broth	**brodo**	vegetables	**legumi, verdure**
beef	**bue**	hare	**lepre**
game	**cacciagione**	tongue	**lingua**
baby squid	**calamaretti**	fruit salad	**macedonia (di frutta)**
squid	**calamari**	pork	**maiale**
kid	**capretto**	beef	**manzo**
artichokes	**carciofi**	apple	**mela**
carrots	**carote**	aubergine (eggplant)	**melanzane**
home-made	**casalinga**	cod	**merluzzo**
chestnuts	**castagne, marroni**	marrow (squash)	**midollo**
cauliflower	**cavolfiore**	honey	**miele**
cabbage	**cavolo**	bilberries (blueberries)	**mirtilli**
gherkins	**cetriolini**	mutton	**montone**
cucumber	**cetriolo**	nuts, walnuts	**noci**
cherries	**ciliege**	goose	**oca**
onions	**cipolle**	oysters	**ostriche**
rabbit	**coniglio**	sweet peppers	**peperoni**
cutlet	**costoletta**	pear	**pera**
mussels	**cozze**	fish	**pesce**
raw	**crudo**	perch	**pesce persico**
dessert (sweet)	**dolce**	swordfish	**pesce spada**
haricot beans	**fagioli**	peaches	**pesche**
French beans	**fagiolini**	veal cutlet	**piccata**
liver	**fegato**	pigeon	**piccione**
fillet steak (tenderloin)	**filetto**	peas	**piselli**
		poultry	**pollame**
fennel	**finocchio**	chicken	**pollo**
cheese	**formaggio**	meatballs	**polpette**
strawberries	**fragole**	tomatoes	**pomodori**
omelette	**frittata**	leeks	**porri**
seafood	**frutti di mare**	parsley	**prezzemolo**
mushrooms	**funghi**		

326

ham	**prosciutto**	*Level railway crossing*	**Passaggio a livello**
plums	**prugne**	*Toll*	**Pedaggio**
rice	**riso**	*Danger*	**Pericolo**
kidneys	**rognoni**	*Slow down*	**Rallentare**
sausage	**salsiccia**	*One-way street*	**Senso unico**
breaded veal cutlet	**scaloppina**	*No entry*	**Senso vietato/Vietato l'ingresso**
celery	**sedano**	*Exit*	**Uscita**
mustard	**senape**	*driving licence*	**patente**
sole	**sogliola**	*car registration papers*	**libretto di circolazione**
stew, stewed	**stufato**	*Green Card*	**Carta Verde**
juice	**succo**	*Are we on the right road for...?*	**Siamo sulla Strada giusta per...?**
turkey	**tacchino**	*Is there a car park nearby?*	**C'è un parcheggio qui vicino?**
tunny (tuna)	**tonno**	*Can I park here?*	**Posso parcheggiare qui?**
red mullet	**triglia**	*Full tank, please.*	**Il pieno, per favore.**
trout	**trota**	*super (premium)/ normal (regular)*	**super/normale**
egg	**uovo**	*unleaded/diesel*	**senza piombo/gasolio**
grapes	**uva**	*Check the oil/water/ tyres/battery, please.*	**Per favore, controlli l'olio/l'ac qua/i pneumatici/ la batteria.**
veal	**vitello**	*I've had a breakdown.*	**Ho avuto un guasto.**
clams	**vongole**	*There's been an accident.*	**C'è stato un incidente.**
pumpkin	**zucca**		

On the Road

Use headlights (in tunnel)	**Accendere le luci/ i fari (in galleria)**
Stop (pay toll)	**Alt (stazione)**
Falling rocks	**Caduta massi**
Dangerous bend (curve)	**Curva pericolosa**
Diversion (Detour)	**Deviazione**
No overtaking (passing)	**Divieto di sorpasso**
Customs	**Dogana**
Access	**Entrata**
Crossroads (Intersection)	**Incrocio**
Road works	**Lavori in Corso**
Hospital	**Ospedale**

Accommodation

Do you have any vacancies?	**Avete camere libere?**
I'd like a single/ double room with bath/shower	**Vorrei una camera singola/doppia con bagno/doccia**
What's the rate per night/week?	**Qual è il prezzo per una notte/una settimana?**
What's my room number?	**Qual è il numero della mia stanza?**
I'd like to leave this in your safe.	**Vorrei depositare questo nella vostra cassaforte.**

327

Information to Help You Have a Good Trip

Embassies and Consulates (*ambasciata; consolato*)

Embassies and consulates in Rome (prefix 06):

Australia
Via Alessandria 215
Tel. 832 721

Canada
Via G. Battista de
  Rossi 27
Tel. 855 341/841 5341.
Consulate: Via Zara 30
Tel. 440 3028.

Eire
Largo del Nazareno 3
Tel. 678 2 541

New Zealand
Via Zara 28
Tel. 851 225

South Africa
Via Tanaro 14–16
Tel. 841 9794

United Kingdom
Via XX Settembre 80
Tel. 482 5441

USA
Via Vittorio Veneto
  119
Tel. 46741

Tourist Information Offices

The Italian National Tourist Office (ENIT, Ente Nazionale Italiano per il Turismo) is represented in Italy and abroad. The organization publishes detailed brochures with up-to-date information on accommodation, means of transport, general tips and useful addresses for the whole country.

**Australia and New
  Zealand**
c/o Italian State
  Tourist Office
Lions Building
1–1–2 Moto Akasaka
  Minato-Ku
Tokyo 107
Tel. (3) 478 2051.

Canada
Italian Government
  Travel Office
1 place Ville-Marie
Suite 1914
Montreal
Quebec, H3B 3M9
Tel. (514) 866 7667.

Eire
Italian State Tourist
  Office
47 Merrion Square
Dublin 2
Tel. (01) 766 397.

South Africa
Italian State Tourist
  Office
PO Box 6507
Johannesburg 2000.

United Kingdom
Italian State Tourist
  Office
1 Princes Street
London W1R 8AY
Tel. (071) 408 1254

USA
Italian Government
  Travel Office
630 Fifth Avenue
Suite 1565
New York NY 10111
Tel. (212) 245 4822

Italian Government
  Travel Office
500 North Michigan
  Avenue
Suite 1046, Chicago
IL 60611
Tel. (312) 644 0990

Italian Government
   Travel Office
12400 Wilshire
   Boulevard
Suite 550
Los Angeles CA 90025
Tel. (310) 820 0098.

In Italy, each region has its own tourist board (azienda regionale del turismo or azienda regionale per la promozione turistica):

Abruzzo
Viale G Bovio 425
65100 Pescara
Tel. (085) 7671.

Aosta Valley
Piazza Narbonne 3
11100 Aosta
Tel. (0165) 303725.

Basilicata
Via Anzio 44
85100 Potenza
Tel. (0971) 332601.

Calabria
Vico III Raffaelli 9
88100 Catanzaro
Tel. (0961) 8511.

Campania
Via Santa Lucia 81
80132 Naples
Tel. (081) 7961111.

Emilia-Romagna
Via Aldo Moro 38
40127 Bologna
Tel. (051) 283386.

Friuli-Venezia Giulia
Via San Francesco
   d'Assisi 37
34133 Trieste
Tel. (040) 3771111.

Lazio
Via R Raimondi
   Garibaldi 7
00145 Rome
Tel. (06) 54571.

Liguria
Via Fieschi 15
16121 Genoa
Tel. (010) 54851.

Lombardy
Via Fabio Filzi 22
6 piano
20124 Milan
Tel. (02) 67651.

Marches
Via Gentile da Fabriano
60100 Ancona
Tel (071) 8061.

Molise
Via Mazzini 94
86100 Campobasso
Tel. (0874)
   9491/949502.

Piedmont
Via Magenta 12
10128 Turin
Tel (011) 43211.

Puglia
Corso Italia 15
70122 Bari
Tel. (080) 5213134.

Sardinia
Viale Trieste 105
09100 Cagliari
Tel. (070) 6061.

Sicily
Via Emanuele
   Notarbartolo 9
90141 Palermo
Tel. (091) 6961111.

Trentino-Alto Adige
Corso 3 Novembre 132
38100 Trento
Tel. (0461) 895111.

Tuscany
Via di Novoli 26
50126 Florence
Tel. (055) 4383680.

Umbria
Corso Vannucci 30
06100 Perugia
Tel. (075) 5041.

Veneto
Palazzo Balbi
Dorsoduro 3901
30123 Venice
Tel. (041) 792834.

In addition, each city and principal town has a local tourist office where you can get information on sightseeing, transport and accommodation.

Rome
Via Parigi 11
Tel. (06) 488 1851
Via Parigi 5 (Tourist
Assistance)
Tel. (06) 488 3748.

Florence
Via Manzoni 16
Tel. (055) 2346284/5.

Milan
Via Marconi 1
Tel. (02) 870016.

Naples
Piazza del Gesù
Tel. (081) 323328.

Venice
San Marco
Ascensione 71c
Tel. (041) 522 6356.

Sports
Information on specific sports activities in Italy is available from the

following organizations:

Boating

Sea

Federazione Italiana
    Motonautica
Via Piranesi 44b
20100 Milan.

Lakes

Ufficio Navigazione
    Interna
Ministero dei Trasporti
    e Aviazione Civile
Via Cristoforo
    Colombo 420
00100 Rome.

Fishing

Federazione Italiana
    Pesca Sportiva
Viale Tiziano 70
00196 Rome.

Golf

Federazione Italiana
    Golf
Via Flaminia 388
00196 Rome.

Horse riding

Riding tours

Federazione Italiana
    Sport Equestri
Viale Tiziano 70
00196 Rome

Riding schools

Associazione Nazionale
    per il Turismo
    Equestre
Largo Messico 13
00100 Rome.

Hunting

Federazione Italiana
    Caccia
Via C. Da Ancona 27
Rome.

Mountaineering

Club Alpino Italiano

Via Fonseca Pimental 7
Milan.

Tennis

Federazione Italiana
    Tennis
Viale Tiziano 70
00196 Rome.

Water-skiing

Federazione Italiana
    Sci Nautico
Via Piranesi 44b
20137 Milan.

Winter sports

Federazione Italiana
    Sport Invernali
Via Piranesi 44b
20137 Milan.

National Parks

Accessible by rail and
road, Italy's national
parks are open to every-
body. Accommodation
is provided in overnight
rest areas or nearby ho-
tels, while meals can be
taken at rural inns.

**Parco Nazionale
d'Abruzzo**

East of Rome. Some
400km^2 (155 square
miles), surrounded by a
protected zone of
600km^2 (230 square
miles). For informa-
tion, contact:
Abruzzo National Park
    Administration
Via Piave
Pescasseroli
Tel (0863) 91461.

**Parco Nazionale della
Calabria**

Near Cosenza. 170km^2

(66 square miles).
Calabria National Park
    Administration
Viale della Repubblica
    26
Cosenza
Tel. (0984) 26544.

**Parco Nazionale del
Circeo**

In Lazio, on the
Tyrrhenian coast mid-
way between Rome
and Naples. Approxi-
mately 84km^2 (32
square miles).
Circeo National Park
    Adminstration
Via Carlo Alberto 6
04016 Sabaudia
Tel. (0773) 57 251.

**Parco Nazionale del
Gran Paradiso**

In Aosta Valley.
700km^2 (270 square
miles).
Gran Paradiso
    National Park
    Administration
Via della Rocca 47
10123 Turin
Tel. (011) 871 187.

**Parco Nazionale dello
Stelvio**

In Lombardy and
Trentino-Alto Adige
on the Swiss border.
1,350km^2 (520 square
miles).
Stelvio National Park
    Administration
Via Monte Braulio 56
23032 Bormio
Tel. (0342) 901 582.

The Right Place at the Right Price

Hotels

While hotels and restaurants throughout the world are becoming more and more similar day by day, in Italy they usually continue to provide a unique experience, something that stays in the mind long afterwards, and which is discussed on cold evenings back at home with nostalgia and pleasure. In order to help you choose a suitable hotel, we have tried to provide an initial selection based on the criteria of price, attraction and location.

We have ranged the hotels into three broad price bands according to the cost of a double room with bath:

  ▌ Below L.150,000
  ▌▌ L.150–250,000
  ▌▌▌ Above L.250,000

Central Italy

Rome

Cesari ▌
Via di Pietra 89/a (near Corso)
00186 Rome
Tel. (06) 6792386; fax 67900882
51 rooms. Pleasant hotel dating from the 18th century which numbers Stendhal, Mazzini and Garibaldi among its famous past visitors.

Columbus ▌▌
Via della Conciliazione 33
00193 Rome
Tel. (06) 6865435; fax 6864874
105 rooms. Tastefully furnished hotel in 15th-century palace. Situation is convenient for the Vatican.

Forum ▌▌▌
Via Tor de' Conti 25
00184 Rome
Tel. (06) 6792446; fax 6786479
81 rooms. Spectacular view of the Imperial Forum from the roof-garden restaurant. Restaurant closed Sunday.

Le Grand Hotel ▌▌▌
Via Vittorio Emanuele Orlando 3 (near Termini Station)
00185 Rome
Tel. (06) 4709; fax 4747307
170 rooms. One of Rome's most sophisticated hotels with monumentally proportioned salons and ornate decor.

Gregoriana ▌▌
Via Gregoriana 18 (near Spanish Steps)
00187 Rome
Tel. (06) 6794269; fax 6784258
19 rooms. A converted convent in a pleasant location. Distinctive Art Deco style and pretty, comfortable rooms.

Hassler Villa Medici ▌▌▌
Piazza Trinità dei Monti 6
00187 Rome
Tel. (06) 6782651; fax 6789991
100 rooms. One of the world's most romantic locations, above the Spanish Steps, with furnishings, service and a roof-top view.

Holiday Inn ▌▌▌
Crowne Plaza Minerva
Piazza della Minerva 69
(Corso/Piazza Navona)
00186 Rome
Tel. (06) 69941888; fax 6794165
133 rooms. A 17th-century palazzo that has been a lodging place since Napoleonic times. It is now Rome's newest luxury hotel.

Lord Byron ▌▌▌
Via Giuseppe De Notaris 5
00197 Rome
Tel. (06) 3220404; fax 3220405
37 rooms. Elegant hotel in Rome's Parioli district, hosting one of Rome's most distinguished restaurants, Relais le Jardin.

Majestic ▌▌▌
Via Veneto 50
00187 Rome
Tel. (06) 486841; fax 4990984
95 rooms. Luxury hotel recently renovated and beautifully refurbished. All bathrooms complete with Carrara marble and Jacuzzi. Popular with Rome's glitterati.

Scalinata di Spagna ▌▌
Piazza Trinità dei Monti 17
(above Piazza di Spagna)
00187 Rome
Tel. (06) 6793006; fax 6799582
14 rooms. A fantastic view over the city and down the Spanish Steps. No restaurant.

Sole Al Biscione ▌
Via del Biscione 76 (near Campo dei Fiori)
00186 Rome
Tel. (06) 68806873
59 rooms. Large and in a convenient location. Garage.

Sole Al Pantheon ▌▌▌
Piazza della Rotonda 63 (near the Pantheon)
00186 Rome
Tel. (06) 6780441; fax 69940689
26 rooms. An inn for 500 years, the hotel has recently been refurbished, retaining its Renaissance charm while adding modern comforts.

Lazio

Borgo Paraelios ▌▌▌
Localitá Villa Collicchia
02040 Poggio Mirteto Scalo
Tel. (0765) 26267; fax 26268
14 rooms. In the heart of the Sabine Hills. All rooms have their own terrace. Indoor and outdoor swimming pools, golf, tennis. Restaurant. Minibus to Rome.

Grand Hotel Villa Florio ⏐⏐
Viale Dusmet 28
00046 Grottaferrata
Tel. (06) 9459276; fax 9413482
*20 rooms. Pleasant hotel. Small
park with swimming pool. Outdoor
dining.*

Duca degli Abruzzi ⏐
Viale Giovanni XXIII 10
67100 L'Aquila
Tel. (0862) 28341; fax 61588
*120 rooms. Comfortable hotel.
Restaurant Il Tetto has a
panoramic view.*

Tuscany, Umbria and The Marches

Florence
Grand Hotel Baglioni ⏐⏐⏐
Piazza Unità Italiana 6
50123 Florence
Tel. (055) 218441; fax 215695
*195 rooms. Large hotel near the
station. Splendid view of the city
from the roof-garden restaurant
and terrace.*

Bernini Palace ⏐⏐⏐
Piazza San Firenze 29
50122 Florence
Tel. (055) 288621; fax 268272
*86 rooms. Elegant hotel near
Palazzo Vecchio, with historic
associations. Italy's parliament
met here in the breakfast room
during the five years when Florence
was the newly united nation's
capital.*

Excelsior ⏐⏐⏐
Piazza Ognissanti 3
50123 Florence
Tel. (055) 264201; fax 210278
*203 rooms. Luxury hotel in 19th-
century palace on the banks of the
Arno. Superb restaurant, Il Ces-
tello. Outdoor dining on roof-top
terrace in summer.*

Il Guelfo Bianco ⏐⏐
Via Cavour 57r
50129 Florence
Tel. (055) 288330; fax 295203
*29 rooms. Small hotel housed in
16th-century building with all
modern comforts.*

Lungarno ⏐⏐⏐
borgo Sant'Jacopo 14
50125 Florence
Tel. (055) 264211; fax 268437
*66 rooms. Modern hotel overlook-
ing the Arno. Boasts its own collection of modern paintings. No
restaurant.*

Regency ⏐⏐⏐
Piazza Massimo D'Azeglio 3
50121 Florence
Tel. (055) 245247; fax 2342938
*38 rooms. Elegant luxury hotel
with charming garden and
renowned restaurant,* Relais le
Jardin *(closed Sunday).*

Sheraton Firenze Hotel ⏐⏐⏐
(Off A1 Firenze Sud)
50126 Florence
Tel. (055) 64901; fax 680747
*321 rooms. Recently opened hotel
on the outskirts of Florence. Swimming pool, tennis.*

Silla ⏐
Via dei Renai 5
50125 Florence
Tel. (055) 2342888; fax 2341437
*32 rooms. A small, unpretentious
hotel situated near the Arno. No
restaurant.*

Torre di Bellosguardo ⏐⏐⏐
Via Roti Michelozzi 2
50124 Florence
Tel. (055) 2298145
*13 rooms. Elegant hotel set in a
peaceful location in the hills above
Florence with splendid views of the
city and surroundings. Beautiful
gardens and swimming pool. No
restaurant.*

Villa Belvedere ⏐⏐
Via Benedetto Castelli 3
50124 Florence
Tel. (055) 222501; fax 223163
*27 rooms. Modern, quiet hotel just
outside Florence. Splendid views.
Garden with swimming pool, tennis.
Open March to November.*

Grand Hotel Villa Medici ⏐⏐⏐
Via Il Prato 42
50123 Florence
Tel (055) 2381331; fax 2381336
*103 rooms. Luxury hotel in 18th-
century villa, completely modernized within. Garden, outdoor dining
and swimming pool.*

Tuscany
Minerva ⏐
Via Fiorentina 6
52100 Arezzo
Tel. (0575) 370390; fax 370390
*118 rooms. Comfortable hotel on
the outskirts of the town. Restaurant closed for three weeks in
August.*

Tenuta di Ricavo ⏐⏐⏐
53011 Castellina in Chianti
(Siena)
Tel. (0577) 740221; fax 741014

*25 rooms. A medieval village con-
verted into a luxury hotel, complete
with swimming pools and gardens.
Open April to October. Restaurant
closed Wednesday.*

Oasi G. Neumann ⏐
Via Contesse 1
52044 Cortona
Tel. (0575) 630354; fax 630354
*36 rooms. Quiet hotel in park set-
ting just beyond the city walls.
Good view of valley below. Open
April to October. Restaurant.*

Villa San Michele ⏐⏐⏐
Via Doccia 4
50014 Fiesole
Tel. (055) 59451; fax 598734
*28 rooms. Pleasant luxury hotel in
a 15th-century monastery. Incomparable view of Florence and the
Arno Valley Park. Outdoor dining,
heated swimming pool. Open April
to November.*

Universo ⏐
Piazza del Giglio 1
55100 Lucca
Tel. (0583) 493678; tlx 501840;
fax 954854
*62 rooms. Elegant hotel right in the
heart of Lucca's centro storico.
Recently renovated. Restaurant:
Del Teatro (closed Thursday).*

Villa la Principessa ⏐⏐⏐
55050 Massa Pisana (Lucca)
Tel. (0583) 370037; fax 379019
*44 rooms. Attractive, quiet hotel in
19th-century villa just outside
Lucca. Park, outdoor swimming
pool. Restaurant closed Wednesday.*

Grand Hotel e la Pace ⏐⏐⏐
Via della Torretta 1
51016 Montecatini Terme
Tel. (0572) 75801; fax 78451
*150 rooms. Elegant 19th-century
hotel favoured by the spa town's
VIP visitors. Park with heated
outdoor swimming pool, tennis.
Restaurant. Open April to October.*

Il Marzocco ⏐
Piazza Savonarola
53045 Montepulciano
Tel. (0578) 757262; fax 757530
*16 rooms. Small hotel in the centre
of town. Closed for two weeks in
late November. Restaurant.*

Il Bottaccio ⏐⏐⏐
Via Bottaccio 1
54038 Montignoso
Tel. (0585) 340031; fax 340103
*Excellent restaurant also provides
luxury accommodation in five
apartment suites.*

Ariston I
Via Maffi 42
56125 Pisa
Tel. (050) 561834; fax 562891
33 rooms. A stone's throw from the Leaning Tower. No restaurant.

Jolly Hotel Cavalieri III
Piazza Stazione 2
56125 Pisa
Tel. (050) 43290; fax 502242
100 rooms. Comfortable modern hotel near the station. Restaurant.

Don Pedro I
58018 Port'Ercole
Tel. (0564) 833914; fax 833914
44 rooms. Comfortable hotel with view. Outdoor dining. Open Easter to October.

Il Pellicano III
Località Cala dei Santi
58018 Port'Ercole
Tel. (0564) 833801; fax 833418
34 rooms. Pleasant, quiet hotel with view of sea and cliffs. Heated outdoor swimming pool, garden, tennis and private beach. Outdoor dining. Open Easter to December.

Hermitage III
Biodola
57037 Portoferraio (Isola d'Elba)
Tel. (0565) 936911; fax 969984
110 rooms. Open early May to early October. Quiet hotel at Biodola, west of Portoferraio, with private beach, swimming pool, garden and tennis. Restaurant.

La Cisterna I
Piazza della Cisterna 23
53037 San Gimignano
Tel. (0577) 940328; fax 942080
50 rooms. Lovely hotel in the heart of town. Le Terrazze restaurant affords splendid view of streets and countryside. Open early March to early November. Restaurant closed Tuesday and Wednesday lunch.

Pescille I
Verso Castel San Gimignano
53037 San Gimignano
Tel. (0577) 940186; fax 940186
40 rooms. Charming hotel in a converted farmhouse just outside San Gimignano. Garden, swimming pool and tennis. Restaurant, I Cinque Gigli, offers outdoor dining with a view of the town and surrounding countryside. Closed November to mid-March.

Relais Fattoria Vignale II
Via Pianigiani 9
53017 Radda in Chianti
Tel. (0577) 738300; fax 738592
27 rooms. Elegant hotel in 18th-

century farmhouse. Closely associated with Chianti wine, there is a bottle in each room on arrival. Good restaurant, swimming pool.

Certosa di Maggiano III
Strada di Certosa 82
53100 Siena
Tel. (0577) 288180; fax 288189
14 rooms. Pleasant, quiet hotel in a converted 14th-century monastery just outside Siena. Heated outdoor swimming pool and tennis. Restaurant (closed Tuesday).

Duomo I
Via Stalloreggi 38
53100 Siena
Tel. (0577) 289088; fax 43043
22 rooms. Small, central hotel (near Cathedral). No restaurant.

Villa Scacciapensieri III
Via di Scacciapensieri 10
53100 Siena
Tel. (0577) 41441; fax 270854
26 rooms. Comfortable hotel in a converted country house just outside Siena. Outdoor dining in pretty garden in summer. Park with view of city and hills. Outdoor swimming pool, tennis. Closed mid-November to mid-March. Restaurant closed Tuesday.

Locanda dell'Amorosa III
53048 Sinalunga (near Cortona)
Tel. (0577) 679497; fax 678216
10 rooms. This country restaurant in a restored farmhouse also offers pleasant accommodation. Good regional cuisine. Reserve. Restaurant closed Monday, Tuesday lunch and from late January to late February.

Villa Nencini I
Borgo Santo Stefano 55
56048 Volterra
Tel. (0588) 86386; fax 80601
14 rooms. Quiet small hotel with pleasant garden. No restaurant.

Umbria
Subasio II
Via Frate Elia 2
06081 Assisi
Tel. (075) 812206; fax 816691
70 rooms. Assisi's first hotel, opened 1868. Guests have included Charlie Chaplin and Marlene Dietrich. Near the Basilica with views over town. Garden, outdoor dining.

Umbra I
Vicolo degli Archi 6
06081 Assisi
Tel. (075) 812240; fax 813653
25 rooms. Quiet hotel in a 16th-century building. Outdoor dining in

summer. Closed mid-January to mid-February. Restaurant closed Tuesday and from mid-November to mid-December.

Bosone Palace I
Via 20 Settembre 22
06024 Gubbio
Tel. (075) 9220688; fax 9220522
28 rooms. Comfortable hotel housed in the old Palazzo Raffaelli. Closed February.

La Badia II
Località La Badia 8
05019 Orvieto
Tel. (0763) 90359; fax 92796
28 rooms. Charming, quiet hotel housed in a 13th-century abbey just outside the town. Beautiful courtyards and garden, plus outdoor swimming pool and tennis courts. Closed January and February. Restaurant closed Wednesday.

Brufani III
Piazza Italia 12
06100 Perugia
Tel. (075) 5732541; fax 5720210
24 rooms. Central hotel housed in a 19th-century palazzo. Restaurant.

Gattapone II
Via del Ponte 6
06049 Spoleto
Tel. (0743) 223447; fax 223448
13 rooms. Pleasant small hotel near the Ponte delle Torri with splendid views of the ancient bridge and ravine. Garden. No restaurant.

Le Tre Vaselle III
Via Garibaldi 48
06089 Torgiano
Tel. (075) 9880447; fax 9880214
64 rooms. Pleasant hotel located about nine miles from Perugia near charming Lake Bettona. Excellent restaurant. Wine Museum nearby.

Hotel Bramante II
Via Orvietana 48
06059 Todi
Tel. (075) 8948381; fax 8948074
43 rooms. Charming hotel near the beautiful Renaissance church. Outdoor dining, swimming pool, tennis.

The Marches
Vittoria III
Piazzale della Libertà 2
61100 Pesaro
Tel. (0721) 34343; fax 65204
36 rooms. Hotel overlooking the sea with old-fashioned charm and modern facilities. Swimming pool, sauna, exercise room. Restaurant (evenings only, closed Sunday from October to May) and grill room.

Bonconte
Via delle Mura 28
61029 Urbino
Tel. (0722) 2463; fax 4782
20 rooms. Comfortable small hotel beside city walls. Small restaurant, breakfast in garden during summer.

The North-East

Venice

Accademia
Fondamenta Bollani 1058
(Dorsoduro)
30123 Venice
Tel. (041) 5237846; fax 5239152
27 rooms. Charming hotel in a small villa bounded by gardens and a canal, not far from the Accademia gallery. No restaurant.

Cipriani
Isola della Giudecca 10
30133 Venice
Tel. (041) 5207744; fax 5203930
105 rooms. Luxury hotel on the island of Giudecca with breathtaking views of the lagoon. A private motor boat service takes guests across the water to San Marco. Facilities include two restaurants, a flower garden with heated outdoor swimming pool, sauna and tennis court. Open March to November.

Danieli
Riva degli Schiavoni 4196
30122 Venice
Tel. (041) 5226480; fax 5200208
231 rooms. Attractive luxury hotel in an ancient palace (with modern additions). Illustrious past guests include Dickens, Ruskin and Balzac. Roof-top restaurant with splendid view of San Giorgio Maggiore.

La Fenice et des Artistes
Campiello de la Fenice 1936
30124 Venice
Tel. (041) 5232333; fax 5203721
65 rooms. Charming hotel near Venice's La Fenice theatre. No restaurant.

Flora
Calle Larga XXII Marzo 2283/a
30124 Venice
Tel. (041) 5225324; fax 5228217
44 rooms. Charming, quiet hotel with small flower garden. Not far from San Marco. Open February to mid-November.

Gabrielli Sandwirth
Riva degli Schiavoni 4110
30122 Venice
Tel. (041) 5231580; fax 5209455

100 rooms. Comfortable hotel with view of the Bacino di San Marco. Pleasant garden and courtyard. Open late February to late November.

Gritti Palace
Campo Santa Maria del Giglio 2467
30124 Venice
Tel. (041) 794611; fax 5200942
87 rooms. Elegant luxury hotel in a 15th-century palace on the Grand Canal. The terrace restaurant on the water makes a splendid setting for dining.

Monaco e Grand Canal
Calle Vallaresso 1325
30124 Venice
Tel. (041) 5200211; fax 5200501
70 rooms. Charming hotel on the Grand Canal, not far from San Marco, with good views of Santa Maria della Salute across the water. Waterside dining in the open in fine weather.

La Residenza
Campo Bandiera e Moro 3608
30122 Venice
Tel. (041) 5285315; fax 5238859
15 rooms. Pleasant small hotel in 14th-century building. No restaurant. Closed early November to early December, and early January to mid-February.

San Cassiano
Santa Croce 2232
30125 Venice
Tel. (041) 5241768; fax 721033
35 rooms. Comfortable hotel on the Grand Canal, near Ca' Pesaro, home of Venice's museum of modern art. No restaurant.

Grand Hotel des Bains
Lungomare Marconi 17
30126 Venice Lido
Tel. (041) 5265921; fax 5260113
191 rooms. Luxury hotel on the Lido, dating from the beginning of the century. The setting for Visconti's film Death in Venice. Facilities include private beach, tennis, sauna and heated swimming pool. Open April to October.

Veneto

Villa Cipriani
31011 Asolo
Tel. (0423) 952166; fax 952095
31 rooms. Superb luxury hotel in a Renaissance villa occupying a prime spot of the Veneto countryside. The hotel is beautifully furnished and has a fine restaurant and attractive garden.

Donatello
Piazza del Santo
35123 Padua
Tel. (049) 8750634; fax 8750829
42 rooms. Comfortable hotel located opposite the cathedral. The hotel restaurant, Sant'Antonio (closed Wednesday and from December to late January) offers terrace dining in summer. Closed from mid-December to mid-January.

Ca' del Galletto
Via Santa Bona Vecchia 30
31100 Treviso
Tel. (0422) 432550; fax 432510
57 rooms. Comfortable hotel just outside the town centre. Tennis. No restuarant.

Due Torri Baglioni
Piazza Sant'Anastasia 4
37121 Verona
Tel. (045) 595044; fax 8004130
81 rooms. Elegantly furnished luxury hotel with old-fashioned charm and modern conveniences. Fine cuisine in restaurant, L'Aquila.

Italia
Via Mameli 58–64
37126 Verona
Tel. (045) 918088; fax 8348028
53 rooms. Comfortable hotel a short distance from the centre. Restaurant closed Sunday.

Campo Marzio
Viale Roma 21
36100 Vicenza
Tel. (0444) 545700; fax 320495
35 rooms. Comfortable modern hotel near the centre. Restaurant (evening only, closed Saturday, Sunday and throughout August).

Villa Michelangelo
Arcugnano
36057 Vicenza
Tel. (0444) 550300; fax 550490
36 rooms. Quiet hotel at Arcugnano, a few miles south of Vicenza. Good views of the surrounding hills. Indoor swimming pool. The hotel restaurant, La Loggia (closed Sunday), overlooks an attractive park.

Friuli Venezia Giulia

Duchi d'Aosta
Via dell'Orologio 2
34121 Trieste
Tel. (040) 7351; fax 366092
50 rooms. Luxury hotel standing on the city's main square, the Piazza Unità d'Italia. The hotel's fine restaurant, Harry's Grill, offers outdoor dining in summer.

Astoria Hotel Italia   ▯▯
Piazza XX Settembre 24
33100 Udine
Tel. (0432) 505091; fax 509070
*80 rooms. Comfortable, centrally
located hotel. Restaurant.*

Dolomites
Park Hotel Laurin   ▯▯▯
Via Laurino 4
39100 Bolzano
Tel. (0471) 980500; fax 970953
*95 rooms. Luxury hotel set in an
attractive park in the centre of
town. Facilities include a heated
outdoor swimming pool. The fine
restaurant,* Belle Epoque *(closed
Sunday), offers outdoor dining in
the park in summer.*

Elefante   ▯▯
Via Rio Bianco 4
39042 Bressanone
Tel. (0472) 32750; fax 36579
*43 rooms. Pleasant hotel in a 16th-
century building, furnished with antiques and paintings. Park with
heated outdoor swimming pool.
Open Christmas to early January
and March to mid-November. Excellent restaurant (closed Monday
except from
August to mid-November).*

Menardi   ▯▯
Via Majon 110
32043 Cortina d'Ampezzo
Tel. (0436) 2400; fax 862183
*48 rooms. Comfortable, elegantly
furnished hotel set in a shady park
with a view of the Dolomites. Open
mid-December to late April and
mid-June to mid-September.*

Miramonti Majestic   ▯▯▯
Località Pezziè 103
32043 Cortina d'Ampezzo
Tel. (0436) 4201; fax 867019
*116 rooms. Splendid luxury hotel
set in an attractive location just
2km (1 mile) south of the town.
View of Cortina and the Dolomites.
Golf, indoor swimming pool, exercise room, sauna, tennis. Open mid-
December to late March and July
to mid-
September.*

Castel Labers   ▯▯
Via Labers 25
39012 Merano
Tel. (0473) 234484; fax 234146
*32 rooms. Set in a hilltop castle just
outside Merano, this charming hotel has a great view of the town,
plus heated outdoor swimming pool
and tennis. Meals served in the garden in summer. Open mid-April to
November.*

Accademia   ▯▯
Vicolo Colico 4
38100 Trento
Tel. (0461) 233600; fax 230174
*43 rooms. Centrally located hotel
in an ancient palazzo near the
cathedral. The hotel's very fine
restaurant is next door.*

Emilia-Romagna
Grand Hotel Baglioni   ▯▯▯
Via dell'Indipendenza 8
40121 Bologna
Tel. (051) 225445; fax 234840
*125 rooms. Elegant luxury hotel in
the centre of Bologna. It boasts Renaissance frescoes by the Carracci
brothers, who have given their
name to the hotel's very fine restaurant,* I Carracci.

Roma   ▯▯
Via Massimo d'Azeglio 9
40123 Bologna
Tel. (051) 226322; fax 239909
*84 rooms. Comfortable, centrally
located hotel. Restaurant closed
first three weeks of August.*

Britannia   ▯
Viale Carducci 129
47042 Cesenatico
Tel. (0547) 672500; fax 81799
*42 rooms. Comfortable hotel with
restaurant, garden terrace, outdoor
swimming pool, private beach and
tennis. Open May to mid-September.*

Ripagrande   ▯▯▯
Via Ripagrande 21
44100 Ferrara
Tel. (0532) 765250; fax 764377
*40 rooms. Hotel housed in a me-
dieval palace providing a mix of ancient charm and modern comforts.
The top-floor bedrooms have splendid views of the city. Outdoor dining in the courtyard in summer.
Restaurant closed Monday and
from late July to late August.*

Canalgrande   ▯▯▯
Corso Canal Grande 6
41100 Modena
Tel. (059) 217160; fax 221674
*78 rooms. Elegant hotel installed in
an ancient palazzo with large, comfortable rooms and a fine restaurant (closed Tuesday and first
three weeks of August).*

Palace Hotel Maria Luigia   ▯▯▯
Viale Mentana 140
43100 Parma
Tel. (0521) 281032; fax 231126
*101 rooms. Modern hotel with good
restaurant,* Maxim's *(closed Sunday and August).*

Centrale-Byron   ▯
Via IV Novembre 14
48100 Ravenna
Tel. (0544) 33479
*54 rooms. Comfortable hotel in
heart of Ravenna. No restaurant.*

Grand Hotel   ▯▯▯
Piazzale Indipendenza 2
47037 Rimini
Tel. (0541) 56000; fax 56866
*169 rooms. Luxurious resort hotel
set in a shady park. Heated outdoor swimming pool, private beach,
tennis and restaurant.*

The North-West
Milan
Carlton Hotel Senato   ▯▯▯
Via Senato 5
20121 Milan
Tel. (02) 76015535; fax 783300
*79 rooms. Comfortable modern ho-
tel situated near Milan's most elegant shopping area, around Via
Monte Napoleone. Closed August.
Restaurant closed Saturday, Sunday and from late December to
early January.*

Casa Svizzera   ▯▯
Via San Raffaele 3
20121 Milan
Tel. (02) 8692246; fax 3498190
*45 rooms. Pleasant, small hotel lo-
cated near Duomo. Closed late
July to August. No restaurant.*

Grand Hotel Duomo   ▯▯▯
Via San Raffaele 1
20121 Milan
Tel. (02) 8833; fax 86462027
*160 rooms. Luxury hotel in the
heart of the city, overlooking, as
the name suggests, Milan's Duomo.
Many rooms have superb views.
Restaurant.*

Manzoni   ▯▯
Via Santo Spirito 20
20121 Milan
Tel. (02) 76005700; fax 784212
*52 rooms. Comfortable small hotel
located in heart of Milan's shopping district. No restaurant.*

Pierre Milano   ▯▯▯
Via Edmondo de Amicis 32
20123 Milan
Tel. (02) 72000581; fax 8052157
*47 rooms. Modern luxury hotel,
opened in 1987, located near the
church of Sant'Ambrogio, a short
way from the centre. The hotel bedrooms boast the very latest in electronic gadgetry. Restaurant closed
August.*

Lombardy

Belvedere
22021 Bellagio
Tel. (031) 950410; fax 950102
*50 rooms. Comfortable hotel with a
view of lake, outdoor swimming
pool and garden. Outdoor dining.
Open April to mid-October.*

Grand Hotel Villa Serbelloni
Via Roma 1
22021 Bellagio
Tel. (031) 950216; fax 951529
*95 rooms. Luxury hotel attractively
set in a large park overlooking the
lake. It offers a heated outdoor
swimming pool, private beach and
tennis. Outdoor dining. Open mid-
April to mid-October.*

Cristallo Palace
Via Betty Ambiveri 35
24100 Bergamo
Tel. (035) 311211; fax 312031
*88 rooms. Comfortable hotel near
the ring road. Restaurant, L'Antica Perosa (closed Sunday).*

Vittoria
Via delle X Giornate 20
25121 Brescia
Tel. (030) 280061; fax 280065
*65 rooms. Luxury hotel in the cen-
tre of town. Restaurant closed Sunday and August.*

Grand Hotel Villa d'Este
22010 Cernobbio
Tel. (031) 3481; fax 348844
*158 rooms. Stupendous luxury ho-
tel in 16th-century villa set in large
park overlooking Lake Como. Terrace dining with superb view of lake
and mountains. Heated outdoor
swimming pool, indoor swimming
pool, tennis courts and exercise
room. Open March to November.*

Villa Flori
Strada per Cernobbio 12
22100 Como
Tel. (031) 573105; fax 570379
*44 rooms. Comfortable hotel a
short distance from Como offering
attractive views of the lake, mountains and town. Terraced garden
and outdoor dining. Closed Christmas to mid-January.*

Grand Hotel Fasano
25080 Fasano del Garda
Tel. (0365) 21051; fax 21054
*70 rooms. Originally a Habsburg
hunting lodge, this pleasant lakeside hotel set in a splendid park has
heated outdoor swimming pool, private beach and tennis court. Outdoor dining. Open May to October. Villa Principe (12 rooms), also
in the park, is open all year round.*

Grand Hotel
25083 Gardone Riviera
Tel. (0365) 20261; fax 22695
*180 rooms. Large luxury hotel
overlooking the lake. Amenities include heated outdoor swimming
pool and private beach. Outdoor
dining. Open April to October.*

San Lorenzo
Piazza Concordia 14
46100 Mantua
Tel. (0376) 220500; fax 327194
*41 rooms. Comfortable, centrally
located hotel. No restaurant.*

Villa Cortine
Via Grotte 12
25019 Sirmione
Tel. (030) 9905890; fax 916390
*55 rooms. Pleasant, quiet hotel in a
19th-century villa set in a lakeside
park. Amenities include heated outdoor swimming pool, private beach
and tennis. Outdoor dining. Open
late March to late October.*

Il Gourmet
Via San Vigilio 1
24100 Bergamo
Tel. (035) 256110; fax 256110
*10 rooms. Charming, family-run
hotel in the upper town, minutes
from historic centre. Restaurant.*

Piedmont

Valle d'Aosta
Corso Ivrea 146
11100 Aosta
Tel. (0165) 41845; fax 236660
*104 rooms. Comfortable hotel on
the edge of town. Closed mid-
November to mid-December. No
restaurant.*

Villa Carlotta
28040 Belgirate (near Stresa)
Tel. (0322) 76461; fax 76705
*148 rooms. Comfortable hotel in
small resort on Lake Maggiore.
Amenities include restaurant,
heated outdoor swimming pool, private beach and tennis.*

Hermitage
11021 Breuil-Cervinia
Tel. (0166) 948998; fax 949032
*32 rooms. Quiet hotel with excep-
tional view. Heated indoor swimming pool, sauna, exercise room,
restaurant and garden. Open mid-
November to mid-May and early
July to mid-September.*

Del Viale
Viale Monte Bianco 74
11013 Courmayeur
Tel. (0165) 842227; fax 844513

*23 rooms. Comfortable hotel with
restaurant, garden and good views
of the mountains. Closed May to
mid-June and late October to early
December.*

Al Sorriso
Via Roma 18
28018 Soriso
Tel. (0322) 983228; fax 983328
*8 rooms. Acclaimed restaurant with
accommodation. Closed mid to late
January and two weeks in mid-August. Restaurant also closed Monday and Tuesday lunch.*

Regina Palace
Lungolago Umberto 27
28049 Stresa
Tel. (0323) 30171; fax 30176
*175 rooms. Large lakeside hotel
with good view of the islands. Park
with heated outdoor swimming
pool, plus tennis, sauna and exercise room. Restaurant. Closed
January.*

Victoria
Via Nino Costa 4
10123 Turin
Tel. (011) 5611909; fax 5611806
*65 rooms. Comfortable hotel with
convenient central location. No
restaurant.*

Villa Sassi
Strada al Traforo del Pino 47
10132 Turin
Tel. (011) 8900556; fax 890095
*15 rooms. Elegant hotel in an 18th-
century villa set in large park.
Restaurant, El Toulà (closed Sunday). Closed August.*

Italian Riviera

Grand Hotel Diana
Via Garibaldi 110
17021 Alassio
Tel. (0182) 642701; fax 640304
*68 rooms. Comfortable hotel
overlooking the seafront. Shady
terrace garden. Indoor swimming
pool, private beach. Self-service
restaurant open at lunchtimes, à la
carte menu is provided in the
evening. Closed December and January (excluding 27 December to 6
January).*

Grand Hotel del Mare
Capo Migliarese
18012 Bordighera
Tel. (0184) 262201; fax 262394
*111 rooms. Quiet hotel with view
of the sea. Roof-garden with outdoor swimming pool, plus private
beach and tennis. Closed October
to mid-December. Restaurant
closed Monday.*

Residenza Punta Est ▯▯
Via Aurelia 1
17024 Finale Ligure
Tel. (019) 600611; fax 600611
40 rooms. Attractive hotel in an ancient building standing in a shady park. Outdoor swimming pool, restaurant. Open May to September.

Agnello d'Oro ▯
Vico delle Monachette 6
16126 Genoa
Tel. (010) 2462084
35 rooms. Modest hotel near Stazione Principe. No restaurant.

Jolly Hotel Plaza ▯▯▯
Via Martin Piaggio 11
16122 Genoa
Tel. (010) 8393641; fax 8391850
97 rooms. Comfortable hotel near Piazza Corvetto in the centre of town. Restaurant.

Hotel Eden ▯▯
16034 Portofino
Tel. (0185) 269261
10 rooms. Quiet, small hotel in centre of town. Outside dining. Open March to early November.

Splendido ▯▯▯
Via Baratta 13
16034 Portofino
Tel. (0185) 269551; fax 269614
63 rooms. Pleasant luxury hotel standing in a wooded park overlooking the sea. Outdoor dining. Heated outdoor swimming pool, sauna and tennis. Open early April to December.

Méditerranée ▯▯
Corso Cavallotti 76
18038 San Remo
Tel. (0184) 571000; fax 541106
62 rooms. Park with outdoor swimming pool. Outdoor dining.

Royal ▯▯▯
Corso Imperatrice 80
18038 San Remo
Tel. (0184) 5391; fax 61445
148 rooms. Pleasant luxury hotel overlooking the seafront. Attractive garden with heated outdoor swimming pool. Outdoor dining in summer. Tennis and exercise room. Closed October to mid-December.

Helvetia ▯
Via Cappuccini 43
16039 Sestri Levante
Tel. (0185) 41175; fax 47216
28 rooms. Quiet hotel with a beautiful view of the bay. Pretty terrace garden. Private beach. Open March to October. No restaurant.

The South

Naples

Excelsior ▯▯▯
Via Partenope 48
80121 Naples
Tel. (081) 7640111; fax 7649743
114 rooms. Luxury hotel, used to accommodating royalty and rock stars. Lovely views over the bay. First-class rooftop restaurant.

Majestic ▯▯
Largo Vasto a Chiaia 68
80121 Naples
Tel. (081) 416500; fax 416500
132 rooms. Quiet, modern hotel near the Villa Pignatelli, away from the noise and bustle of the town centre. Restaurant.

Rex ▯▯
Via Palepoli 12
80132 Naples
Tel. (081) 7649389; fax 7649227
40 rooms. Comfortable hotel in the heart of the Santa Lucia district. No restaurant.

Vesuvio ▯▯▯
Via Partenope 45
80121 Naples
Tel. (081) 7640044; fax 7640044
171 rooms. Late 19th-century grand hotel overlooking the Santa Lucia waterfront. Roof-garden restaurant with view of the bay and Castel dell'Ovo.

Campania

Cappuccini Convento ▯▯
Via Annunziatella 46
84011 Amalfi
Tel. (089) 871008; fax 871886
52 rooms. Charming hotel housed in a 12th-century convent with magnificent cloister. Private beach and restaurant.

Miramalfi ▯
Via Quasimodo 3
84011 Amalfi
Tel. (089) 871588; fax 871588
Comfortable cliff-top hotel with lift to the beach. Restaurant, garden and outdoor swimming pool. Closed November and December.

Santa Caterina ▯▯▯
Via SS Amalfitana
84011 Amalfi
Tel. (089) 871012; fax 871351
70 rooms. Elegant hotel set in beautiful grounds overlooking the Amalfi coast. Attractive rooms, most with balcony, and an excellent restaurant. Swimming pool and private beach.

San Michele ▯
Via Orlandi 1–3
80071 Anacapri
Tel. (081) 8371427; fax 8371420
56 rooms. Comfortable hotel, with pleasant gardens, swimming pool and restaurant. April to October.

Luna ▯▯
Viale Matteotti 3
80073 Capri
Tel. (081) 8370433; fax 8377459
44 rooms. Charming, quiet hotel with traditional furnishings and superb sea views. Terrace and garden with swimming pool. Outdoor dining. Open Easter to October.

Villa Sarah ▯
Via Tiberio 3/a, 80073 Capri
Tel. (081) 8377817; fax 8377215
20 rooms. Very quiet, clean hotel with simple, whitewashed rooms and a beautiful shady garden. Open Easter to October.

Regina Isabella e ▯▯▯
Royal Sporting
Lacco Ameno, 80076 Ischia
Tel. (081) 994322; fax 900190
133 rooms. Luxury twin hotels overlooking the sea in this exclusive resort. Outdoor dining, garden and private beach. Heated outdoor swimming pool, exercise room, sauna and hydrotherapy.

La Villarosa ▯▯
Via Baldassarre Cossa 29
80077 Ischia
Tel. (081) 991316; fax 992425
37 rooms. Quiet hotel in Ischia Porto with garden and heated outdoor swimming pool. Restaurant. Open April to October.

Villa Laura ▯
Via della Salle 13, 80045 Pompeii
Tel. (081) 8631024; fax 8504893
25 rooms. Comfortable small hotel with garden. No restaurant.

Covo dei Saraceni ▯▯
84017 Positano
Tel. (089) 875400; fax 875878
58 rooms. Quiet hotel with good views of the sea and coast. Outdoor swimming pool. Outdoor dining. Open April to October.

Le Sirenuse ▯▯▯
84017 Positano
Tel. (089) 875066; fax 811798
62 rooms. Splendid hotel in converted 18th-century buildings in the centre of Positano. Heated outdoor pool, attractive garden, wonderful views, convenient for the beach. Fine restaurant, outdoor dining.

Palumbo ▥
Via S. Giovanni del Toro 28
84010 Ravello
Tel. (089) 857244; fax 858133
20 rooms. Sumptuous hotel in-stalled in a 12th-century palace. Bedrooms are cool and comfort-able, many with balconies over-looking the sea. Outdoor dining.

Rufolo ▥
84010 Ravello
Tel. (089) 857133; fax 857935
29 rooms. Quiet hotel with attrac-tive views. Terrace-garden with swimming pool. Restaurant closed Friday from November to March.

Grand Hotel Excelsior ▥
Vittoria
Piazza Tasso 34
80067 Sorrento
Tel. (081) 8071044; fax 8771206
106 rooms. Comfortable and ele-gant hotel, once home to the Great Caruso. Fabulous views of the Bay of Naples and Vesuvius. Stylishly furnished rooms. Garden with swimming pool.

La Tonnarella ▯
Via del Capo 31
80067 Sorrento
Tel. (081) 8781153
16 rooms. This villa hotel is a good budget choice. Excellent restau-rant, wonderful views, and a lift down to a small private beach. Open all year. Half-board only in the high season.

Puglia
Dei Trulli ▥
Via Cadore 32
7011 Alberobello
Tel. (080) 9323555; fax 9323560
19 apartments. Pleasant hotel oc-cupying a series of beehive-shaped cottages in the distinctive local trulli-style. Outdoor dining, garden and swimming pool.

Majestic ▯
Corso Umberto 151
72100 Brindisi
Tel. (0831) 222941; fax 524071
68 rooms. Modern hotel situated opposite the railway station. Restaurant closed Friday.

Cicolella ▥
Viale XXIV Maggio 60
71100 Foggia
Tel. (0881) 3890; fax 78984
105 rooms. Modern hotel near the station with restaurant (closed Sunday, from late December to early Janaury and for two weeks in mid-August).

Grand Hotel Costa Brada ▥
73014 Gallipoli
Tel. (0833) 22551; fax 22555
78 rooms. Resort hotel overlooking its own beach. Facilities include garden with heated outdoor swim-ming pool and tennis, sauna, exer-cise room and indoor pool.

Rotary ▯
Via per Pulsano
71037 Monte Sant'Angelo
Tel. (0884) 62146
24 rooms. Small, quiet hotel in pleasant setting. Rooms have good views of the Gulf of Manfredonia. Restaurant closed November.

Grotta Palazzese ▯
Via Narciso 59
70044 Polignano a Mare
Tel. (080) 740677; fax 740767
20 rooms. Small, quiet hotel in coastal resort. Its restaurant is built into a cave overlooking the sea.

Gabbiano ▯
San Nicola di Tremiti
71040 San Domino (Tremiti Is-lands)
Tel. (0882) 663044; fax 663090
37 rooms. Quiet hotel with good sea views, garden, outdoor dining and tennis.

Calabria
Centrale ▯
Via del Tigari 3
87100 Cosenza
Tel. (0984) 73681; fax 75750
48 rooms. Comfortable, centrally located hotel with restaurant.

Baia Paraelios ▥
Località Fornaci
88035 Parghelia
Tel. (0963) 600004; fax 600074
68 rooms. Pleasant resort hotel made up of cottages in a park. Swimming pool, beach and tennis. Full-board only. Open June to September.

Grand Hotel Excelsior ▥
Via Vittorio Veneto 66
89121 Reggio di Calabria
Tel. (0965) 812211; fax 812450
84 rooms. Modern, centrally lo-cated hotel with restaurant (near the Museo Nazionale).

La Pineta ▯
88038 Tropea
Tel. (0963) 61700; fax 62265
59 rooms. Comfortable hotel with restaurant. Tennis. Open April to mid-September.

The Islands
Sicily
Villa Athena ▥
Via dei Templi
92100 Agrigento
Tel. (0922) 596288; fax 402180
40 rooms. Comfortable hotel set in expansive gardens near the temple area. Outdoor dining, swimming pool.

Excelsior ▥
Piazza Verga 39
95129 Catania
Tel. (095) 537071; fax 537015
163 rooms. Large, modern central hotel. Restaurant closed Sunday.

Carasco ▥
Porto delle Genti
98055 Lipari
Tel. (090) 981605; fax 9811828
89 rooms. Comfortable hotel with splendid sea views, swimming pool, garden and beach. Open Easter to mid-October.

Jolly ▥
Corso Garibaldi 126
98100 Messina
Tel. (090) 363860; fax 5902526
96 rooms. Comfortable hotel with a good view of the harbour. Restau-rant.

Astoria Palace ▥
Via Monte Pellegrino 62
90142 Palermo
Tel. (091) 6371820; fax 6372178
325 rooms. Large modern hotel (opened in 1988) with good restau-rant.

Villa Igiea Grand Hotel ▦
Salita Belmonte 43
90142 Palermo
Tel. (091) 543744; fax 547654
117 rooms. Elegant luxury hotel on the outskirts of Palermo set in pleasant grounds overlooking the sea. Splendid terrace restaurant, outdoor swimming pool and tennis.

Jolly ▥
Corso Gelone 43
96100 Syracuse
Tel. (0931) 461111; fax 461126
100 rooms. Comfortable, centrally located hotel with restaurant.

San Domenico Palace ▦
Piazza San Domenico 5
98039 Taormina
Tel. (0942) 23701; fax 625506
101 rooms. Splendid luxury hotel installed in a 16th-century convent. Superb views of Taormina Bay and Mt Etna. Heated outdoor swim-ming pool. Outdoor dining.

Restaurants

Villa Fiorita ▯
Via Pirandello 39
98039 Taormina
Tel. (0942) 24122; fax 625967
24 rooms. Comfortable small hotel with good sea views, swimming pool and garden. No restaurant.

Sardinia
Villa Las Tronas ▯▯
Lungomare Valencia 1
07041 Alghero
Tel. (079) 981818; fax 981044
30 rooms. Attractive hotel in a former royal villa on rocky coast just outside Alghero. Restaurant, swimming pool, private beach.

Club Hotel ▯▯
Baia Sardinia
07021 Arzachena
Tel. (0789) 99006; fax 99286
85 rooms. Comfortable hotel with private beach. Casablanca restaurant offers outdoor dining. Closed early January to Easter.

Mediterraneo ▯▯
Lungomare Cristoforo
Colombo 46
09125 Cagliari
Tel. (070) 301271; fax 301274
136 rooms. Large modern hotel overlooking the sea. Garden. Restaurant closed Sunday.

Moderno ▯
Via Roma 159
09124 Cagliari
Tel. (070) 660306; fax 660260
93 rooms. Comfortable, centrally located hotel. No restaurant.

Su Gologone ▯
08025 Oliena (near Nuoro)
Tel. (0784) 287512; fax 287668
65 rooms. Modern hotel with good restaurant serving typical Sardinian cuisine. Outdoor dining, garden, swimming pool and tennis.

Cala di Volpe ▯▯▯
07020 Porto Cervo
Tel. (0789) 96083; fax 96442
123 rooms. Elegant luxury hotel, designed as a castle and sited on a small bay on the Costa Smeralda. Restaurant, tennis, salt-water swimming pool and private beach. Open mid-May to September.

Sporting ▯▯▯
07020 Porto Rotondo
Tel. (0789) 34005; fax 34383
27 rooms. Elegant hotel sited on the Costa Smeralda. Swimming pool, garden and private beach. Restaurant with outdoor dining. Open mid-April to September.

This is a selection of restaurants from all over Italy. We do not list pizzerias, fast-food outlets and stand-up bars serving *tavola calda* where prices will be lower. Many of the restaurants chosen are well known and have received distinctions for the quality of their cuisine.

The restaurants have been classified according to the price of a three-course meal as follows:

▯   Below L.35,000
▯▯   L.35,000–70,000
▯▯▯ Above L.70,000

Central Italy
Rome
Alberto Ciarla ▯▯▯
Piazza San Cosimato 40
(Trastevere)
00153 Rome
Tel. (06) 5818668
The city's top restaurant for seafood. The fish tank is worth a visit. Outdoor dining. Dinner only. Reserve. Closed Sunday and for two weeks in August and two weeks in December.

Apuleius ▯▯
Via Tempio di Diana 15
(Aventine)
00153 Rome
Tel. (06) 5742160
Quiet restaurant in a 1st century Roman house serving seafood dishes and hearty fare. A good mid-day stopping point for Aventine sightseers. Closed Sunday.

Crisciotti-al Boschetto ▯
Via del Boschetto 30
00184 Rome
Tel. (06) 4744770
Rustic trattoria. Outdoor dining. Closed Saturday and throughout August.

L'eau Vive ▯▯
Via Monterone 85
(near Largo Argentina)
00186 Rome
Tel. (06) 6541095
Splendid French Colonial cuisine in a restaurant run by French nuns and housed in a 16th-century papal palace. Reservations advised. Closed Sunday and throughout August.

Elettra ▯
Via Principe Amedeo 72
00185 Rome
Tel. (06) 4745397
Popular local trattoria. Closed Saturday and for three weeks in August.

Da Sabatino a Sant'Ignazio ▯
Piazza Sant'Ignazio 169
00186 Rome
Tel. (06) 6797821
Good, authentic Roman cooking in the heart of Rome near the Jesuit Church of Sant'Ignazio. Excellent value.

Margutta Vegetariano ▯▯
Via Margutta 119 (near Piazza del Popolo)
00187 Rome
Tel. (06) 6786033
Traditional vegetarian dishes from southern Italy served in pretty surroundings. Closed Sunday.

Da Mario ▯▯
Via della Vite 55 (Corso/Piazza di Spagna)
00187 Rome
Tel. (06) 6783818
Nicely cooked food from Tuscany with strong flavours, rich in meat and game and filling pasta dishes. Closed Sunday and throughout August.

Romolo a Porta Settimiana ▯▯
Via di Porta Settimiana 8 (Trastevere)
00153 Rome
Tel. (06) 5818284
Classic and creative pasta dishes. Outdoor dining in terraced garden in summer. Late-night dining. Reservation advised. Closed Monday and in August.

El Toulà ▯▯▯
Via della Lupa 29/b (Corso/Piazza Navona)
00186 Rome
Tel. (06) 6873750
Elegant restaurant near Piazza del Parliamento, popular with politicians. Notable wine list. Reserve. Closed Saturday at lunch, Sunday and throughout August.

Lazio
Cacciani ▯▯
Via Diaz 13
00044 Frascati
Tel. (06) 9420378
Good cuisine. Outdoor dining on terrace. Closed Tuesday, Sunday evening (November to March) and for two weeks in January and mid-August.

Adriano ‖
Villa Adriana
00019 Tivoli
Tel. (0744) 529174
Pleasant restaurant with accommodation (seven rooms). Conveniently sited for Hadrian's Villa. Outdoor dining in summer. Garden and tennis. Closed Sunday evening.

Il Palestrina ‖
Via Toti 2
00036 Palestrina
Tel. (06) 9534615
Excellent pasta dishes and inventive cuisine. Situated in heart of the town near the cathedral. Closed Monday and during July.

Tuscany and Umbria

Florence
Buca Mario ‖
Piazza Ottaviani 16
50123 Florence
Tel. (055) 214179
Popular cellar restaurant. Closed Wednesday, Thursday lunch and during August.

La Capannina di Sante ‖‖‖
Piazza Ravenna
50126 Florence
Tel. (055) 688345
Florence's best seafood restaurant. Splendid setting on the banks of the Arno. Dinner only, open till late. Closed Sunday, for two weeks in August and one week at Christmas.

Cavallino ‖
Via delle Farine 6
50122 Florence
Tel. (055) 215818
Popular with locals, this restaurant offers outdoor dining in summer. Closed Tuesday evening, Wednesday and for three weeks in August.

Cibreo ‖
Via dei Macchi 118
50122 Florence
Tel. (055) 2341100
Classic Tuscan cuisine is brought up to date in this popular restaurant. Reserve. Closed Sunday, Monday and throughout August.

Enoteca Pinchiorri ‖‖‖
Via Ghibellina 87
50122 Florence
Tel. (055) 242777
One of Italy's finest restaurants. Outstanding cuisine in the elegant setting of a 15th-century palace. Outdoor dining in the pretty court-

yard in summer. Reserve. Closed Sunday, Monday lunch, Christmas and during February and August.

Taverna del Bronzino ‖
Via delle Ruote 25/27
50129 Florence
Tel. (055) 495220
Out-of-the-way restaurant popular with those in the know. Named after the 16th-century Florentine painter. Closed Sunday and throughout August.

Tuscany
Buca di San Francesco ‖
Piazza San Francesco 1
52100 Arezzo
Tel. (0575) 23271
Cellar restaurant in a medieval building. Closed Monday evening, Tuesday and throughout July.

Il Chiasso ‖
57031 Capoliveri (Isola d'Elba)
Tel. (0565) 968709
Seafood restaurant offering outdoor dining in a pleasant setting. Reserve. Open April to October.

Buca di Sant'Antonio ‖
Via della Cervia 1–5
55100 Lucca
Tel. (0583) 55881
Good Tuscan cuisine. Closed Sunday evening, Monday and for three weeks in July.

Da Giulio in Pelleria ‖
Via delle Conce 45 (Piazza San Donato)
55100 Lucca
Tel. (0583) 55948
Popular trattoria tucked away in the back streets of Lucca. Good Tuscan peasant cooking. Reserve. Closed Sunday, Monday, for three weeks in August and from late December to early January.

Cucina da Giovanni ‖
Via Garibaldi 27
51016 Montecatini Terme
Tel. (0572) 71695
Excellent Tuscan dishes and good choice of wines. Closed Monday.

La Chiusa ‖‖‖
Via Madonnina
53040 Montefollonico (near Siena)
Tel. (0577) 669668
Excellent cuisine in converted farmhouse. Reserve. Also offers accommodation (6 rooms). Closed Tuesday, at lunch in July and August, and from early January to late March and mid-November to mid-December.

Al Ristoro dei Vecchi Macelli ‖
Via Volturno 49
56126 Pisa
Tel. (050) 20424
Excellent cuisine in restaurant which takes its name from the old slaughterhouses (macelli) nearby. Reserve. Closed Sunday lunch, Wednesday and for two weeks in August.

La Mora ‖
55029 Ponte a Moriano (near Lucca)
Tel. (0583) 57109
Traditional regional cooking in historic country inn. Closed Wednesday, and for three weeks in October.

Il Gambero Rosso ‖
58018 Port'Ercole
Tel. (0564) 832650
Outdoor dining with view of port. Closed Wednesday, from mid-January to mid-February and for two weeks in November.

Il Piraña ‖
Via Valentini 110
50047 Prato
Tel. (0574) 25746
Good seafood restaurant. Reserve. Closed Sunday, Saturday and Monday lunch, and throughout August.

Il Campo ‖
Piazza del Campo 50
53100 Siena
Tel. (0577) 280725
Restaurant in Siena's beautiful central square. Outdoor dining. Reserve. Closed Tuesday.

Locanda dell'Amorosa ‖
53048 Sinalunga (near Cortona)
Tel. (0577) 679497
Pleasant restaurant in former farm. Good cuisine. Reserve. Also offers accommodation (10 rooms). Closed Monday, Tuesday lunch and from late January to late February.

Etruria ‖
Piazza dei Priori 6
56048 Volterra
Tel. (0588) 86064
Restaurant in the heart of town offering regional specialities. Closed Thursday, for three weeks in June and all of November.

Poggio Antico ‖
Località I Poggi
52034 Montalcino
Tel. (0577) 849200
Excellent cuisine accompanied by wonderful Brunello wine.

Umbria

Buca di San Francesco   ▯▯
Via Brizi 1
06081 Assisi
Tel. (075) 812204
Cellar restaurant with outdoor dining in the garden in summer. Closed Monday, from early January to end of February, and throughout July.

Alla Fornace di Mastro Giorgio   ▯▯
Via Mastro Giorgio 2
06024 Gubbio
Tel. (075) 9275740
Regional cooking in an historic 14th-century building. Closed Sunday evening, Monday and in February.

Le Grotte del Funaro   ▯▯
Via Ripa di Serancia 41
05018 Orvieto
Tel. (0763) 43276
Restaurant located in caves in the volcanic rock beneath Orvieto. Closed Monday.

La Taverna   ▯▯
Via delle Streghe 8
06100 Perugia
Tel. (075) 5724128
Regional specialities in a rustic atmosphere. Closed Monday and for one week in late July.

Il Tartufo   ▯▯
Piazza Garibaldi 24
06049 Spoleto
Tel. (0743) 40236
Good game and truffle dishes. Closed Wednesday and from mid-July to early August.

Nuovo Coppiere   ▯
Via Beato Vescovo Mainardo 5
61029 Urbino
Tel. (0722) 320092
Small, centrally located restaurant. Closed Wednesday and throughout February.

The North-East

Venice

Antico Martini   ▯▯▯
Campo San Fantin 1983
30124 Venice
Tel. (041) 5224121
Elegant restaurant with excellent cuisine. Fine weather sees dining on a pleasant terrace with a view of the nearby La Fenice theatre. Closed Tuesday, Wednesday lunch, and from December to March, except for Christmas, New Year and Carnival.

Da Bruno   ▯
Castello-calle del Paradiso 5731
30122 Venice
Tel. (041) 5221480
Popular local restaurant. Closed Tuesday, for two weeks in late January and for two weeks in late July.

Da Fiore   ▯▯
Calle del Scaleter 2202 (near Campo San Polo)
30125 Venice
Tel. (041) 721308
Popular seafood restaurant. Reserve. Closed Sunday, Monday, from Christmas to 6 January and for three weeks in August.

Al Giardinetto-da Severino   ▯
Ruga Giuffa 4928
30122 Venice
Tel. (041) 5285332
Outdoor dining beneath a pergola in summer. Closed Thursday and from mid-January to mid-February.

Al Graspo de Ua   ▯▯
Calle dei Bombaseri 5094
30124 Venice
Tel. (041) 5200150
Good cuisine in a typical taverna. Closed Monday, Tuesday, for three weeks in late December and early January, and for first two weeks in August.

Harry's Bar   ▯▯▯
Calle Vallaresso 1323
30124 Venice
Tel. (041) 5285777
Famous bar and restaurant, patronized by Hemingway and a host of other big-league celebrities down the years. Excellent cuisine. Closed Monday and for one week in early January.

Harry's Dolci   ▯▯
Giudecca 773
30133 Venice
Tel. (041) 5224844
Popular outpost of Harry's Bar on the island of Giudecca. Outdoor dining in summer on the Canale della Giudecca. Closed Tuesday (except September) and from early November to early March.

Veneto

San Bassiano   ▯▯
Viale dei Martiri 36
36061 Bassano del Grappa
Tel. (0424) 212453
Splendid cuisine in attractive town on the banks of the Brenta River. Reserve. Closed Sunday and during August.

Belle Parti   ▯▯
Via Belle Parti 11
35139 Padua
Tel. (049) 8751822
Good cuisine in the setting of an ancient palazzo. Reserve. Closed Sunday, Monday lunch, for ten days in January and two weeks in August.

El Toulà da Alfredo   ▯▯
Via Collato 26
31100 Treviso
Tel. (0422) 540275
Elegant restaurant with very good cuisine. Closed Sunday evening, Monday and late July to late August.

Arche   ▯▯▯
Via Arche Scaligere 6
37121 Verona
Tel. (045) 8007415
Fine seafood restaurant. Reserve. Closed Sunday, Monday lunch and first two weeks of January.

Il Desco   ▯▯▯
Via Dietro San Sebastiano 7
37121 Verona
Tel. (045) 595358
Splendid variations on regional cuisine, including fish and game. Closed Sunday, Christmas, Easter and last two weeks of June.

Cinzia e Valerio   ▯▯▯
Piazzetta Porta Padova 65–67
36100 Vicenza
Tel. (0444) 505213
Superb seafood restaurant. Closed Sunday evening, Monday, and first week in January and August.

Scudo di Francia   ▯▯
Contrà Piancoli 4
36100 Vicenza
Tel. (0444) 323322
Regional cooking in an ancient palazzo. Closed Sunday evening, Monday and throughout August.

Friuli Venezia Giulia

Antica Trattoria Suban   ▯▯
Via Comici 2
34128 Trieste
Tel. (040) 54368
Good regional cuisine in the hills on the outskirts of town. Outdoor dining in summer in a pleasant bower. Closed Monday, Tuesday and three weeks in August.

Là di Moret   ▯▯
Viale Tricesimo 276
33100 Udine
Tel. (0432) 545096
Excellent regional cooking. Closed Sunday evening and Monday lunch.

Dolomites

Da Abramo ☐☐
Piazza Gries 16
39100 Bolzano
Tel. (0471) 280141
Good cuisine. Outdoor dining in summer. Closed Sunday and during August.

El Toulà ☐☐☐
Via Ronco 123
32043 Cortina d'Ampezzo
Tel. (0436) 3339
Good cuisine. View of Cortina and the Dolomites. Reservations required. Open late December to mid-April and mid-July to late September.

Tivoli ☐☐
Località Lacedel
32043 Cortina d'Ampezzo
Tel. (0436) 8666400
Excellent cuisine, good views of the Dolomites. Outdoor terrace dining in summer. Reservations required. Open from early December to mid-April and mid-July to late September. Closed Monday (during January).

Andrea ☐☐☐
Via Galilei 44
39012 Merano
Tel. (0473) 37400
Excellent cuisine in elegant surroundings. Reserve. Closed Monday, February and mid-June to early July.

Flora ☐☐
Via Portici 75
39012 Merano
Tel. (0473) 231484
Excellent cuisine, including very fine seafood and game. Reservations usually required. Evenings only. Closed Sunday and from mid-January to the end of February.

Chiesa ☐☐
Via San Marco 64
38100 Trento
Tel. (0461) 238766
Regional specialities in a medieval building. Closed Sunday evening and during September.

Emilia-Romagna

Il Trigabolo ☐☐☐
Piazza Garibaldi
44011 Argenta
Tel. (0532) 804121
One of Italy's leading restaurants, situated in this small town on the road between Ferrara and Ravenna. Closed Sunday evening, Monday and during July.

Notai ☐☐☐
Via de' Pignattari 1
40124 Bologna
Tel. (051) 228694
Elegant restaurant near the Duomo serving excellent regional cuisine. Reserve. Closed Sunday.

**Antica Trattoria
del Cacciatore** ☐☐
Via Caduti di Casteldebole 25
40132 Bologna
Tel. (051) 564203
Good, traditional cooking. Outside dining in summer. Closed Sunday evening, Monday, and first week of January and August.

La Buca ☐☐
Corso Garibaldi 41
47042 Cesenatico
Tel. (0547) 82474
Seafood restaurant offering outdoor dining. Closed Monday, for ten days in January and three weeks in November.

La Providenza ☐☐
Corso Ercole I d'Este 92
44100 Ferrara
Tel. (0532) 205187
Regional specialities. Outdoor dining in summer. Closed Monday and for one week in mid-August.

Vecchia Chitarra ☐
Via Ravenna 13
44100 Ferrara
Tel. (0532) 62204
Reasonably priced regional cuisine. Closed Tuesday, for one week in January and first three weeks of August.

San Domenico ☐☐☐
Via G. Sacchi 1
40026 Imola
Tel. (0542) 29000
Outstanding cuisine in the setting of a 16th-century Dominican convent. Reserve. Closed Monday, first two weeks in January and first three weeks of August.

Borso d'Este ☐☐
Piazza Roma 5
41100 Modena
Tel. (059) 214114
Excellent cuisine, including fine seafood and game dishes. Reserve. Closed Saturday lunch, Sunday and in August.

Parma Rotta ☐☐
Via Langhirano 158
43100 Parma
Tel. (0521) 581323
Relaxed trattoria offering open-air dining in summer. Closed Monday.

Antica Osteria del Teatro ☐☐☐
Via Verdi 16
29100 Piacenza
Tel. (0523) 23777
Excellent cuisine. Reserve. Closed Sunday evening, Monday, first two weeks in January and in August.

Tre Spade ☐☐
Via Faentina 136
48100 Ravenna
Tel. (0544) 500522
Excellent cuisine in the town's best restaurant. Reserve. Closed Monday, first three weeks of July and also Sunday evening from November to March.

The North-West

Milan

Bagutta ☐ ☐☐
Via Bagutta 14
20121 Milan
Tel. (02) 76002767
Atmospheric trattoria with an artistic clientele whose paintings and caricatures decorate the walls. Closed Sunday, late December to early January and last three weeks of August.

I Matteoni ☐☐
Piazzale Cinque Giornate 6
20129 Milan
Tel. (02) 55188293
Popular local restaurant sited east of the Duomo. Closed Sunday and throughout August.

Osteria del Binari ☐☐
Via Tortona 1
20144 Milan
Tel. (02) 89409428
Outdoor dining, old-fashioned atmosphere and excellent cuisine at this reasonably priced restaurant near the Porta Genova railway station. Reserve. Open evenings only. Closed Sunday and one week in mid-August.

Savini ☐☐☐
Galleria Vittorio Emanuele II
20121 Milan
Tel. (02) 72003433
Old-fashioned elegance sums up the ambience of this famous and expensive restaurant on three levels in the Galleria. Reasonably priced set menu for lunch and dinner. Reserve. Closed Sunday, Christmas to early January and mid-August.

La Scaletta ☐☐☐
Piazzale Stazione Genova 3
20144 Milan
Tel. (02) 58100290

Humble local specialities get the gourmet treatment in this elegant and expensive restaurant – probably Milan's best eating establishment. Reserve. Closed Sunday, Monday, late December to early January, Easter and August.

Lombardy

Taverna dei Colleoni ▯▯▯
Piazza Vecchia 7
24100 Bergamo (Città Alta)
Tel. (035) 232596
Excellent cuisine in this restaurant housed in the Palazzo del Podestà. Outside dining in summer. Closed Monday and two weeks in August.

La Sosta ▯▯▯
Via San Martino della Battaglia 20
25100 Brescia
Tel. (030) 295603
Good regional specialities served in a 17th-century building. Closed Monday and most of August.

Aquila Nera ▯▯
Via Sicardo 3
26100 Cremona
Tel. (0372) 25646
Excellent cuisine beside the Duomo. Reserve. Closed Sunday evening, Monday, first ten days in January and three weeks in August.

Al Bersagliere ▯▯▯
Via Statale 258
46044 Goito (near Mantua)
Tel. (0376) 60007
Excellent traditional cuisine. Closed Monday, Tuesday lunch, Christmas, one week in early January and three weeks in August.

L'Aquila Nigra ▯▯
Vicolo Bonacolsi 4
46100 Mantua
Tel. (0376) 350651
Excellent local cuisine in a restaurant housed in a former medieval convent. Reserve. Closed Sunday, Monday, first 12 days of January and during August.

Locanda Vecchia Pavia ▯▯▯
Via Cardinal Riboldi 2
27100 Pavia
Tel. (0382) 304132
Excellent cuisine near the Cathedral. Very reasonable set lunch menu. Reserve. Closed Monday, Wednesday lunch, ten days in January and throughout August.

Del Sole ▯▯▯
Piazza Venezia 5
21020 Ranco
Tel. (0331) 976526

Outstanding cuisine in acclaimed lakeside restaurant-inn. Closed Monday evening, Tuesday and from January to mid-February.

Gualtiero Marchesi ▯▯▯
Via Vittorio Emanuele 11
25030 Erbusco (nr. Brescia)
Tel. (030) 7760550
A new venture for the 'king' of Italian gastronomy. Excellent cuisine. Gourmets' menu is highly recommended. Reasonably priced set lunch menu. Closed Monday and first two weeks of January.

Grifone-da Luciano ▯▯
Via delle Bisse 5
25019 Sirmione
Tel. (030) 916097
Lakeside dining in attractive restaurant. Open mid-March to October. Closed Wednesday.

Piedmont

Vecchia Aosta ▯▯
Via Porte Pretoriane 4
11100 Aosta
Tel. (0165) 361186
Good food and wine in this attractive restaurant set in the old Roman walls of the Porta Pretoria. Closed Wednesday.

Al Sorriso ▯▯▯
Via Roma 18
28018 Soriso
Tel. (0322) 983228
Outstanding cuisine at this elegant restaurant (with accommodation). Reserve. Closed Monday, Tuesday lunch, mid- to late January and two weeks in mid-August.

L'Emiliano ▯▯▯
Corso Italia 50
28049 Stresa
Tel. (0323) 31396
Excellent cuisine. Reserve. Closed Tuesday (except in summer), Wednesday lunch, and second half of November and February.

Del Cambio ▯▯▯
Piazza Carignano 2
10123 Turin
Tel. (011) 546690
Famous restaurant with 19th-century décor. Reserve. Closed Sunday and during August.

Vecchia Lanterna ▯▯▯
Corso Re Umberto 21
10128 Turin
Tel. (011) 537047
Elegant restaurant with outstanding cuisine. Closed Saturday lunch, Sunday and mid-August.

Italian Riviera

Palma ▯▯▯
Via Cavour 5
17021 Alassio
Tel. (0182) 640314
Outstanding cuisine. Outdoor dining. Reserve. Closed Tuesday, November and first week in December.

Paracucchi-Locanda dell'Angelo ▯▯▯
Via XXV Aprile
19031 Ameglia
Tel. (0187) 64391
Famous restaurant offering excellent cuisine and tranquil accommodation. Closed Monday and three weeks in January.

La Reserve Tastevin ▯▯
Via Arziglia 20
18012 Bordighera
Tel. (0184) 261322
Fine trattoria with a good sea view plus its own private beach. Outdoor dining. Closed Sunday evening and Monday (except mid-June to mid-September), and mid-October to mid-December.

Da Giacomo ▯▯▯
Corso Italia 1/r
16145 Genoa
Tel. (010) 369647
Elegant modern restaurant. Outdoor dining. Closed Sunday and two weeks in mid-August.

Del Mario ▯▯
Via Conservatori del Mare 35/r
16123 Genoa
Tel. (010) 297788
Good trattoria near the port. Local specialities. Open all week.

The South

Naples

Amici Miei ▯
Via Monte di Dio 78
80132 Naples
Tel. (081) 7646063
Small, intimate restaurant in the Mergellina area, serving homely regional food, including some delicious pasta dishes. Closed Sunday evening, Monday and throughout August.

La Cantinella ▯▯
Via Cuma 42
80132 Naples
Tel. (081) 7648684
Excellent waterfront restaurant with fine seafood specialities. Closed Sunday, Christmas, New Year and throughout August.

La Cantina di Triunfo
Riviera di Chiaia 64
80100 Naples
Tel. (081) 668101
The Triunfo family have converted their famous wine cellar into a 'kitchen with wine' – for every dish a different wine.

Dante e Beatrice
Piazza Dante 44
80135 Naples
Tel. (081) 349905
Popular local trattoria with Neapolitan specialities. Closed Wednesday and last week in August.

La Sacrestia
Via Orazio 116
80122 Naples
Tel. (081) 664186
Famous and fashionable restaurant located up on the hills of Posillipo. Superb seafood and pasta, and impeccable service. Outdoor dining on the terrace with panoramic view of the city and bay. Closed Sunday in July and Monday during the rest of the year. Also closed during August.

Campania
La Caravella
Via Matteo Camera 12
84011 Amalfi
Tel. (089) 871029
Good seafood restaurant. Closed last three weeks in November and Tuesday from October to May.

Giardini Eden
Località Ischia Ponte
Via Nuova Cartaromana
80070 Ischia
Good seafood and other dishes in a superb setting with incredible view. Closed from October to April.

Il Principe
Piazza Longo 8
80045 Pompei
Tel. (081) 8633242
Good Neapolitan cuisine and fine wines. Closed Mondy and three weeks in August.

La Capannina
Via Le Botteghe 14
80073 Capri
Tel. (081) 8370732
Restaurant offering a wide choice of local specialities, with particularly good pasta, fish and desserts. Reserve for evening dining. Open mid-March to early November. Closed Wednesday (except August).

Chez Black
Via del Brigantino 19
84017 Positano
Tel. (089) 875036
Stylish restaurant on the seafront offering surprisingly good value for money. Excellent pasta and pizzas and a huge choice of seafood. Closed early November to late December.

Cumpa' Cosimo
Via Roma 44
84010 Ravello
Tel. (089) 857156
Homely, unpretentious trattoria serving pizzas (evenings only), pasta and fish, and homemade wine. Closed Monday from November to March.

Don Alfonso 1890
Piazza Sant'Agata
80064 Sant'Agata sui due Golfi
Tel. (081) 8780026
Highly esteemed restaurant set in lovely surroundings high in the hills above Sorrento. A good choice of traditional regional food, plus many original and inventive dishes. Reservations required. Also accommodation (two apartments). Closed Sunday evening and Monday (from June to September), Tuesday, and most of January and February.

O'Parrucchiano
Corso Italia 71
80067 Sorrento
Tel. (081) 8781321
Beautiful old family-run restaurant with splendid décor and pretty terraced gardens. Traditional Campanian food, with particularly good pasta and desserts. Closed Wednesday in low season.

Puglia
Il Poeta Contadino
Via Indipendenza 21
70011 Alberobello
Tel. (080) 721917
Excellent regional cuisine. Closed Sunday evening and Monday (except July and September), two weeks in mid-January and first two weeks in July.

La Pignata
Corso Vittorio Emanuele 173
70122 Bari
Tel. (080) 5232481
Bari's best restaurant offering excellent cuisine, superb desserts and good local wines. Closed Sunday evening, Monday and during August.

Ai Due Ghiottoni
Via Putignani 11
70121 Bari
Tel. (080) 5232240
Popular restaurant serving local specialities. Closed Sunday and first three weeks in August.

Bacco
Via Sipontina 10
70051 Barletta
Tel. (0883) 571000
Elegant restaurant serving outstanding regional cuisine. Reserve. Closed Sunday, Monday, throughout August and at Christmas.

Barbablu
Via Umberto I, 7
73100 Lecce
Tel. (0832) 241183
Situated near Lecce's most important Baroque church, Santa Croce, this elegant restaurant offers good regional cooking. Closed Monday.

La Darsena
Contrada Costa Merlata
Strada statale 379
72017 Ostuni
Tel. (0831) 339585
Housed in a typical Puglian farm, this restaurant offers good seafood dishes. Ice-cream and Grappa served on terrace with sea view. Closed Monday and November.

Taverna degli Artisti
70013 Castellana Grotte
Tel. (080) 8968234
Regional cuisine in tavern near the caves. Outdoor dining. Closed throughout December and Thursday from October to June.

Il Gambero
Lungmare degli Eroi 1
73028 Otranto
Tel. (0836) 801107
Excellent seafood restaurant. Closed Wednesday (except March to September) and from mid-November to mid-December.

La Cemener
Via Garibaldi 20
70037 Ruvo di Pugila
Tel. (080) 811794
Cordial atmosphere, good food and local wines. Closed Sunday and in August.

Fagiano
72010 Selva di Fasano
Tel. (080) 9331157
Good cuisine. Outdoor dining. Closed November and Monday evening and Tuesday from October to June.

344

Basilicata

Taverna Rovita ⌷⌷
Via Rovita 13
85046 Maratea
Tel. (0973) 876588
Good food, excellent desserts and wines. Closed from November to mid-March, except for 18 December to 6 January.

Basilico ⌷⌷
Via San Francesco 33
75100 Matera
Tel. (0835) 330502
Good seafood and traditional dishes from Matera. Regional wines and home-made desserts. Closed during first three weeks of August.

Calabria

Alla Antica Trattoria ⌷⌷
La Locanda Da Alia
Via Jetticelle 69
87012 Castrovillari
Tel. (0981) 46370
Excellent regional cuisine. The restaurant also has 16 rooms. Restaurant closed Sunday.

Rodrigo ⌷⌷
Via XXIV Maggio 25
Reggio di Calabria
Tel. (0965) 20170
Good regional cuisine. Closed Sunday.

La Collina dello Scoiattolo ⌷⌷
Località Gallina
Via Provinciale 34
89061 Reggio Calabria
Tel. (0965) 682255
Superb seafood straight from the fishermens' boats. Closed Wednesday and the first two weeks in November.

Scilla ⌷
Lungomare Cristoforo Colombo
89058 Scilla
Tel. (0965) 754889
Fresh seafood served in typical fishermens' restaurant right on the seafront. Good local wines available. Closed Monday and in November.

Barini ⌷
Via Stazione
88038 Tropea
Tel. (0963) 61654
Fresh seafood prepared according to traditional fishermens' recipes. Try the particularly good spaghetti 'alla Corte d'Assise'. Good local wines. Closed Sunday (except in summer).

The Islands

Sicily

Il Delfino-da Angelo ⌷⌷
Mazzaro
98030 Taormina
Tel. (0942) 23004
Good seafood restaurant at the beach in Mazzaro a few miles east of Taormina. Outdoor dining. Open mid-March to October.

Parco dei Principi ⌷⌷
Via delle Ginestre 1
95019 Zafferane Etnea
Tel. (095) 7082335
Excellent local cuisine in this friendly restaurant on the slopes of Etna (try the volcano's famous boletus mushrooms). Closed Tuesday (excluding summer).

Filippino ⌷⌷
Piazza Municipio
98055 Lipari
Tel. (090) 981102
Excellent cuisine. Outdoor dining. Closed from mid-November to mid-December and Monday from October to May.

Alberto Sporting ⌷⌷
Frazione di Mortelle
Via Nazionale
Messina
Tel. (090) 321009
Excellent local cuisine and good seafood. Wonderful Sicilian desserts and impeccable service. Closed Monday and last two weeks of January.

La Botte ⌷⌷
Contrada (on S186)
90046 Monreale
Tel. (091) 414051
Excellent open-air dining. Closed all of July and August; Monday and at lunch (except Saturday, Sunday and throughout June).

L'Approdo da Renato ⌷⌷
Via Messina Marine 224
90123 Palermo
Tel. (091) 6302881
Excellent restaurant a short distance from the centre of town. Seafood specialities. Outdoor dining. Closed Wednesday and for two weeks in mid-August.

Charleston ⌷⌷⌷
Piazzale Ungheria 30
90141 Palermo
Tel. (091) 321366
Elegant restaurant with Art Nouveau ambience and excellent cuisine. Closed Sunday and from June to late September.

A' Rutta e' Ciauli ⌷⌷
Riviera Dionisio il Grande 194
96100 Syracuse
Tel. (0931) 65540
Good restaurant overlooking the sea and serving typically Sicilian cuisine. Outdoor dining on the terrace in summer. Closed Tuesday, Christmas, New Year and last two weeks in August.

Le Caprice ⌷⌷
Strada Panoramica dei Templi 51
92100 Agrigento
Tel. (0922) 26469
Outdoor dining in the temple area. Closed Friday and first two weeks in July.

Al Poggio Ducale ⌷⌷
Via Paolo Gaifami 7
95126 Catania
Tel. (095) 330016
Excellent Sicilian cuisine. Closed Sunday evening, Monday lunch and in August.

Puntazzo ⌷⌷
98050 Ginostra
Stromboli
Tel. (090) 9880665
Excellent cuisine in wonderful surroundings. Good value. Closed from November to April.

Sardinia

La Lepanto ⌷⌷
Via Carlo Alberto 135
07041 Alghero
Tel. (079) 979116
Good seafood restaurant with outdoor dining. Closed Monday (excluding summer).

Dal Corsaro ⌷⌷
Viale Regina Margherita 28
09124 Cagliari
Tel. (070) 664318
Popular restaurant near the seafront offering excellent regional cuisine. Closed Sunday, Christmas to Epiphany and throughout August.

Su Gologone ⌷⌷
08025 Oliena (near Nuoro)
Tel. (0784) 287512
Good restaurant serving typical Sardinian shepherds' cuisine.

Canne al Vento ⌷⌷
Via Nazionale 23
07028 Santa Teresa Gallura
Tel. (0789) 754219
Popular restaurant offering typical Sardinian cuisine. Closed October, November and Saturday in the low season.

Index

Page references in *italic* refer to illustrations.

039/605 RP